The
Presidential
Advisory
System

The
Presidential
Advisory
System

edited by

THOMAS E. CRONIN
UNIVERSITY OF NORTH CAROLINA
AT CHAPEL HILL

and

SANFORD D. GREENBERG
EDP TECHNOLOGY, INC.,
WASHINGTON, D.C.

Harper & Row, Publishers
NEW YORK, EVANSTON, AND LONDON

THE PRESIDENTIAL ADVISORY SYSTEM

LIBRARY OF CONGRESS CATALOG CARD NUMBER: 69-18487

Contents

Notes on Contributors

Part I

THEODORE C. SORENSEN, formerly Special Counsel to President John F. Kennedy, is currently in private law practice in New York and an Editor-at-large for *Saturday Review*.

RICHARD E. NEUSTADT served as government civil servant and later as a White House staff assistant during the Truman Administration and as a consultant to both the Kennedy and the Johnson Administrations. He is now the Director of the John F. Kennedy Institute of Politics and Professor of Government at Harvard University.

RICHARD F. FENNO, author of several books on Congress and the Presidency, is a Professor of Political Science at the University of Rochester.

WALTER W. HELLER served as President Kennedy's chief economic adviser and as Chairman of the Council of Economic Advisers. He is presently Professor of Economics at the University of Minnesota.

HARVEY BROOKS is Dean of the Division of Engineering and Applied Physics at Harvard University and has served in numerous capacities as a science adviser, including service on the President's Science Advisory Committee and the National Science Board.

KERMIT GORDON served on the Council of Economic Advisers under Kennedy and acted as Director of the Bureau of the Budget in both the Kennedy and the Johnson Administrations. He is now President of The Brookings Institution.

WILLIAM GORHAM, a former RAND Corporation economist and sub-Cabinet officer in both the Department of Defense and the Department of Health, Education and Welfare, was selected in 1968 to serve as the first President of The Urban Institute in Washington, D.C.

VIRGINIA HELD teaches Philosophy at Hunter College of the City University of New York.

Part II

ADAM YARMOLINSKY served the Government in various capacities as a Special Assistant to Secretary Robert McNamara in the Department of Defense and also as a White House consultant during the Kennedy and Johnson Administrations. He is now a Professor of Law at Harvard University and associated with the John F. Kennedy Institute of Politics.

ALAN L. DEAN, formerly a Management Analyst with the Bureau of the Budget, has recently served as the Assistant Secretary for Administration in the Department of Transportation.

DANIEL BELL has served on a number of White House Commissions and Task Forces. Author of several books on sociology, he is Professor of Sociology at Columbia University and a founder and co-editor of *The Public Interest*.

NORMAN C. THOMAS spent 1967–1968 as a Visiting Research Scholar at The Brookings Institution and is a Professor of Political Science at the University of Michigan. HAROLD L. WOLMAN serves on the faculty of Political Science at the University of Pennsylvania.

HENRY FAIRLIE is a free-lance British journalist currently based in Washington, D.C. JEROME B. WIESNER, former Science Adviser to President Kennedy, is now Provost at M.I.T. ARTHUR J. GOLDBERG, former Cabinet member, Supreme Court Justice, and Ambassador to the United Nations, is currently in private law practice in New York. NORMAN COUSINS serves as Editor-in-chief of the *Saturday Review*. WALTER C. CLEMENS, JR., of Boston was an Executive Officer of the Committee on Arms Control. JOHN F. WHITE is an educational administrator and president of the National Educational TV and Radio Center in New York City. LUTHER EVANS is a political scientist, government adviser, and former chief librarian of the Library of Congress.

JOSEPH KRAFT, long a reporter and author on foreign affairs and politics, is now a nationally syndicated political columnist.

HENRY A. KISSINGER is the author of several books on national security. He has taken a leave of absence from Harvard University to serve as President Nixon's Special Assistant for National Security Affairs.

Part III

AARON WILDAVSKY, author of several political research studies, is Professor of Political Science and Department Chairman at the University of California at Berkeley.

MORTON H. HALPERIN, while on leave from the Department of Government at Harvard University, has served as a Deputy Assistant Secretary of Defense in the Johnson Administration.

JOHN C. DONOVAN was an Executive Assistant to Secretary of Labor W. Willard Wirtz. He has recently returned to Maine as the Chairman of the Department of Government at Bowdoin College.

THOMAS E. CRONIN, a former White House Fellow–White House staff assistant, currently teaches Political Science at the University of North Carolina at Chapel Hill.

LEE RAINWATER is Professor of Sociology and Anthropology at Washington University. WILLIAM L. YANCEY is Instructor of Sociology and Anthropology at Washington University and Research Assistant at the Social Science Institute at Washington University, St. Louis.

GILBERT STEINER taught and conducted a number of political research studies at the University of Illinois before becoming the Director of the Governmental Affairs Research Division of The Brookings Institution in Washington, D.C.

Part IV

MICHAEL D. REAGAN taught at Syracuse University for several years and is now a Professor of Political Science at the University of California at Riverside.

ROGER HILSMAN, former Director of the State Department Bureau of Intelligence and Assistant Secretary for Far Eastern Affairs, is now a Professor of Government at Columbia University.

THOMAS C. SCHELLING, adviser to both the Department of Defense and the State Department is a Professor of Economics at Harvard University.

DON K. PRICE has served in numerous capacities in government and as an adviser to the White House. A former Vice-President of the Ford Foundation, he is currently Dean of the John F. Kennedy School of Government at Harvard University.

CHARLES J. HANSER is the author of an extensive historical treatment on British Royal Commissions entitled *Guide to Decision,* 1965.

HUBERT H. HUMPHREY, former Mayor of Minneapolis, United States Senator, and Vice-President of the United States, is now serving as a Visiting Professor of Social Sciences and International Relations at The University of Minnesota and Macalester College.

NELSON A. ROCKEFELLER, was a White House Special Assistant and Under-Secretary of the Department of Health, Education and Welfare under President Eisenhower. Serving as Governor of the State of New York since 1958, he has occasionally sought the Republican Party Presidential nomination.

Introduction

The Presidency is the most centralized American political institution and symbolically and actually the most conspicuous. Not surprisingly, the Presidency is constantly under journalistic and scholarly scrutiny. America's attentive public continually watches and argues over the use of Presidential power and, more often, over the style of Presidential leadership. Yet the Presidency is no easy subject for analysis, because it is inevitably changing, not only from incumbent to incumbent but also from one political season to the next. It is a hydra-like subject: having discussed one aspect, immediately another aspect springs up to take its place. To discuss and assess every facet of every Presidency would be a difficult, if not an impossible, assignment; for the rapidly changing, highly personal, and often secretive relationships that constitute the Presidency do not readily lend themselves to rigorous comparative or quantitative analysis.

We have many excellent studies of the Presidency from historical, legal, or biographical viewpoints. Historical works usually concentrate on describing the key decisions and turning points that typify or characterize a particular Presidency. Historians try, to the best of their ability, to place in perspective the political and policy consequences of these key decisions or key personality traits of a President and his administration. Legal studies of the Presidency focus on the Constitutional provisions and the legal precedents which tend to guide Presidential decision making. Biographical treatments predominantly emphasize the President as an individual and the role which his personality plays in interactions with Congress, the Courts, the press, and so forth. In recent years, several political studies of the Presidency have begun to focus attention on the political bargaining strategies and personal political styles manifest in Presidential behavioral patterns. Neustadt and Barber are good representatives of this latter school.[1]

[1] Richard E. Neustadt, *Presidential Power*, New York, Wiley, 1960 and Richard E. Neustadt, "White House and Whitehall," *The Public Interest*, Winter, 1966, pp. 55–69. See also: James D. Barber, "Adult Identity and Presidential Style: The Rhetorical

Such research developments have been essential for the comprehension of the contemporary Presidency. A further aspect of the Presidency, however, has seriously been ignored—the area of Presidential policy intelligence capabilities. Up to now, the many excellent studies of the Presidency have rarely explored in detail the functioning of Presidential policy processes, the sub-institutions within the Presidency, the formal and informal networks of advisers and support staffs which can facilitate or inhibit responsive Presidential policy leadership. There are obvious reasons why this has been the case. It is always difficult to analyze systematically an intangible such as personality and the way it affects or obscures essential policy outputs. It is even more difficult to trace and discuss the genesis of political and policy invention. Often, too, even the materials for such a study are unavailable. And, of course, it is only recently —within the last three administrations—that we have witnessed the burgeoning of specialists, advisers, task forces, commissions, and White House conferences, whose role it is to gather intelligence, organize it into coherent, manageable form, analyze it, and then try to translate it into recommendations for action programs for the President or his Cabinet.

Every President has had his entourage of formal and informal advisers, but the recent geometric increase in the number and functions of these advisers has been remarkable. Speaking of the 1964 effort to fashion Great Society programs, Stephen K. Bailey went so far as to suggest that:

> Within a few weeks' time the President and White House staff organized the largest, most detailed, and most highly differentiated *ad hoc* mobilization of expertise in our country's history.[2]

Presidential contact with the universities, foundations, and other nongovernmental research institutions has received some considerable praise. Journalist Theodore White has observed that, "Never have ideas been sought more hungrily or tested against reality more quickly." [3] Political scientist Aaron Wildavsky substantially concurred when he asserted that:

> In foreign affairs we may be approaching the stage where knowledge is power. There is a tremendous receptivity to good ideas in Washington. Most anyone who can present a convincing rationale for dealing with a hard world finds a ready audience. . . . The man who can build better foreign policies will find Presidents beating a path to his door.[4]

Emphasis," *Daedalus*, Summer, 1968, pp. 938–968 and James D. Barber, "Classifying and Predicting Presidential Styles: Two 'Weak' Presidents," *Journal of Social Issues*, vol. 24, July, 1968.

[2] Stephen K. Bailey, "A White House–Academia Dialogue" in Bertram M. Gross, ed., *A Great Society?*, New York, Basic Books, 1968. p. xii.

[3] Theodore H. White, "The Action Intellectuals," *Life*, June 9, 1967, p. 44.

[4] Aaron Wildavsky, "The Two Presidencies," *Trans-action*, December, 1966, p. 14.

Despite such admiring interpretations of White House receptivity toward the modern "action intellectual," there are just as many analysts proclaiming executive branch "intelligence gaps" or an "alarming weakness" and asserting that appropriate talent and ideas are too often noticeably lacking.[5]

This anthology of essays and articles has as its central interests: (1) How do Presidents and the White House staff secure intelligence, advice, and general expertise? (2) How is new intelligence and information evaluated? (3) How are ideas translated into proposals for policy? (4) What are the norms and the strategies of Presidential advising? (5) Who are the President's men or the President's educators and why? (6) Who is taken into account and how? (7) Why do certain types of people and ideas gain ready access to the White House, while others are overlooked, bypassed, or avoided? (8) What seem to be the evolving patterns of advice gathering and appraisal?

As Wildavsky has suggested, it becomes useful at this point to distinguish among *policy politics* (which policy will be adopted?), *partisan politics* (which political party will be assisted in gaining office?), and *system politics* (how will decision structures be set up?).[6] Our interest here is primarily with system politics: the processes and milieux which affect the way in which decisions are made; occasionally, it will be useful to examine policy politics to gain a more refined understanding of the consequences of system politics.

It hardly needs to be emphasized that the Presidency has become the pre-eminent policy planner and legislative program architect for both foreign and domestic policy. While this is somewhat more true for the former than the latter, the contemporary Presidency is expected to attract the most talented advisers in both areas for the purpose of generating social and technological invention and innovation. This is not to suggest that the other branches of government are collapsing or going out of the business of initiation and innovation. Such is not the case. But we wish to underscore the reality that as expanding external expectations on the Presidency have escalated, so too has a growing bureaucracy within the Presidency, a bureaucracy heavily made up of "in and outers" and part-time consultants who make their base the university, the foundation, or some similar nongovernmental institution.

It has often been pointed out that Congress is essentially a collection of decentralized committees and subcommittees; at one count in recent years it was estimated that about three hundred such committees operated on Capitol Hill. Although considerably less publicized and, until quite recently, much less studied, Presidential use of committees (both internal federal interagency com-

---

[5] See, for example, Bertram Gross, *et al.*, "What Another Hoover Commission?," *Public Administration Review*, vol. XXVIII, March/April, 1968, pp. 168–180 and, Mc-George Bundy, *The Strength of Government*, Cambridge, Harvard University Press, 1968, pp. 27–61.

[6] Aaron Wildavsky, "The Political Economy of Efficiency," *The Public Interest*, Summer, 1967, p. 41.

mittees and committees made up of outside professionals and consultants) far exceeds Congressional "government by committee."

President John F. Kennedy was very fond of using task forces, particularly for promoting and refining provocative new projects. He viewed these as part of the "theater of government" and did not appear to mind if they called for legislative action which went beyond that which he knew he could secure. Kennedy valued the task force process both for long-range planning and for educating more people to the major problems that faced our government. He enjoyed meeting with the outside task forces and was clearly at home among their participants. By the summer of 1968, President Lyndon B. Johnson was reported to have created about one hundred special task forces to assist in the development of his legislative programs. Illustrative of the White House temperament toward this process is the following account by former Special Assistant to the President, Joseph A. Califano:

> Why the increasing use of the task force? Because as society becomes more complex, problems become many-faceted and can no longer be attacked by one or two skills. We have long recognized this in our systems analyses of airplanes and weapons. But we are now applying it to help solve the problems of our people.
>
> Take, for example, the problem of juvenile delinquency. It requires more than judges and probation officers alone. Properly addressed, the problem also requires the talents of sociologists, doctors, psychiatrists, lawyers, educators, city planners, religious leaders and many others. . . .
>
> The Presidential task force has its counterpart in the committees and hundreds of individual consultants that advise his cabinet officers and their principal assistants. From across the country, from the universities and corporations, from the law firms and the labor movements, comes the individual consultant to the Government. These experts deal with an unbelievably wide range of complex matters—from surplus stockpile materials to space projects, from metal fatigue in aircraft to the effects of mental fatigue on a broken family; from city blight to rural poverty; from cancer and heart disease to crime and pollution.[7]

Presidents have always had to employ a number of federal interagency committees to help coordinate overlapping programs. But at one tally during the early Johnson years, it was learned that there were more interagency or

---

[7] Address by Joseph A. Califano, Jr., College of New Rochelle, Rye, New York, October 25, 1966. "The Challenge of Ideas in the Great Society," mimeographed White House press release copy, pp. 4–5.

[8] See Carroll Kilpatrick, "LBJ Asks Fewer Committees," *The Washington Post,* March 5, 1965, p. A4.

interdepartmental committees in Washington than there were Senators and Congressmen combined![8] President Johnson is also credited with having the responsibility of appointing advisers to over one hundred and seventy White House level advisory commissions or boards. Close to twenty-five hundred citizens serve by appointment of the President on boards such as the Advisory Commission on Intergovernmental Relations, the President's Science Advisory Committee, the Commission on International Commodity Trade, the National Commission on Reform of Federal Criminal Laws, and the Water Pollution Control Advisory Board, etc.

Thousands of additional nongovernmental professionals report as part-time advisers to White House staff officials or to Cabinet and sub-Cabinet officers. For example, in recent years approximately two hundred scientists and engineers have served as part-time consultants to the President's Science Adviser who heads up the relatively compact Office of Science and Technology. Twenty-seven different education advisory councils, with a total membership somewhere in the neighborhood of three hundred, report to the Commissioner of the U.S. Office of Education in the Department of Health, Education, and Welfare. These examples mirror similar types of arrangements in all the other departments and agencies of the executive branch.

Examples of some of the more formal or typical White House advisory channels might be listed as follows:

1. *The President's Cabinet, and Sub-Cabinet Committees*
2. *White House Personal Staff:*
   A. Policy and program advisers
   B. Legislative liaison staffs
   C. Political and appointment advisers
   D. Press secretaries and speech-writing staffs
   E. Special Counsels and Special Consultants
3. *White House Support Staffs: An Inside Network*
   A. The Bureau of the Budget
   B. Council of Economic Advisers
   C. National Security Council and Staff
   D. Central Intelligence Agency
   E. Foreign Intelligence Board
   F. National Security Agency
   G. Office of Science and Technology
   H. Office of Emergency Planning
   I. Civil Service Commission and Talent Bank/Recruitment Office
   J. National Committee Staff (of the President's political party)
4. *White House Support Staffs: An Outside Network*

A. President's personal friends and political allies
B. White House advisory commissions, councils, or boards
C. White House conferences
D. White House task forces
E. White House special study commissions (short term)
F. White House consultants
G. White House staff visits to universities and foundations
H. White House interagency committees
I. White House initiated contracts with advisory institutions: (e.g., RAND, The Brookings Institution, Stanford Research Institute, The Urban Institute, etc.)

As Harold Laski noted in his introductory remarks to *The American Presidency,* "The processes of government are very like an iceberg: what appears on the surface may be but a small part of the reality beneath." [9] Few people are aware of the physical magnitude of the Presidential advisory system or of the extent of its influence (and potential influence). Of all the aspects of the Presidency, this is, to date, the least explored and the least understood, or, to continue the analogy, the most "submerged." Yet, it is one of the most important segments of the Presidency since it is at this level, not at the Congressional level or at the more visible Presidential level, that the major portion of the policy agenda is acted upon and recast.

The exact extent of the influence of Presidential task forces and commissions is far too difficult to measure at this time. However, selective interviewing of Congressmen and of senior members of the bureaucracy reveals that more and more of the policy initiatives emanate from these White House appointed collectivities. Because of this development, selection to such groups has become a sought after symbol of prestige as well as a form of patronage. Inevitably, jealousies have developed, even to the point where an occasional Congressional committee has decided to appoint its own commission, as in the cases of the 1967 and 1968 Selective Service and civil disorders investigations. Then too, there are many complaints from Cabinet and sub-Cabinet officials who feel that the White House has greatly centralized and almost monopolized the ablest experts (at the White House level) to discretely assess and oversee ongoing programs and recommend new ones. Clearly, then, there are liabilities, as well as advantages, inherent in the expanding Presidential advisory system.

With the social and technological revolutions that have occurred during the recent Presidential Administrations, specialists in every field are deemed essential to the intelligent formulation of policy. It is at this level of government, in what might be called a "Parliament of Experts," that the future planners and inventive leaders meet and join to initiate national policy goals

[9] Harold J. Laski, *The American Presidency,* New York, Grosset & Dunlap, 1940, p. 2.

and programs. It is this stratum of government which ultimately propels ideas and innovations into the appropriate decision-making circles of the executive branch. Of necessity, this professional subinstitution is a flexible one, incorporating its own myriad political "trade offs" and concomitantly arising bargaining tactics and strategies.

While the precise consequences of these new processes and subinstitutions are not entirely understood, a resulting number of practical and normative considerations have become quite apparent. In an era of continual vigils, protests, "Marches on Washington," and even civil disorders, it is quite evident that a vast number of people feel that they are not being taken into consideration. It is also quite obvious that the Presidential advisory system, as organized under Presidents Eisenhower, Kennedy, and Johnson, was extraordinarily skewed in composition in favor of the best educated and the professionally well established. It is perfectly normal for members of a "participatory civic culture" to question who is taken into account by Presidents and why. One can readily wonder whether the "Parliament of the People" once dreamed of by Woodrow Wilson is being still further emasculated when our Chief Executives grow more and more dependent on a nonelected parliament of future planners, chosen not for their representativeness, nor for their ideology, but rather for their professional education and specializations. Or whether this is indeed the most efficient and the only realistic way to respond to the policy requirements of our rapidly changing and increasingly future-oriented nation.

One can even question whether the Presidency is the proper locus of an elaborate intelligence and advisory system. Why not have it attached to Congress? Why not have it decentralized to the states? Or why not use private institutions? How secret or how public should future planning in a participatory democracy be? What types of future planning and institutions for future planning should be developed and funded? To whom should such institutions be responsible and accountable? These are still open questions which require academic and public investigation. These are the questions which have motivated this anthology. Hopefully this book will serve as a first step for those who will join in the development of a more systematic understanding of Presidential advisory system politics, and for those who are interested in becoming involved in a society which will itself be able to choose among alternative futures.

Harold Lasswell once posed some similar questions to his colleagues in the social sciences when he urged them to consider a greater policy orientation in their research activity. His concerns and questions are still the relevant ones today:

> The continuing crisis of national security in which we live calls for the most efficient use of manpower, facilities, and resources of the American people. Highly trained talent is always costly. Hence the crisis poses the problem of utilizing our intellectual resources with the wisest economy. If our policy needs are to be served, what topics of research are most worthy of pursuit?

What manpower and facilities should be allocated to official agencies and to private institutions for the prosecution of research? What are the most promising methods of gathering facts and interpretating their significance for policy? How can facts and interpretations be made effective in the decision-making process itself? [10]

THE EDITORS

[10] Harold D. Lasswell, "The Policy Orientation" in Daniel Lerner and Harold D. Lasswell, eds., *The Policy Sciences*, Stanford, Stanford University Press, 1951, p. 3.

—⟋— I

Presidential Advisory System: An Inside Network

The central concern here is the relationship between "intelligence" and the Presidency. By intelligence, we refer to the problem (or role) of gathering, processing, evaluating, and interpreting facts and information for the decision-making process.[1] Political analysts have often written of these roles being performed by "kitchen cabinets," assistant Presidents, or alter egos of the President. Much of this literature kindles the imagination with visions of FDR's "brain trust" of university professors or the imperial entourage of an Akbar the Great or a Haile Selassie. And no doubt, there are some distinct parallels. But the glamor and mystique attached to these visions could and should be set aside. The demystification of the White House staff and the Executive Office of the President can readily be achieved without diminishing in the least the appropriate dignity and importance of the responsibilities of these offices.

[1] See the usage of the term "intelligence" by Harold Wilensky, *Organizational Intelligence*, New York, Basic Books, 1967, and by Harold Lasswell, "The Public Interest: Proposing Principles of Content and Procedure" in Carl J. Friederich, ed., *The Public Interest*, Nomos V, New York, Atherton Press, 1962, pp. 54–79.

"Inside network," as used here will refer to the President's personal staff and those staff members with whom the President is likely to come into close and frequent contact. Selections here also treat some of the chief professional advisers who, necessarily, have close association with Presidential policy making and with some of the procedures which have been developed to assist in advisory/evaluative work.

Interest in this section revolves around the following questions: With whom does the President talk and consult? With whom does his staff confer and on whom do they rely for new ideas, information, and policy appraisal? What is the division of labor at the White House? In short, what strategies are preferred and frequently relied upon for getting the jobs of the White House staff done? Also, who gets the President's attention, and why, and how? The selections which follow have been chosen because they treat these questions and raise similar ones.

1

Presidential Advisers

THEODORE C. SORENSEN

. . . [E]ach President must determine for himself how best to elicit and assess the advice of his advisers. Organized meetings, of the Cabinet and National Security Council, for example, have certain indispensable advantages, not the least of which are the increased public confidence inspired by order and regularity and the increased esprit de corps of the participants.

President Kennedy, whose nature and schedule would otherwise turn him away from meetings for the sake of meeting, has sometimes presided over sessions of the full Cabinet and National Security Council held primarily for these two reasons. Regularly scheduled meetings can also serve to keep open the channels of communication. This is the primary purpose, for example, of the President's weekly breakfast with his party's legislative leaders.

But there are other important advantages to meetings. The interaction of many minds is usually more illuminating than the intuition of one. In a meeting representing different departments and diverse points of view, there is a greater likelihood of hearing alternatives, of exposing errors, and of challenging assumptions. It is true in the White House, as in the Congress, that fewer votes are changed by open debate than by quiet negotiation among the debaters. But in the White House, unlike the Congress, only one man's vote is decisive, and thorough and thoughtful debate *before* he has made up his mind can assist him in that task.

Reprinted by permission from Theodore C. Sorensen, *Decision-Making in the White House,* New York, Columbia University Press, 1963, pp. 58–76.

That meetings can sometimes be useful was proven by the deliberations of the NSC executive committee after the discovery of offensive weapons in Cuba. The unprecedented nature of the Soviet move, the manner in which it cut across so many departmental jurisdictions, the limited amount of information available, and the security restrictions which inhibited staff work, all tended to have a leveling effect on the principals taking part in these discussions, so that each felt free to challenge the assumptions and assertions of all others.

Everyone in that group altered his views as the give-and-take talk continued. Every solution or combination of solutions was coldly examined, and its disadvantages weighed. The fact that we started out with a sharp divergence of views, the President has said, was "very valuable" in hammering out a policy.

In such meetings, a President must carefully weigh his own words. Should he hint too early in the proceedings at the direction of his own thought, the weight of his authority, the loyalty of his advisers and their desire to be on the "winning side" may shut off productive debate. Indeed, his very presence may inhibit candid discussion. President Truman, I am told, absented himself for this reason from some of the National Security Council discussions on the Berlin blockade; and President Kennedy, learning on his return from a midweek trip in October, 1962, that the deliberations of the NSC executive committee over Cuba had been more spirited and frank in his absence, asked the committee to hold other preliminary sessions without him.

But no President—at least none with his firm cast of mind and concept of office—could stay out of the fray completely until all conflicts were resolved and a collective decision reached. For group recommendations too often put a premium on consensus in place of content, on unanimity in place of precision, on compromise in place of creativity.

Some advisers may genuinely mistake agreement for validity and coordination for policy—looking upon their own role as that of mediator, convinced that any conclusion shared by so many able minds must be right, and pleased that they could in this way ease their President's problems. They may in fact have increased them.

Even more severe limitations arise when a decision must be communicated, in a document or speech or diplomatic note. For group authorship is rarely, if ever, successful. A certain continuity and precision of style, and unity of argument, must be carefully drafted, particularly in a public communication that will be read or heard by many diverse audiences. Its key principles and phrases can be debated, outlined, and later reviewed by a committee, but basically authorship depends on one man alone with his typewriter or pen. (Had the Gettysburg address been written by a committee, its ten sentences would surely have grown to a hundred, its simple pledges would surely have been hedged, and the world would indeed have little noted or long remembered what was said there.)

Moreover, even spirited debates can be stifling as well as stimulating. The homely, the simple, or the safe may sound far more plausible to the weary ear in the Cabinet room than it would look to the careful eye in the office. The most formidable debater is not necessarily the most informed, and the most reticent may sometimes be the wisest.

Even the most distinguished and forthright adviser is usually reluctant to stand alone. If he fears his persistence in a meeting will earn him the disapprobation of his colleagues, a rebuff by the President, or (in case of a "leak") the outrage of the Congress, press, or public, he may quickly seek the safety of greater numbers. At the other extreme are those who seek refuge in the role of chronic dissenter, confining their analytical power to a restatement of dangers and objections.

Still others may address themselves more to their image than to the issues. The liberal may seek to impress his colleagues with his caution; idealists may try to sound tough-minded. I have attended more than one meeting where a military solution was opposed by military minds and supported by those generally known as peace-lovers.

The quality of White House meetings also varies with the number and identity of those attending. Large meetings are less likely to keep secrets—too many Washington officials enjoy talking knowingly at social events or to the press or to their friends. Large meetings are also a less flexible instrument for action, less likely to produce a meaningful consensus or a frank hard-hitting debate. President Kennedy prefers to invite only those whose official views he requires or whose unofficial judgment he values, and to reserve crucial decisions for a still smaller session or for solitary contemplation in his own office.

The difficulty with small meetings, however, is that, in Washington, nearly everyone likes to feel that he, too, conferred and concurred. For years agencies and individuals all over town have felt affronted if not invited to a National Security Council session. The press leaps to conclusions as to who is in favor and who is not by scanning the attendance lists of meetings, speculating in much the same fashion (and with even less success) as the Kremlinologists who study the reviewing stand at the Russian May Day Parade or analyze which Soviet officials sat where at the opening of the Moscow ballet.

Yet in truth attendance at a White House meeting is not necessarily a matter of logic. Protocol, personal relations, and the nature of the forum may all affect the list. Some basic foreign policy issue, for example, may be largely decided before it comes to the National Security Council—by the appointment of a key official, or by the President's response at a press conference, or by the funds allocated in the budget. Yet personnel, press conference, and budget advice is generally given in meetings outside the National Security Council.

Expert Advisers

Many different types of advisers, with differing roles and contributions, attend these meetings. President Kennedy met on his tax policy in the summer of

1962, for example, with professional economists from both inside and outside the government, as well as with department heads and White House aides. To the key meetings on Cuba were invited highly respected Foreign Service officers as well as policy appointees, retired statesmen as well as personal presidential assistants.

There is no predictable weight which a President can give to the conclusions of each type. The technical expert or career specialist, operating below the policy making level, may have concentrated knowledge on the issue under study which no other adviser can match. Yet Presidents are frequently criticized for ignoring the advice of their own experts.

The reason is that the very intensity of that expert's study may prevent him from seeing the broader, more practical perspective which must govern public policy. As Laski's notable essay pointed out, too many experts lack a sense of proportion, an ability to adapt, and a willingness to accept evidence inconsistent with their own. The specialist, Laski wrote, too often lacks "insight into the movement and temper of the public mind. . . . He is an invaluable servant and an impossible master."

Thus the atomic scientist, discussing new tests, may think largely in terms of his own laboratory. The career diplomat, discussing an Asian revolt, may think largely in terms of his own post. The professional economist, in urging lower farm price supports, may think more in terms of his academic colleagues than of the next presidential election.

But not all experts recognize the limits of their political sagacity, and they do not hesitate to pronounce with a great air of authority broad policy recommendations in their own field (and sometimes all fields). Any President would be properly impressed by their seeming command of the complex; but the President's own common sense, his own understanding of the Congress and the country, his own balancing of priorities, his own ability to analyze and generalize and simplify, are more essential in reaching the right decision than all the specialized jargon and institutionalized traditions of the professional elite.

The trained navigator, it has been rightly said, is essential to the conduct of a voyage, but his judgment is not superior on such matters as where it should go or whether it should be taken at all. Essential to the relationship between expert and politician, therefore, is the recognition by each of the other's role, and the refusal of each to assume the other's role. The expert should neither substitute his political judgment for the policy-maker's nor resent the latter's exercising of his own; and the policy-maker should not forget which one is the expert.

Expert predictions are likely to be even more tenuous than expert policy judgments, particularly in an age when only the unpredictable seems to happen. In the summer of 1962, most of the top economists in government, business, and academic life thought it likely that a recession would follow the stock-market slide—at least "before the snows melted" was the cautious forecast by one economist from a cold northern state. But, instead, this year's thaw brought with it new levels of production—and, naturally, a new set of predictions.

In the fall of 1962, most specialists in Soviet affairs believed that long-range Soviet missiles, with their closely guarded electronic systems, would never be stationed on the uncertain island of Cuba, nearly 6,000 miles away from Soviet soil and supplies. Nevertheless, each rumor to this effect was checked out; increasing rumors brought increased surveillance; and when, finally, the unexpected did happen, this did not diminish the President's respect for these career servants. It merely demonstrated once again that the only infallible experts are those whose forecasts have never been tested.

Cabinet Advisers

In short, a Cabinet of politicians and policy-makers is better than a Cabinet of experts. But a President will also weigh with care the advice of each Cabinet official. For the latter is also bound by inherent limitations. He was not necessarily selected for the President's confidence in his judgment alone—considerations of politics, geography, public esteem, and interest-group pressures may also have played a part, as well as his skill in administration.

Moreover, each department has its own clientele and point of view, its own experts and bureaucratic interests, its own relations with the Congress and certain subcommittees, its own statutory authority, objectives, and standards of success. No Cabinet member is free to ignore all this without impairing the morale and efficiency of his department, his standing therein, and his relations with the powerful interest groups and congressmen who consider it partly their own.

The President may ask for a Secretary's best judgment apart from the department's views, but in the mind of the average Secretary (and there have been many notable exceptions) the two may be hardly distinguishable. Whether he is the captive or the champion of those interests makes no practical difference. By reflecting in his advice to the President his agency's component bureaus, some of which he may not even control, he increases both his prestige within the department and his parochialism without.

Bureaucratic parochialism and rivalry are usually associated in Washington with the armed services, but they in fact affect the outlook of nearly every agency. They can be observed, to cite only a few examples, in the jurisdictional maneuvering between the Park Service and the Forest Service, between the Bureau of Reclamation and the Army Engineers, between State and Treasury on world finance, or State and Commerce on world trade, or State and Defense on world disarmament.

They can also be observed in Cabinet autobiographies complaining that the President—any President—rarely saw things their way. And they can be observed, finally, in case studies of an agency head paying more heed to the

Congress than to the President who named him. But it is the Congress, after all, that must pass on his requests for money, men, and authority. It is the Congress with which much of his time will be spent, which has the power to investigate his acts or alter his duties. And it is the Congress which vested many of his responsibilities directly in him, not in the President or the Executive branch.

White House Staff Advisers

The parochialism of experts and department heads is offset in part by a President's White House and executive staff. These few assistants are the only other men in Washington whose responsibilities both enable and require them to look, as he does, at the government as a whole. Even the White House specialists—the President's economic advisers or science adviser, for example—are likely to see problems in a broader perspective, within the framework of the President's objectives and without the constraints of bureaucratic tradition.

White House staff members are chosen, not according to any geographical, political, or other pattern, but for their ability to serve the President's needs and to talk the President's language. They must not—and do not, in this Administration [Kennedy's]—replace the role of a Cabinet official or block his access to the President. Instead, by working closely with departmental personnel, by spotting, refining, and defining issues for the President, they can increase governmental unity rather than splinter responsibility. A good White House staff can give a President that crucial margin of time, analysis, and judgment that makes an unmanageable problem more manageable.

But there are limiting factors as well. A White House adviser may see a departmental problem in a wider context than the Secretary, but he also has less contact with actual operations and pressures, with the Congress and interested groups. If his own staff grows too large, his office may become only another department, another level of clearances and concurrences instead of a personal instrument of the President. If his confidential relationship with the President causes either one to be too uncritical of the other's judgment, errors may go uncorrected. If he develops (as Mr. Acheson has suggested so many do) a confidence in his own competence which outruns the fact, his contribution may be more mischievous than useful. If, on the other hand, he defers too readily to the authority of renowned experts and Cabinet powers, then the President is denied the skeptical, critical service his staff should be providing.

Outside Advisers

Finally, a President may seek or receive advice from outside the Executive branch: from members of the Congress; from independent wise men, elder statesmen, academic lights; from presidentially named high-level commissions or special agents; or merely from conversations with friends, visitors, private interest leaders, and others. Inevitably, unsolicited advice will pour in from the mass media.

This is good. Every President needs independent, unofficial sources of advice for the same reasons he needs independent, unofficial sources of information. Outside advisers may be more objective. Their contact with affected groups may be closer. They may be men whose counsel the President trusts, but who are unable to accept government service for financial or personal reasons. They may be men who are frank with the President because, to use Corwin's phrase, their "daily political salt did not come from the President's table."

Whatever the justification, outside advice has its own limitations. As national problems become more complex and interrelated, requiring continuous, firsthand knowledge of confidential data and expert analysis, very few outsiders are sufficiently well informed. The fact that some simple recommendation, contained in an editorial or political oration or informal conversation, seems more striking or appealing or attention-getting than the intricate product of bureaucracy does not make it any more valid.

Moreover, once the advice of a distinguished private citizen or committee is sought and made public, rejection of that advice may add to the President's difficulties. The appointment by the last three Presidents [Truman, Eisenhower, Kennedy] of special advisory committees on civil rights, world trade, and foreign aid was, in that sense, a gamble—a gamble that the final views of these committees would strengthen, not weaken, the President's purpose. Should the outside report not be made public, the Gaither report being a well-known example, a President who rejects its advice may still have to face the consequences of its authors' displeasure.

Qualifications of Advisers

Finally, a President's evaluation of any individual's advice is dependent in part on the human characteristics of both men. Personalities play an intangible but surprisingly important role. Particular traits, social ties, recreational interests or occupational backgrounds may strengthen or weaken the bonds between them. Some Presidents pay more attention to generals, some to businessmen, some to politicians, some even to intellectuals who have "never met a payroll and never carried a precinct."

In truth, a political background, not necessarily at the precinct level, is helpful. It gives the adviser a more realistic understanding of the President's needs. Those without such experience will tend to assume that the few congressmen in touch with their agency speak for all the Congress, that one or two contacts at a Washington cocktail party are an index of public opinion, and that what looms large in the newspaper headlines necessarily looms large in the public mind.

Those with a political base of their own are also more secure in case of attack; but those with political ambitions of their own—as previous Presidents discovered—may place their own reputation and record ahead of their President's. (Such a man is not necessarily suppressing his conscience and forgetting the national interest. He may sincerely believe whatever it is most to his advantage to believe, much like the idealistic but hungry lawyer who will never defend a guilty man but persuades himself that all rich clients are innocent.)

Other advisers may also be making a record, not for some future campaign, but for some future publication. "History will record that I am right," he mutters to himself, if not to his colleagues, because he intends to write that history in his memoirs. The inaccuracy of most Washington diaries and autobiographies is surpassed only by the immodesty of their authors.

The opposite extreme is the adviser who tells his President only what he thinks the President wants to hear—a bearer of consistently good tidings but frequently bad advice.

Yet there is no sure test of a good adviser. The most rational pragmatic-appearing man may turn out to be the slave of his own private myths, habits, and emotional beliefs. The hardest-working man may be too busy and out-of-touch with the issue at hand, or too weary to focus firmly on it. (I saw first hand, during the long days and nights of the Cuban crisis, how brutally physical and mental fatigue can numb the good sense as well as the senses of normally articulate men.)

The most experienced man may be experienced only in failure, or his experience, in Coleridge's words, may be "like the stern lights of a ship which illumine only the track it has passed." The most articulate, authoritative man may only be making bad advice sound good, while driving into silence less aggressive or more cautious advisers.

All this a President must weigh in hearing his advisers.

2

Approaches
to Staffing
the Presidency

RICHARD E. NEUSTADT

It has been a quarter century since the President's Committee on Administration Management, chaired by Louis Brownlow, blessed by Franklin Roosevelt, heralded a major innovation in our constitutional arrangements: substantial staffing for the Presidency distinct from other parts of the Executive
establishment, in Edwin Corwin's phrase an "Institutionalized Presidency." The
Executive Office, which throughout our prior history had been essentially a
"private office" in the English sense, was to become a "President's Department."
So it did. Presidential agencies have filled the building which in 1937 housed
the State Department (and in 1913 had housed War and Navy, too). Presidential aides outrank in all but protocol the heads of most Executive departments.

I. The Brownlow Report

We date this development from Brownlow's Report. In the sphere of Presidential staffing, its proposals for the most part were put into practice with
promptness and fidelity. And practice, for the most part, has been kind to the
proposals, has sustained—indeed has vindicated—key ideas behind them. What

Reprinted by permission from Richard E. Neustadt, "Approaches to Staffing the Presidency," *The American Political Science Review*, vol. LVII, No. 4, December, 1963, pp.
855–863. Originally a paper delivered at the Annual Meeting, American Political Science
Association, New York, September 6, 1963.

rare experience for an advisory report! It gives the work of the Committee special standing which we properly acknowledge as we meet professionally in 1963, the Silver Anniversary of their decided service to the country and to our profession.

As Brownlow cheerfully acknowledges, his group was in effect a White House "chosen instrument." The Committee urged what Roosevelt wanted. They wrote, he edited. In the election year of 1936 he gave them a "non-political" assignment, "administrative management." After his reelection they couched their response in appropriate terms, PODSCORB terms, Gulick-and-Urwick terms, shades of Taylorism, with "administration" set apart from "policy" and "politics." Roosevelt thought it politic that they should do so. But he took care that their proposals met his purposes which were emphatically, essentially political. He wanted to enhance his own capacity to rule. And when he undertook to implement what they proposed, the product seemed to fit him like a glove, to be but an enlargement and refinement of his style of operation circa 1936. So I think it was.

The Brownlow report and what followed, the first stages of the institutionalized Presidency, must be taken to reflect this President's matured approach after a term in office—to say nothing of his seven years in Wilson's Washington. Did Brownlow educate the President? How much was it the other way 'round? Or Harold Smith, whom Brownlow helped make Budget Director under the new dispensation: did he teach FDR or Roosevelt him? At this distance it is hard to be precise about the educative interchange among these three. With all credit to Brownlow and to Smith, my money is on Roosevelt as the one who gave more than he took.

To characterize the FDR approach we cannot rest content with the Brownlow Report. Its language is too "managerial." The same thing can be said of Roosevelt's formal documents, or of Smith's public statements (his among others). For the sake of analysis—and comparison—it becomes necessary to construct a characterization out of what they and their colleagues did, not what they said in public, as revealed piecemeal by memoirs, by case studies, and by retrospective conversations. For 18 years I have made something of a hobby of such conversations.

Let me draw on these, and on the published works as well, to characterize as best I can. In doing so I grant the risks of retrospection, still more those of oversimplification. But since our commentator, Arthur Schlesinger, has yet to give us for the later FDR a characterization as effective as he offered for the earlier, our purposes today demand a temporary substitute. However risky, here it is.

II. The Roosevelt Approach

So far as I can find, Roosevelt did not theorize about the principles which underlay his operating style in later years. But he evidently had some principles, or at least premises, or touch-stones, or instincts, for his practice was remarkably consistent in essentials.

The first of these "principles," I would suggest, was a concern for his position as *the* man in the White House. If he began the institutionalized Presidency, he did not for a moment mean that it should make an institution out of *him*. The White House was *his* House, his home as well as office. No one was to work there who was not essential for the conduct of his own work, day by day. "This is the White House calling" was to mean *him*, or somebody acting intimately and immediately for him. The things he personally did not do from week to week, the trouble-shooting and intelligence he did not need first-hand, were to be staffed outside the White House. The aides he did not have to see from day to day were to be housed in other offices than his. This is the origin of the distinction which developed in his time between "personal" and "institutional" staff. The Executive Office was conceived to be the place for "institutional" staff; the place, in other words, for everybody else.

Not only did he generally try to keep second-string personnel out of his house, he also shied away from second-string activities which smacked of the routine (except where *he* chose otherwise for the time being). This seems to be one of the reasons—not the only one—why he never had "legislative liaison" assistants continuously working at the White House. Reportedly, he foresaw what came to be the case in Eisenhower's time, that if the White House were routinely in the liaisoning business, Congressmen and agencies alike would turn to *his* assistants for all sorts of routine services and help. "It is all your trouble, not mine," he once informed his Cabinet officers, with reference to the bills that *they* were sponsoring. This was his attitude toward departmental operations generally, always excepting those things that he wanted for his own, or felt he had to grab because of personalities or circumstances.

For routine, or preliminary, or depth staff-work that his White House aides could not take on (or should not, in his view), Roosevelt usually looked to the Budget Bureau or, alternatively, to a man or group he trusted in the operating agencies. In many ways the modern Bureau was his personal creation. And in most of his later years it was, as well, the only "institutional" staff of substantial size under his own control.

Theoretically he might have looked instead to interdepartmental mechanisms, to standing committees and secretariats. Indeed, he had begun his Presidential career by doing so. He created our first "cabinet secretariat" with the National Emergency Council of 1933. But after experimenting elaborately in his first term, Roosevelt lost taste for interagency committees. Thereafter, he never seems to have regarded any of them—from the Cabinet down—as a vehicle for doing anything that could be done by operating agencies or by a staff directly tied to him. This left small scope for such committees *at his level*. He used the Cabinet as a sounding board *sometimes*, and sometimes as a means to put his thinking, or his "magic" on display. Otherwise, his emphasis was on staffs and on operating agencies, taken one by one or in an *ad hoc* group.

The second "principle" I would note is FDR's strong feeling for a cardinal fact in government: that Presidents don't act on policies, programs, or personnel in the abstract; they act in the concrete as they meet deadlines set by due dates—or the urgency—of documents awaiting signature, vacant posts awaiting appointees, officials seeking interviews, newsmen seeking answers, audiences waiting for a speech, intelligence reports requiring a response, etc., etc. He also had a strong sense of another fact in government: that persons close to Presidents are under constant pressure—and temptation—to go into business for themselves, the more so as the word gets out that they deal regularly with some portion of his business.

Accordingly, he gave a minimum of fixed assignments to the members of his personal staff. Those he did give out were usually in terms of helping him to handle some specific and recurrent stream of action-forcing deadlines he himself could not escape.

Thus, before the war, he had one aide regularly assigned to help him with his personal press relations and with those deadline-makers, his press conferences: the Press Secretary. Another aide was regularly assigned to schedule his appointments and to guard his door: the Appointments Secretary. Early in the war he drew together several scattered tasks and put them regularly in the hands of Samuel Rosenman as "Special Counsel." (The title was invented for the man; Rosenman, a lawyer and a judge, had held a similar title and done comparable work for FDR in Albany.): pulling together drafts of Presidential messages, speeches, and policy statements, reviewing proposed Executive Orders, Administration bill drafts, and action on enrolled bills—in short, assisting with the preparation of all public documents through which Roosevelt defined and pressed *his* program.

These fixed assignments, and others like them in the Roosevelt staff, were sphere-of-action assignments, *not* programmatic ones. They were organized around recurrent Presidential obligations, not functional subject matters. They were differentiated by particular sorts of actions, not by particular program areas. This had three consequences:

1. The men on such assignments were compelled to be generalists, jacks-of-all-trades, with a perspective almost as unspecialized as the President's own, cutting across every program area, every government agency, and every facet of *his* work, personal, political, legislative, administrative, ceremonial.

2. Each assignment was distinct from others but bore a close relationship to others, since the assigned activities, themselves, were interlinked at many points. Naturally, the work of the Press Secretary and the Special Counsel overlapped, while both had reason for concern and for involvement, often enough, with the work of the Appointments Secretary—and so forth. These men knew what their jobs were but they could not do them without watching, checking, jostling one another. Roosevelt liked it so. (Indeed, he liked it almost too much; he positively encouraged them to jostle. He evidently got a kick out of bruised egos.)

3. Since each man was a "generalist" in program terms, he could be used for *ad hoc* special checks and inquiries depending on the President's needs of the moment. So far as their regular work allowed, the fixed-assignment men were also general-utility trouble-shooters. No one was supposed to be too specialized for that.

There were some spheres of recurrent action, of activities incumbent on the President, where Roosevelt evidently thought it wise to have *no* staff with fixed, identified assignments. One was the sphere of *his* continuing relations with the leaders and members of Congress. Another was the sphere of his own choices for the chief appointive offices in his Administration. A third was the sphere of his direct relations with Department Heads, both individually and as a Cabinet. Every Roosevelt aide on fixed assignment was involved to some degree in all three spheres. These and other aides were always liable to be used, *ad hoc,* on concrete problems in these spheres. But no one save the President was licensed to concern himself exclusively, or continuously, with FDR's Congressional relations, political appointments, or Cabinet-level contacts.

The third thing I would emphasize is Roosevelt's sense of need for mobile manpower and multiple antennae. In addition to his aides with fixed assignments, FDR took full advantage of the Brownlow Report's proposal for a number of "Administrative Assistants" on his personal staff, each with a "passion for anonymity." After 1939 and on into the war years, he had several men so-titled—and so enjoined—about him, all of them conceived as "generalists," whom he could use, *ad hoc,* as chore-boys, trouble-shooters, checker-uppers, intelligence operatives and as magnets for ideas, gripes, gossip in the Administration, on the Hill, and with groups outside government. These men were also used, as need arose, to backstop and assist the aides who did have fixed assignments.

FDR intended his Administrative Assistants to be eyes and ears and manpower for *him,* with no fixed contacts, clients, or involvements of their own to interfere when he had need to redeploy them. Naturally, these general-purpose aides gained know-how in particular subject-matter areas, and the longer they worked on given *ad hoc* jobs the more they tended to become functional "specialists." One of them, David Niles, got so involved in dealings with minority groups that Truman kept him on with this as his fixed specialty. Roosevelt's usual response to such a situation would have been to shake it up before the specialization grew into a fixed assignment.

The "passion for anonymity" phrase, which caused such merriment in Washington when Brownlow's report came out, did not seem funny in the least to FDR. He evidently thought it of the essence for the men inside his House whom he would use as general-purpose aides. Fixed, functional assignments interfered with anonymity as well as with his freedom of deployment.

Roosevelt had never wanted in his House more general-purpose men for

ad hoc missions than he personally could supervise, direct, assign *and reassign.*
During the war, however, as his needs and interests changed, his White House
staff inevitably tended to become a two-level operation, with some aides quite
remote from his immediate concerns or daily supervision. How he might have
met this tendency, after the war, we have no means of knowing.

It never seems to have occurred to FDR that his only sources of such
ad hoc personal assistance were the aides in his own office. He also used
Executive Office aides, personal friends, idea-men or technicians down in the
bureaucracy, old Navy hands, old New York hands, experts from private life,
Cabinet Officers, Little Cabinet Officers, diplomats, relatives—especially his
wife—toward the end his daughter—as supplementary eyes and ears and manpower. He often used these "outsiders" to check or duplicate the work of
White House staff, or to probe into spheres where White House aides should not
be seen, or to look into things he guessed his staff would be against.

He disliked to be tied to any single source of information or advice on
anything. Even if the source should be a trusted aide, he preferred, when and
where he could, to have alternative sources.

Put these three operating "principles" together and they add up to a
fourth: In Roosevelt's staffing there was no place for a Sherman Adams.
Roosevelt made and shifted the assignments; *he* was the recipient of staff work;
he presided at informal morning staff meetings; *he* audited the service he was
getting; *he* coordinated A's report with B's (or if he did not, they went un-
coordinated and he sometimes paid a price for that). Before the war, reportedly, he planned to keep one of his Administrative Assistants on tap "in
the office," to "mind the shop" and be a sort of checker-upper on the others.
But he never seems to have put this intention into practice. From time to time,
he did lean on one aide above all others in a given area. In wartime, for example, Harry Hopkins was distinctly *primus inter pares* on a range of vital
matters for a period of time. But Hopkins' range was never as wide as the
President's. And Hopkins' primacy was not fixed, codified, or enduring. It
depended wholly on their personal relationship and Roosevelt's will. In certain
periods their intimacy waxed; it also waned.

III. FDR in Wartime

This brings me to the matter of wartime innovations, unforeseen in 1937,
which profoundly changed the atmosphere and focus of the preexisting White
House operation.

From 1941 to 1943 Roosevelt brought new staff into the White House.
Superficially, the new men and their new assignments made the place look
different. But as he dealt with wartime staff, he operated very much as he had
done before. He let his prewar pattern bend; despite appearances, he did not
let it break.

The principal new arrivals were Hopkins, Rosenman, Lubin, Leahy, a "Map-Room," and Byrnes. Rosenman, as Counsel, has already been mentioned. Hopkins evolved into a sort of super (very super) administrative assistant, working on assignments without fixed boundaries in the conduct of the wartime Grand Alliance, and collaborating with Rosenman on major speeches. Lubin, nominally a Hopkins assistant, was Roosevelt's counterpart to Churchill's wartime Economic Section, the President's personal statistician, an independent source and analyst of key data on production of munitions, among other things. Leahy, as Chief of Staff to the Commander-in-Chief, became an active channel to and from the services, and kept an eye upon the White House Map-Room. This was a reporting and communications center, staffed by military personnel, in direct touch with the services, with war fronts, with intelligence sources, and with allied governments. As for Byrnes, he left the Supreme Court to be a "deputy" for Roosevelt in resolving quarrels among the agencies concerned with war production and the war economy. Byrnes' assignment was relatively fixed, but limited, temporary and entirely at the pleasure of the President, dependent on their personal relationship. In 1944, when Congress turned his job into a separate, statutory office (OWMR), Byrnes hastened to resign.

A final wartime innovation deserves mention: Charles Bohlen's designation as State's White House liaison. Until Sumner Welles' departure from the Undersecretaryship, Roosevelt had resolved his chronic inability either to make use of Cordell Hull or to dispense with him partly by ignoring State Department services, partly by using Welles as personal adviser and as link to the Department. Once this painful arrangement had been ended, there was no replacing it while Hull endured. But Hull's ill-health and ultimate departure paved the way for new arrangements. These embody Roosevelt's notions in the last months of his life on the ever-present issue of White House–State relations: Edward Stettinius became Hull's successor on the evident assumption that he would keep house and "front" for the Department; Bohlen was confirmed in a liaison role and given formal status as the active link through which the White House was to get staff work from the Department and the Foreign Service orders from the White House. How this might have worked nobody knows.

The striking common feature in these wartime innovations is that none of the new aides, from first to last, had irreversible assignments, or exclusive jurisdictions, or control over each other, or command over remaining members of the peacetime staff. Regarding all of them, and as he dealt with each of them, Roosevelt remained his own "chief of staff." And he continued to employ outsiders for assistance. Winston Churchill, among others, now became an alternative source. Anna Boettiger became a window to the world of personalities and politics beyond the terribly confining realm of war-making.

The war, in short, brought new men and new facilities into the Presidential orbit, reflecting the new needs and new preoccupation of the President. Compared with 1939, the staff of 1944 had far more scope, more varied skills, incomparably better technical resources, a wider and a *different* range of interests, wider reach for policy, and on the part of leading members an enormous although variable share in exercising Presidential powers. To members of the pre-existing peacetime staff it often seemed that everything had changed, that Roosevelt's operation was transformed. But from his standpoint looking down, not up, nothing had changed save his preoccupations. Despite the surface differences—and making due allowance for the differences in substance, risk, and process—Roosevelt ran the war in the same way, with the same style, responsive to the same instincts or "principles" as during those preceding years when he and Louis Brownlow educated one another about "management." Or so it seems to me.

IV. Wartime Complications

In peace and war Roosevelt's approach to Presidential staffing was consonant with his approach to Presidential power. He sought to maximize the office as a vehicle for *him*. His interest lay in strengthening his own hold over policy. He put his faith, as always, in a competition among men and ideas both; his staff facilities gave institutional expression to the operating style he had developed during his first term, a style which Schlesinger has brilliantly described, a style which was intended to enhance his personal power. He conceived of Presidential staff in the same terms.

This is not to say that his approach to staffing brought the same results in wartime as in peacetime. On the contrary, his war experience exposed a host of difficulties which had been undreamed of—or at least left unexplored—when he and Brownlow started their collaboration.

Wartime, for one thing, changed the size and pace of Executive operations. We have got used to the Pentagon, but it was then the symbol of a new dimension. The New Deal had substantially enlarged and quickened the Executive establishment of Hoover's time. War government towered over the New Deal. With the change in scale came changes in physical proximity, in direct contact, in human scope, in ease of interchange. Rooseveltian staff work called for intimacy, informality, word-of-mouth, walking-through, not only in the White House but around the town. War made it a much bigger town.

Wartime also imposed secrecy and censorship. No longer could the President look anywhere and everywhere for scraps of information and advice on his preeminent concerns, his most compelling choices. No longer could he pick up any aide or friend he chose to spy out the terrain of his official advisers. His instinct for alternative sources, his avid curiosity, his reach for information and ideas, now had to be confined to men with a "need to know."

Moreover, his instinct for competitive administration had to be confined—at least in cardinal spheres of policy—to men whose quarrels with one another were imperfectly observable to him through press reports, men whose opposing views, alternative approaches were veiled from public notice, public argument. As Schlesinger has pointed out, Roosevelt in peacetime relied on contention underneath him to produce a show and test of bureaucratic stresses, congressional reactions, interest-group alignments, political pressures, which he could weigh *before* he chose *his* timing and *his* course. Rooseveltian staffing obviously was designed to help him make full use of competition in these terms. But that peacetime practice took one thing for granted: an open field, a visible arena, with affected interests in the stands and audience—reactions audible to him. Secrecy—and censorship—shadowed the field, reduced the audience, blunted reactions.

In a closed arena, competitive administration gave Roosevelt less protection, fewer clues than it had done before. The inhibitions secrecy imposed upon staff services but added to the problem. Harold Stein's case-books, the new one and the old, provide us classic instances of the pain in that problem. Roosevelt never solved it. Nor—to anticipate—has Kennedy.

Secrecy did something more: it put the President into a world of knowledge *different* from the world the press inhabited. And not the press alone but his old friends, his political associates, many of his aides, the bulk of his bureaucracy, most members of his Cabinet knew less of what was happening and knew it differently, in different sequence, at a different time than he did. Now that we have lived with secrecy for a full generation, all of us have got accustomed to it and some of us have come to discount it. Numbers of my academic colleagues seem to think that if one reads the *New York Times* with care one misses nothing of importance, secrecy or not.

Numbers of Washingtonians appear to share this view. But this, I submit, is an illusion even now. Certainly it was so then when secrecy was new and censorship in force.

Roosevelt's approach to staff-work had assumed a wide array of "knowledgeable men," outside the White House as well as in, communicating freely with the President. But when most of them know less than the President, or know it differently, communication scarcely can be free and often is not useful in his business. So Roosevelt evidently found.

Not only was the President removed from most of his associates by what he knew—and when—but also by the nature of his personal responsibility. This had always been the case to a degree; wartime made it more so. FDR was spared the burden of a Kennedy that his choice, or the lack of it, might devastate a hemisphere; for the most part he was even spared the burden of a Lincoln that his judgment, or its lack, might lose a war. But in the winning of the war the burden of his choices was severe enough to chain him to his desk, exhaust his energy, cut short his life. The perspective he acquired with that burden on his back was not shared fully, could not be, by even his most intimate assistants. He remained his own "chief of staff," but tended less and less to put his mind on his assignment. Toward the end, he seems a man apart from all his principal associates. Neither individually or collectively were they abreast of his preoccupations and intentions. When Truman asked what Roosevelt meant to do, the answers were as speculative as the question.

The war had still a further consequence: the great bureaucracies it fostered, in their tangle of arms-length relationships, felt ever-more compelling need—the more compelling with each increment of size, distance, impersonality, and "brass"—for service from the White House as a source of arbitration in their combats with each other. Wartime responsibility entangled bureaucratic jurisdictions even as it added scope and scale. The War Power, meanwhile, enhanced the Presidency as a Court of Ultimate Appeal. But Roosevelt's presidential institution had been built to serve his purposes in mastering the bureaucrats, not theirs in getting service out of him. Orderly procedure, dutiful response, written records binding on the signer, firm decisions in behalf of others at *their* option—these were not often easy to obtain from Roosevelt's White House, and were not meant to be. Grudgingly, belatedly, he yielded ground sector by sector, when and as he felt impelled by bureaucratic and congressional politics, or by strained limits on his own attention. So Hopkins became arbiter-by-delegation on the inter-allied sharing of munitions, so Byrnes became, in time, an arbiter for the home-front economy; so Smith was handed, privately, complete control of budgeting for Fiscal 1946.

But in the most important spheres of all Roosevelt was adamant: On main matters in the conduct of the war and of allied relations he kept White House decision-making intimate, personalized, *ad hoc,* "disorderly," and in *his* hands. This suited him but caused great pain at Pentagon and State.

The pain Roosevelt inflicted in the war years has left a lasting imprint on our government. Officialdom retaliated, after he was gone. To some degree or other—oftener than not to a large degree—organizations at the Presidential level which were written into statute in the later 1940's were intended to assure against just such Rooseveltian free-wheeling. "Never again." It is no more than mild exaggeration to call NSC "Forrestal's Revenge," or NSRB (now OEP) "Baruch's Revenge" with Eberstadt as agent. Even in the 1950's White House organization was, in part, the product of reactions against Roosevelt. Eisenhower, too, had been a victim.

There was no need for Roosevelt to face squarely the pain his practice caused to his officialdom. Their difficulties never grew so great as to impair his own ability to function, to make use of them. The war itself while sharpening their hurt provided its own palliatives. The White House might be loath to settle a dispute, decide on policy, clarify authority, or choose priorities, but warfare and the aim of winning helped enormously to keep issues in focus, and in bounds. Money helped as well; officials operating in the cardinal spheres of policy had ample funds. As students of the Pentagon are well aware, nothing is more conducive to rational behavior, orderly discussion, give-and-take. Talent helped too; the best of the New Deal mingled with the best of Wall Street gave officialdom as much ability, as widely spread, as we have ever seen.

Meanwhile the War Power kept Congressional committees relatively muted; Congressional tempers relatively checked. And wartime unity drove underground, much of the time, the clash of interests and of parties in our politics. The war, in short, did much to ease the usual tensions among "separated institutions sharing powers," much to enhance and clarify the President's central position. With so many peacetime pains removed, or lightened, Roosevelt's wartime bureaucrats could well afford increased discomfort from his persistent "untidyness."

But suppose a President whose operating instincts were not unlike FDR's faced complications of the sort I have ascribed to wartime Washington without the wartime benefits I have just mentioned? There is no need to be suppositious. This, roughly speaking, is John Kennedy's plight.

V. The Kennedy Approach

President Kennedy has been in office a year and a half less than Roosevelt when the latter edited Brownlow's proposals; he has worked inside the White House four years less than Roosevelt when the latter fully implemented those proposals. To speak of Kennedy's "approach" to Presidential staffing is to deal with something which no doubt is still evolving in his practice and his mind. One cannot characterize what has not happened. Yet Kennedy moved swiftly to create a staffing pattern, show an operating style, and he has held to these with quite remarkable consistency for some two years. In retrospect this may turn out to have been an interim approach. But this, at least, one can attempt to characterize. Let me try.

There are some obvious affinities between the operating "principles" in Kennedy's own mind and those I earlier ascribed to FDR. His staffing demonstrates this rather plainly. He evidently shares Roosevelt's concern for the distinction between "personal" and "institutional" staff. From Administration to Administration White House staff has grown inexorably; "this is the White House calling" has less meaning every decade. But Kennedy quite consciously has tried to slow the trend; he cut back Eisenhower's growth and started small.

Kennedy, moreover, has run his personal staff with a feeling as keen as Roosevelt's (or was it Brownlow's?) for organizing around action-forcing processes. Like FDR, this President has operated with a small core of senior aides on relatively fixed assignments, and as with Roosevelt's men these have been action-sphere, not program-area assignments. Theodore Sorensen, as Special Counsel, is a Rosenman-writ-large. McGeorge Bundy is a sort of pinned down Harry Hopkins, standing astride the stream of operational actions in the conduct of diplomacy and of defense which now flows to a President routinely with no less intensity or volume than had been "exceptional" as late as 1940. And so it goes for Kenneth O'Donnell, for Pierre Salinger, for Lawrence O'Brien, for Ralph Dungan—each handles a distinctive aspect of the work-flow which the

President must get through, day-by-day. Like their Rooseveltian counterparts these men also do other things, *ad hoc*. And as in Roosevelt's day their general-purpose services are supplemented by the services of others who do not have comparable fixed-assignments, our commentator for one.

Titles have changed but style is similar. "Administrative Assistant" has less novelty and dignity; almost everyone is now a "Special Assistant." The fine old title "Secretary" is now held only by Salinger. But do not be confused by nomenclature. The pattern is much the same. So are the operating consequences for the staff. And Kennedy is very much his own chief-of-staff.

This personal staff is *unlike* FDR's in one particular: thirty-two months have passed without much feuding. These men have managed the deliberate overlapping of their work and their bilateral relations with the President in remarkable self-discipline. The lack of "personalities" is striking; the lack of bureaucratic paranoia even more so. This presumably reflects the President. His taste for competition, for alternative sources, is stronger than in any President since Roosevelt. But he seems to have no taste for ego-baiting and low tolerance for egoism, even perhaps his own. Comparing Presidential styles is tricky business. In this respect, as obviously in others, the Kennedy White House is not simply Roosevelt's reproduced.

The differences grow greater as one moves beyond the personal staff toward the realms of institutional staff and departmental relations. Roosevelt was lucky, he wrote on a clean slate and then he got a second slate "war government." Roosevelt innovated, Kennedy inherited.

From Truman he inherited an Executive Office larger and much more diffuse than Roosevelt's Budget Bureau, encompassing by statutory mandate NSC staff, CEA, and what we now call OEP. From Eisenhower he inherited a complex "staff system" and cabinet-committee structure, as well as a variety of specialized staff units. From both his predecessors he inherited classic and unresolved dilemmas of relationship between a President and certain key departments, notably Defense, State, Justice, Treasury. Kennedy's approach to staffing has been shaped in major part by his attempts to cope with this inheritance. The outcome naturally resembles Roosevelt's less than does the White House staff, *per se*.

Commotion over Kennedy's deliberate dismantling of his predecessor's staff and cabinet system has obscured the fact that he retained and has elaborated on four features of the Eisenhower era. For one thing, Kennedy disposes of his time with much the freedom Eisenhower painfully acquired from a heart attack. It is only thirty years since Hoover, once a week, received whatever citizens desired to shake hands. It is little more than a decade since Truman's days were crowded by obligatory interviews with Congressmen, with lobbyists, with spokesmen for good causes. One of Eisenhower's greatest contributions to the Presidency—and to the sanity of future Presidents—lay precisely in this: the gift of time.

But Eisenhower's cut-back on the set-appointments list is not the only way in which his practice has been carried forward. Kennedy has also kept, indeed enlarged upon, the White House staff for legislative liaison, a notable departure from Rooseveltian practice, which Eisenhower was the first to introduce in a serious way. Similarly, Kennedy has followed and indeed elaborated Eisenhower's staff for science and technology. The Executive Office now has a new component, OST, and its Director keeps the White House status Eisenhower had conferred. Further, the Special Projects Fund which Eisenhower added to White House resources has been used by his successor, very much as he had done, to bring assorted special staffs with special purposes—including status-recognition for an interest-group or program—into presidential orbit as need be from time to time. This evidently has become an indispensable adjunct of presidential life as it will be lived from now on.

In his relations with departments and department heads, JFK has sought to steer a course between Roosevelt's "disorder" and Eisenhower's "system." Kennedy appears to view the formal meeting-with-fixed-membership and ponderous procedures much as Roosevelt did: a waste of energy and time and a restriction on the President. But Kennedy also appears far less inclined than FDR to keep his senior ministers at arm's length, or at odds with one another, or in the dark about his plans and interventions. On the contrary, with those of his department heads whose work is most bound up with his from day to day—Defense, State, Justice, above all—he has sought a relationship as close and confidential and collegial as with his staff, and he has delegated tasks to them and their associates as though they all were members of his staff. With Justice and Defense, especially, he has devolved on Cabinet members staff-work which a Roosevelt almost surely would have held within the White House. Evidently this is Kennedy's preferred course; if he has not done it everywhere or equally the signs are that he does it where and as he finds he can.

What this suggests is not merely that Kennedy's own personal proclivities depart in these respects from FDR's. Their situations differ, their options differ; personalities aside, their approaches could not be the same. Roosevelt, we are always hearings, was his own Secretary of State. To the same degree, he also was his own Secretary of Defense, insofar as such a role existed in his time. But no President, not excepting Roosevelt if he were to reappear (which the two-term amendment was enacted to prevent), could manage this under contemporary conditions. This is not Roosevelt's wartime, nor is it what he knew before as "peacetime." It is, instead, a time when [the] government exhibits disadvantages of both with few of the advantages of either. It is, indeed, late in the second decade of that disadvantaged time.

In governmental terms, Kennedy's time (to date) is marked by what I once tried to encompass in the phrase "emergencies in policy with politics-as-usual." It is a time marked also by the presence of intractable substantive problems and immovable bureaucratic structures. A Kennedy must operate from day to day under restraints upon administrative free-wheeling as tight as the restraints upon large policy departures.

On neither score has he a Roosevelt's freedom for maneuver. Kennedy's approach to Presidential staffing suggests that he knows this very well.

VI. Concluding Note

Where do we go from here? I leave the question to our commentator and the panel, adding only this: A quarter-century ago, members of our profession dealt with staffing the Presidency as a problem in "management" which the President in question took to mean scope for himself through control over others. Those students of administration and that politician found themselves quite able to agree, despite implicit differences in terms of reference. But their agreement rested on a shaky base: the premise that both democratic theory and constitutional prescription put the President, by right, "in charge" of the Executive establishment as though it were a business corporation and he its chief executive. "All power to the boss" was thus a principle of "good administration" which the students could endorse and FDR could hide behind.

But neither as a document nor as accreted precedent does the American Constitution give the President of the United States exclusive warrant to be "boss" of the Executive establishment. It gives him but a warrant to contest for that position, agency by agency, as best he can. Congress and its committees have their warrants too; so do department heads and bureau chiefs. And every bureaucrat swears his *own oath* to preserve and defend the Constitution.

As for me, I know what side I'm on and think I have good grounds to be there. But I make no claim that my side has superiority of *right* drawn from the Constitution!

Nor would I claim that any sort of Presidential staffing—personal or institutional—or any sort of operating style can meet, at once and equally, a President's own needs for service from officialdom and bureaucratic needs for service from the President. What wartime Washington experienced is with us still, in aggravated form: to a degree the needs of bureaucrats and Presidents are incompatible. The better one is served the worse will be the other. Yet each is bound to have a stake in satisfaction for the other. So each is bound to be dissatisfied.

In Kennedy's Washington, as in Eisenhower's and Truman's, to say nothing more of FDR's, honorable and able men inside departments fume in frustration at White House "unwillingness" to be "decisive," while their White House counterparts fume in frustration at bureaucracy's "unwillingness" to be "responsive." Why do these feelings persist (and grow)? For answer, one must probe beneath the surface of "machinery," even beneath the surfaces of "personality," to the perspectives and compulsions generated by the combination of "big government" and "separated powers."

====⟋⟍ *3*

Presidential
Cabinet
and Advisory
Politics

RICHARD F. FENNO

President Truman once described the Cabinet as "a body whose combined judgment the President uses to formulate the fundamental policies of the administration . . . a group which is designed to develop teamwork wisdom on all subjects that affect the political life of the country."[1] The historians of the Cabinet concluded, similarly though earlier, that, "The rule may be laid down that the President ordinarily consults the Cabinet on matters of grave public importance."[2] The Cabinet has been described by observers and participants as "the board of directors of the nation," as "a combination of qualified experts that have stood behind every President," and as producers of "committee government."[3] Pictures have been painted of the family circle thrashing out the great issues of the day under conditions of closest intimacy. "In fact, it is assumed today simply as a matter of course that the Secretary of a new department

Reprinted by permission from Richard F. Fenno, *The President's Cabinet*, Cambridge, Harvard University Press, 1959, pp. 154–156, 247–249.

[1] Louis W. Koenig (ed.), *The Truman Administration* (New York, 1956), p. 360.
[2] Mary Hinsdale, *A History of the President's Cabinet* (Ann Arbor, 1911), p. 326.
[3] James A. Farley, *Jim Farley's Story: The Roosevelt Years* (New York, 1948), p. 38; Henry B. Learned, *The President's Cabinet* (New Haven, 1912), pp. 4–7.

will become as such an intimate adviser and associate of the President."[4] Since it is impossible to obtain conclusive data on Cabinet proceedings, dogmatic conclusions are not in order, but on the available evidence of the last forty-five years, at least, these versions of Cabinet activity do not square with the facts. It is, perhaps, significant that President Truman's comment was made in December 1945, at a time when he had been in office less than a year. With respect to all of its possible functions, the group's [Eisenhower's Cabinet] performance has been haphazard and its success has been sporadic. This is not to say that the Cabinet should be classified as an ornamental antique. It is not. But neither does it correspond to the over-idealized discussions of its activity which have acquired, from time to time, substantial currency.

Instead of exaggerating its importance or relegating it to the dust bin, it is of more purpose to examine its activity in order to distinguish its areas of greatest strength and those of greatest weakness. It is weakest in performing the function of interdepartmental coordination and in making direct contributions to decisions through a well-informed, well-organized discussion of policy alternatives. It is most useful as a presidential adviser, in the sense of a political sounding board equipped to provide clues as to likely public or group reactions, and as a forum in which some overall administrative coherence can be secured. Neither of the latter two functions requires a high degree of institutionalization. The first can be carried on in the face of departmentalism; the second operates to combat it. With regard to administrative coherence, the importance of the Cabinet meeting may well be measured by the extent to which it prevents the degree of Cabinet-level disunity from becoming any greater than it is.

What is perhaps the most striking part of the over-all picture is the number of factors which operate to *prevent* the Cabinet from fulfilling its potential functions. They are factors, however, which cannot be eliminated at the level of the Cabinet meeting. Insofar as the President's behavior, e.g., his differentiation among members, constitutes a limitation on the effectiveness of the meeting, that behavior is grounded in the American conception of executive leadership. The limiting behavior of the department heads, e.g., departmentalism, stems from the basic pluralism of the American political system. The low degree of institutionality characteristic of the Cabinet meeting is not an independent limiting factor, but a political derivative determined by the interaction of President and Cabinet members.

The problem of greater or lesser institutionalization must be put in perspective as one possible method for capitalizing on assets or minimizing liabilities, but *not* as a fundamental solution to Cabinet weakness. Thus, one can find changes such as the Eisenhower ones to be helpful under the existing circumstances; but they should not be looked upon as permanent cure-alls. This is so because the President-Cabinet nexus will always be an unstable accommoda-

[4] Henry B. Learned, *The President's Cabinet, ibid.,* p. 6.

tion rather than a fixed relationship. What seems necessary for a successful accommodation is a degree of institutionality sufficient to hold the group together, coupled with a degree of resiliency sufficient to convince the President that he can use it. Insofar as this kind of relationship can be maintained, the successes of the Cabinet meeting are likely to underwrite its continuance, while its limitations are likely to guarantee the coexistence of other avenues of presidential assistance.

● ● ●

The investigations which we have made into Cabinet-member activity in the areas of public prestige, party, Congress, and departmental administration lead to a few conclusions about the Cabinet and the political system in which it operates. One striking circumstance is the extent to which the Cabinet concept breaks down in the course of the members' activities outside the Cabinet meeting. In matters of prestige, partisan politics, and legislative relations alike, the Cabinet as a collectivity has only a symbolic value, a value which readily disappears when the need for action supersedes the need for a show window. In the day-to-day work of the Cabinet member, each man fends for himself without much consideration for Cabinet unity. His survival, his support, and his success do not depend on his fellow members. His performance is judged separately from theirs. This condition is but another result of the combination of the centrifugal tendencies in our political system with the low degree of institutionalization which characterizes the Cabinet.

The political help which the President receives comes not from the group but from individual Cabinet members, who can and do augment the President's effectiveness in his leadership roles. It would be a serious mistake not to emphasize the possibilities for crucial assistance by individuals. But probably most striking is the fact that the possibilities for such assistance are very frequently negated by the number of limitations which surround them. There are pervasive limitations of a personal or a situational nature, and there are limitations inherent in the political system—all of which make it neither easy for a Cabinet member to help the President nor axiomatic that he should do so. In the final reckoning, the President receives much less assistance of a positive, non-preventive type from his individual Cabinet members than one might expect. This fact serves to accent the high degree of success which is represented by preventive assistance. It also helps to underline the tremendous gap which separates the presidential level of responsibility from that of his subordinates. It demonstrates, too, the extent to which the two levels are subject to the pulls of different political forces.

The President-Cabinet power-responsibility relationship is . . . inadequate as a total explanation for the extra-Cabinet performance of the individual member. As a group the Cabinet draws its life breath from the President, but as individuals the Cabinet members are by no means so dependent on him. In many instances, we are presented with the paradox that in order for the Cabinet member to be of real help to the President in one of his leadership roles, the member must have non-presidential "public" prestige, party following, legislative support, or roots of influence in his department. And in any case, the problems of his own success and survival will encourage him to consolidate his own nexus of power and will compel him to operate with some degree of independence from the President. For his part, the President's influence over the Cabinet member becomes splintered and eroded as the member responds to political forces not presidential in origin or direction. From the beginnings of his involvement in the appointment process, the President's power is subject to the pervasive limitations of the pluralistic system in which he seeks to furnish political leadership.

One final conclusion takes the form of a restatement of the pluralism of American politics. In every area we have noted the diffusion, the decentralization, and the volatility of political power. The same kaleidoscopic variety which characterized the factors influential in the appointment process is evident in the political processes which engulf the Cabinet member. Each member interacts with a great variety of political units, interest groups, party groups, and legislative groups, and each has his own pattern of action and his own constellation of power. The feudal analogy is an apt one. It frequently makes more sense to describe the Cabinet member as part of a "feudal pattern of fiefs, baronies, and dukedoms than . . . an orderly and symmetrical pyramid of authority."[5]

Here, then, is an underlying explanation for Cabinet-meeting behavior. Departmentalism is a condition whose roots are grounded in the basic diversity of forces which play upon the individual member. By the same token, this pluralism generates centrifugal influences which help to keep the Cabinet in its relatively non-institutionalized state. The greatest problems for Cabinet and President, like the greatest problems in American politics, are those which center around the persistent dilemmas of unity and diversity.

[5] Pendleton Herring, "Executive-Legislative Responsibilities," *American Political Science Review*, December, 1944, p. 1160.

4

Economic
Policy
Advisers

WALTER W. HELLER

I doubt that a new chairman of the Council of Economic Advisers will ever again be asked, as I was late in 1960: "Will you handle this from Minnesota, or will you have to go to Washington?" And never again will a member of the Council call his position, as one did in the 1950's, the "highest paid fellowship in the profession." The detached, Olympian, take-it-or-leave-it approach to Presidential economic advice—the dream of the logical positivist—simply does not accord with the demands of relevance and realism and the requirements of the Employment Act.

Advisory Functions

What *are* the Presidential adviser's responsibilities to the President, to the public, to the profession, and to himself? I do not, by the way, necessarily identify "economic adviser" with "Council of Economic Advisers." The President receives economic advice from many other sources both inside and outside of the government—I don't know why, but the Treasury readily comes to mind—and even from sources that are "independent in, but not of, the Government." Yet, the forces of both law and practice make it increasingly natural

Reprinted by permission from Walter W. Heller, *New Dimensions of Political Economy*, Cambridge, Harvard University Press, 1966, pp. 15–26, 51–56.

that the major focus of Presidential economic advice should be in the Council. So even when I use the term "economic advisers" generally, the reader will usually be right if he subconsciously adds the prefix, "Council of."

The major functions of the economic adviser, as I have seen and known them, are to analyze, interpret, and forecast; to give policy advice; to educate; and to adapt and translate.[1]

ECONOMIC ANALYSIS, INTERPRETATION, AND FORECASTING.   The unique function of the Council of Economic Advisers is to put at the President's disposal the best facts, appraisals, and forecasts that economic science, statistics, and surveys can produce. Under the terms of the Employment Act, the Council assesses for the President both "current and foreseeable economic trends" and the levels of economic activity needed to carry out the policy of the act.[2] Beyond this, the advisers supply him—at times, he must think, bombard him —with a steady stream of searching memoranda on the whole spectrum of economic issues. Important economic developments and events are analyzed and interpreted, not merely in the sense of how and why they occurred, but what they signify, and what their future consequences are likely to be. In addition, President Johnson has assured himself of a continuous flow of current economic intelligence by setting up a system of thrice-weekly "economic news notes"—brief reports of economic news, both good and bad, with interpretive comments by CEA members. In recent years, a substantial part of the economic analysis undertaken within the Administration has been made available to the Congress and the public through the Council's *Annual Report,* testimony, statements, and speeches.

POLICY ADVICE.   On a foundation of such analysis and fact, and in the normative environment of Employment Act mandates and basic Presidential philosophy, the economic adviser weighs the contributions of various courses of action to the competing objectives of economic policy. Not ignoring administrative and political feasibility, he presses the case for some measures and against others. Often he serves up alternatives and points up conflicting economic and political hazards. But when the President asks what, all things considered, is his advice, he must be prepared to answer. As Gardner Ackley recently put it:

---

[1] The role of the economist in government has been the subject of many articles and books. A recent probing study is by Edward S. Flash, Jr., *Economic Advice and Presidential Leadership: The Council of Economic Advisers* (New York: Columbia University Press, 1965). Earlier volumes of particular interest are *Economics and Public Policy* (Washington, D.C.: The Brookings Institution, 1955); and W. A. Johr and H. W. Singer, *The Role of The Economist as Official Adviser* (London: Allen & Unwin, 1955).

[2] Employment Act of 1946, sec. 3.

"If his economic adviser refrains from advice on the gut questions of policy, the President should and will get another one."[3] Happily for the economic adviser, politics and economics are often in harmony rather than conflict. For him, happiness is a political need that can be filled by an economic good.

EDUCATION. Experience of recent years has demonstrated that education—of the President, by the President, and for the President—is an inescapable part of an economic adviser's function. The explanatory and analytical models of the economist must be implanted—at least intuitively—in the minds of Presidents, congressmen, and public leaders if economic advice is to be accepted and translated into action. I deal with this important function at some length below.

ADAPTATION AND TRANSLATION. In listing this as a separate function, I run the risk of overlap with the analysis and education functions. Nonetheless it is such a vital activity of the adviser—and yet one so often dimly perceived by observers—that it merits separate listing. To take the highly refined and purified concepts of economics and to convert them into workable and digestible form for service as policy guides and focal points for consensus—that is, to move economics from a point several abstractions away from the real world right to ground zero—involves a constant process of adaptation, translation, and innovation. The operational concepts of the "production gap," "full-employment surplus," the "fiscal drag," and "fiscal dividends" illustrate this process.[4] The terms in which problems are put, even their simple semantics, have an important bearing on the fixing of political objectives and the formation of policy. As Irving Babbitt said, "All great revolutions are preceded by a revolution in the dictionary."[5]

Issues in Advisory Responsibility

The foregoing functions inevitably raise some issues of responsible behavior for the economic adviser. They involve him in value choices, in advocacy of Presidential programs, and in balancing what is ideal against what is practicable. And they push him to the outer limits of his data and analysis, and sometimes beyond. Let me offer a few personal observations on how one resolves some of these issues. If, perchance, there is a grain or two of eternal truth in these observations, so much the better.

[3] Gardner Ackley, "The Contribution of Economists to Policy Formation," *The Journal of Finance* (May, 1966), Vol. 21, p. 176.
[4] These concepts are spelled out in Chapter II (Walter W. Heller, *New Dimensions of Political Economy*).
[5] As quoted in Norton E. Long, *The Polity* (Chicago: Rand McNally, 1962), p. 104.

VALUE CHOICES.   Implicit in a great deal of what I have already said is that value judgments are an inescapable, obligatory, and desirable part of the life of an economic adviser.

Value judgments are *inescapable,* because, as Arthur Smithies pointed out some years ago, "Concern with policy . . . must be based on ethical or political presuppositions derived from the non-economic world."[6] Merely selecting objectives for economic policy, as one must, involves us in normative choices. "Full employment," "high growth," and "price stability" may have a hard economic ring, but they are only proxies, if you will, for such social goals as personal fulfillment, a rising quality of life, and equity between fixed and variable income recipients. As we said in the 1962 *Annual Report:* "The ultimate goals of the Nation are human goals, and . . . economics is merely instrumental to the making of a better life for all Americans. Involuntary unemployment is a sign of economic waste, but the fundamental evil of unemployment is that it is an affront to human dignity."[7]

Value judgments are *obligatory* under the Employment Act, which requires the setting of target levels of employment, production, and purchasing power. Where? At unemployment rates of 5 percent, or 4, or 3? At average factory operating rates of 90, or 92, or 94 percent of capacity? At annual growth rates of 3, or 4, or 5 percent? In answering those questions, we are not making coldly scientific judgments, but value choices between higher prices and more jobs, between current consumption and investment in the future, and so on.

Value judgments are *desirable,* for to say anything of importance in the policy process requires such judgments. For example, meeting the added costs of Vietnam by higher taxes rather than Great Society cutbacks is not just an economic but a social choice. The choice of higher taxes gives content to President Johnson's eloquent pledge to "call for the contribution of those who live in the fullness of our blessing, rather than try to strip it from the hands of those that are most in need."[8] Technical advice divorced from such value preferences will have a hollow ring to those in authority.

The intimate connection between values and analysis, between technical and social goals, was well illustrated in the original economic thinking that underlay the poverty program. As early as May 1963, Kenneth O'Donnell told me: "Stop worrying about the tax cut. It will pass—and pass big. Worry about something else." We did. We turned to the question of those whom the tax

---

[6] Arthur Smithies, "Economic Welfare and Policy," in *Economics and Public Policy* (Washington, D.C.: The Brookings Institution, 1955), p. 1.

[7] *Economic Report of the President, Transmitted to the Congress January 1962, Together With The Annual Report of the Council of Economic Advisers* (Washington, D.C.: Government Printing Office, 1962), p. 37.

[8] President Lyndon B. Johnson, State of the Union Message, January 12, 1966.

cut would leave behind. Our analysis showed that the tax cut would create two to three million additional jobs and thus open many new exits from poverty. But those caught in the web of illiteracy, lack of skills, poor health, and squalor would not be able to make use of these exits.

A full-fledged response to the Employment Act's insistence on "useful employment opportunities . . . for those able, willing, and seeking to work" had to go beyond tax cuts and fiscal policy to entirely new measures focused sharply and specifically on removal of the roadblocks of poverty. By mid-1963, I had sent President Kennedy our economic and statistical analysis of the groups beyond the reach of the tax cut and had offered some groping thoughts on "an attack on poverty." Obviously, we were deep in the realm of social goals and values. But much of the problem, and much of the solution, was economic in nature. I do not feel that I strayed beyond my preserve as economic adviser.

The danger, then, does not lie in admitting, or even welcoming, values to the economic advisory process. Danger would exist were value choices permitted to warp the economist's advice and slant his facts and analysis. If the adviser were to cloak his value preferences in the guise of scientific findings, he would of course be unfit to serve.

ADVOCACY. Much has been written about the hazards of open advocacy—of explanation and defense of Presidential policy—by economic advisers. The fear is that they may lose their professional objectivity and integrity in the process. But as the Kennedy CEA said in its first appearance before the Joint Economic Committee of Congress in March 1961 (in which it set new precedents both by appearing in open, rather than executive, session and by submitting and releasing a prepared statement): "The Council has a responsibility to explain to the Congress and to the public the general economic strategy of the President's program, especially as it relates to the objectives of the Employemnt Act."[9]

Such explanation, it seems to me, is essential to the understanding, acceptance, and adoption of sound economic policy. Some have said, "Explanation, yes; defense, no." But to draw a line between the two is next to impossible. And within reasonable bounds, it is unnecessary. Again, as we stated in 1961: "The Council is, and necessarily must be, in harmony with the general aims and direction of the President and his Administration. A member of

[9] *January 1961 Economic Report of the President and The Economic Situation and Outlook,* Hearings Before the Joint Economic Committee, Congress of the United States, 87th Cong., 1st Sess. (Washington, D.C.: Government Printing Office, 1961), p. 291. The varying conceptions of earlier Councils and their chairmen on responsibility toward the public, the Congress, and the President are examined in Flash's study, *op. cit.,* in *The President's Economic Advisers* by Corinne Silverman, The Inter-University, Case Program, no. 48 (University of Alabama Press, 1959), and in Edwin G. Nourse, *Economics in the Public Service: Administrative Aspects of the Employment Act* (New York: Harcourt, Brace, 1953).

the Council who felt otherwise would resign." And we added: "This general harmony is, of course, consistent with divergences of views on specific issues."[10]

Advocacy poses no insoluble problems of integrity and few of objectivity (though silence may occasionally be golden) under circumstances that surely characterize the years since 1961: first, a general harmony of objectives between President and Council; second, a Presidential readiness to heed (if not always to follow) the Council's analysis and advice; and third, an Administration economic policy bearing the Council's imprint in both content and direction.

Of course, the adviser will not always get his way—nor should he. Some policy measures may be ruled out at a given time—perhaps by a conflicting Presidential commitment, by an insurmountable congressional obstacle, or by an unready public opinion wedded to shibboleths not yet unlearned. In that case, the ideal solution may have to yield to "second best." To explain and defend a *good* policy measure under circumstances where the *best* is beyond the political pale need not offend the conscience of the economist.

At times, the view of the economic advisers *does* diverge from that of the President. It did in 1962 when the Council was privately urging a large tax cut that President Kennedy was not yet ready to endorse. Under such circumstances, selective silence, publicly, is the adviser's best defense of integrity and credibility. "Where politics has necessarily overruled economics," Theodore Sorensen has observed, ". . . the economic adviser should not use his skills and reputation to justify the unjustifiable if he is to retain his effectiveness with his professional colleagues, the Congress, the public, and ultimately the President."[11] In this context, advisers need to keep in mind the warning voiced by Allan Sproul: "The silence which should occasionally be golden may succumb more and more to the lure of the lectern as the warmth of a place near the throne inflames the blood."[12]

Open advocacy carries with it certain other discomforts. When the adviser takes to the economic stump, he has to make a more conscious effort to stay within the bounds of his professional competence. And the public makes no fine distinctions—in advocacy, the political economist is seen as more "political" than "economist."

He should also be prepared to serve as a lightning rod for the angry charges generated by offended vested interests and prejudices—a consequence that is as convenient for Presidents as it is uncomfortable for advisers. The wage-price guideposts have been a prolific source of such charges against the Council, and the AFL-CIO carried them to a new peak of intensity in 1966. Accusations of fiscal irresponsibility reached their peak early in 1963, just

---

[10] Hearings Before the Joint Economic Committee (1961), p. 292.
[11] Letter to the author, May 12, 1966.
[12] Letter to the author, June 13, 1966.

after President Kennedy proposed a massive tax cut in the face of a rising deficit, rising expenditures, and a rising economy. Hugh Sidey's book, *John F. Kennedy, President,* reminds me that the President interrupted our conversation one day during that period and said, "Walter, I want to make it perfectly clear that I resent these attacks on you."[13]

MAINTAINING OBJECTIVITY AND PERSPECTIVE. Difficult as it may be for the citizen to discern, there is a deep professional commitment that serves as a safeguard against loss of professional objectivity. The adviser knows he has to answer not only to himself but to his profession as well. This commitment is strengthened by our American practice—one might almost say our "system"—of moving advisers back and forth between academic and government life. The close tie with his professional base and the prospect of returning to it after a period of service in government prevent the subtle accretion of hostages to a political environment—hostages, not to special interest groups, but to Presidential preferences—which might eventually impair objectivity and bias judgment. This "in-and-out" characteristic of American economic advising substitutes, in a sense, for the British career-service tradition as insurance of objectivity.

In addition to objectivity, modesty becomes advisers. They need to recognize the limitations of their tools, the role of luck, the role of the private sector, and the restrictions imposed by various "realities":

• Staying within the technical limits of his analysis and information is essential to confidence in the adviser. This means that he sometimes has to say "I don't know" even when an educated guess might seem a manlier way out. At other times, it means identifying (both to himself and to others) the gaps in his data and analysis. But it does *not* mean that he has to forswear judgments and advice until all the facts and analyses are in. If it did, he would stand mute a good part of the time. In the course of a hearing before the Joint Economic Committee in 1959, I observed that "policy itself must be made humbly and hesitantly in the light of imperfect knowledge . . . policy decisions cannot wait until knowledge is perfected." Senator Douglas quickly replied in the words of Justice Oliver Wendell Holmes: "Every year, if not every day, we have to wager our salvation upon some prophecy based on imperfect knowledge."[14]

• Aptness in government economic policy is based not only on good facts, good analysis, and good timing—it also requires good judgment, good nerves,

13 Hugh Sidey, *John F. Kennedy, President: A Reporter's Inside Story* (New York: Atheneum, 1963), p. 378.

14 *Employment, Growth and Price Levels,* Hearings Before the Joint Economic Committee, Congress of the United States, 86th Cong., 1st Sess., (Washington, D.C.: Government Printing Office, 1959), part 9A, p. 2988.

and above all, good luck. For example, though the tax cut chiefly reflects the first five items in the list, it was the Council's good luck—just when the skeptical, not to say hostile, spotlight was full upon it—to have the 1964 tax cut come when the economy was still moving forward. If the impact of the tax cut had instead offset an incipient downturn, holding the economy up but not moving it spectacularly ahead, we would have lost the force of the *post hoc, ergo propter hoc* reasoning that has undoubtedly played an important role in gaining popular acceptance for positive fiscal policy.

• Economic advisers are sometimes accused of acting as though they alone were carrying and balancing economic expansion on their shoulders. This accusation goes too far. But the view from the third floor of the Executive Office Building does not always have the private economy in sharp focus. The political economist is well advised to recognize that a key factor, not only in the length and strength but particularly in the balance of the great expansion of the 1960's, has been the impact of effective private policies—better inventory and cost control, less speculation, better matching of plant capacity to markets, and more restrained wage-price policies than we have had in any previous expansion in our history.

• The economist on the policy firing line clearly has fewer options than the academic economist because he has to operate within the limits not only of his scientific knowledge but of political reality, public understanding, and institutional rigidities (like fixed exchange rates, a lengthy legislative process, and so forth). Unlike his academic colleague who can abstract from reality, deal with ultimates, and envision quantum jumps in our progress toward the ideal economic state, the economic practitioner has to operate deep in the heart of realism, has to deal with movement *toward* rather than *to* the ideal, and has to be at all times multidimensional in his objectives. The lump-sum tax— economically, the best of all taxes—will never replace the lump of taxes we now live with. And the principle that a change is good if the gainers could more than compensate the losers—the central policy precept of formal welfare economics—is a sterile guide when, in practice, the compensation can never be made. All this exaggerates my point, particularly since many academic economists are themselves at the forefront in providing realistic analysis and policy proposals. But it does illustrate the gulf that often separates economic science, with its limitations, from economic practice, with its. Although the gulf will never be entirely bridged, an important part of the adviser's job is to push out the boundaries of the possible in public policy, especially those that are set by lack of economic understanding.

• • •

Advisory Machinery

An understanding of U.S. economic policy making and the professional adviser's place in it requires at least a brief review of the advisory machinery, the conduits through which advice flows to the President. My observations here will be centered on the CEA, which is "a professional but political economic arm of the presidency that has no counterpart in any other country."[15]

Other advanced countries typically couple the economic advisory function with a cluster of operating functions, assigning responsibility for both to an established agency in the hierarchy, even in the Cabinet. This is true of the new Ministry of Economic Affairs in Great Britain, the German Economic Ministry, and the French Ministry of Finance and Economics. They sit astride a flow of business that supports them from below. The Council of Economic Advisers, in contrast, is suspended from above. That may be their strength and CEA's weakness. But it is also CEA's strength and their weakness in that the Council is, and they are not, part of the Executive Office per se. This position in the scheme of things offers the advisers easy and direct access to the Chief Executive. And, in turn, it puts at his disposal a catholic, not a parochial, approach to economic policy—an undivided, rather than a competing, loyalty (though professional integrity *could* become a competitor).

The President knows that the Council's expertise is fully at his command, undiluted by the commitments to particular programs and particular interest groups that, in the nature of things, tend to build up in the various line agencies of government. So although no law and no hierarchical flow of business force a President to rely on the Council of Economic Advisers—not even the Employment Act, which places the Council at his disposal but does not require him to use it (except in preparation of his annual *Economic Report*)— it is his most natural ally in economic matters.

Yet, the Council's access to the President is potential, not guaranteed. Unless personalities click; unless the economic adviser is both right and relevant; unless he gets off of his academic high horse without falling obsequiously to the ground—his usefulness will be limited and his state of proximity to the President will gradually wither away.

My preoccupation with the Presidency will not have gone unnoticed. This concern is natural enough in an agency that is suspended, as I say, from above. It has no trouble generating plenty of busy-ness on its own, even if the President rarely calls. But it is the business with and for the President that makes the standard 80-to-90 hour week of Council members productive, rewarding, and memorable.

Access not just to the person but to the mind of the President is crucial. The Council's major instrument of access to a modern President is the development of economic concepts, targets, and policies that fit his philosophy and further his high purposes—indeed, sometimes give concrete shape to those purposes, as did the concepts of economic potential and the GNP gap and the targets of 4-percent unemployment and 4½-percent annual growth. All of

15 *Business Week,* March 5, 1966, p. 152.

these were imprinted with the Presidential seal in Kennedy's first year and thereby became Administration policy. As Tobin has observed,

> It was of no small importance that the Council's definition and estimation of the targets of government policy under the Employment Act became Administration doctrine, adopted throughout the Executive Branch. . . . Whether in interagency debate or in public discussion, it became difficult for government spokesmen to advocate policies that held no prospect of reaching the target in a reasonable time.[16]

The *Economic Report,* memoranda, general policy sessions with the President, Cabinet meetings, direct or indirect responsibility for Presidential messages and pronouncements all afford the economic adviser important opportunities to influence Administration economic policy. But in the early months of the Kennedy Administration, we found that on many specific decisions involving economic policy, the Council had become only a flag stop on the policy-making track. Unless the White House took a hand in directing economic traffic through the Council, the policy train often flashed past before we could get out the flag to stop it. One of our major tasks was to establish constructive relationships with the men around the President to help insure that the Council's voice would be heard before final decisions were made, even if it had not been drawn into the early stages of the policy-making process. The corridors to power in domestic affairs ran through the offices of people like Sorensen, O'Donnell, Ralph Dungan, and Lawrence O'Brien. Their confidence and their conviction that the Council had something important or even unique to offer to Presidential decision making were essential.

The Council relied on this relationship in particular for an opportunity to be heard on the economic implications of issues and programs outside the mainstream of economic policy for stability and growth. Examples that come to mind are housing programs and their financing, agricultural price supports, maritime subsidies, transportation regulations, social security benefits, and payroll tax increases. As the importance of this function became more evident, the Council was brought into the year-end legislative planning process in the White House to advise on the economic aspects of all phases of the President's domestic program, much as the Bureau of the Budget advises on the budgetary aspects.

Only as the network of relations within the Executive Office of the President, with White House assistants, and with Cabinet and sub-Cabinet members was gradually built could the Council feel that its position in the economic policy process was reasonably secure. As an alumnus of the Council, I can only hope that enough of a tradition is developing so that the process of

[16] James Tobin, "The Intellectual Revolution in U.S. Economic Policy Making," Noel Buxton Lecture, University of Essex, England, January 18, 1966, p. 16.

reconstructing this network in another Administration one day will come rather more easily than it did to us. But tradition or no, the role of the Council will surely change from one Administration to the next, and its levers of power will have to be renewed and rebuilt each time there is a change of scene and a new cast of characters.

In spite of the somewhat uncertain and changing nature of the Council's role—resulting from its heavy dependence on the President's favor and its own ability to make itself useful—I do not favor buttressing its position with specific program responsibilities. I mention this because in the early days those who were advising Kennedy on the management of the Presidency wanted to assign the Council advisory functions in the fields of manpower and public works consumer protection. Initially, this idea appealed to me. But experience soon convinced me that if the Council is to be put to its best uses in general policy advising, and if it is to maintain the compactness and flexibility that small size makes possible—it has a total staff of only forty, of whom fifteen are economists—such an enlargement of scope would be unwise. We had a test of this principle in the period when the Consumer Advisory Council was attached to the CEA. We found that this program, or operating, responsibility not only diverted energies and efforts from the Cooncil's central purpose and competence but threatened to get it entangled in the conflicts and cross fire of special interest groups. The Council should stand above these.

Almost four years of service as Council chairman kindled in me no burning desire for changes in the formal organization of economic advice in the Federal government. After a year and a half's perspective on the matter as a nonparticipant, I have not changed my view. I do not see, for example, that a National Economic Council paralleling the National Security Council would serve an essential need which is now being neglected.

This conclusion is not a vote for no change in the economic advisory machinery, but a vote for fluidity. I do not contend that the present arrangements are the best of all worlds. Each President will recast the Council in his own image.[17]

[17] For an extensive examination of the advisory machinery and how it was used in three different administrations, see Flash, *op. cit.*

5

The Scientific Adviser

HARVEY BROOKS

Throughout American history the federal government has used scientific advisory committees made up of part-time outside consultants. Since World War II this practice has flourished, and has even become institutionalized in the form of statutory scientific advisory committees. The function of giving scientific advice to the federal government has begun to assume a professional status, and, as Gilpin points out,[1] a hierarchy of part-time advisory groups has emerged that parallels the bureaucratic hierarchy within the structure of government. This interesting development has accompanied the rapid increase in the use of contracts and grants by federal agencies to support research and development in the private sector—in industry, universities, and research institutes. It is difficult to decide which is cause and which is effect, but there is little doubt that federal support for private research and development and scientific advising have gone hand in hand.

Government scientific advisory committees form a complex interlocking network and many scientists and engineers are members of committees at several different levels in the hierarchical structure. In some cases this overlap is de-

Reprinted by permission from Harvey Brooks, "The Scientific Adviser," in R. Gilpin and C. Wright, eds., *Scientists and National Policy-Making*, New York, Columbia University Press, 1964, pp. 73–96.

[1] See Robert Gilpin, "Introduction: Natural Scientists in Policy-Making" in Robert Gilpin and Christopher Wright (eds.) *Scientists and National Policy-Making*, (New York, Columbia University Press, 1964.) pp. 1–19.

liberate; for example, in the Department of Defense the chairmen of the advisory committees to the three military services are automatically members of the Defense Science Board, which advises the Secretary of Defense. In other cases the overlap is accidental; the same individual is co-opted for different committees on the basis of his individual talents and experience. In both instances, this overlap forms a parallel communication network within the federal government which to a very considerable extent circumvents the customary bureaucratic channels. This bypassing of the bureaucracy is probably one of the most important and useful functions of scientific advisory committees. In science and engineering no level of the bureaucracy has a monopoly on new ideas, and the loose nature of the advisory system provides one means by which ideas originating at a low level in the bureaucratic structure can be brought directly to the point of decision without going through regular channels, and new ideas from outside the federal structure can be introduced quickly into government operations.

We shall begin with an examination of some functions of scientific advisers, and will then examine the roles of scientists in the advisory process, the qualities and skills of scientists that are called upon when they give advice. Finally, we shall discuss a number of problems and conflicts which arise in scientific advising.

Functions of Scientific Advisory Committees

The term "scientific advisory committee" is used generally although such committees are often as concerned with technology and engineering as with science and include many engineers or other applied scientists among their members. The role of the adviser varies greatly, depending upon the level in the federal hierarchy at which his advice is sought and implemented. In general, the lower the level, the more strictly technical the nature of the advice sought, although this is not always the case.

We may distinguish five advisory functions:

1. To analyze the technical aspects of major policy issues and interpret them for policy-makers, frequently with recommendations for decision or action. At the highest levels this often involves the analysis of political issues to determine which issues are political and which can be resolved on a technical or scientific basis. It also involves interpreting the policy implications of technical facts, opinions, or judgments. Familiar examples of this type of advice are such questions as whether to seek a nuclear test ban or whether to resume nuclear testing and, if so, when.

2. To evaluate specific scientific or technological programs for the purpose of aiding budgetary decisions or providing advice on matters affecting public welfare or safety. Many important decisions involving choice between alternate weapons systems, or determinations of whether to proceed with major

technological developments such as civilian nuclear power are of this nature. The review function of the Advisory Committee on Reactor Safeguards of the Atomic Energy Commission (AEC) is an example of such use of scientists in the area of public safety.

3. To study specific areas of science or technology for the purpose of identifying new opportunities for research or development in the public interest, or of developing coherent national scientific programs. Such studies may be science-oriented, that is, concerned with specific scientific disciplines as in the work of the Committee on Oceanography of the National Academy of Sciences (NAS)[2] or the Panel on High Energy Physics of the President's Science Advisory Committee (PSAC). They may also be need-oriented, that is, concerned with the use of science for a specific social purpose, as in the case of the recent study on natural resources made by the National Academy.[3] These studies may be conducted either on a continuous or *ad hoc* basis.

4. To advise on organizational matters affecting science, or a particular mission of an agency involving the use of science or scientific resources. The continuing advisory boards of the military services and the Defense Science Board serve mainly this function. A recent example is the recommendation of a PSAC panel which led to the establishment of the National Aeronautics and Space Administration (NASA), or the recommendation of another panel for the creation of the Federal Council on Science and Technology (FCST).[4]

5. To advise in the selection of individual research proposals for support, as in the so-called "study sections" of the National Institutes of Health, or the Advisory Panels of the National Science Foundation.

With the possible exception of the fifth designation, none of these functions is purely scientific in nature or depends purely on technical knowledge or expertise. All recommendations involve nontechnical assumptions or judgments in varying degrees. In some cases the nontechnical premises are provided by the policy-maker seeking the advice, but more often they have to be at least partly supplied by the scientist himself. For instance, in the judgment as to the safety of a nuclear reactor installation, "safety" itself is a relative term. In a sense the only truly safe reactor is the one which is never built. Every technical judgment on safety is actually a subtle balancing of risk against opportunity—the tiny risk of injury to the public against the advantages of nuclear power. Yet the administrator seldom makes clear to the adviser just how this balance between advantage and risk is to be achieved. Much of the apparent disagreement among scientists over the danger of fallout from bomb tests

[2] NAS-NRC, Committee on Oceanography, *Oceanography 1960 to 1970* (Washington, D.C., NAS-NRC, 1959).

[3] NAS-NRC, Committee on National Resources, *Natural Resources; A Summary Report* (Washington, D.C., NAS-NRC, 1962), Publ. No. 1000.

[4] PSAC, *Strengthening American Science* (Washington, D.C., USGPO, 1958).

stems not from a conflict as to actual technical facts, but rather from a difference of views as to the relative weight to be assigned, on the one hand, to the political and military risks of test cessation and, on the other hand, to the possible threat to human welfare resulting from the continuation of testing in view of the large uncertainties in our knowledge about radiation effects.

In a somewhat oversimplified way, the functions of the scientific adviser may be divided into those concerned with science in policy and those concerned with policy for science. The first is concerned with matters that are basically political or administrative but are significantly dependent upon technical factors —such as the nuclear test ban, disarmament policy, or the use of science in international relations. The second is concerned with the development of policies for the management and support of the national scientific enterprise and with the selection and evaluation of substantive scientific programs. It is not possible to draw a sharp line between these two aspects. For example, the negotiations over a nuclear test ban—which certainly involved science in policy —led directly to recommendations for a greatly expanded program of federally supported research in seismology, with quite specific suggestions as to the particular areas of promise—which is obviously policy for science. Conversely, the proposal for an International Geophysical Year, which was essentially a very interesting and exciting scientific proposal, involved highly significant political considerations and in many ways became an important tool of U.S. foreign policy.

Roles of Scientific Advisers

What are the particular qualities and skills demanded of scientific advisers? What kind of knowledge and experience do they bring to bear? Although the public image of the scientific adviser is primarily that of expert or specialist, the way in which he is actually used is much broader. One may distinguish at least seven different roles which closely relate to the above five functions.

The scientist or engineer is used for his expert knowledge or particular technical subject matter, as in the study sections of the National Institutes of Health whose function it is to rate research proposals.

He makes use of his general "connoisseurship" of science and scientific ways of thinking. In this role he is required to transfer his scientific experience from fields in which he is expert to fields of science and technology with which he is only generally familiar. He is used for his ability to understand and interpret quickly what other experts say, to formulate general policy questions involving scientific considerations in terms suitable for presenting to a group of experts, and to detect specious or self-serving arguments in the advice of other experts.

He makes use of his wide acquaintance within the scientific community and his knowledge of scientific institutions and their manner of operation. In this role he often helps by suggesting key technical people to serve in full-time government positions, and even in persuading the preferred candidate to accept the appointment. He may also predict the effects of government policies or actions on scientific institutions, and serve the ends of both government and science by defending the scientific community against ill-advised or inappropriate administrative procedures of government affecting the conduct of research and development.

The public administrator often makes use of the confidence and prestige enjoyed by scientists in order to obtain backing for projects or policies which he has already decided to undertake. While this particular use of scientific advisers is not necessarily to be deplored, it is subject to abuse. In many cases the administrator may "stack" his committee to obtain the advice he wants, or to obtain a "white-wash" for doubtful decisions. On the other hand, an advisory committee may often legitimately be used to help an administrator rescind an unwise decision without humiliation or embarrassment. A famous example is the appointment of an advisory committee of the NAS to investigate the National Bureau of Standards at the time of the battery additive controversy.

The scientist is increasingly being used as a specialist in policy research. This practice began during World War II with the development of the science of operations research, mainly by physicists in Great Britain and the United States. It involves the construction of mathematical models of varied military situations and the quantitative prediction of the military results of the use of varied weapons sysems and strategies. During the postwar period this methodology was extensively elaborated by mathematicians, economists, and theoretical physicists, and has been institutionalized in such organizations as the RAND Corporation, or the Weapons System Evaluation Group which serves the Joint Chiefs of Staff. A number of amateur and professional groups have also developed to carry on policy research in the field of disarmament or arms control. In all these examples natural and social scientists collaborated in order to bring to policy problems the methods of analyzing problems which are characteristic of the physical sciences.

Scientists are often sought for policy advice merely because the scientific community provides a convenient and efficient process for selecting able and intelligent people. One is reminded of Macaulay's dictum that he wanted "to recruit university graduates in the classics not because they had been studying the classics, but because the classics attracted the best minds, who could adapt themselves to anything."[5] If one substitutes nuclear physics for classics in this quotation, one has a basis for the selection of certain kinds of advisory committees. It is also probably true that physicists have a way of simplifying prob-

[5] See Don K. Price, "The Scientific Establishment" in Gilpin and Wright (eds.), *op. cit.,* pp. 19–41.

lems which is especially useful to harassed administrators—a capacity which has its pitfalls, since the temptation to oversimplify is always present.

According to C. P. Snow, science is more oriented toward the future than most other disciplines, and scientists are animated by a belief that problems are soluble.[6] Such natural optimism, even when unjustified, is an asset in attacking disarmament problems which have resisted solution for such a long time. It is undoubtedly a characteristic which has brought scientists into policy advisory roles even in areas where they are not especially qualified. Similarly, science forms the most truly international culture in our divided world, and scientists probably enjoy better communication with their counterparts throughout the world than members of any other discipline. Consequently, it was natural that scientists should lead in the cultural penetration behind the iron curtain, and in organizing and promoting joint international activities and exchanges.

Problems in Scientific Advising

The preceding discussion demonstrates that specific expertise is only a small part of the scientist's role as adviser. It is this very fact that is responsible for much of the controversy surrounding the present role of scientists in government and especially their role in the White House and the Executive Office of the President. The criticism of scientists is epitomized by Harold Laski's stricture on expertise:

> It is one thing to urge the need for expert consultation at every stage in making policy; it is another thing, and a very different thing, to insist that the expert's judgment must be final. For special knowledge and the highly trained mind produce their own limitations which, in the realm of statesmanship, are of decisive importance. Expertise, it may be argued, sacrifices the insight of common sense to intensity of experience. It breeds an inability to accept new views from the very depth of its preoccupation with its own conclusions. It too often fails to see round its subject. It sees its results out of perspective by making them the centre of relevance to which all other results must be related. Too often, also, it lacks humility; and this breeds in its possessors a failure in proportion which makes them fail to see the obvious which is before their very noses. It has also a certain caste spirit about it, so that experts tend to neglect all evidence which does not come from those who belong to their own ranks. Above all, perhaps, and this most urgently where human problems are concerned, the expert fails to see that every judgment he makes not purely factual in nature brings with it a scheme of values which has no special

[6] C. P. Snow, *Science and Government* (Cambridge, Mass., Harvard University Press, 1961). See also Warner R. Schilling, "Scientists, Foreign Policy and Politics" in Gilpin and Wright (eds.), *op. cit.,* pp. 144–174.

validity about it. He tends to confuse the importance of his facts with the importance of what he proposes to do about them.[7]

The view so eloquently expressed by Laski is sometimes echoed by political scientists and government administrators in referring to the present influence of scientists in the high councils of government. While it is a valid warning against the uncritical acceptance of scientific advice, particularly where tacit ethical and political judgments are involved, it is not exactly a fair description of the way in which the senior scientific advisers have exercised their responsibilities. Scientists in government have not claimed that their advice should be overriding, but they do insist on the value and importance of this advice in reaching a balanced decision in matters involving the use of scientific results. This is true even when the scientist is speaking primarily as a citizen outside his area of special competence. Especially on matters of military technology, scientists are often in a position to exercise their political and ethical judgments as citizens in a more realistic and balanced manner than other citizens. Precisely because they are so familiar with the technological aspects, they are able to concentrate more on the other issues involved without becoming bemused by mere technical complexities. While scientific advice is not free of bias, or even of special pleading, it is probably more free of prejudice than much other professional advice, and at least has the virtue of providing a fresh perspective unprecedented in government councils.

A number of problems arise in scientific advising which are, in one way or another, related to the type of problem raised by Laski in the above quotation. Discussion of these problems can be organized under eight topical headings: (1) the selection of advisers, (2) the scientific adviser as the representative of science, (3) communication between the scientist and the policy-maker, (4) the relation between advice and decision, (5) the responsibility of the adviser, (6) the resolution of conflicting viewpoints, (7) executive privilege, and (8) conflict of interest.

Selection of Advisers

Although the method of selecting members of a scientific advisory committee depends strongly on the function of the committee, the usual procedures are rather informal and based, for the most part, on personal acquaintance. This is especially true of committees that operate at the higher levels of policy discussion. The final selection is made by the executive to whom the committee is responsible, but usually the executive accepts the suggestions of present members of the committee or of other advisory committees. Thus the advisory

---

[7] Quoted by I. L. Horowitz, "Arms, Policies, and Games," *American Scholar,* XXXI, No. 1 (January, 1962), 94. The original source of the quote is Harold Laski, "The Limitations of the Expert," *Fabian Tract* No. 235.

role tends to become self-perpetuating, and constitutes a kind of subprofession within the scientific professions. Certainly administrative skills and some degree of political sophistication are factors almost as vital as scientific competence and reputation in the selection of members for the top committees. Experience in one of the major wartime laboratories, especially the M.I.T. Radiation Laboratory and the laboratories of the Manhattan Project, or an apprenticeship on one or more of the military "summer studies," still appears to be a useful qualification for scientific advising. There is as yet little sign of a change of generations that would affect this pattern. Even the relatively few younger scientists who have filtered into the higher level advisory committees are often students of one of the wartime giants like Rabi, Teller, Oppenheimer, or Fermi. Full-time administrative experience in the federal government or long experience on lower-level advisory committees or panels are also important qualifications. One of the most common methods of evaluating possible candidates for membership on the PSAC is a tryout on one of its numerous specialized panels. In this process of selection for advisory committees the characteristics deplored by Laski often tend to be weeded out.

Representation of the Scientific Community

The higher-level committees are often criticized for inadequately representing some particular disciplines, certain kinds of institutions, or some points of view on major national questions such as disarmament. For example, the PSAC has been criticized for having too many physicists and not enough engineers, too many academic scientists and too few industrial scientists, too many scientists from the east and west coasts and too few from the central areas of the nation, too many scientists who are prepared to negotiate with the Soviets and too few representing the school of thought of which Professor Edward Teller is the most articulate spokesman. All of these criticisms have some factual basis and yet it is essential to remember that scientific advisory committees are not legislative bodies, that the ability to reach a large measure of consensus and settle matters by a good deal of give and take in rational argument is much more important to the policy-maker than assurance of equal representation for all the "estates" of science and technology. People with very strong viewpoints which are impervious to rational argument or compromise merely tend to lead to a hung jury which does not help the decision-maker. A majority vote is much less useful than a well-reasoned consensus in providing scientific advice.

Many of the criticisms regarding lack of representation are either untrue or grossly exaggerated. For instance, there have always been industrial scientists on the PSAC. Although a majority of the Committee are physicists, it also consists of engineers, life scientists, and members of the medical profession. A high representation of academic scientists on the presidential committees and panels is balanced by a predominant representation of industrial scientists and research directors on the Defense Science Board and the top advisory committees of the military services. Yet to some extent this is beside the point. The members of the Committee are supposed to be selected for their ability to look at problems in broader terms than those of their own corner of science. The advice of a committee is not the sum of the individual expertise of its members, but a synthesis of viewpoints of people accustomed to looking at problems in the broadest terms. The high proportion of physicists stems from their wartime experience and their subsequent military advisory experience, for it must be remembered that scientists came into the top advisory role in government via their contributions in the national security field, and it was only later that they became concerned with the broader problems of basic science policy and the impact of science on international affairs.

It is important to bear in mind that on any given problem it is the practice of most scientific advisory committees to delegate much of the groundwork to panels whose memberships are carefully chosen to reflect the scientific and engineering skills required in the solution of particular problems. Furthermore, if the issue to be resolved is politically controversial, a special effort is made to ensure representation of a wide spectrum of viewpoints on the panel even though such a variety may not be represented on the parent committee. At the same time it is important to avoid people who are so committed to one view that a discussion of real significance is impossible. A surprising measure of agreement can be reached by a group of scientists of divergent views when they are partially protected by individual anonymity and not constrained by the need to be consistent with previously voiced public positions.

The Special Assistant to the President for Science and Technology, as well as the PSAC, is often thought of as the "spokesman" of science. It is sometimes said by both scientists and nonscientists that the members of the PSAC should be lobbyists for the interests of the scientific community and promoters of science. This feeling came about partly because the creation of the Office of Special Assistant was the result of public concern over inadequate national attention to the cultivation of national scientific strength. An important part of the task initially facing the Special Assistant was to promote the support of science, particularly basic science, in every way possible.[8] Actually, the PSAC and the Special Assistant are not, and should not be, official spokesmen for science but are organs of government. They regard themselves not as advocates of science, but as mediators between science and government. In this function they feel an obligation to take into account the needs and interests of the government as a whole and not just the needs of the scientific community. It is the NAS and its committees which are and should be the

8 See Robert N. Kreidler, "The President's Science Advisers and National Science Policy" in Gilpin and Wright (eds.), pp. 113–144.

advocates of science. The enthusiasts for a particular field of science are represented on these committees, but their reports are criticized and reviewed by the Special Assistant, by the PSAC and its special panels, and by panels of the FCST. This process is an attempt to balance the demands of a special field against the over-all requirements of science, and to adjust the requirements of a special program to the fiscal and administrative limitations of the federal government. It is still an imperfect process which has not yet been fully tested. In recent years science budgets have been rising so rapidly that the problems of maintaining balance between fields of science within the confines of severely limited resources have not had to be faced.

Communication With the Policymaker

. . . The science adviser cannot always be blamed when he steps outside the technical area. Too often the politician or administrator is tempted to throw the onus of difficult or controversial political decisions onto his scientific advisers. An important decision may be much more palatable to the public and to Congress if it is made to appear to have been taken on technical grounds. In the early days of the negotiations on a nuclear test ban, both scientists and diplomats fell into the trap of believing that the basic issues were primarily technical ones which could be resolved by discussions among experts, if not at the time, then later on as new scientific knowledge became available. Subsequently, it became increasingly clear that the really difficult issues were related to the degree of assurance which the United States felt it must have against the conduct of clandestine underground tests, and to the Soviet judgments as to what would be the acceptable degree of penetration of their military security. The importance of detecting clandestine underground tests has been differently estimated by the United States, depending on judgment as to the military decisiveness of tactical nuclear weapons. The winds of public and governmental opinion appear to be too much influenced by day-to-day changes in technical developments and ideas such as the "Latter hole" or the Tamm "black boxes."[9]

The nonscientist often has an exaggerated faith in the exactness of physical science, and has great difficulty in distinguishing between what is known with a high degree of certainty and what is only a matter of reasonable probability or scientific hunch. Under pressure to make concrete recommendations, the scientist has often tended to exaggerate the validity of his data and to permit the administrator to erect an elaborate superstructure of policy on a very flimsy technical base. Something of this sort happened twice in the nuclear test ban negotiations when much too general conclusions were drawn from

[9] U.S. Disarmament Agency, State Department, *Geneva Conference on the Discontinuance of Nuclear Weapons Tests; History and Analysis of Negotiations* (Washington, D.C., USGPO, 1961), Publ. No. 7258.

fragmentary data obtained from one particular U.S. underground test. As in military decisions, policy decisions can seldom be made with all the necessary information available, and the scientist who refuses to commit himself until he considers his data completely adequate is not very useful to the administrator. He does, however, have an obligation to explain the areas of uncertainty to his political master and to prepare him as best he can for technical surprises.

Advice Versus Decision

Political scientists writing about the PSAC and other advisory groups have often tended to confuse advice with decision, thereby investing the PSAC with a power and responsibility which it does not in fact possess. It is true that the scientist's public prestige occasionally gives his advice an influence and authority with decision-makers. He thus has power which is in some respects equivalent to, though not identical with, political power. Ultimately the scientific adviser recognizes that his influence in government rests solely on the degree to which his views are verified by subsequent events. He has no true constituency to give his advice political force, and perhaps to a greater degree than in the case of any other type of adviser his influence must rest with the persuasiveness of his arguments. Professor Bethe's prestige as an adviser was, perhaps unjustifiably, dimmed by his failure to anticipate the possibility of decoupling in underground nuclear explosions. At the same time, his prestige would have suffered much more if he had not been so quick to accept the new technical suggestion and examine it on its own merits without reference to its effect on his own deeply held political convictions regarding the desirability of a test ban.

Congressman Melvin Price has publicly attacked the PSAC for its role in the decision to abandon the aircraft nuclear propulsion program (ANP),[10] implying that it alone was responsible for this decision and that its recommendation was based on political and budgetary grounds. While there is no doubt that nontechnical considerations played an important role in the actual decision, the PSAC's part was to give advice on primarily technical grounds, as has been clearly stated by Kistiakowsky.[11] Contrary to Congressman Price's implications, the responsibility for the ANP decision was shared by many administrators and advisers; the voice of the PSAC was only one among many voices, and this voice was probably not decisive. Such decisions within the executive branch are seldom reached through the advice of a single group or individual but are the result of a gradually evolving consensus among many advisers.

[10] Melvin Price, "Atomic Science and Government—U.S. Variety," an address delivered to the American Nuclear Society in Washington, D.C., on June 14, 1961.

[11] George B. Kistiakowsky, "Personal Thoughts on Research in the United States," in *Proceedings of a Conference on Academic and Industrial Basic Research* (Washington, D.C., USGPO, 1960), NSF 61–39, pp. 49–53.

The Problem of Responsibility

The scientific adviser differs from the military adviser in government in that he is seldom responsible for carrying out his own advice, or even for the consequences of the advice he has given. This situation has both advantages and disadvantages. It can lead to the particular type of irresponsibility which Laski describes above so graphically, or it can permit a degree of detachment and objectivity which would be difficult to achieve if the adviser were more deeply concerned with the consequences of his advice. The advice given by the Joint Chiefs of Staff has always been plagued by parochial service interests.

The problem of the responsibility of advice comes to the fore in the field of budgetary decisions affecting science. Unfortunately, advisory committees of scientists are seldom presented with the hard choices between attractive alternatives which usually concern the budgetary officer or administrator. The competing claims of different fields of science have yet to be squarely presented to a scientific advisory committee. When confronted with the virtually unlimited opportunities in a scientific field, the advisory committee is tempted to recommend expansion without much reference to other alternatives. The balance between scientific fields in the past has been determined by the somewhat accidental resultant of many pressures, both political and scientific. The committees that recommend expansion, while not achieving all they hoped for, generally see enough effect from their recommendations to be reasonably satisfied. In an era of expanding scientific budgets this has worked fairly successfully, and the general balance of scientific effort seems to have been preserved. The scientific adviser may find himself faced with an entirely different responsibility when the time comes, as it inevitably will, that scientific budgets level off. The scientist who has to live with his professional colleagues outside government, especially in universities, will find himself torn between his natural inclination to appear as the champion and promoter of science on every occasion and his sense of responsibility as a government adviser.

Resolution of Conflict

In controversial issues the ideal advisory committee is one which succeeds in enlarging the area of agreement and reaching as wide a consensus as possible. A wise committee or panel can often succeed in narrowing the disagreements on a complex issue to a few technical issues which might be resolved by further research or to a clean-cut set of political alternatives which can then be resolved by the administrator. The committee which strives for consensus at all costs usually ends up with a series of pious platitudes which are useless to the policymaker—and useless in a peculiarly irritating and frustrating way. Having reached the widest possible area of agreement the committee should then attempt to formulate the disagreements as clearly and objectively as possible. Recommendations should generally be formulated in terms of forecasts of the probable consequences of alternative actions rather than in terms of exhortation. The responsibility for these tasks rests, for the most part, with the chairman, on whom usually falls the further duty of interpreting both the agreements and the disagreements to the policy-maker. This calls for unusual objectivity and detachment on the part of the chairman. In some cases it is wise for the policy-maker himself to hear the arguments of both sides directly from the proponents rather than filtered through the chairman.

It has sometimes been suggested that major issues involving technical advice should be resolved by a sort of adversary procedure, as in a court of law. There are instances when this is desirable, as, for example, when the rights or interests of individuals or groups may be in jeopardy as a result of the decision to be made. However, on broader policy issues the advisory process should be designed to encourage convergence rather than divergence of views. An adversary procedure tends to produce a polarization of viewpoints which then must be resolved by the policy-maker himself. The administrator would be forced to immerse himself in the technical details of every decision as does a judge in patent litigation. Given the many decisions which have to be made by every administrator, and especially by the President, such a process would be ludicrously cumbersome and would paralyze decision-making.

The alternative suggestion that every advisory committee should include a devil's advocate, is probably a good one. There are times when the chairman should deliberately assume this role. Sometimes it is the only way that the strongest arguments for the committee's final position can be brought out and potential objections to its recommendations anticipated.

On the whole the greatest occupational hazard of advisory committees is not conflict but platitudinous consensus.

Executive Privilege

No aspect of the PSAC has received as much criticism as the sheltering of its deliberations and recommendations under executive privilege. Other scientific advisory committees enjoy varying degrees of privilege, but never to the extent of those operating directly under the aegis of the White House. Of course, this is only a part of a more general source of irritation between the executive and legislative branches. The irritation has been directed at the PSAC only because its advice has frequently been followed, and has sometimes been against important agencies or congressional positions and projects. In practice, Congress, and for that matter, the public, have seldom been denied access to the technical and nontechnical considerations on which the PSAC advice was based; only questions of who said what are withheld. In some instances the PSAC panels have actually been reconstituted as panels of other agencies in order that their views could be made public without revealing the advice precisely as it was given to the President. In the early days of the PSAC, the Special Assistant, Dr. Killian, frequently advised the heads of agencies about the recommendations he intended to make to the President, and this has remained a common practice.[12] The decision to drop the ANP project, for example, was actually concurred in by the Director of Defense Research and Engineering and a panel of the General Advisory Committee of the AEC. Most of the technical and military considerations involved in that decision were covered in testimony before Congress by Dr. Herbert York and others.

There is a general feeling in the scientific community that J. Robert Oppenheimer was persecuted because of the unpopularity of his advice, supposedly given in private. The protection of executive privilege is sometimes necessary to induce scientists to join panels. They feel, rightly or wrongly, that their private interests may be vulnerable to reprisal by Congress or by powerful agencies which may be adversely affected by their recommendations.

A different type of problem has arisen when scientific advisers have chosen to speak out publicly on issues with which they have also been concerned as scientific advisers under the mantle of executive privilege. People opposed to their views feel that advisers who take public stands on controversial issues are trying to have their cake and eat it too. These advisers have, however, been willing and even eager to testify before Congress, with the exception of specifics like who recommended what to the President. The suspicion may remain that their testimony is filtered or distorted by the omission of privileged matter, but it is hard to see how this problem is any different for a presidential adviser than for an agency or department head who also gives privileged advice to the President. Perhaps the principal difference is that the part-time adviser does not consider himself under political or administrative discipline, and so may feel more free to volunteer a public statement at variance with the official line of the moment. The administrator who differs from the official line is constrained from expressing his difference except when called upon to do so while testifying under oath.

This is a complex question, but its facets are not peculiar to scientific advisers, except insofar as scientists may enjoy greater public prestige than other experts. Because of their relative newness in the higher government councils, the reputation of scientists is less tarnished by special pleading or self-serving, and it is hoped that in their public statements scientific advisers will bear in mind their responsibility to preserve the reputation for objectivity which scientists generally enjoy, and which is their greatest asset in the political arena.

Speaking out on public issues should not in itself be considered an abuse of executive privilege. Under the Eisenhower administration, the Special As-

---

[12] See Robert Gilpin, "Introduction: Natural Scientists in Policy-Making" in Gilpin and Wright (eds.), *op. cit.*, pp. 1–19.

sistant often felt hampered by the rigidity of the practice of executive privilege, which is even more enforced when the Executive and Congress are controlled by different parties. There were times when the Special Assistant was unable to testify although it would have been to the interest of the government for him to do so. Reorganization Plan No. 2, which became effective in June, 1962, created the Office of Science and Technology and gave the Special Assistant two hats—one as a confidential White House adviser and the other as statutory Director of the Office, subject to Senate confirmation. One of the purposes of providing such statutory underpinning to the science advisory role was to permit the Director to testify before Congress and thereby formally defend administration positions on new science legislation, on budgetary matters affecting basic science, and on the coordination of federal scientific programs. As a result of this reorganization, the area which we have called "policy for science" can become the subject for congressional testimony, while the area which we have called "science in policy" remained under executive privilege.

In the reorganization, the PSAC remained in the White House and continued to enjoy the protection of executive privilege. It is possible that if all the PSAC members had been made subject to Senate confirmation, this might ultimately have led to political control of science and to a serious threat to the independent and apolitical nature of the Committee. This nonpartisan character was explicit in the PSAC's original charter from President Eisenhower, and was recognized by President Kennedy through his continuation of the membership after the change in administration. Offsetting the fear of partisan control is the historical fact that there has so far been no problem of partisan politics with respect to the National Science Board, whose membership is subject to Senate confirmation.

A possibly more serious problem resulting from the new status of the Special Assistant is the amount of time involved in congressional relations that must now be added to that required for all the other responsibilities of the office. A major part of the past effectiveness of the whole presidential science advisory operation has been due to its compactness and lack of bureaucratization. The Special Assistant and the PSAC were able to be highly selective in the problems undertaken for study. With greater congressional visibility the Special Assistant may find himself forced to know less and less about more and more, and to depend increasingly on staff work rather than first-hand study for his expression of views. Since he has no decision-making or executive responsibility, other than for his own small staff, he can, I believe, avoid this dilemma by proper selectivity with respect to the type of things on which he chooses to testify. The Director of the Bureau of the Budget is in an analogous situation, and has so far lived with it successfully by delimiting his areas of testimony.

The preservation of executive privilege is clearly essential if the President is to get honest and independent advice. Too frequently the violently unpopular position of today becomes government policy tomorrow. If the adviser could not look ahead without fear of political crucifixion, policy would soon become frozen in a static mold. Furthermore, it would be ossified at the very moment of generation, when it should be most fluid and dynamic.

Conflict of Interest

Nearly two-thirds of all the nation's research and development is financed by the federal government, and 55 percent of the work is carried out through contracts and grants from the government to the private sector. Much of this work is of a nature that is unique to government financing. It is usually impossible to recruit advisers in these fields unless they are closely associated with institutions whose work is heavily financed by the federal government. In its modern guise, the problem of conflict of interest is much more subtle and complicated than envisioned in the conflict of interest statutes, which were designed originally to prevent government officials from directly and personally benefiting from their official position.

• • •

No government adviser can be free of bias. Although no statute recognizes the possibility of a conflict of interest within government, every administrator is well aware of the agency biases harbored by federal employees who give scientific advice. The scientists of the three military services tend to favor strategies and weapons systems which lead to the aggrandizement of their service, and the professional military scientist can seldom be depended on for unbiased advice on disarmament.

In fact it is often to counteract the effects of conflicts of interest within government that administrators have sought advice from the private scientific community. This community, in turn, has its own bias toward contracting out as much research as possible rather than doing it within government. Government scientists generally favor government laboratories and are opposed to the practice of contracting out either research or development. University scientists have a bias favoring basic research. These biases are seldom consciously self-serving; they are merely a part of human nature. "What's good for General Motors is good for the country" is not a sentiment unique to a famous Secretary of Defense; there is a little bit of it in every institution and profession. Some advisers are more able than others to recognize this sentiment in themselves and consciously strive to discount it in formulating their advice. These are generally the people that make good advisers. There is also an opposite danger of leaning over backwards, of failing to defend the interests and values of science because of a fear of the appearance of pleading the cause of a special interest.

Issues of the kind described above are much more important in scientific advising than are the obvious conflicts of interest involving personal profit. Yet it is basically impossible to resolve such issues by any legislative prescription.

As long as the federal government retains the necessary competence within its own full-time administrative and technical staff, it has less to fear from advice subtly or overtly biased by self-interest than it does from loss of the benefit of a perspective from outside government. The answer to the conflict of interest problem in scientific advice is not restrictive and negative legislation but positive legislation and administrative action to improve working conditions within government so that it can continue to attract people capable of properly using outside scientific advice. With respect to scientific advisers acting at the higher policy levels, it is important to develop a professional code of ethics connected with the advisory function. Fortunately, among basic scientists there is a stern ethical code associated with the question of scientific credit and priority which is powerfully sanctioned by public opinion within the scientific community. It provides a model for a similarly sanctioned, though unwritten, code with respect to the objectivity of scientific advice.

Conclusion

The reader may conclude that this essay has presented an unduly rosy picture of the beneficial effect of scientific advisers in government, and particularly of the operation and influence of the PSAC. There are certainly many critics, especially among those who have disagreed with the influence exerted by the PSAC in the field of disarmament and weapons policy, who would emphatically and sincerely disagree concerning the beneficial effects. Only history will tell who was right with respect to policy.

A major criticism would be of the tendency toward self-perpetuation among the most influential committees, and especially the consequent preservation through two administrations of a single viewpoint on many questions of policy. Furthermore, critics would argue, the presidential advisers have, through their influence on major appointments, gradually imposed their policy viewpoints throughout the upper levels of the scientific agencies and in the Bureau of the Budget. Although there may be superficial evidence for such an analysis, it will scarcely stand historical examination. The diversity of viewpoints and institutions represented on high-level advisory committees has been much broader than the critics claim. If it can be said that any policy viewpoints have become dominant in government, this has been imposed more by the logic of events than by any particular group of advisers. The advisers merely foreshadowed what would probably have been brought about by events anyway: the creation of an invulnerable retaliatory force; the inadequacy of the policy of massive retaliation; the importance of limited and guerrilla warfare and of conventional arms; the creation of the NASA, the Arms Control and Disarmament Agency, and a research and development section in the foreign-aid program; the centralization of research and development responsibility in the Department of Defense; increased support for basic research and graduate education; the fostering of international scientific activities and of scientific exchanges with the Soviet bloc; the creation of the FCST and its interagency committees; and the creation of the Office of Science and Technology by reorganization plan.

In matters of armament policy the critics have had their day in court and indeed have spoken from a much more firm base of power and influence than the various scientific advisers. Perhaps where the advisers have won out they have done so because their case was more persuasive, rather than because of illegitimate pressures or some sort of inside track to policy.

The scientific community and its influence in government is in a politically exposed position if only because of the magnitude of the scientific enterprise and the success of scientists, especially university scientists, in influencing policy despite their lack of a true constituency or base of power. To an increasing degree the country is looking to the Special Assistant and his supporting advisory staff, and, rightly or wrongly, there will be a growing tendency for Congress to blame his office for everything that goes wrong in the manifold scientific activities of the government. Whether the office can maintain its ability to concentrate on the key issues and not become lost in a rash of bureaucratic brush fires is the crucial question for its future success. It seems probable that the test of the political viability of the present network of advisory committees, and particularly of the presidential advisory structure, will come during the next few years, when budgetary ceilings may put a greater strain than ever before on the advisory committee's task of judging, and when the accountability of scientists to Congress and to the public will be more carefully probed than it has been in the past.

=== 6

The Budget Director

KERMIT GORDON

Consideration of the realities of the budget process must begin with the role of the President, for the budget is his plan, and the implied priorities are his priorities. The extent of the President's personal involvement in the minutiae of budgetary decision-making is less significant than it is sometimes made to seem. The President must in any case make the grand budgetary choices, for these are the direct expressions of his highest policy judgments. He cannot personally involve himself in every one of the thousands of secondary judgments which must be made each year—though I must grant that President Johnson came close to upsetting this axiom in his first assault on the federal budget. However, the secondary judgments are made by the Budget Director and the White House staff within a field of forces which provides reasonable assurance that the decisions will faithfully reflect Presidential attitudes, values, and priorities. The budget is the President's budget, in a real as well as in a formal sense.

The Budget Director, in his relations with the President, enjoys one high privilege and bears two paramount obligations. The privilege is the right to have his day in court with the President: to argue his own position on any matter which involves spending policy, whether in support of other Administration views or in opposition to them. No matter how well or poorly he exercises this

Reprinted by permission from Kermit Gordon, "Reflections on Spending," in J. D. Montgomery and A. Smithies, eds., *Public Policy*, vol. XV, Cambridge, Harvard University Press, 1966, pp. 11–22.

privilege, however, his usefulness to the President will and should be judged mainly by the faithfulness with which he discharges his two major obligations.

The first of these is the obligation to help guard against the bias of the many *ex parte* representations which pour in on the President from all sides, by assuring that the President has before him all of the relevant facts and analysis before he makes his decision. When the President decides an issue against the recommendations of the Budget Director, the latter will be disappointed, but he should save his genuine distress for those inevitable lapses when he has failed to lay the full story before the President in advance of a Presidential decision. His responsibility to inform is more vital to his role than his right to advise.

His second central responsibility is to use such secondary decision-making authority as the President allows him to exercise in accordance with the President's attitudes, values, and priorities as he discerns them—even when, on occasion, they may differ from his own. The assurance that he will act in this manner rests not only on his own sense of duty but on a very powerful built-in sanction. Any agency head is always free to appeal to the President any recommendation of the Budget Director, and such appeals are likely to be fairly numerous in the Budget Director's first year. If the President concurs with his Budget Director in the great majority of cases, the appeals will thereafter subside, for the word will have spread that the Budget Director is accurately reading the President's mind. If the President reverses his Budget Director fairly frequently, the latter's usefulness to the President will be gravely impaired if not destroyed, for it will have become evident that he has failed in his effort to tune in on the President's wavelength, and his desk will become only a temporary resting place for problems on their way to the President.

Watching and working with two Presidents does not qualify one to pronounce with authority on the institution of the Presidency, even as it relates to budgetary matters; for what one sees is all too obviously the product of an interplay between the man and the office, and the clear analytical separation of the two forces is extremely difficult. But, having made this disclaimer, let me go on to say that I think I have observed the working of a powerful chemistry which bubbles up from the office itself and transforms the budgetary thinking of the man who occupies it. Whereas the budget may have looked from the perspective of the Senate like an intricate collection of compromises among the interests of separate and often conflicting constituencies, it is suddenly seen from the White House as the central focus of efforts to achieve the Presidential vision of national purpose. What appears from lower vantage points to be a catalogue of discrete decisions is viewed from the highest perspective as a series of *choices* among alternatives, many of them perplexing and some of them agonizing. Expenditure on objects of questionable merit tends to be perceived not merely as improvidence but as the sacrifice of more urgent alternatives. While the President cannot ignore the claims and entreaties of the organized interests which clamor for a share in the budget, he tends to see his task as that of minimizing those concessions which conflict with his own conception of the national interest; and his own conception of the national interest is conditioned by the fact that he, among all public officials, has the broadest constituency and the broadest horizon of choice. To approach the budget in this manner is to look at it with a *Presidential perspective.*

As one moves down through the officials in the executive hierarchy, the Presidential perspective fades rapidly, and parochial conceptions take its place. Consider the official who directs the day-to-day operations of even a broadly defined program; let us call him the bureau chief. He directs the work of large numbers of people, he disposes of large sums of money, he deals every day with weighty, intricate, and delicate problems. He has probably spent most of his adult years in the highly specialized activity over which he now presides. He lives at the center of a special world inhabited by persons and groups in the private sector who stand to gain or lose by what he does, certain members of Congress who have a special interest in his actions, and a specialized press to which he is a figure of central importance. The approbation which is most meaningful to him is likely to be the approbation of the other inhabitants of this special world. The rest of the federal government may seem vague and remote, and the President will loom as a distant and shadowy figure who will, in any event, be succeeded by someone else in a few years.

It would be unreasonable to expect this official to see his program in the Presidential perspective. The President wants him to be a zealot about his mission, to pursue the goals of his program with skill, enthusiasm, and dedication. To ask him at the same time to be Olympian about his role and his claim on resources—to see in a detached way that he is a part of a hive in which many other bees have missions of equal or greater urgency—is to ask him to embrace a combination of incompatible attitudes. There are few Olympian zealots. One has to live with the truth which is known in Washington as Miles' Law, which holds that where you stand depends on where you sit.[1]

The President is entitled, however, to ask loyalty of the bureau chief—to expect that subordinate officials will accept Presidential decisions and support them faithfully, no matter how strenuously they may have sought a different decision. In my experience, the President does in fact enjoy such loyalty from the great majority of bureau chiefs and comparable officials. The exceptions, however, are sufficiently numerous to be disquieting. They typically take the form of more or less surreptitious efforts by the bureau chief to induce the Congress—often with outside support—to fund his program more generously than the President desires or to authorize new programs which the President has not requested. These breakdowns of discipline are most likely to occur in

---

[1] Named for its discoverer, Rufus E. Miles, until recently Assistant Secretary for Administration of the Department of Health, Education and Welfare.

those cases where the department or agency is weakly managed from the top, where the Congress has seen fit to lodge statutory authority in the bureau chief rather than in the agency head, where the bureau chief is the object of powerful and one-sided pressures from a private constituency and from influential members of Congress to upset a Presidential decision, or where the bureau chief's zeal to achieve the goals of his program has become a passion.

While such lapses from executive discipline are uncommon among bureau chiefs, they are even more rare among agency heads and those Presidential appointees directly subordinate to agency heads. But they are not unknown. It is worth a moment to consider the forces and circumstances which influence the relations between the agency head and the President, particularly as they relate to spending.

A Budget Director of some years ago told me that he followed the custom of his day, which required that each new Budget Director repair to the Chicago offices of the first federal Budget Director, General Charles G. Dawes, there to acquire nuggets of budgetary wisdom from the founder himself. At the end of the audience, General Dawes escorted his visitor to the door and said, "Young man, if you retain nothing else that I have told you, remember this: Cabinet members are vice presidents in charge of spending, and as such they are the natural enemies of the President. Good day."

General Dawes, I am told, was given to hyperbole, and that is certainly one of the better examples. But he did manage to communicate to his visitor an important insight—that Cabinet members and agency heads are not wholly immune to the disease of parochialism, and cannot be routinely assumed to share the Presidential perspective on broad budgetary strategy. Whether this has come about because the Cabinet as a corporate body has never amounted to much in the American system—thereby denying to Cabinet members the full exposure to the rationale underlying the Presidential perspective—or whether the Cabinet is kept weak because Cabinet members sometimes fall victim to the virus of parochialism, I leave to wiser heads than mine to judge.

The degree to which any agency head will perceive his own task in the Presidential perspective will depend both on the nature of the task and on the kind of man he is. If he harbors career ambitions, political or otherwise, which would be advanced by uniting his agency's clientele in his support, the danger is somewhat increased that he will take a view of his agency's programs which differs from that of the President. Quite apart from his own ambitions, he may lack the managerial skill to assert effective control of the policies of his agency; in the extreme case of managerial weakness, the agency head may become the instrument of determined subordinates whose objectives diverge from those of the President. Or he may simply become so entranced with the importance of his agency's mission that he is unable to maintain a balanced view of his agency's place in the total scheme.

But the extent to which the agency head succeeds in maintaining budgetary rapport with the President depends as much on the nature of his mission as on the nature of himself. If the agency has no substantial clientele which covets federal funds, or if the acquisitive clientele is poorly organized and weak, or if there is an effective adversary relationship among segments of the clientele, a competent agency head will be able to keep in step with the President without heroic effort. At one end of the federal spectrum are agencies which experience little difficulty in maintaining budgetary rapport with the President, while at the other end are agencies so exposed to the forays of their clientele that the agency head can hold the Presidential line only by risking personal martyrdom.

Over the years, it has become clear in which sectors of the line the President's defenses are weakest, and an informal second line of defense has been mounted in the Executive Office to reinforce these weak spots. Thus the Budget Bureau has for years maintained a special surveillance over day-to-day decision-making in certain agencies which are particularly vulnerable to clientele pressures. The Bureau sometimes works in quiet collusion with an agency head who wants to make a sound but unpopular decision which would strain his relations with a bureau chief or the agency's clientele; the Bureau, exploiting its more secure sanctuary, will make no denial when word is passed to the protesting parties that the objectionable action was pressed on the agency by the Bureau of the Budget.

So much for the stresses and strains which complicate the budgetary process in the executive branch. Nothing, of course, moves from plan to performance without the concurrence of the Congress, for Congress must provide the funds. Let me go on, then, to a consideration of the manner in which Congress goes about supplying the funds.

There exists no Congressional perspective on the composition of the budget to weigh against the Presidential perspective. Choice-making on the scale of the federal budget requires hierarchy, whereas power in the Congress is widely diffused laterally. Moreover, the responsibilities of members of Congress to special-interest constituencies must introduce into Congressional decision-making a greater element of bargaining and compromise than need be accepted at the White House. The Congress can review and amend the President's budget, but it can scarcely substitute a budget of its own making.

Even to speak of Congressional decision-making on the budget is to speak elliptically. Floor action on appropriations bills tend to be perfunctory and un-eventful. The real locus of decision-making on spending is the Appropriations Committee, more particularly the twelve subcommittees of the House Committee. Once a bill issues from a subcommittee—usually with bipartisan support—it will typically move through the full committee and floor action with few challenges and even fewer changes.

The Appropriations Committee is a semi-autonomous province in the House which exercises great power, possesses high prestige, and lives with its own deeply entrenched traditions and attitudes. Assignments to membership on Appropriations are eagerly sought, for it is not recorded that any Congressman's district has ever suffered by reason of his membership on Appropriations. The Committee is itself a loose confederation of principalities, each ruled by a subcommittee chairman who by reason of his office is a major power in the House.

Of the twelve subcommittee chairmen, six have served in the House for a quarter-century or more, and eight of the twelve are from the South or the Southwest. It has been observed that the average Southern Congressman is not only more conservative than his colleague from the big city in the North but also tends to be more astute, to work harder at his Congressional job, and to stay longer in the House of Representatives. The case of the eight Southerners who chair appropriations subcommittees lends support to this observation. They have learned their trade well, and they sometimes are better informed on the small details of agency programs than are the agency heads who testify before them.

The ritual of the Appropriations Committee requires that the Committee cut the President's budget. One subcommittee chairman said to President Johnson, only partly in jest, "Mr. President, I accuse you of having usurped the powers of the Congress. You have given me a budget I can't cut." The chairman subsequently proved, however, that he was equal to the challenge; he managed to do the impossible.

Knowing that the Appropriations Committee will assuredly cut their budgets, some agencies try to add a little padding to their estimates so that the inevitable cuts will not cause discomfiture. This is a practice which the Budget Bureau has always combatted, largely on the pragmatic grounds that, when each adversary comes to understand the strategy of the other, the size of the padding and of the cuts is likely to escalate wildly.

The tradition that the Committee must cut the budget undoubtedly derives from the Committee's image of itself as the taxpayer's shield against bureaucratic extravagance, incompetence, and aggrandizement. Those chairmen who take a jaundiced view of government spending in general have little difficulty in achieving the necessary cuts in the budget. They will pore over the details of proposed expenditures on administrative personnel, or travel, or public buildings, or supplies, and they will not infrequently put their fingers on legitimate opportunities for modest savings. Sometimes, however, they will cut deeply into the substance of a program because they regard it, for one reason or another, as undesirable.

Other chairmen, not temperamentally averse to public spending, will have a more difficult time of it. Though they may be favorably disposed toward the programs over which they preside, and though they may wish to support these programs even more generously than the President proposed, they cannot easily brush aside the tradition that the House cuts the budget. This dilemma, however, has been resolved over the years by the development of techniques—the details of which I shall not bore you with—which make it possible to increase the budget in fact while seeming to reduce it. If these techniques should be insufficient, it is always possible to cut high-priority programs in the House, knowing that the Senate will restore the cuts and that the matter can be worked out in conference.

Every season seems to be open season for criticism of Congressional budgetary procedures. It is frequently held, for example, that the process is subject to inordinate delays, such that executive agencies often do not receive their funds until a quarter or a third of the fiscal year has passed into history; that the need to mobilize a Congressional majority frequently makes it impossible to provide federal funds to areas in which the need is great without at the same time spreading the funds among other areas where the need is considerably less urgent; that executive discretion is so tightly circumscribed by the fine detail of appropriations acts that agencies are frequently unable to respond to unpredictable developments by even a modest reprogramming of funds; and that Congressmen pursue federal projects for their districts with such determination that the government often builds projects for which the need is not apparent or locates them in the wrong places.

While there is truth in each of these indictments, they add up, in my judgment, to a misdemeanor rather than a felony. The splintering of authority in the House Appropriations Committee seems to me a more disquieting matter. Given the sterility of floor consideration of appropriations bills, and the inactivity of the Appropriations Committee as a corporate body, the effective appropriations power goes by default in twelve segments to twelve small groups of Congressmen, each dominated by a powerful chairman. No one is able to make the broadest and most critical choices, because no one has in his hands all the ingredients of choice. Though there are important interdependencies among programs in different agencies, it is virtually impossible to take these connections into account when the agencies fall under the jurisdiction of different subcommittees. Most important, the present system lends itself to capricious inconsistencies of treatment, for one agency's program may grow rapidly under the benign oversight of a generous chairman, while another's may be starved by a hostile or penurious chairman. The reactivation of the full Appropriations Committee as a vital force in appropriations policy would help to correct some of these shortcomings and would provide a forum in which the broad budgetary strategy of the President could be reviewed and appraised in meaningful fashion.

Having made the circle of the principal participants in the fashioning of spending policy, one returns inevitably to the Presidency. If the pattern of public spending is to be related to a broad vision of national purpose, if the budget is to be infused with public-interest judgments which supersede private-interest claims, then the process must be molded to fit the perspective of the Presidency.

As Paul Appleby has said, in a somewhat wider context:

> For all the executive government—and indeed for the political government as a whole—the obligation to support integrity is greatest on the President and on his staff, who partake of his influence. . . . Lower levels are more vulnerable, and on them there is a moral obligation in behalf of responsible government to bend to Presidential guidance. The President is actually in [the] best position to take the highest moral ground, his obligation and dependence alike being pinned to the widest public.[2]

Molding the budget process to fit the Presidential perspective serves the cause of integrity and morality in government. But good will alone bakes no budgetary bread. Purity of motivation is no substitute for accuracy of analysis. And no one who has struggled with the baffling issues of program evaluation which are flushed up by the budget process can be content with the traditional tools of analysis.

The last few years have seen the emergence in Washington of a new determination to build a sounder system of program analysis and evaluation. The influences have been several: the McNamara–Hitch success in applying the tools developed at the RAND Corporation to the problems of program evaluation in the Defense Department has influenced the thinking of everyone in Washington concerned with better management in federal affairs. The increasing stress in the budget process on the critical evaluation of old and new activities of the federal government has led many agencies to place greater emphasis on self-analysis. The establishment in the Budget Bureau of a new program-evaluation unit under the leadership of RAND alumni has established a new center for innovative thinking and leadership. The insistent prodding of agency heads by the President to trim obsolete programs in order to release funds for more urgent activities—climaxed by the recent Presidential order directing each agency head to establish in his organization a formal program-evaluation unit—has produced a visible intensification of activity.

Thus, if I read the signs correctly, we are now in the early stages of an intensive and contagious drive to elevate the quality of program evaluation in the federal government. These developments are overdue. As they take hold, they promise major changes in the way federal programs are planned and managed.

The importance of moving to higher standards of program analysis is underscored by a review of some of the makeshift techniques upon which budget decision-making must rely in the absence of systematic program evaluation. Where serious program analysis is absent, budget decision-making must perforce rest on considerations which impinge on the issues without ever going to their heart.

There is first and foremost the blight of incrementalism—the sum of money

---

2 Paul Appleby, *Morality and Administration in Democratic Government* (Baton Rouge: Louisiana State University Press, 1952), p. 130.

allotted to a program this year will tend to be based on what the program received last year, plus or minus a small amount determined by over-all budgetary guidelines, a "feel" for broad priorities, workload indicators, productivity estimates, tactical judgments, and other such partial or shaky considerations. Sometimes the rate at which a program is allowed to expand is dictated by judgments as to the likely capacity of the organization involved to administer the activity. Often the judgment rests on the presumed absorptive capacity of the recipients of public funds—the level of activity in cancer research, for example, may be dictated mainly by the number of qualified cancer researchers willing to take the money. Throughout, there may run unconsciously an effort to equalize the degree of dissatisfaction felt by the directors of the various programs.

By contrast, it is easy to say what kinds of judgments ought to play the dominant role in budgetary decision-making. In the best of all possible worlds, the federal government would launch or continue a program only when the resources employed yielded greater aggregate benefits in the public sector than they would have yielded in the private sector. It would review the alternative means of pursuing each program goal, and it would choose the means which accomplish the goal at least cost. It would settle on a scale for each program such that the benefits yielded by the marginal dollar were equal in all applications.

To set the standards for program evaluation this high would obviously be unrealistic. So long as the government takes from some and benefits others, there is an inevitable conceptual fuzziness in any cost-benefit calculations. But even more important, of course, is the fact that the absence of a market test of benefits greatly complicates rational calculation in the management of public programs.

Nevertheless, we can do a great deal better than we are now doing. Some benefits of government programs can be quantified in dollar terms. There have been systematic efforts in this direction in the field of water resources, and scattered efforts have been made in a number of other fields. In my experience, even when the quantification rests on shaky assumptions and heroic simplifications, the results if used with good judgment can usually make a positive contribution to the illumination of the problem. Even when we have not been able to quantify goals in dollar terms, we can still analyze alternative strategies for achieving the goals and thus select the least-cost strategy. The problems one encounters in this activity are less difficult conceptually than in the dollar quantification of benefits, and the opportunities for useful analysis are very great. Finally, we can test the rationale of particular programs, usually by tracing their effects through primary, secondary, and tertiary consequences. Even in the absence of data permitting a precise comparison of costs and benefits, it is often the case that public judgment on the merits of a particular program would be altered positively or negatively by full disclosure of the direct and indirect consequences of the program.

The expanding efforts to introduce greater precision into the evaluation of federal programs will inevitably meet with setbacks and disappointments. Intuition does not yield passively to systematic analysis, particularly when the latter results in findings which are usually less than conclusive. Nevertheless, I believe that the next few years will see a major advance in the application of rational calculation to federal expenditures. No other development which is visible on the Washington scene offers as much hope for improving the clarity and strengthening the authority of the Presidential perspective on public spending.

$\approx$ 7

A Social
Report
and Social
Policy
Advisers

WILLIAM GORHAM

MR. CHAIRMAN AND MEMBERS OF THE COMMITTEE:

I am particularly happy to testify at this hearing, for it deals with a subject
that is at the center of my interests and responsibilities. The President's Message
to the Congress on Domestic Education and Health of March 1, 1966, directed
the Secretary of Health, Education, and Welfare to develop social statistics and
indicators to supplement those prepared by the Bureau of Labor Statistics and
the Council of Economic Advisers. One of my responsibilities, as Assistant
Secretary for Program Coordination in the Department of Health, Education,
and Welfare, is to oversee this research on what is sometimes now called
"social indicators" or "social accounts," and so I am naturally particularly
pleased that these hearings are being held.

The first problem was definitional and conceptual. It was obviously not
possible to develop a single indicator that would precisely measure every aspect

A statement made when Mr. Gorham was Assistant Secretary for Program Coordination, Department of Health, Education and Welfare before the Senate Subcommittee
on Government Research, Committee on Government Operations on July 26, 1967.

of the quality of human life. We had to subdivide human experience into categories. Each category had to be composed of somewhat similar phenomena if we were to be able to say anything meaningful about it, yet be broad enough to be of general interest. Then we had to search for any quantitative measures of developments within each category, and determine how the qualitative information could be organized and assessed.

Evidently broad conceptual problems of this sort demand the attention of many minds and the theoretical tools of several different disciplines. Our first step was therefore, to seek the counsel of leading social scientists in a variety of disciplines. This was not the fastest way to proceed, but it made it possible to draw on the broad spectrum of exceptional talent. It was, moreover, obviously not possible to draw the many outstanding men whose help we wanted into full-time Government service, so we secured their counsel on an *ad hoc* basis by making them consultants to the Government. In this way we obtained the services of more than a score of first-rate scholars. Additional consultants are being added as new talents and scholarly specialties are required.

These consultants are organized into a "Panel on Social Indicators," which meets periodically to exchange ideas, to organize research and writing, and to criticize any outlines, indicators, or drafts that have been prepared. Professor Daniel Bell of the Department of Sociology at Columbia University and I share the chairmanship of this Panel.

The Panel on Social Indicators is now engaged in a "trial run" attempt to produce a "Social Report." One of the initial steps in this attempt was to divide the Panel on Social Indicators into sub-panels, each of which was to take a special interest in a particular part of the Report and submit outlines, draft chapters, and social indicators for the consideration of the Panel as a whole. One sub-panel specializes in problems of poverty and levels of living, and is headed by Professor Howard Freeman of the Department of Sociology at Brandeis University. Another specializes in opportunity and social mobility, and is headed by Professor Otis Dudley Duncan, Sociologist and Demographer at the University of Michigan. A third sub-panel considers health and life, and is headed by Professor Phillip Hauser. Professor Hauser, who recently testified before your Committee, is a Demographer at the University of Chicago, and has in the past been Deputy Director of the Bureau of the Census and an Assistant Secretary of Commerce. A fourth sub-panel focuses on the quality of the environment, and is chaired by Harvey Perloff, an Economist at Resources for the Future in Washington. A fifth sub-panel considers the extent to which different groups of our citizens participate in, or are left out of, the organized life of our society, and it has been chaired by Bertram Gross, Professor of Political Science at Syracuse University. Meanwhile, we have an effort under way in our Department to produce a draft of a section of the Report on education, and are making plans for a section of the Report on crime and other social costs.

The Panel is off to a promising start. Some sections of the Report—

particularly those on opportunity and on the quality of the environment—have been extensively outlined. Others are in less formative stages with conceptual problems still unresolved.

Once the initial reconnaissance of the Panel consultants had been carried out, and some hopeful lines of inquiry begun, it seemed proper to accelerate the pace by obtaining someone on a full-time basis who could help coordinate the effort to produce a Report. Thus a new position—that of the Deputy Assistant Secretary for Social Indicators—was created. The first incumbent of this position has just assumed his new duties. He is Mancur Olson, Jr. His primary responsibility will be to work with me and the Panel and to attempt to increase the tempo of the work on the Report.

Since the problems involved in applying the Planning-Programming-Budgeting System to socio-economic problems are intimately related to those involved in finding useful social indicators, it is expected that members of my staff in the Office of Program Coordination who have had experience with the Planning-Programming-Budgeting System, will also be able to make important contributions to this endeavor.

Fortunately, the inevitable limits on the resources directly available can in part be overcome by enlisting the participation of a number of agencies and offices throughout the Government. This participation of other departments of the Government is desirable on other grounds as well. The task the President set before us relates to the whole range of the nation's socio-economic problems, rather than only to the particular programs of the Department of Health, Education, and Welfare. Accordingly, representatives of several departments and agencies have participated in the meetings of the Panel on Social Indicators, and many of the offices in the Government that gather statistics on social and economic phenomena have provided statistical series which we will use in the preparation of our indicators and reports.

Now that I have described the endeavor we have under way, I want to turn to the specific questions that Senator Harris asked in his letter inviting me to testify. Your first question, Senator Harris, asked whether a useful national social accounting system could be established, and whether it was possible to design a set of reliable social indicators. My answer is that we can't know the answer until we have tried, that we are in the process of trying, and that I will be able to give you a full answer when our report has been completed. But the answer, even when it can be given, will, I would guess, probably not be entirely in accord with either the most sweeping claims of the bolder advocates of the creation of "social accounts," who seem to assume that we can take the measure of every sparrow's fall, or with skepticism of any who would deny the need for the inquiries you and we are making, and thus rely solely on convention, cliche, or political power to determine our social and economic policy. Surely it is better that policy be chosen in the light of whatever relevant information can be obtained, however incomplete it may have to be.

Another of Senator Harris' questions asked about the problem of invasions of privacy in the course of research for a social report. A vigilant concern about the individual's right to privacy is necessary to preserve the freedom and civility of any society, but I think that in this particular area the problem is not as difficult as it is in some others. A Social Report would dwell on aggregates and averages, not on particular individuals. There would be no need to violate the anonymity of any particular source of information. The sort of information which is normally collected by credit bureaus, tax collectors, and police officials is of a more sensitive nature than that which we would need. Nonetheless, the protection of privacy is so vital that special safeguards may be in order. Perhaps the law should prohibit the release of any information on any particular individual and provide serious penalties for noncompliance.

Senator Harris also asked some questions about the role that State and local governments should play in the collecting of data about, and participating in, the formation of a national social policy. The American nation is not a homogeneous mass: it has many local variations and purely parochial problems which may benefit from the individual attention of a particular unit of government. Moreover, some of the socio-economic problems of this nation are so profound and difficult that we must sometimes simultaneously experiment with a wide variety of methods of dealing with them. The number, diversity, and independence of our State and local governments may bring about variations in policy that can expand our knowledge and thereby light the way to better policies. Thus such governments must play a significant role, both in the collection of information about, and in the formulation and execution of many of our social and economic policies.

Finally, Senator Harris asked three more questions which I should answer together, since my answers to these three questions are intimately interrelated. He asked what might be done to excite the American people about social goals, inquired whether a Council of Social Advisors was the best organizational structure to achieve the objectives of the "Full Opportunity and Social Accounting Act," and asked for specific or detailed comments about this Act.

The basic point is that I am in enthusiastic accord with this Bill's worthy purposes. The distinguished Senators who have authored this Bill, and the Subcommittee that has held these informative hearings, have, in my opinion, perceptively discerned the urgent need for the systematic collection and analysis of social and economic intelligence. I think that the concern of these Senators and this Subcommittee about the need for social research, and the parallel concern in the academic community, is a sign that the work on social indicators that the President directed us to undertake is particularly necessary. Hopefully so many people have decided to shake this particular branch because they think that it may bear rich fruit. It has long been recognized that our military strategy should be based on all of the intelligence that we can feasibly obtain, and should benefit from the best analysis that science and scholarship can offer. Organizations such as the RAND Corporation, designed in large part to give the military services the benefit of a research capability in the social sciences, have for sometime been commonplace. Some of our country's domestic socioeconomic difficulties, such as the problem of racial discrimination, go back for more than a century, and stem from prejudices of extraordinary tenacity. Such problems are as difficult and profound as any the nation faces, and there is surely as much need for the systematic collection of information, and the careful analysis of this information with the best tools that science can provide in this area as in any other.

In addition to the goal of giving the Government the benefit of more social science research, the Bill apparently has still other noble purposes. It is evidently designed, in the words of Senator Harris' question, to excite and commit the American people to social goals—that is to serve a hortatory or journalistic function as well as a strictly scientific purpose. In addition, the Bill is evidently designed in part to overcome what Senator Mondale has called "bureaucratic channel vision" by supplanting or supplementing the research input and advice the President already gets from particular departments and agencies with the hopefully disinterested and centralized advice and research capability of a Council of Social Advisors.

These are all creditable objectives. But I fear that with all of these very different purposes the Bill suffers from an embarrassment of riches. When the apparent purposes of this Bill are distinguished, it becomes clear that they may not all be properly served by the single Council that the Bill provides, that some of these purposes might better be served by separate bills and different institutions, and that the Bill raises many fundamenal questions that cannot be properly answered without more experience, more study, and additional hearings.

This point is best illustrated by considering whether the proposed Council of Social Advisors composed of professional social scientists would be the best way of dramatizing the moral urgency of the nation's socio-economic problems. Though social science has not yet reached the stage where there are no longer any conflicting schools of thought or intellectual traditions, it is probably true that a majority of social scientists agree that they should aspire to be "scientific." This means that they strive for detachment rather than commitment and that they conceive their task to be to study the consistency of means and ends, raher than to specify what ends or values should be sought. According to this conception, the social scientist engages in positivistic studies of the way given social, political, and economic systems function, and asserts that on normative questions—those that ask what we ought to do in some moral sense—he has, as a social scientist, no *professional* opinion, and like everyone else can claim only one vote. The fact that many social scientists strive to be objective and scientific means that they may not be especially good as advocates for the disadvantaged, nor adept at making an appeal to the public's higher sympathies and moral aspirations.

Moreover, the social scientist is trained to avoid sensationalism, and the word "journalistic" is in his language an epithet when applied to any supposedly scholarly study. Partly as a result of this, and partly because of the desire to be scientific, the prose of modern social science is famous for jargon and complexity rather than fire and spirit. At the same time the fact that the social scientist researcher earns his daily bread by working at the frontier of knowledge gives him a lively sense of the limits of our knowledge. He is therefore inclined to plead for further research before committing himself. One of the things I have already learned from our Panel on Social Indicators is that some liberal and distinguished social scientists feel that a Social Report should emphasize the profundity of our socio-economic problems so that the public will understand why these problems can't be solved quickly.

For these as well as other reasons, a Council composed of social scientists might not be the best institution for dramatizing the urgency of the nation's socio-economic problems. Perhaps this is why some of the witnesses before this Committee have recommended that some members from the humanities be added, or that the representatives of the disadvantaged groups be given special representation on it, or that the Council undertake regular surveys to determine the wishes of the poor. It is perhaps even conceivable that some of the purposes of the "Full Opportunity and Social Accounting Act" could be served by a body composed of elder statesmen, distinguished clergymen, civil rights activists, and others distinguished by their sympathy for the disadvantaged. Possibly such a body should be entirely separate from whatever institutions are responsible for social science research on policy problems.

The emphasis in some statements on the need to separate the activities [the proposed] Council of Social Advisors would perform from [those of] any particular agency or department may suggest that one of its purposes would be to compare the merits and effectiveness of the programs of different departments of the Government. Any body that is designed to pass judgment on the performance of particular departments, and help decide which should be expanded and which should be contracted will by definition have an impact on the budgetary process. It is also inevitably related to the task of assessing the results of the Planning-Programming-Budgeting System studies under way throughout the Government. The Planning-Programming-Budgeting System is designed to facilitate a comparison of the merits of additional expenditures on different programs, including alternative programs to deal with socio-economic problems. Both the budgetary process and the assessment of the results of the Planning-Programming-Budgeting System studies in different departments are now centralized in the Bureau of the Budget. If a Council of Social Advisors is to advise the President which social programs to emphasize, it should perhaps either be a part of the Budget Bureau, or else take over some of the present functions of the Budget Bureau. It would seem to me that any organizational decisions of this importance should be undertaken, if at all, only after much more study. I realize that the separation of the Budget Bureau's Planning-Programming-Budgeting System activities and any Council of Social Advisors is contemplated, but I am not sure such a separation could be maintained in practice.

The division of responsibility between any Council of Social Advisors and the Council of Economic Advisers also poses an unsolved problem. At first glance it seems reasonable that if there is a Council of Economic Advisers studying economic policy, there should naturally also be a Council of Social Advisors studying social policy. But this prescription is not quite as simple or symmetrical as it sounds. For there is no clear-cut distinction between economic and social policies. Is the question of how we allocate scarce funds among competing programs designed to deal with poverty any less an economic question than the question of how we deal, say, with the problem of unemployment? And even if it is, how do we separate other ways of dealing with the poverty problem from the basic problem of unemployment with which the Council of Economic Advisors has an obvious and long-standing concern. Just as there is a fundamental economic dimension to any so-called social decisions, so there is also an obvious social element in most economic issues. Reality is not neatly divided into departments in the ways that universities are. If there is no clear and logically defensible distinction between that which is social and that which is economic we should think carefully before making any final decision to separate policy oriented analysis and advice according to whether it is arbitrarily deemed to be economic or social. This argument is not sufficient to show that there should *not* be a Council of Social Advisors. The point is rather that this matter is a great deal less obvious than it might seem.

It seems to me that we can make a better decision about how we should organize the research and advice on how to solve our socio-economic problems after we have had more experience and more time for thought. In time, too, we will, because of the undertaking we already have well under way in my office, know more about what are now sometimes too vaguely described as social accounts or social indicators. Our own efforts, and those of the Panel on Social Indicators, will also give us an idea what a Social Report can convey and what functions it can serve. Thus, I respectfully suggest, despite the warmth of my agreement with the spirit and purpose of the Full Opportunity and Social Accounting Act, that any decision to create a Council of Social Advisors should be postponed until we have learned what can be learned from the effort that we already have well under way, and which seems to me to have had a most auspicious beginning. I naturally expect that our initial effort will have the special sympathy and attention of the proponents of the Bill under discussion today, and that it may continue to benefit from the constructive and useful hearings of this Subcommittee. . . .

x

≈ *8*

PPBS Comes
to Washington

VIRGINIA HELD

In May 1966, all departments and most agencies of the U.S. government, in submitting to the Budget Bureau their rough spending plans for the fiscal year starting fourteen months later, began using for the first time the Planning-Program-Budgeting System, or PPBS. The change has its source in the summer of 1965, when Lyndon B. Johnson ordered them to institute what he called a "revolutionary" new system, one which demands that departments and agencies define clearly the major objectives (or "programs") which they choose to pursue, that they apply systematic analyses to the alternative ways in which these objectives are being—or may be—sought, and that they plan their spending in long-range as well as one-year-ahead terms. This doesn't sound very revolutionary; indeed, it sounds merely sensible. Oddly enough, it may actually be both.

RAND and the D.O.D.

In initiating this new approach, the President is applying throughout the government an approach toward more rational decision-making which has already swept through the Defense Department. "Program budgeting" was introduced into the Department of Defense in 1961. Previously, defense expenditures had

Reprinted by permission from Virginia Held, "PPBS Comes to Washington," *The Public Interest,* No. 4, Summer, 1966, pp. 102–115. Copyright © 1966 by National Affairs, Inc.

been considered in traditional line-item form, focusing on categories such as maintenance, supplies, personnel, and equipment; and the budget presented by the Secretary of Defense was really a combination of Army, Navy, and Air Force budgets. The deficiencies, as explained by Alain C. Enthoven, Deputy Assistant Secretary of Defense for Systems Analysis, were that the whole question of how much a weapon system *cost* was not brought in systematically, either to determine the feasibility of the program or to evaluate its efficiency. By 1960 it was apparent that the troublesome decisions of the Defense Department centered around the choice of vast weapon systems, each enormously expensive, designed for various military missions (such as strategic retaliation and continental defense). In order to be able to consider the "worth" of a weapon system as a whole, and to relate longer range planning to annual budgets, the Defense Department's comptroller, Charles J. Hitch, at Secretary of Defense Robert McNamara's direction, instituted a new system of program budgeting. The U.S. defense effort has, as a result, been broken down into nine basic "programs": Strategic Retaliatory Forces, Continental Air and Missile Defense Forces, General Purpose Forces, Airlift and Sealift Forces, Reserve and National Guard Forces, Research and Development, General Support, Military Assistance, and Civil Defense. Each is composed of certain "program elements" (such as Polaris submarines and Minutemen missiles) which are intended to accomplish a common military mission.

The groundwork for the reorganization of the Defense Department budget had been laid by several studies. The Hoover Commission on Organization of the Executive Branch of the Government had made a general recommendation in its 1949 report that the government adopt a budget based upon functions, activities, and projects—which it designated a "performance budget." David Novick of the RAND Corporation presented in 1954 a systematic exposition of how the new technique could be applied effectively to military spending. In his RAND study, called *Efficiency and Economy in Government Through New Budgeting Procedures,* and on subsequent occasions, Novick proposed a method of "program budgeting" and recommended its adoption by the Defense Department. The Committee for Economic Development issued a policy statement in 1955, called *Control of Federal Government Expenditures,* also advocating a refashioning of the entire federal budget along "program" lines. The term "program," as then used by the Bureau of the Budget, designated combinations of activities, such as procurement of equipment, training of personnel, and so forth, rather than their objectives. With the 1954 RAND study for the Defense Department, however, the term "program" came to mean the ultimate goal of many interdependent activities.

When Charles Hitch first took office as Defense Department Comptroller in 1961, he expected to introduce program budgeting over a period of several years. But McNamara speeded up the process and decided that the budget for fiscal 1963 should be formulated in terms of major programs and weapons systems. The results of this reorganization, and of the evaluations it has made possible, led to recommendations that the approach be extended to civilian affairs. David Novick suggested that RAND conduct research on the government-wide applicability of program budgeting; this led to a collection of papers edited by Novick, and recently published by Harvard University Press under the title, *Program Budgeting—Program Analysis and the Federal Budget,* and the advice "to introduce into the nondefense areas of the federal government the kind of program analysis that has been installed in the Department of Defense as an integral part of the planning, programming, and budgeting process." In line with this and other recommendations, the government is now in the process of doing just this.

The Role of the Budget

Since every governmental program is only as extensive as the money put into it, the place where the decisions—whether rational or not—over how to divide up the national effort are most apparent, is in the federal budget. The budget is the central expression of how the government's finite resources will be allocated, the terms of the annual cease-fire, as it were, within the executive branch, between the competing claims of different advocates for more money for defense, or agriculture, or new welfare programs.

Once the amounts have been fixed in the budget, which the President will then present to Congress, the major decisions have for the most part been made. Congress can, of course, upset the settlement temporarily by decreasing or increasing some aspects of some programs, and dissatisfied agencies can breach the cease-fire and help one congressional faction or another. But as George A. Steiner puts it in his chapter of the recent RAND study, "despite the wide publicity frequently given to changes made by the Congress in the budget presented by the President, important alterations are usually relatively few and minor." Hence it is in the executive process of putting together a budget that the impact of the new approach will be most apparent.

The greater part of a federal budget is what it is because of what it was. All those programs already made mandatory—such as farm price supports or veterans' pensions—have to be paid for. Defense expenditures, which have used up over half of the total of federal expenditures for the past 15 years, have not changed drastically from year to year. The region of discretion, then, is distinctly limited. But as in other human affairs, it is those few decisions that are open to conscious choice which cause anguish. And it is to the resolution of such anguish that the new intellectual techniques are directed.

What Is a Program?

Establishing just what a program may or may not be involves the conceptual distinguishing and grouping of various objectives and activities; alternative conceptualizations are always possible, and are often floating about. Charles Hitch and Roland McKean, whose book *The Economics of Defense in the Nuclear Age* (published as a paperback last year by Atheneum) has become a classic in its field, discussed the problem of discerning a defense program:

> Let us illustrate the distinction between a program and an object [of expenditure]. . . . Certain activities of the Air Force, the Army, and the Navy produce retaliatory striking power or deterrence, and these activities might be grouped together and called a program. In providing deterrence, the Services use missiles, manpower, food, paper clips, and transportation—intermediate items which might be called "objects of expenditure. . . ."
>
> Just what one means by an "end product" or a "program" is not unambiguous. The line of demarcation between programs and objects is not clear-cut. Is the Military Air Transport Service a program or simply an activity supporting, say, the Tactical Air Program? Or is even the latter merely something to be purchased for a program that might be called "deterrence and fighting of limited wars"? Even such tasks as providing nuclear striking power and providing forces for limited war have interrelationships. Neither is solely a supporting activity of the other, yet each can influence the credibility and effectiveness of the other. It may seem that one is driven to regard every military item and activity as an object purchased for and contributing to one program—national security.
>
> Despite these complexities, officials do find it helpful to think in terms of several programs, and there is hope of developing categories that will be even more meaningful. After all, our only chance of pondering the gains as well as the costs of defense budgets is to think in terms of rather broad aggregations of activities.

The Defense Department budget has thus been divided into the nine major programs already mentioned and over 800 "program elements," which are the forces, weapons, or support systems, and other types of integrated activities by means of which the programs are to be achieved. But the possibilities of regrouping are almost endless.

Officials trying to decide what to consider part of and what to exclude from various civilian programs face analogous difficulties. Education, for instance, is one of the most dispersed activities of the government. In the fiscal 1965 budget, funds for education were dispersed through more than forty agencies. The U.S. Office of Education's expenditures constituted only about one-fifth of the total federal education budget, and efforts are only now under way to distinguish what could be conceived of as *the* education program of the federal government.

A member of the executive involved with the new system has said that the president's directive on program budgeting is forcing some agencies to consider, virtually for the first time, just what their objectives are. Officials of the Justice Department, for example, being lawyers, traditionally think it is their clients, not they themselves, who have objectives. But formulations of what the Department of Justice is trying to do are now being considered in terms of such categories as reduction and prevention of crime, protection of internal security, assurance of civil rights under law, maintenance of competition in the business community, and so on.

Melvin Anshen, in the opening chapter of RAND's *Program Budgeting* sums up the scope of the undertaking:

> The central issue is, of course, nothing less than the definition of the ultimate objectives of the federal government as they are realized through operational decisions. Set in this framework, the designation of a schedule of programs may be described as building a bridge between a matter of political philosophy (what is government for?) and the administrative function of assigning scarce resources among alternative governmental objectives. The unique function of a program budget is to implement the conclusions of a political philosophy through the assignment of resources to their accomplishment. . . . In a number of areas no clear objectives have ever been laid down. This undesirable condition has prevailed in the field of international aid and investment, but it can also be found in many domestic areas including, among others, agriculture, transportation, education, and unemployment.

One problem which may become troublesome is that of frankness. How honest can an agency be in declaring its intentions without getting into difficulties, how open about its criteria of evaluation? If the Department of Agriculture, for instance, is trying to shift a lot of people out of farming, will it be wise to advertise this objective? If the State Department values a program that induces in the leaders of foreign countries a healthy respect for U.S. power, should it say so in a public analysis? How much program budgeting may aggravate "the honesty problem" remains to be seen.

The End of Absolutes

The importance of thinking in program terms is that, in addition to clarifying objectives, it helps move discussion away from the fairly useless absolutes of (a) what fixed amounts of money to spend no matter what the goals, or (b) what fixed objectives to achieve no matter what the costs.

Starting out with an immovable sum, and deciding how to spend it makes little sense for an entity such as the U.S. Government. (It appeared to be the favored approach of President Eisenhower's Budget Director, Maurice Stans, who liked to tell department secretaries to be sure not to exceed certain fixed amounts of money in their requests.) Critics of this approach point out that, since revenues are subject to being increased, it should be acknowledged that, if the nation's security requires stronger defenses, or its soundness a program to combat unemployment, no fixed amount of spending should be imposed as a precondition to which all subsequent decisions must conform.

But the opposite approach, taking needs or objectives as thoroughly immovable, is no more satisfactory. Congressmen often ask military officials to tell them, honestly, what they "really need." Senator Chavez, for instance, said to General Maxwell Taylor, in Congressional hearings on appropriations for Eisenhower's defense program, "We would like to know what you need and not what the Budget Bureau thinks you should have." The question, however, in isolation, is unanswerable. If money is no problem at all, some people need Cadillacs and caviar pretty badly, and generals and department heads are no exception. Governments, like individuals, traditionally find ways to spend what is available.

Alan Peacock and Jack Wiseman, in their book *The Growth of Public Expenditure in the United Kingdom,* published in 1961, tried to assess the validity of the "law" of ever-increasing state expenditures formulated by the German economist Adolph Wagner in 1883. Wagner had said, on the basis of observations of Western European countries, that pressures for social progress inevitably lead to increasing state activity and hence to a growth of governmental expenditures, and that "in the long run the desire for development of a progressive people will always overcome . . . financial difficulties." Peacock and Wiseman found upon analyzing British figures that it seemed to be the other way around: expenditures increase because revenues increase. With a given tax system and constant tax rates, government revenues grow as the economy grows, and governments arrange to use up their incomes. But discovering which is cause and which effect may be less important than acknowledging the disutility of taking the levels of either revenues or expenditures as absolute in trying to make the decisions that a federal budget transfixes.

Explaining the point with regard to defense plans, Hitch and McKean say:

> There is no budget size or cost that is correct regardless of the payoff, and there is no need that should be met regardless of cost.
>
> On the one hand, there is no presumption that the defense budget is now, or should be, near any immovable upper limit. As far as physical and economic feasibility is concerned, national security expenditures could be raised (within a two- or three-year transition period) by, say, $30 billion per year. With appropriate changes in tax rates and monetary policy, this could be done without causing severe inflation.
>
> From existing levels, in other words, outlays for defense activities can be raised if we really want to raise them—if we feel that we need extra defense programs more than other things.
>
> On the other hand, [Hitch and McKean continue] there is no particular national security program that we need in an absolute sense. . . . A list of the "desirable" items that could strengthen our defense would be almost endless. Where does one draw the line [without reference to cost] between what is needed and what is not? There are no clear-cut "minimal" needs, either for defense as a whole or for particular programs. . . . Outlays for various programs *can* be cut if we feel that we need other things even more. It is up to us to choose.

The Methods of Choice

Along with facilitating an awareness of the objectives to be sought, PPBS provides for the application of a battery of new techniques, such as systems analysis and cost-benefit analysis, to try to increase the possibilities of making rational choices between alternative means of pursuing these objectives. The terms used to designate these techniques are not yet at a stage of precise definition. As Gene H. Fisher states in his chapter on "cost-utility analysis," the term he favors, in the RAND study on program budgeting, the terms "cost-benefit analysis," "cost-effectiveness analysis," "systems analysis," "operations research," and "operations analysis" all "convey the same general meaning but have important different meanings to different people."

David Novick explains one important distinction:

> Cost-effectiveness analysis of alternative forces and weapon systems . . . stems basically from operations research in World War II. But operations research is concerned with the analysis of alternative tactics with basically given weapon systems [e.g., in bombing a bridge, whether to go across it or down the middle], while the emphasis in cost-effectiveness analysis is on forward planning. Freedom to allocate one's resources is usually severely limited in typical problems of operations research, whereas the purpose of cost-effectiveness analysis is to examine the effects of such alternative resource allocations. . . .

While these techniques remain in their present healthy state of disorderly and inventive and sometimes exuberant development, precise definitions may be of less interest than a few glimpses at how they may be shaped and used in specific decision-making situations.

One of the most useful books for this purpose, partly because of its conceptual openness, is a collection of papers edited by Robert Dorfman under the title *Measuring Benefits of Government Investments* (Washington, D.C., The Brookings Institution, 1965). The authors attempt to expand and apply cost-benefit concepts to various areas of federal and local governmental activity, such as providing outdoor recreation, preventing high school dropouts, investing in highways, and undertaking urban renewal, where questions of how to quantify social "costs" and "benefits" become crucial. "It is no accident," the editor explains, "that benefit-cost analysis had its origin and highest development in the field of water resources. That is the field in which . . . the highest proportion of outputs—water and power—are saleable commodities bearing relevant market prices." This volume steers clear of the relatively easy cases of dams and levees, where costs and benefits are more quantifiable in terms of money, and enters foggier territory. Dorfman notes that the book's "preoccupation with conceptual problems and comparative neglect of technical expedients is probably a symptom of the youngness of the field. . . . The work of extending the methods of benefit-cost analysis and of criticizing and appraising these extensions has only just begun."

For the purpose of grasping a few basic concepts of cost-benefit analysis, however, it may be useful to revert to reservoirs for a moment and to look at one simple case offered by Otto Eckstein, who has written two books on cost-benefit analysis in connection with water resource development. In his little book *Public Finance* (Prentice-Hall, 1964), he gives the following table showing, for a Brink Valley, estimated flood damage without protection in a typical year and the lowered damage figures with progressively more ambitious flood protection plans:

PLAN	ANNUAL COST OF PROJECT	AVERAGE ANNUAL DAMAGE	BENEFIT (REDUCTION OF DAMAGE)
Without protection	0	$38,000	0
Plan A—levees	$ 3,000	32,000	$ 6,000
Plan B—small reservoir	10,000	22,000	16,000
Plan C—medium reservoir	18,000	13,000	25,000
Plan D—large reservoir	30,000	6,000	32,000

With all plans, benefits exceed costs, but it is Plan C that is the best one because with it the marginal benefit of going from the lesser plan to it continues to exceed the marginal cost of spending the extra money. Although it costs $8,000 more than Plan B, it will avert $9,000 worth more of damages. But a further increment, going to Plan D, would cost an extra $12,000, yet yield only $7,000 in additional benefits. Hence it would fail the test of having marginal benefits exceed marginal costs.

In the Dorfman volume, a paper by Ruth P. Mack and Sumner Myers, of the Institute of Public Administration and National Planning Association, respectively, attempts to provide an analysis in cost-benefit terms that could be used to evaluate governmental expenditures on outdoor recreation. Benefits are calculated on the basis of what the authors call "merit-weighted user-days," which take into account various sorts of recreation for various sorts of people under varying conditions. The simple measure of "user-days"—a function of the numbers of people expected to use a park and of the lengths of time of their stays—is weighted to take account of evaluations that some user-days are better than others. The weighted figures include such judgments of social merit as that a day spent by a child in the wilderness has more lasting value than an adult's picnicking in a crowded, noisy park; that the marginal utility of additional recreation declines as larger amounts are made available; that equity requires government to provide relatively more recreational opportunities to those who most need them and can least afford private alternatives, plus many others. In ways too complex to examine here, alternative parks under consideration for a given expected number of users are then evaluated in terms of the merit-weighted user-days which they could be expectd to provide.

Hitch and McKean in their book present conceptual frameworks, together with a mathematical appendix which becomes impossible for the non-specialist, for choices between alternative military forces. In a simplified hypothetical example, they take a situation with one input, say a fixed budget of B billion dollars and two possible outputs. A planner is assumed to be deliberating about what proportion of the B billion dollars to spend on a strategic bombing force and what proportion on an air defense force. Using enemy targets that could be destroyed and the number of attacking enemy bombers that could be shot down as the two outputs to which he would attach values, the planner could construct a curve showing maximum combinations which could be bought with the B billion dollars. Each point on the curve then represents an "efficient" use of resources, because at any point on it, it is possible to increase one valuable output only by decreasing the other. To select a point on the curve representing the "optimal" use of his budget amount, a planner needs what the economists call "indifference curves" to intersect it. Indifference curves reflect preferences for some combinations of target destruction and kill potential over others. The optimal point is a point of intersection of the original curve with as high an indifference curve as possible.

In many actual situations, an analysis can only yield calculations on efficient systems, trying to choose optimal ones may largely require reliance on intuitive judgment. But the range within which such judgment must be made can often be narrowed.

One of the central problems of any analysis is the choice of a criterion, or test of preferredness, which suggests the best combination of things distinguished as desirable. Simultaneously maximizing gain while minimizing cost looks appealing, but is no criterion because, as Hitch and McKean point out, "there is no such policy" as one that would accomplish it. "Maximum gain is infinitely large, and minimum cost is zero. Seek the policy that has that outcome, and you will not find it." One common preference is to choose that policy which has the highest ratio of "effectiveness," or achievement of objectives assumed to be desirable, to cost. The maximizing of this ratio is then the criterion, but choices should be bounded by common sense from extreme forms, as for instance in overkill situations. It often happens that the ratio reduces itself to maximum effectiveness for a given budget.

What are usually required are analyses that straddle a problem, that calculate what, given a certain scale of objectives, can minimize costs, or that calculate what, given assumed amounts of money to spend, can maximize achievements. Which formulation to use, here as in other deliberations, tends to depend on which it seems more feasible to choose intuitively "reasonable" levels for.

An example of an analysis that is to be made when the data is in, as the use of analytic techniques expands from the Defense Department, where most actual analyses are classified, to other areas of government, is an evaluation of the Office of Economic Opportunity's Job Corps and Neighborhood Youth Corps. The two corps are alternative ways of pursuing certain of the Poverty Program's objectives. The Job Corps takes youngsters and puts them in residential camps, keeping them there 24 hours a day, seven days a week. It teaches them to read and write, and it trains them for a job. The Neighborhood Youth Corps takes youngsters of the same age group, and gives them work for 35 hours a week, paying them the minimum wage. They live at their own homes. Although very different, and designed for different kinds of enrollees, the objective of both organizations is to make youngsters employable, and attempts can be made to measure their relative effectiveness.

It is known already that the Job Corps costs about four times as much per youth as the Neighborhood Youth Corps. "The large differential in costs," an OEO working memorandum states, "makes assessment of payoff critical. It is, for example, estimated that $100 increase in annual income, discounted at 5%, justifies the expenditure of $1,500 in training." Although economic considerations need not constitute the basis on which a decision to expand or decrease either program is made, they are at least worth looking into in planning future efforts to combat poverty.

Kermit Gordon, a former member of the Council of Economic Advisers, and Budget Director under Presidents Kennedy and Johnson, has recently suggested a series of possible applications of economic analysis to existing governmental programs. One suggestion is for an evaluation of the program the U.S. has for sugar.

> The U.S. sugar program [Gordon says] incorporates import quotas, domestic production quotas, import duties, an excise tax on sugar refining, and graduated subsidies to U.S. cane and beet sugar producers. Over the years, the program has been used to promote increased domestic production at the expense of imports. On the average, over the past decade or so, domestic prices have been roughly double the world price of sugar. The present combined costs to the U.S. Government and to the U.S. sugar consumer of our sugar program have been estimated at about $500 million a year; that is, we spend on sugar $500 million more than we would spend if there were no U.S. sugar program. (This does not include the Federal subsidy for irrigation water to sugar beet growers.) Estimated net income of all U.S. cane and beet growers is about $140 million per annum. Thus, the total cost of the program is more than three times the net income of products.
>
> Presumably, [Gordon continues] the purpose of the program is to support the incomes of U.S. sugar growers and to assure to U.S. consumers a reliable supply of sugar at relatively stable prices. It should not exceed the talents of economists to devise alternative programs which would achieve these objectives at substantially lesser costs than the present program.

One of the most imaginative attempts to evaluate the effectiveness of programs with hard-to-assess objectives is a method devised by David Osborn, Deputy Assistant Secretary of State for Educational and Cultural Affairs. Built into this system, which is being programmed by the Franklin Institute Research Laboratory in Philadelphia, is the view that the agency's various activities have multiple and overlapping objectives, and that a conceptual structure delineating end programs aimed at through alternative means does not adequately reflect such overlapping. Osborn recommends a scheme of cross-multiplying the costs of the activities with a number representing the rank of its objectives on a scale. For instance, the exchange of Fulbright professors may contribute to "cultural prestige and mutual respect," "educational development," and gaining "entrée," which might be given scale numbers such as 8, 6, and 5, respectively. These numbers are then multiplied with the cost of the program, and the resulting figure is in turn multiplied with an ingenious figure called a "country number." The latter is an attempt to get a rough measure of the importance to the U.S. of the countries with which we have cultural relations. It is arrived at by putting together in complicated ways certain key data, weighted to reflect cultural and educational matters, such as the country's population, Gross National Product, number of college students, rate of illiteracy, and so forth. The resulting numbers are then revised in the light of working experience, as when, because of its high per capita income, a certain tiny middle-eastern country turns out to be more important to the U.S. than a large eastern European one. At this point, country numbers are revised on the basis of judgment and experience, as are other numbers at other points. But those who make such revisions have a basic framework to start with, a set of numbers arranged on the basis of many factors, rather than single arbitrary guesses. As Osborn explains it:

> We debate the numerical results we come up with but it becomes a revision process. The analysis gives us approximations to work with. If you break up your judgment into various parts you have something to talk about.

Because of the imaginative, and sometimes conceptually playful nature of these techniques, which nearly all agree still constitute an art rather than a science, critics sometimes contend that the attempt to assign numerical values to such amorphous objectives as what an educational exchange program is aiming at, or what urban renewal is trying to accomplish, are of little use, and may be misleading. Misused, the techniques may lead to a focus on less important but measurable factors, such as dollar costs and miles of highway constructed, let us say, and to the neglect of less quantifiable factors such as the social and aesthetic costs and benefits of programs.

One point of such analyses may be, however, that when many guesses go into a calculation, the deficiency of any one of them is less crucial than if the only thing guessed at, intuitively, is the outcome, such as that exchanging professors is more valuable than exchanging dance troupes, or that programs for preschoolers will do more to ease poverty than money spent on housing.

William Gorham, an Assistant Secretary in the Department of Health, Education and Welfare and an economist who recently moved up from the Defense Department to introduce into HEW the kind of analyses that have been helpful in resolving defense decision problems, finds non-quantifiable considerations already so profuse in an agency such as HEW that there is hardly a danger for some time of introducing too much calculation.

In efforts such as those to prevent high-school dropouts, for instance, about all that is known now is how much is being spent. To evaluate them one has to specify objectives—which may not amount to doing away with dropping-out altogether—and then to compare the merits of achieving different levels of high-school education. One of the principal benefits of finishing high-school is the higher expected earning capacity of graduates. The more that is spent to reduce the drop-out rate, the greater the expected income of the population. Looked at in this way, the economic benefits and costs of achieving different levels of high school completion can be compared and can at least help determine the efficacy of such programs.

Gorham says of his experience in dealing with military problems that the dominant characteristics in a decision are often not those that can be measured, but if one does what is possible with numbers, it leads those involved in a decision to be clear about the non- or less-quantifiable factors on which the decision may be based, and such an influence is often useful.

The Locus of Decision

The problems of defining what is rational and what is not and of deciding whether rational choices—if possible at all—are better than those made on the basis of intuitive feelings, involve high-level philosophical complexities. But to assert that it is advisable to know what one is doing may be a modest claim susceptible of general approval. What the new intellectual techniques, such as those used in PPBS, attempt to provide are methods by which those who make the decisions about how the government should direct its efforts can increase their awareness of the conditions and consequences of their choices and can clarify the elements that, explicitly or implicitly, enter into their judgments.

Various unforseeable and irrational factors will continue, sometimes rightly, to influence final decisions. And debates about just which sorts of considerations *are* the rational ones are bound to remain lively. Congress, for instance, may cut an unpopular engineering project which the Department of the Interior declares rewarding, or, because of the pressures upon it, vote more money for a given defense component than Administration calculations deem effective. A department head may override his professional advisers for political reasons, good or bad. But the knowledge which the new techniques can provide may be used to raise the contests over such issues to a more responsible level. And those who object to the language of game-playing and payoff may simply not yet have understood the extent to which these techniques can embody a distinctively moral concern for alternative values.

Several of those RAND and Defense Department alumni now preparing to apply quantitative analyses to broader domains have made the point that the factors to be considered are probably more measurable in the case of domestic programs than in the case of defense. It is at least easier to measure jobs created, or numbers of people moved across an income figure taken as a "poverty line," than it is to measure "deterrence."

Joseph Kershaw, now analyzing poverty programs, recently compared the problem for the two fields. He finds it easier to make such analyses for poverty programs because there is already so much information available—population and income and other statistics—even though the information is often not quite what one wants. He thinks objectives are somewhat easier to define and to quantify, for the poverty program than for the defense program, and furthermore, he observes, "we're playing the game against nature, whereas the Defense Department is playing, of course, against a very active player, or coalition of players," who can design their policies to confound those of the United States, and this "makes it possible for us to do things with more confidence than the Defense Department can."

To the extent that various forces lead those with political power to look to those with expert knowledge for advice on ways to increase the effectiveness with which government pursues its objectives, and thus to rationalize its efforts, the role of new intellectual techniques such as PPBS is likely to grow. And as the influence of government in shaping the national society continues to expand, any possible improvement in its capacity to make "better" choices becomes more significant.

There appears to have been in recent years a significant shift in the kind of advice the politicians call upon most. The supervisory outlook of New Deal government, shaped by lawyers apt to think in terms of governmental regulation and control of the nation's enterprises, has receded. Those that seem to have come to the fore are the economists, who think in terms of the effective management and development not only of the American economy but of the enterprise of government itself.

Participants in governmental decisions concede that foolish and wasteful choices are often made simply because those who make them do not know many of the things intelligent analyses can tell them. Yet even if those holding a political power of decision which continues to be primary develop no greater good-will nor desire to be rational, increased reliance upon the new techniques remains probable because, as Kermit Gordon expresses it, "analyses become powerful weapons in the arsenal of persuasion," as political wills confront one another and grapple toward resolution.

II

Presidential Advisory System: An Outside Network

The phrase "outside network" is used here in a general sense to refer to those individuals, groups, or advisory institutions who contribute to White House intelligence and decision-making processes, but who are not generally employed by either the White House or the federal government. As has quite frequently been pointed out lately, the boundaries between "public" and "private" are sufficiently blurred today to make distinctions of this sort somewhat hazardous, but the reader should readily be able to understand our inside/outside usage. The outside network is likely to be part-time, consultative, and usually of a more temporary duration than formalized White House staff roles or support agencies such as the Bureau of the Budget.

As the agenda of the New Deal became successfully accomplished, and hence, exhausted, Presidents began to look beyond the Washington bureaucracy for new intelligence for national policy. And as we have mentioned earlier, it has become commonplace for the White House to establish and consult with a growing number of task forces, advisory councils, commissions, conferences, and advisory corporations. Such extensions of the Presidential intelligence and advisory network are not entirely new; President George Washington, for example, relied on appointed laymen advisers for policy guidance in his Administration. But the extensiveness of their present use, while sometimes exaggerated, is unprecedented in American history and deserves careful systematic attention.

Twenty-five years ago, Carl Marcy suggested the importance of studying Presidential commissions, but little has been done since to heed his proposition:

> Presidential commissions created by the President upon his own authority and for his own purposes are governmental devices of increasing importance. Presidents rely on them more today than ever in the past. Their activities are news and their findings may profoundly affect the life of the nation. They have been used by Presidents as instruments to guide public opinion and to influence the Congress. They have also been used by Presidents to confuse the public and to avoid important issues.
>
> Presidential commissions have not received the attention as an instrument of government that their importance and influence warrant.[1]

The contributions in this second part will help to introduce some of the outside advisory processes which have been in frequent use in the past three Administrations. The implications and political consequences of these processes are explored and evaluated. These articles contribute an important beginning to the framework for the needed future research—research which would include comparative studies, empirical examinations of alternative advisory network roles, and the varied outcomes and effects of these roles.

---

[1] Carl Marcy, *Presidential Commissions*, New York, King's Crown Press, 1945, Preface.

1

Ideas
into
Programs

ADAM YARMOLINSKY

We were informed by the late T. S. Eliot that, "Between the idea/ And the reality/ Between the motion/ And the act/ Falls the shadow." It is not too much to say that the principal business of government, at least in the Executive Branch, is to grapple with the shadow—to make it possible for action to follow thought in orderly sequence.

Of course, the problem of moving from ideas to achievement is not unique to government (or even to the world of affairs). It was one of the great French post-impressionist painters who observed to a poet friend, "I have the most wonderful ideas for poems," and was properly rebuked by the reply, "You don't write poems with ideas, you write them with words." But what is true is that government, and particularly big government, provides an environment particularly hostile to the cultivation of new ideas. This is not because government officials are more likely than most men to be sterile, or even stodgy. It is rather because the circumstances in which they live and work are extraordinarily unfriendly to innovation.

To begin with, our big government—the federal government—is bigger than any other kind of organization in the world. Now, big government is not just little government writ large. You cannot build a large organization

Reprinted by permission from Adam Yarmolinsky, "Ideas Into Programs," *The Public Interest,* No. 2, Winter 1966, pp. 70–79, Copyright © 1966 by National Affairs, Inc.

simply by increasing the dimensions of a small organization, anymore than you can build a mansion by taking the blueprints for a cottage and multiplying every measurement. There are a number of break-points along the growth curve and at each break-point organization becomes significantly more complex and communication becomes significantly more difficult.

One of the hardest lessons for a newcomer to the governmental bureaucracy to learn in Washington is that a communication from, say, the Secretary of State to the Secretary of Defense is nothing like a letter from one individual to another. It is rather an expression of the shared views of a large group of people in one department, which it is expected will be pondered by another large group of people in the other department for days and, I am afraid in some cases, weeks—all this before it reaches its ultimate addressee, with a reply prepared for his signature. In fact, if the person who happens to be the Secretary of State wants to address a personal communication to the Secretary of Defense, he has to resort to extraordinary means to do so.

But not all of the complexity of government is a consequence of its size, by any means. The tasks of government today are themselves more complex, I submit, than those of any private undertaking. Nowhere can a man more easily be overwhelmed by the flow of paper than in government, and nowhere can one experience a greater delay, in distance and time, between initiating an action and seeing its concrete results. I am prepared to concede without argument that writing a serious book or developing a mathematical theorem or composing a sonata is harder work than any undertaken by a civil servant or a politician. But, in a sense, these are also simpler tasks—more unified, involving fewer discontinuities. People in government are constantly moving back and forth, not only between ideas and events, but between significant events and trivial ones. In my own experience, I have been called out of a meeting on U.S. policy in outer space to discuss an urgent, if perhaps not equally important, question of the allocation of inner space within the Pentagon; and within one half-hour I have had to discuss the assignment of astronauts and automobile drivers.

It is these complexities and these distractions which produce that figure of fun, the greatest enemy of new ideas, without whom no new idea in government can be put into action—the government bureaucrat.

When I speak of the government bureaucrat, I mean the person whose career is contained within the institution he serves, whether it is the civil service, the military service, or one of the quasi-military bodies like the Public Health Service or the Foreign Service. Because his career is bounded by the institution of which he is a part, and because of the size and complexity of that institution, he tends to see the institution as a sharply defined structure against a dimly perceived background of the world outside. Happenings in the outside world are not as clearly noticed, and, accordingly, their effects on the inside world are less likely to be anticipated or even appreciated when they occur. The bureaucrat is shaped by the immediate demands of his job, and his job is primarily to see that things get done, within the existing institutional framework. Significantly, the military refer to the officer in charge of a particular project as "the action officer," and the question, "Who is responsible for a particular project?" is phrased as, "Who has the action?" Because the primary responsibility of the bureaucrat is not to figure out the best way to do something, but to get it done.

If this definition appears to be inconsistent with the facts of bureaucratic delays and bureaucratic resistances, I believe the inconsistency is only superficial. The bureaucrat's constant concern is to keep the system moving, and he, more than anyone else, is aware of its enormous inertia, and the difficulty of changing course or starting up again if it is stopped even momentarily. Bureaucrats realize better than anyone else how difficult it is to get anything done in government, and they adopt the devices of routinizing and systematizing—and bureaucratizing, if you will—in order that certain things, at least, will be done. Planners in the three military departments are naturally resistant to coordination, not because they really expect that the Army, Navy, and Air Force would fight separate wars if it came to it, but rather because the difficulty of turning plans into programs is great enough within each military service. It is their very commitment to getting things done that makes them resist new and perhaps better ways of doing things.

The good bureaucrat is an expert at something called completed staff work. Staff work is what a bureaucrat does with a piece of paper before he sends it on to his superior, whom he usually refers to as "the decision-maker." Completed staff work means that before the paper goes to his superior, it has attached to it a memorandum that describes all the alternative courses of action that can be taken with the paper—approve, disapprove, modify, send back for further information; indicates the arguments for each course of action; explains who else has been consulted, and what each one thinks; recommends one alternative course of action; and finally attaches a piece of paper for the decision-maker to sign which will put that course of action into effect. Many frustrated decision-makers spend their entire official careers reacting to other people's completed staff work. But what should not be overlooked is that the purpose and end of completed staff work is to produce action, and it is by focusing on that end that the bureaucrat keeps the enterprise moving ahead. The effect of completed staff work, like the effect of the presence of bureaucrats in the system, is to encourage attention to business at hand. It is also frequently a useful antidote to sloppy thinking. But it emphatically does not encourage the production of new ideas, or the suspension of judgment until new ideas can sink in.

Where Do Ideas Come From?

Still, despite all of the resistances in the system, new ideas do appear, and some of them develop into new operating programs. Where do these ideas come from, and what determines whether they jump the gap or just sputter out? How are they changed as they emerge into the outside world? And what can we do to make the government more hospitable to the best of the new ideas?

In examining sources of new ideas in government, one observes that the theory of simultaneous—and seemingly spontaneous—invention applies here as elsewhere. The successful new ideas seem to crop up all at once from a number of sources; in fact, people have almost come to blows in Washington about who invented poverty. No one can say today where the ideas for the test ban treaty, the trade bill, or the tax cut first originated. And there seems also to be some current dispute as to which party first came up with the idea of returning Federal tax money to the States.

But ideas do have to come from somewhere, and the greatest source of important and successful ideas is probably still in the academic community. The Poverty Program owes a great deal to Robert Lampman of the University of Wisconsin, and he, in turn, to the whole University of Wisconsin school of economists. The Department of Defense has been living off the intellectual capital of the RAND Corporation and its scholars for the last five years. Recent revisions in the conflict of interest laws have drawn heavily on the work of Dean Manning of the Stanford Law School and of Dean Bernstein of the Woodrow Wilson School at Princeton.

It is interesting to note, also, that in each of these examples there has been a productive interaction between the academic community proper and the worlds of the private research organizations, foundations, and professional associations, before the ideas under discussion ripened for consideration as governmental programs. The concept of the community action program as a central element in the anti-poverty program—a concerted, coordinated attack on all the tangled roots of poverty in a particular community—was the result of academic research and experimental development fostered by Paul Ylvisaker's Gray Areas Program at the Ford Foundation. The RAND Corporation provided men like Albert Wohlstetter, Herman Kahn, Henry Rowen, and Alain Enthoven with a research base that also offered them the opportunity to explore practical problems under RAND's Air Force contract. And the Manning-Bernstein study of conflict of interest was conducted under the auspices of a committee of the Association of the Bar of the City of New York.

On the other hand, relatively few ideas seem to come from within government itself. The contribution of government people is likely to be more in detail and in implementation, matters I shall come to shortly. The so-called policy planning staffs of departments and agencies usually serve merely as a conduit for ideas from outside. To be sure, this is not always the case. The proposal for a multilateral force, for example, seems to have been conceived within the bosom of the State Department's Policy Planning Council, and nurtured there with the assistance of the Council's then chairman, Robert Bowie, who later returned to academic life, retaining close ties with the Department, however, even through changes in the Administration. And the fallout shelter program proposed by President Kennedy was developed by Carl Kaysen, now Associate Dean of the Littauer School at Harvard, when Kaysen was serving as a National Security Council staff member.

Lastly, successful ideas come occasionally—but too infrequently—from individuals in private life. Burke Marshall's proposal for the institution of voting registrars in civil rights voting cases is an example of an idea that quickly struck fire, and, in part, led to Marshall's later selection as Assistant Attorney General in charge of the Civil Rights Division of the Department of Justice.

What then does it take for an idea to be adopted by decision-makers in government, and to become a program? There is an essential difference between an idea or a proposal, on the one hand, and a program on the other. A program has a dollar sign attached to it, and the dollar sign is placed there by a person who is responsible also for competing programs, each with its own dollar sign attached. Economists distinguish between an "economic good" and a "free good." An idea is a free good; a program is an economic good.

The Preconditions of a Program

All programs may not succeed. Some will go down to legislative defeat, and others may be abandoned even before they reach the legislative threshhold. But once they have been "priced out" in competition with other programs, they have left never-never land and entered the real world. When Secretary McNamara began insisting on cost-benefit studies in connection with new weapons systems, he was not confusing the processes of military analysis with the processes of bookkeeping; rather, he was requiring that an essential element of every program decision be made articulate. He wanted to know how the particular proposed solution to a military problem compared with other solutions in its demand on the available resources.

Given the pressure of competing ideas on available resources, the first pre-condition for a new program must be the existence of a genuine national need—and it must be a deep-seated and pressing need. While the immediate occasion for the introduction of a program may be the decision-maker's response to a particular pressure group, or even his desire to find a positive theme for the work of his agency, when it comes to a decision whether to proceed, he will look for the national need before he moves—or somebody may be looking for a new decision-maker. The choice of a particular solution can be a good deal more debatable than the existence of the underlying problem, and that debate may itself conceal the fundamental consensus on the need. (Few, if any, of those who oppose the Multilateral Force would deny the need to find new answers to the question of NATO nuclear policy.) But once the President had called the country's attention to the problem of poverty in the

United States, even the strictly partisan opposition to the anti-poverty program focused on the means, rather than the goal, and ended up offering an alternative bill.

If the first requirement for transformation of an idea into a program is the existence of a deeply felt—even if inadequately perceived—national need, the second requirement is that the idea can, in fact, be made flesh, that is to say, that it can be transformed into a program that would produce visible results *within a limited period of time.*

Again, an unhappy case in point is the proposed fallout shelter program. Here the events of the summer of 1961, together with some remarks of President Kennedy, unfortunately amplified by the media, produced an immediate short-term concern almost amounting to hysteria, which a proposed middle- or long-term program of incentives for shelter construction could not begin to meet. The Administration's attempt to fill the gap by outlining a self-help program, or what to do until the community shelter comes, was equally unsuccessful, apparently making greater demands on American self-reliance than the national psychology warranted.

A similar danger that the near-term results will not be, or appear to be, adequate to the need, looms for the President's Poverty Program. The stated purpose of the program is to help the poor pull themselves out of poverty more rapidly. We have reduced the size of the poverty class in the United States from Roosevelt's one-third of the nation to one-fifth—using the rough yardstick of the Council of Economic Advisers. But the rate of decrease has fallen off in recent years, and in some groups of the population—households headed by a woman, for example—it has stabilized, and the proportion of such families below the poverty line has actually increased significantly. The Poverty Program should increase the rate at which families and individuals are emerging from poverty—but how can one show visible results from year to year, since the Act contains only a one-year authorization? This question haunts all those engaged in the war on poverty.

As it happens, the Poverty Program to some extent did try to protect itself on this flank. There was a fundamental strategic decision to be made in attacking the problem of poverty. People are poor because they lack the capacity or the opportunity to perform services that society values sufficiently to reward them with a decent living. In attacking the overall problem, we can begin either with the lack of opportunity or with the lack of capacity; that is to say, we can begin by preparing jobs for people, or by preparing people for jobs. A decision was made to begin by concentrating on the latter, in part, because the tax cut already represented the first step towards decreasing unemployment generally, but also because the process of preparing people to get and hold decent jobs itself created an extra margin of time to find the job opportunities for the people. No one could reasonably expect instant results; and this fact made the program more workable.

It would be a gross misreading to regard this process of decision-making as "political" in any pejorative sense. Rather, the search for results here as elsewhere is part of the calculus of cost and benefit in a world of limited resources—including the resource of time. Clearly, the first responsibility of the administrator of a new program is to keep it alive. While he must be prepared to let his program go down to a martyr's death, if necessary, he must also realize that a useful life is generally to be preferred to early martyrdom. Moreover, emphasis on early and visible results is not only politically expedient; it also provides a useful discipline for the administrator, by requiring him, in effect, to be prepared to pay an interest penalty for delayed returns on the original investment

Thinking Programmatically

The shape of a program, then, is affected by its relation to the visible results it is expected to produce. Another pressure that affects the shape of the program is the desire to appeal to a number of constituencies in order to maximize public and congressional support. Mishandled, such an effort may only result in each constituency feeling it has been short-changed, or the program itself may be destroyed because resources are allocated too thinly to achieve a critical mass in any area. But the pressure is there, and the program planner ignores it at his peril. Here the program planner's art consists, not in dividing the available resources into smaller shares, but rather in finding ways of allocating resources that genuinely serve more than one purpose. In diversifying program appeal, he may in fact create a new constituency. It seems unlikely, for example, that the Indian Bureau could find a sufficiently powerful constituency to set up an active program of Job Corps camps on Indian reservations. But by incorporating these camps into the much larger Job Corps program, a new constituency is identified, one concerned with more rapid elimination of poverty and the building of the Great Society in the United States. Similarly, the Job Corps Conservation Camps conserve human values by helping prepare the enrollees for permanent jobs; at the same time, they conserve natural resources through the work the enrollees are doing on public lands of the United States—a fact that did not escape the attention of the important conservation lobby while the bill was before the Congress.

The primary effects, then, of political constraints on program planning are rather like the effects of fiscal or economic constraints. They tend to require more economic use of the resources available.

Program planners like to talk about the need to think programmatically, and they tend to measure the value of an innovator by his ability to do so. In a sense they are wrong, because the idea must precede the program, and without new ideas there will be no new programs. But they are right too, in the sense that before an idea can be used, *someone* must think about it programmatically, determining the resources needed to accomplish the objective and measuring the value of the resources against the results. Programmatic thinking is like completed staff work. It must be watched carefully to see that it doesn't eliminate remote but striking possibilities, yet it does serve to focus attention unrelentingly on what must happen in the here and now.

Having said this, one is left with the question: what can we do to improve the climate for new ideas in government so that the shadow falls less heavily between the idea and the action? Here I have three suggestions, or groups of suggestions.

First, we need to make it easier for people to move back and forth between the world of ideas and the world of action. In my own experience, the best program planners, the people best able to bridge the gap, are the in-and-outers in government, the people who come to government from a university or a foundation or a law office or an industrial concern, for a tour of three or four years, and then go off to a university or a foundation or a law office or an industrial concern, returning after a period for a second or a third or a fourth tour in government—people whose allegiance is not primarily to an institution, but to a discipline, an area of intellectual concern. These people are important both as program planners and as sources of the original ideas that must precede programs. If we continue to draw people away from the universities and hold them in government for too long, we are draining their creative potential, as we drain their sense of the realities of politics if we keep them too long away from responsibility for action.

There are some practical steps that need to be taken in this direction. One of the most important was the Executive Pay Act last year, and the provisions of that act will undoubtedly have to be supplemented in years to come so that government pay scales do not again fall behind those of the universities and the professions. Another step would be to devise a system for transfer of pension rights and other fringe benefits without any penalty to the transferee. Delayed vesting of pension rights, particularly in industrial concerns, is one of the most troublesome remaining vestiges of involuntary servitude since the ratification of the Thirteenth Amendment. I am inclined to give less weight to schemes for broadening the horizons of career public servants, whom I have already described, I hope without giving offense, as bureaucrats. In the nature of our system, I do not believe that they can generally broaden their horizons to the point where they can perform the essential mediating function between the world of action and the world of ideas, for which we must depend primarily on the in-and-outers. On the other hand, I am not suggesting that programs for advanced study for civil servants are of little value: policy is made interstitially as well as structurally, and if career public servants are not likely to build new structures, they are quite capable of tearing them down.

Lastly, there are a number of institutional arrangements that expose young people to government service without committing them to a government career or to a particular specialty. Arrangements like the Defense Department's Management Intern Program, and the Justice Department's Honor Law Graduates Program, and the new White House Fellows Program, offer exciting possibilities to produce more in-and-outers and broader-gauged career people.

Laboratories and Start-up Costs

My second group of suggestions attempts to deal with the problems of size and complexity in government as obstacles to new ideas. We ought to expand the area of governmental and public affairs activity in which new ideas can be tried out as limited-scale programs. As Justice Brandeis observed: "It is one of the happy incidents of the federal system that a single courageous state may, if its citizens choose, serve as a laboratory; and try novel social and economic experiments without risk to the rest of the country." One hears too much nowadays about state government as an obstacle to progress in new programs; we tend to lose sight of some of the current and valuable laboratory experiments like Terry Sanford's Governor's School, for example, in North Carolina; or the new Youth Opportunity Camps in Indiana. Cities like New Haven and Boston and East St. Louis have already led the way with community action programs of the kind that are now receiving substantial support from the Federal Government. And city and state governments can enter into partnerships with private resources—as in the Ford Foundation's Gray Areas Program—perhaps more easily than the Federal Government can. What I am suggesting is that we need to think of state and local government more explicitly as laboratories for new program ideas, which if successful can then be tried on at the Federal level. If we are looking for creative Federalism, here is a chance to create it.

The Federal Government may also delegate operating programs to private institutions. The Job Corps, for example, contracts with universities and even (confounding the proponents of the conventional wisdom) with private companies to operate training centers. By making the generators of new ideas responsible for trying them out, we may be able to build additional bridges between ideas and programs.

My third suggestion is a painfully practical one. After an idea has been accepted for adoption within government as an operating program, there is still a good deal to be done in order to put it into programmatic form. All of its elements must be developed and "costed out" in some detail, legislation must be drawn up, and at least some thought must be given to staffing. All of these activities cost money. They don't cost a lot of money, but the kind of talent that is required to do the job is not freely available. If the new program is being developed within the bosom of an existing department or agency, there may be sufficient funds available to cover it. But if it is an independent enterprise, the very limited discretionary funds at the disposal of the President simply will not stretch that far. The Peace Corps was fortunate in its planning stages that money was available from foreign aid appropriations. The domestic Peace Corps proposal had a much more difficult time, and that planning effort was, in fact, the target of legislative riders preventing departments and agencies from lending people or services. The Anti-Poverty Task Force struggled along with something like $30,000 from the President's discretionary funds, and with volunteers recruited from private life or lent by their companies or unions.

This kind of sacrifice should not be necessary, and in any event it does not make for efficiency. But I confess to having no ready prescription for this problem. Congress is naturally reluctant to appropriate funds for enterprises on which it has not yet passed. On the other hand, Congress might well be receptive to new ideas on how to translate new ideas into programs.

In short, and in sum: we not only need new ideas, we also need new ideas about how to turn new ideas into programs.

2

Ad Hoc *Commissions for Policy Formulation?*

ALAN L. DEAN

The use of *ad hoc* commissions and committees as an aid in the development of public policies has become commonplace in recent decades, and some of these groups have achieved considerable national prominence. However, there are so many kinds of boards, commissions, and committees now being used for public purposes, that it will help keep our discussion within reasonable bounds to pause long enough to define the "nature of the beast." Once we have decided what an *ad hoc* policy commission is, it will be possible to consider the advantages and disadvantages associated with their use within a tolerably coherent framework.

The principal characteristics of *ad hoc* policy commissions, as they are treated [here], are the following:

1. *They are multi-member in composition.* This may seem to be stating the obvious, but it is important to keep in mind that *ad hoc* commissions consist of three or more members, all of whom share equally the responsibility for findings and recommendations.

2. *They are temporary.* To be considered an *ad hoc* commission, a group must have been given a more or less definite time within which to complete

Reprinted by permission from Alan L. Dean, "Advantages and Disadvantages in the Use of *Ad Hoc* Commissions for Policy Formulation," a paper presented at the Annual Meeting, American Political Science Association, New York, September 5–7, 1957.

its work and depart from the scene. Continuing advisory committees, of which there are many, are not considered *ad hoc* commissions.

3. *They have a policy formulation responsibility limited to a particular issue or group of related policy questions.* Groups established to investigate wrong-doing, to find responsibility for a disaster, or to make detailed studies of internal management are outside the range of our topic.

4. *They must have official status.* The *ad hoc* commissions with which we are concerned are created by governmental action. In the Federal Government, such action can be by the President alone, by the Congress, or by joint action. Private committees established by private efforts are excluded.

5. *They are purely advisory and have no power to implement their find-ings or recommendations.* Ad hoc commissions do not have administrative authority of any kind, other than the powers conferred to assist them in gathering information.

6. *They are composed in whole or in part of persons drawn from private life.* Congressional select committees and interagency committees consisting solely of executive officials are, therefore, not considered *ad hoc* commissions. The Cabinet committees which have received so much attention in recent years are interagency committees and do not fall within the scope of this paper.

The following discussion will also be limited, possibly arbitrarily, in a number of other respects. First, we shall focus our attention on the use of *ad hoc* commissions by the National Government of the United States. It is realized that British Royal Commissions, Canadian commissions of inquiry, and other foreign counterparts of the American *ad hoc* commission play important roles in other governments. It is also acknowledged that the States and many cities make use of *ad hoc* commissions for policy purposes.

Second, within the National Government, the paper deals only with *ad hoc* commissions established by the President or created by legislation. Department heads from time to time create commissions to consider policies or programs within their jurisdiction. Such groups usually receive comparatively little public attention and tend to be concerned primarily with agency management, administrative problems, or the review of established programs. The Citizens Advisory Committee on the Food and Drug Administration (1955) and the Secretary of State's Public Committee on Personnel (Wriston Committee) are examples of *ad hoc* commissions at the departmental level concerned with substantive or administrative policy.

Third, primary attention will be focused on the use of *ad hoc* commissions during the Truman and Eisenhower administrations. Although references will be made to the use of commissions under earlier Presidents, our main concern is with the advantages and disadvantages of the device under present day conditions.

In spite of the frequency with which they have been used, *ad hoc* commissions in the United States have received relatively little systematic treatment by political scientists and students of public administration. One of the few works in this area is Carl Marcy's pamphlet on Presidential Commissions, published in 1945. More recently, in 1952, Fritz Morstein Marx prepared for use in the Bureau of the Budget a staff paper on "Temporary Presidential Advisory Commissions." Dr. Marx's paper has never been published, but is available for reference by interested persons. In addition, several of the better known commissions have been treated in articles appearing in various periodicals.

Ad hoc commissions for policy formulation, as opposed to commissions to study specific problems of maladministration, disaster, or wrongdoing, are largely a development of the current century. Theodore Roosevelt was the first President to employ the device extensively, and he promptly became involved in controversy with the Congress over their use. Presidents Hoover, Roosevelt, Truman, and Eisenhower have all relied on *ad hoc* commissions as an important supplement to other techniques of policy development. No reliable compilation has ever been made of the total number of *ad hoc* commissions established since 1900, partly because of problems of definition and partly because of the extreme informality and lack of public notice which has characterized some past *ad hoc* policy groups. A few statistics will, however, give some idea as to their importance and prevalence.

President Hoover is reported to have established some 62 commissions, boards and similar bodies during the first 16 months of his administration, most of which were clearly *ad hoc* policy bodies as defined in this paper. More than 100 commissions are said to have been established in the first two terms of Franklin Roosevelt's administration.

The Truman administration witnessed a falling off in the number of *ad hoc* policy commissions, with *Business Week* estimating in 1953 that only 20 major commissions were established during his nearly eight years in office. However, the continued importance of the device under Truman is indicated by merely citing some of the commissions established while he was in office; for example, the first Commission on Organization of the Executive Branch of the Government (Hoover Commission), the President's Materials Policy Commission, the President's Water Resources Policy Commission, the President's Commission on Higher Education, the President's Advisory Commission on Universal Training, the President's Committee on Civil Rights, the President's Air Policy Commission, and the Missouri Basin Survey Commission, and the Commission on the Application of Federal Laws to Guam.

During the Eisenhower administration *ad hoc* policy commissions have been created at about the same rate as in the Truman administration. The past four and one half years have witnessed the establishment of 11 groups which clearly have all the characteristics of an *ad hoc* policy commission. Among these have been the second Commission on Organization of the Executive Branch of the Government (Hoover Commission), the Commission on Intergovernmental Relations (Kestnbaum Commission), the Commission on

Foreign Economic Policy (Randall Commission), the Commission on Government Security, the President's Committee on Government Housing Policies and Programs, the President's Commission on Veterans' Pensions (Bradley Commission), and the President's Committee on Civilian National Honors.

Advantages of Ad Hoc Commissions

Only a few of the advantages ascribed to *ad hoc* commissions in this paper are applicable to all groups of this kind. Suffice it to say that those attributes of *ad hoc* commissions which are known to have facilitated the development or acceptance of public policies are included in the list of advantages. Some of these advantages are derived from characteristics which can also detract from the usefulness of the device under some circumstances.

1. *Capacity to focus public attention on a problem. Ad hoc* policy commissions are more often established to focus public attention on a policy area or problem than for any other single purpose. Intragovernmental staff work, however competent, necessarily takes place with little or no public awareness of what is going on, and staff studies are rarely made public. When an *ad hoc* commission is set up by law, Executive order, or Presidential letter, the fact of establishment is usually widely publicized. The work of the commission may involve public hearings and interim reports, and the final report is usually given substantial newspaper and other publicity. The existence of the commission, its public findings, and the discussion engendered thereby tend to increase public understanding of a policy problem and to improve the prospects of successful action to deal with it.

2. *Freedom from domination by the permanent agencies of the Government.* A very important advantage, and one that is most marked when the members are drawn entirely from private life, is the *ad hoc* commission's independence of the preoccupations, jurisdictional aspirations, and established dogma of the regular departments and agencies.

Presidents and the Congress rely heavily on the departments and agencies for policy proposals and the facts to support them. This is only proper, for who can be expected to know more about reclamation problems than the staff of the Department of the Interior and where can more knowledge of agricultural needs be found than among the 85,000 officials and technicians of the Department of Agriculture. Yet there are times when a new look is needed, either to restore public confidence or to escape traditional and possibly rigid departmental attitudes. The poor success of interagency committees when charged with policy formulation in contrast to the occasional good results from *ad hoc* commissions demonstrates that there are times when more is needed than the compromising out of agency differences. Interagency compromises can sometimes produce such timid and watered-down conclusions as to be of little real help to the President or the Congress.

3. *Ability to represent diverse interests and points of view.* The multiple membership of *ad hoc* commissions makes it possible to broaden public support and confidence and to add to the range of competence represented through the careful selection of commissioners. This can, of course, be overdone with a consequent failure of the commission to reach agreement. But when the effort succeeds in producing a consensus on significant recommendations, the report is likely to command more respect than the findings of a single individual committed to a particular point of view. The Water Resources Policy Commission and the President's Advisory Committee on Government Housing Policy and Programs are but two instances in which the good will and sincerity of the commissioners resulted in a surprising amount of agreement in highly controversial areas of public policy.

4. *Effectiveness in enlisting persons of national reputation and competence.* Ad hoc commissions often make a major contribution by bringing into the service of the Government, for a short time and for a particular purpose, persons whose assistance could not otherwise be obtained. Many national leaders in business, labor, agriculture, conservation, and other important fields would not accept permanent Government posts or would not be suitable for roles as permanent advisers. They often can and will serve as one of a group having the prestige of a commission established by law or by Presidential action for a short period of part-time service.

5. *Ability to collect and publish important information. Ad hoc* commissions are often helpful in the resolution of policy problems through the collection, organization, and presentation of important facts bearing on the issues. A group such as the President's Materials Policy Commission can pull together from many sources data of grave import to the Nation and publish them in useable form. It has been said that some commissions have rendered their greatest service not through the quality of their recommendations but rather through the excellence of their fact gathering. Here, again, a word of caution is needed. Commissions are not normally able to do fundamental research or to collect much in the way of basic data. The regular departments and agencies are infinitely better equipped to do such work than a temporary *ad hoc* commission and its usually very limited staff. However, the Commission, if it approaches the problem resourcefully, is in a good position to take data from many agencies and private sources and to so organize and present the facts that they have maximum utility and impact.

6. *Value in forestalling precipitate action.* The creation of an *ad hoc* commission not only provides machinery for increasing public understanding and presenting facts, but it also tends to forestall precipitate action pending the completion of the study. Because relatively firm deadlines are set for the completion of the commission's work, advocates of a policy may be willing to relax their demands until the report of the commission is available. Of course, great caution is necessary in using commissions for such a purpose, for

if it is felt that they are being employed to block action in an already well-understood policy area, then sharp criticism will follow and the commission's work will be carried on in an unpropitious atmosphere of disapproval and distrust.

7. *Effectiveness in increasing public pressure for governmental action.* An advantage of *ad hoc* commissions which is not infrequently a factor in their creation is their value in generating or intensifying public demands for a given course of action. This is particularly important in the case of commissions established by action of the President, who may hope that the prestige of its members and the facts publicized by the commission will make possible forward steps which would not otherwise succeed. It is congressional awareness of this role of *ad hoc* policy commissions which has occasionally led the legislative branch to show something less than enthusiasm for temporary Presidential commissions.

The above list of advantages is by no means exhaustive, but it does cover those which in recent years have attended the use of commissions and have led to their becoming a permanent feature of our machinery of government. It is also clear that what may seem an advantage to those whose objectives are furthered by a commission's report may not be viewed as such by an agency head, a member of Congress, or an interest group opposed to what the commission proposes in the way of policy.

Disadvantages in the Use of Ad Hoc Commissions

As with the advantages, only a few disadvantages in the use of *ad hoc* commissions are of general applicability, for there are ways of minimizing or compensating for most of the more prevalent shortcomings of this device for policy formulation. The most frequently encountered disadvantages are the following:

1. *Multi-member composition.* All *ad hoc* commissions, by definition, consist of several members, and while such composition has certain advantages already noted, it can entail significant disadvantages. First, it is often hard to find from three to twenty-five qualified commissioners and to induce them to serve. It may be difficult to arrange meetings, it may be hard to achieve a common understanding of objectives, the deliberations of the commission may be time consuming, and a special effort may be required to give the ultimate report real weight. The larger the commission, the more serious these problems tend to become. They can best be minimized by holding the membership to the smallest number compatible with providing for the breadth of representation determined to be necessary, and by the proper use of the chairman and staff. Presidential commissions have had memberships as small as three and have often had but five or seven members. At the other extreme, commissions with Congressional members or members appointed by legislative officials usually

consist of from twelve to twenty-five members. In recent years, the trend has been toward larger commissions, and the problems of commission selection and operation have consequently become more difficult.

Larger commissions may also result in one or more of the members taking his duties lightly. There have been cases in which some members have failed to attend a single meeting of a commission on which they accepted appointment. In other instances, members have attended the opening and closing sessions and have missed most or all of the meetings in which the hard work was done. The members of small commissions usually take their assignments most seriously and tend to assume greater personal responsibility for the quality of work performed.

Of course, no commission can be expected to act with the speed, decisiveness, and unity of a single official. If these factors are overruling, and *ad hoc* commission should not be used.

2. *The members usually serve part-time.* Bringing in commissioners from private life for part-time service entails the distinct advantages already described, but the intermittent character of their work also generates problems in accomplishing the assigned task. Attendance at meetings separated by days, weeks, or even months, makes it hard for some members to maintain a high pitch of interest or even to remember what has been accomplished. This part-time status of members also tends to prolong the duration of commissions, because meetings have to take into account the commitments of persons with responsible private positions. The seriousness of this disadvantage can, fortunately, be substantially reduced by a competent staff director, effective leadership from the chairman, and careful preparation for meetings.

3. *Difficulties encountered in organization.* Ad hoc policy commissions usually experience frustrating obstacles in getting organized to do the work assigned them. Such commissions are really Government agencies, usually functioning under tight deadlines. Yet, the commission when appointed has no staff, and often knows little about how to get space, office services, and other essential help and facilities. Even when an established agency or the Executive Office of the President provides assistance, *ad hoc* commissions often waste much of their allotted time just getting ready to do their work. An established agency doesn't face this problem, for it is a going concern with staff and experience in Government operations.

The temporary character of *ad hoc* commissions may also make it harder to get competent staff help. Career professionals may not wish to take the risk of accepting a job which will last but a few months or, at most, a couple of years. Staff loaned by other agencies may be divided in their loyalties, for they will be reluctant to do anything which may impair their standing in their regular posts.

4. *Obstacles to financing.* Throughout the history of their use, *ad hoc* policy commissions have been plagued by problems of financing their essential

costs of operation. Early commissions were particularly handicapped in this regard, and some went out of existence with their work uncompleted simply because the money ran out. President Taft's problems on financing the Commission on Efficiency and Economy and President Hoover's difficulty in getting appropriations for the Wickersham Commission are well known.

Congress has enacted a number of laws which may make it difficult for the President to finance *ad hoc* commissions not specifically authorized by legislation. The first of these was a rider attached to the Sundry Civil Act of 1909 as a protest against President Theodore Roosevelt's frequent use of *ad hoc* commissions. That provision, which remains in effect today (31 U.S.C. 673), prohibits the use of public moneys for the compensation or expenses of any commission, council, board or any similar body, or the payment of expenses, or the detail of employees from other agencies unless the particular body is authorized by law.

Another, and more recent, restriction is the so-called Russell Amendment (31 U.S.C. 696) passed in 1944. It prohibits the payment of the expenses of any instrumentality of the executive branch (including *ad hoc* commissions) for more than one year unless Congress has specifically appropriated funds for, or authorized the expenditure of funds by, such instrumentality. This legislation is one reason why some commissions must complete their work within a twelve-month period and why speed in organizing can be so important.

Theodore Roosevelt and Herbert Hoover responded to Congressional efforts to prohibit the use of their public funds for their commissions with a number of successful expedients. President Roosevelt relied on voluntary service by commissioners and the use of staff of existing agencies to do the supporting work. President Hoover financed his numerous commissions with private grants whenever public funds were not available. Marcy estimates that Hoover used at least $2,000,000 from private sources in this way. President Franklin Roosevelt had ample authority in emergency legislation, including the National Industry Recovery Act and the Emergency Relief Appropriation Acts, under which he was able to finance the large number of commissions established during his first two terms. The Committee on Administrative Management was, for example, supported by emergency relief funds, while the funds for the Committee on Social Security came from NIRA appropriations.

President Truman relied heavily upon the Emergency Fund of the President, an appropriation which authorizes the President to waive provisions of law regarding the expenditure of Government funds, including the provisions of the 1909 Sundry Civil Act referred to above. Among the Commissions supported in whole or in part from the Emergency Fund during the Truman administration were the President's Water Resources Policy Commission, the Missouri Basin Survey Commission, the President's Committee on Civil Rights, the President's Committee on Higher Education, and the Special Committee on Foreign Aid.

President Truman's use of the Emergency Fund for the support of *ad hoc* commissions which did not appear to involve great urgency resulted in considerable criticism from members of Congress, together with warnings that the Emergency Fund would be curtailed if the practice persisted.

President Eisenhower has been especially careful to enlist Congressional support for the commissions established during his administration. Presidential commissions established without the participation of Congress have been few in number. Of the eleven *ad hoc* commissions created during the Eisenhower administration, seven were established by law. These naturally became eligible for regular appropriations, and the President has been generally successful in getting the needed funds from the Congress. Two other *ad hoc* commissions, those on Government Housing Policies and Programs and Veterans Pensions, were supported in whole or in part from specific appropriations, although they were not created by special acts of Congress. Only one Eisenhower commission used money from the President's Emergency Fund. This was the President's Commission on Veterans' Pensions which was initially financed from this source, but was subsequently supported by a specific appropriation. A relatively new White House appropriation, the Special Projects Fund, was used to defray the very limited costs of the President's Committee on Civilian National Honors.

Thus, while Presidents have had their troubles in financing *ad hoc* commissions, especially when the Congress is unsympathetic, a determined chief executive can usually find the means of supporting any commission that he feels to be needed. His first hope is for Congressional sanction. If this fails, he can use emergency or other funds not subject to the 1909 Statutory restraints. Occasionally, he can rely on the authority of an agency. If forced to it, he can depend on voluntary service by commissioners, assistance from the staff of regular agencies, or funds from private sources. Under some circumstances, the President can achieve the benefits desired from the use of an *ad hoc* policy commission and still avoid financing problems by creating an interagency committee and adding private citizens to the representation from the member agencies.

5. *Limitations on implementing findings and recommendations.* Because an *ad hoc* policy commission usually ceases to exist upon the completion of its study and the rendering of its report, it cannot do much directly about the implementation of its recommendations. Agency officials and special assistants to the President do not suffer from this handicap, for they can be charged with taking the leadership in carrying out their own recommendations if the President so desires. The disappearance of the commission not only deprives the Government of the continued assistance of most or all of the members, but it also requires the taking of specific steps to assign responsibility for further action. Delay in acting on the report once it has been submitted or an unfortunate assignment of responsibility for effectuation can greatly reduce the impact of the commission's work.

The solution to this problem does not call for assigning implementation functions to *ad hoc* commissions, for they are not adapted to the efficient discharge of executive functions. What is called for is a recognition that some responsible official must take or be given the task of advising the President on next steps. The role which Mr. Meyer Kestnbaum has played in assisting the President in implementing the comprehensive reports of the second Hoover Commission and the Commission on Intergovernmental Relations provides an example of one type of arrangement which has shown promise. In other cases, a department or agency can logically be given the assignment of following up the report.

An unusual development in connection with the Hoover Commissions has been the organization of the Citizen's Committee for the Hoover Report. This group is privately organized and supported and conducts a vigorous campaign on behalf of the recommendations of the Commissions on Organization of the Executive Branch of the Government. Its work is done in consultation with persons who have served on one or both of the commissions, thus giving the former members a means of promoting the adoption of the proposals which they formulated as commissioners.

Special Problems in the Use of Ad Hoc Commissions

In addition to the advantages and disadvantages discussed above, a number of special problems have arisen in connection with the use of *ad hoc* commissions for policy formulation. These problems are significant because the way in which they are anticipated and resolved can be decisive in determining the quality of a commission's work and the respect accorded its recommendations.

1. *Inclusion of Federal officials and members of Congress on* ad hoc *commissions.* It has already been indicated that *ad hoc* commissions of the kind under consideration must have a substantial portion of their membership drawn from private life. In recent years, there have been several cases in which such commissions have also included federal officials, or members of Congress, or both in their membership.

The inclusion of executive officials has the apparent advantage of assuring that the private members will have the benefit of the views of persons who are, in all probability, concerned with the administration of programs in the area under the study. There is also the hope that the implementation of findings will be more vigorously and successfully pushed by the heads of affected agencies if they, or their designees, have participated in the formulation of the commission's recommendations and concur in them. There are examples of commissions with agency representation which were highly successful in their work. One was the President's Advisory Committee on Government Housing Policies and Programs, which was chaired by the Housing and Home Finance Administrator. Other commissions with executive branch members were the two Hoover Commissions, the Commission on Intergovernmental Relations, and the President's Advisory Commission on Government Office Space.

However, the appointment of executive officials can impair, rather than enhance, the effectiveness of an *ad hoc* policy commission. If too many such officers are appointed, the group becomes more an interagency committee than an *ad hoc* commission, and the private members and their views may become subordinated. There is also the danger that some of the major values of *ad hoc* commissions may be lost, namely those derived from a reasonably detached and independent outside approach to the issues at stake. A further factor in the use of agency officials as commissioners is the severity of other demands on their time. There have been cases in which members appointed from the executive branch have been so burdened by their regular duties that they have contributed little or nothing to the work of the commissions on which they were nominally serving. Still another obstacle to effective service by executive officials is the awkwardness which arises when the members from private life are inclined to positions in conflict with the policies of an administration. Executive officials are first and foremost members of the President's team, and it is not easy for them to join in public espousal of recommendations at variance with the policies of the administration. Finally, it may be preferable to keep the most directly concerned heads of agencies from involvement in a commission's findings so that such officials may later review the report and advise the President and Congress with reasonably uncommitted minds.

Congressional membership has characterized such groups as the Hoover Commissions, the Kestnbaum Commission, the Randall Commission, and the Missouri Basin Survey Commission. The principal argument for including members of Congress has been the alleged greater ease in winning Congressional acceptance of the commission's report.

As in the case of executive officials, care should be given to the ability of Congressional members to serve effectively in the light of the heavy demands on their time from legislative duties. There is also a constitutional question raised by prohibitions against members of Congress being appointed to offices created during the times for which they were elected and against the holding of an office under the United States while serving in Congress. Senator McClellan, who served on both Hoover Commissions, highlighted still another problem when he inserted in the reports the following reservation reflecting his sensitivity to his dual capacity:

> In view of the dual position which I occupy as a member of the Commission and also as a member of the Congress who has the duty of considering and acting upon the reports and recommendations, I feel constrained to reserve the right to further consider in my legislative capacity all recommendations made by the majority, and in such capacity to oppose those which in my judgment may be unsound or impractical, or may be determined to be inadvisable.

It might be tentatively said that *ad hoc* policy commissions should consist of private citizens appointed by the President. However, the inclusion of executive branch officials or members of the Congress may be indicated when special circumstances suggest that their participation will help the commission accomplish its purpose.

2. *Selection and organization of commission staff.* An *ad hoc* commission must rely on staff, borrowed from the agencies or recruited from private life, if it is to do its job well. Usually the key appointment is that of study director or executive director of the commission. Experience indicates that the commission as a whole is usually slow and ineffective in finding and appointing staff. On the other hand, unless specifically given the authority, the chairmen are reluctant to exercise the appointing power. This problem can be eased if the law, executive order or other instrument creating the commission provides, first, that the chairman shall be appointed by the President and, second, that the chairman shall be responsible for the appointment and assignment of staff.

In rare cases, notably the Hoover Commissions, the study is broken up and assigned to task forces, each of which recruits its own staff. This approach is expensive and places a heavy burden of coordination on the commission. Experience suggests that independently staffed task forces should be used only when the scope of a commission's assignment is extraordinarily broad.

3. *Conflict of interest.* The integrity of administration in the Federal Government is safeguarded by a number of statutes prohibiting conflicts of interest, the most important of which are sections 281, 283, 284, 434, and 1914 of Title 18 of the United States Code and section 190 of the Revised Statutes (5 U.S.C. 99). A Federal official may not take salary for his Government service from any other source, he may not have an interest in the profits or contracts of any business entity if he is transacting business with that entity, and for two years after leaving the Government he may not prosecute or aid in prosecuting any claim against the United States which was pending during his employment.

When a commission is established by law, the authorizing legislation customarily provides that service on the commission shall not constitute service or employment within the meaning of the conflict of interest statutes. Section 2(b), for example, of Public Law 108, 83rd Congress, establishing the second Hoover Commission, contains such an exemption.

If the nature of the commission's assignment or the occupation or interests of its prospective members could give rise to conflict of interest questions, the securing of an exemption may be quite important. One instance exists in which a Presidential commission failed to get off the ground for this reason. This was the President's Commission on Internal Security and Individual Rights established by President Truman by executive order in January 1951. When Congress refused to pass legislation exempting the commission from conflict of interest laws, the members resigned without having met and the study was abandoned.

4. *Cooperation with the departments and agencies.* Ad hoc commissions usually rely heavily on assistance from the established departments and agencies.

The agencies may detail staff, provide administrative services, and furnish technical advice. Much of the information on which the commission's report is based may originate in the agencies, either as a by-product of normal work or as the result of special efforts to be helpful.

Temporary Presidential commissions rely on the support of the President as an inducement to the agencies to be cooperative. Moreover, it is the practice for the President to include in an Executive order or letter a directive calling upon the regular agencies to assist the commission in its work and to furnish information. A commission established by legislation can usually point to a section of the authorizing legislation authorizing it to secure from the departments and agencies the information necessary to carry out its functions and in turn authorizing the agencies to furnish such information. Problems have arisen as to the right of *ad hoc* commissions with legislative charters to insist on information which an agency believes should not be disclosed in the public interest. As a general rule, legislation should simply authorize agencies to furnish information requested by *ad hoc* commissions and should leave to the agencies the responsibility for deciding whether or not the requested information should be supplied.

Cooperation with an agency should not be permitted to go so far that the agency does all the work for the commission, writes its report, and determines the content of the recommendations. The commission should have independent advice and diversified sources of information if it is to make a contribution beyond what could be expected of the agencies.

5. *Power of subpoena.* Commissions set up by Presidential action without authorizing legislation do not have the power to administer oaths or to compel the attendance of witnesses or the production of documents from outside the Government. In most cases, the lack of such power does not impair the functioning of the commission.

Commissions set up by law are often given subpoena authority. The second Hoover Commission was, for example, authorized to "hold hearings and sit and act at such times and places, administer such oaths, and require, by subpoena or otherwise the attendance and testimony of such witnesses, and the production of such . . . documents as the Commission . . . may deem advisable." Subpoena powers are rarely used by *ad hoc* commissions charged with formulating policy proposals even when granted. On the other hand, *ad hoc* commissions investigating alleged wrongdoing, malfeasance, or catastrophe could find such powers to be essential.

6. *Reporting relationships.* Because *ad hoc* policy commissions in the Federal Government vary so widely in origin, authority, composition and purpose, no standard method of submitting reports has emerged. Commissions established by the President ordinarily submit their reports to the President, who then decides as to further publicity and distribution. The President customarily transmits the report to the Congress with such comments as he feels

to be appropriate. Rarely, the classified nature of the subject matter of an *ad hoc* commission, such as the Committee on International Information Activities (1953), prevents the President from releasing the report.

Commissions established by authorizing legislation are often empowered to submit their reports directly to the Congress. For example, the acts establishing the Hoover Commissions provided that reports would go directly to the Congress, and no mention is made of the President. The legislation establishing the Commission on Intergovernmental Relations, on the other hand, provided that the final report should be submitted to the President for transmittal to the Congress. It also authorized such other reports to the President as he might request or the Commission might deem appropriate. Still another variation is provided by the Commission on Foreign Economic Policy, which was directed by its authorizing statute to make a report of its findings "to the President and to the Congress." Accordingly, its report of January 23, 1954, was transmitted simultaneously to the President of the United States, the President of the Senate, and the Speaker of the House of Representatives.

Experience suggests that reports prepared by commissions appointed by the President from private life should be submitted first to the President, regardless of whether or not the study was authorized by Congress. In all but extraordinary cases, the President will promptly transmit the report to the Congress with such comments and recommendations as he may choose to make. Commissions with Congressional members in addition to members appointed by the President can appropriately submit their reports to the President for transmittal to the Congress, or to the President and the Congress jointly.

7. *Preparation of action documents.* As a commission nears the end of its work and reaches agreement as to its conclusions and recommendations, the question often arises as to how far the group should go in drafting bills, Executive orders, and other action documents. Some commissions fear that their reports will simply gather dust, unless they supplement them with the papers required to implement their recommendations.

Work on action documents does have the advantage of forcing a commission to think through recommendations in the light of the specific language required by draft bills and orders. Occasionally, a group, such as the President's Committee on Civilian National Honors, will be charged with coming up with legislative language and will do so successfully.

When an *ad hoc* commission attempts the preparation of action documents, it should take into account the risks involved. The President's Water Resources Policy Commission, for example, prepared and informally submitted to the President a draft bill which would certainly have aroused strong opposition had it been a part of the report. The President declined to release the draft until there had been adequate public discussion of the basic report, and he thereby kept the bill from becoming the center of public debate. The report of the Commission on Government Security, which was submitted to the President and the

Congress on June 21, 1957, includes drafts of five bills and three Executive orders designed to implement certain of its recommendations. It remains to be seen how these drafts will fare in the course of executive branch and congressional consideration.

When a commission submits its report, the President normally desires the advice of the interested agencies and of his immediate staff before deciding on next steps. After getting views from many sources, he then decides what recommendations he will support, how he will do it, and at what time. He may prefer to push at once for adoption of measures designed to meet urgent needs, and he may choose to delay action on contested proposals until a propitious time. Thus, the action documents as they eventually emerge from the executive branch may bear little resemblance to what a commission would have drafted from its relatively detached position and its freedom from ultimate political responsibility. Ad hoc commissions may be best advised to make policy proposals and to support them with facts, but to avoid attempting to impose on officials concerned with implementation action documents which may be ill-adapted to their needs.

Concluding Observations

We can conclude with reasonable certainty that ad hoc commissions for policy formulation are here to stay. There has, however, been little standardization of the features, organization, or procedures of such groups, and there appears little likelihood that the near future will find that any particular type of ad hoc policy commission has come to dominate the field.

Ad hoc commissions have attained a position of considerable importance in the arsenal of devices and techniques for policy formulation in the Federal Government. The policies of the Nation are, and will continue to be, formulated and proposed by other organs such as the committees of the Congress, interagency committees of the executive branch, and the numerous public advisory committees that have been established to counsel executive officials. Federal officials, representing the interests of the great departments and agencies of the executive branch, still provide the bulk of the policy recommendations which reach the President, and they still carry the burden of explaining these proposals to the public and defending them before the committees of Congress. Another relatively recent device, the appointment of special assistants to the President, is showing promise as an aid to policy formulation. The recent work of Mr. Edward P. Curtis on aviation facilities provides an example of how effectively a Presidential assistant, aided by a small staff and the resources of the executive agencies, can function in areas involving urgent policy problems and complicated private and public interests.

The creation of an ad hoc commission should, therefore, be the result of a well-considered decision that it can do a better job of resolving the policy problems in the field of its assignment than the other machinery available to the President and Congress. In making the decision, the advantages and disadvantages in the use of *ad hoc* commissions should be reviewed and their applicability to the case at hand established with reasonable certainty.

Care should also be taken to avoid debasing the *ad hoc* commission by excessive use. Only a few commissions can successfully compete for public attention at one time, and an administration can act upon only so many reports in an effective manner. Too many commissions will inevitably produce charges of "government by commission," will make it more difficult to hold congressional support, will produce problems of financing, will complicate the always difficult task of finding qualified commissioners, and will impair the prestige so important to the success of most *ad hoc* commissions. Three or four *ad hoc* policy commissions per year would seem to be about as many as the President and the Congress can establish and still expect optimum results.

$\rightsquigarrow$ *3*

Government
by Commission

DANIEL BELL

The National Commission on Technology, Automation and Economic Progress was, as they say, a "blue ribbon" Commission. It had, among its fourteen members, such public luminaries as Walter Reuther, Thomas J. Watson, and Edwin Land. The Commission itself had been created by Congressional act and its members, though chosen by the President, were subject to Senate confirmation. It had a million dollars to spend as it willed, and a professional staff of eleven, plus the resources of a dozen governmental agencies to assemble whatever data is needed.

The tasks of the Commission, as set forth by the enabling Act, were:

. . . to assess the past effects and the current and prospective role and pace of technological change . . . to describe the impact of technological and economic change on production and employment, including new job requirements and major type of worker displacement which are likely to occur during the next ten years . . . to define those areas of unmet community and human needs toward which application of new technologies might be most effectively directed. . . .

The Commission worked hard. It met regularly in Washington for a minimum of two full days a month, for about eleven months, to hear witnesses, consider research reports, and discuss policy. About five of the more affluent

Reprinted by permission from Daniel Bell, "Government by Commission," *The Public Interest*, No. 3, Spring, 1966, pp. 3–9. Copyright © 1966 by National Affairs, Inc.

members (including two labor representatives) regularly brought down personal staff assistants to prepare detailed briefs supporting their points of view. A considerable amount of homework was done by the Commission members in preparation for the sessions; and towards the end of the year, the four academic members, who had the assignment of drafting the report, were closeted regularly in Cambridge, New York, Los Angeles, and Washington with the professional staff for the purpose of reviewing research material and weighing comments from various consultants to which sections of the report had been submitted. A kaleidoscopic array of witnesses were heard, including Robert Theobold of the *Ad Hoc* Committee on the Triple Revolution, Buckminister Fuller, Leon Keyserling, Francis Keppel, Otto Eckstein of the Council of Economic Advisors, James Russell of General Electric's Tempo (long-range forecasting) division, and, during one long lunch hour—witnesses were often heard during and after the lunch hour to economize on time—three representatives of the C.I.A. who briefed the Commission on developments in cybernetics in the Soviet Union. The thirty or so research reports commissioned directly by the Commission—to be published separately as appendices to the Report itself—on such topics as the Rate of Diffusion of Technology, the Prospects of Numerical Process Control Computers, Commercial Information Processing Networks, Technological Forecasting, Manpower Requirements in 1975, etc.—add up to what is probably the most comprehensive set of materials on technology and the American economy ever assembled.

The final report of the Commission was presented to the White House at the end of January. In the several months before, when successive drafts of the report were being reviewed, staff assistants at the White House had been kept informed of progress made, and drafts of the report had circulated through top government agencies. Yet the reception of the report was curious indeed. The Commission members had been told that the report would be presented in person, to the President, sometime at the end of the month, and were asked to keep three days open in the middle of the week, to come to Washington for the presentation. But, on two days notice, the Commission members were asked to come to Washington on a Saturday afternoon. When the White House was told that the notice was peremptory, the date was changed to Monday—which, ironically enough, was the day of the greatest snowfall of the year in Washington, and all government activities were cancelled. On Thursday of that week, the executive secretary of the Commission was telephoned by the White House press office, and was told that the Commission report would be released that afternoon; and, at the end of Bill D. Moyers' regular press conference, the report was in fact released to the press, in desultory fashion, with no member of the Commission on hand to answer questions, and no prior advance notice to the press that the report would be forthcoming—an advance notice which is usually given when the

White House wants its press corps to reserve space with its city editors about important stories.

How explain the discrepancy between the scope and intensity of the Commission's efforts and the reception of its report by the White House? The ostensible reason, as one was told it, was that the "automation" issue, which had been a burning one when the Commission was created, was no longer important in the face of a steadily decreasing unemployment rate. The private reason, one learned, was that the report was thought to be too "controversial," and that the White House did not want to become identified too directly with some of the proposals that had been put forward by the Commission.

The irony in all this is that the Commission had made truly strenuous efforts to reach a consensus in order to gain the strongest possible support for its recommendations. Divisions among Commission members, while never extreme, had been sufficiently sharp for some persons, on occasion, to talk of writing a minority report. It had been a "leak" to the press by the labor members, during the AFL-CIO convention in December, of such a possibility, that had brought considerable press attention to the Commission and a bird-dogging of the Commission sessions by the *New York Times*. In fact, however, there was never any real possibility of a minority report; for those who muttered most about it, the labor members, had every reason to be most satisfied with the report. The one section they did not like—the section which reported that, while there had been some acceleration of technological change, this was not of sufficient magnitude to create a socio-economic crisis if simple fiscal policies of maintaining adequate demand were followed—did undercut the "ideological" basis of many trade union arguments; but it did not really affect the substantive recommendations of the Commission, which dealt with the considerable gaps and flaws in the operation of a genuine welfare state.

There is little doubt that the proposals put forth by the Commission will find their way into public policy in the next decade. . . . Among the more than twenty recommendations, there is a proposal that the Government should become the "employer of last resort" for individuals who have exhausted unemployment insurance benefits and should provide jobs for them in communal services (a survey done for the Commission found that 5,300,000 useful jobs, mainly unskilled, could be filled in health, education, and recreation tasks if monies were available to local agencies); that the government provide a "floor" under family incomes by some such devices as the negative income tax or a guaranteed minimum income; that free public education for fourteen years (through the second year of college) be provided for all qualified students, with special financial subsidies for children from disadvantaged homes; that a computerized job-man matching system on a national, regional, and local labor market level be created, in order to expedite job searchers; and that some system of social accounts, to supplement the present system of national economical accounts, be explored, in order to assess the social costs and benefits of change as well as to provide "performance budgets" of accomplishment in such areas as health, housing, etc.

And yet, what may be most important in the long run is not the proposals themselves, or the graceless manner in which the White House brushed them temporarily under the rug, but the fact that so crucial a social problem had been turned over to a Commission in the first place.

The idea of government commissions is, of course, an old one. In the United States, in the first decades of this century, the numerous Industrial Commissions were important bodies in hearing evidence on labor conditions and their work led to significant reforms. But in recent years, the number and variety of Government commissions have expanded enormously, and these commissions seem to be developing into a new and unanticipated mechanism of government. Curiously, there is no full record available, in government, of the number of government commissions, statutory and *ad hoc,* created in the last half-dozen years. Inquiry at the Records Office of the White House, the personnel office of the White House, and other government agencies has revealed that no such inventory exists.

One can say, perhaps schematically that five different kinds of functions are served by Government commissions. There are, broadly, the *advisory* kind of commission, such as the President's Science Advisory Committee (PSAC) or the Labor-Management Advisory Commiteee, which are statutory bodies with fixed-term memberships; the *evaluation* commissions, such as that headed by Dean Woolridge to assess the operations of the National Institutes of Health or the one headed by Emanuel Piore of I.B.M. to assess the work of government science laboratories; the *fact-finding* bodies, the most typical of which are those created to deal with national strikes; the *public relations* groups, such as the White House conference on education to call public attention to various problems; and the *policy recommendation* Commissions, such as the DeBakey Commission on Health, which recommended a national policy to focus research and treatment on Heart, Cancer, and Stroke, the Linowitz Commission on Foreign Aid, or the National Commission on Technology, Automation and Economic Progress.

To some extent such bodies take over, duplicate, or compete with the functions of Congressional Committees, whose role[s] as watch-dog agencies, or as public hearing bodies, have also expanded considerably in the last few decades. But, as mechanisms of the Executive branch, they have several new functions:

(a) To provide a means for the direct representation of "functional constituencies" in the advisory process. There is an increasing tendency for the American polity to be organized in functional terms, and it is increasingly thought to be useful and proper to seek the "advice and consent" of such groups.

(b) To permit the Government informally to explore the "limits" of action by taking soundings within various bodies (such as the Labor-Management Advisory Commission) and to enable the government to exert pressure more directly within such bodies for particular policies.

(c) To serve as a direct relations device to call attention to certain issues and to generate public sentiment for support of various policies. In the past, it was not unknown for government to encourage the formation of "independent" citizens groups which served as "fronts" for government-desired policies. The White House Conferences represent an advance upon this procedure; they are less a marked "pressure" device, and permit more open scope for discussion and confrontation with government spokesmen.

(d) And finally, the creation of various government bodies on public problems fosters what the political scientists call "elite participation" in the formulation of government policy.

All of these devices present certain dangers. The evident danger is that they simply become one more means of increased government manipulation of "public opinion." This danger is less real than it might seem, however, for government is not a monolith, shooting out orders from some central source, but a hydra-headed body with diverse interests and looking in different directions. Moreover, the plain fact remains that National Commissions often are one of the few places where a central debate over specific policy issues can be conducted. In the normal play of politics, the effort to formulate coherent policies, even by such disinterested bodies . . . as the National Planning Association or Resources for the Future, or the more technical study groups such as the Brookings Institution, necessarily remain partial in their focus. The distinctive virtue of the Government Commission arrangement is that there is a specific effort to involve the full range of elite or organized opinion in order to see if a real consensus can be achieved. In the National Commission on Technology, Automation and Economic Progress, for example, the process of debate was, in some ways, as important as the conclusions that were finally reached. The labor people, for example, had to confront the hard, technical data which belied some of their ideological presuppositions; the industry people, in turn, had to grapple with the problems of providing for the "hard-core" unemployed, the failure of the market mechanism to meet various community needs, especially in health, air, and water pollution, and various other social deficiencies in the system. The desire to deal with concrete problems, in a nondoctrinaire way, did mean, in part, the surrender of older prejudices, and the emergence of some new, imaginative social proposals. Even hard-shell conservative opposition to certain ideas was worn down quickly by the argument that new ideas were at least worth testing in some pilot fashion, while the facile and sometimes doctrinaire argument that "the government" should undertake all kinds of across-the-board programs was whittled away by the demonstration of ineptitude or heavy-handed institutional rigidity on the part of many government agencies. Increasingly, both arguments led to a conviction that more and more public functions had to be taken over by "new social forms"—be they regional authorities, interstate compacts, decentralized authorities, and other devices which would assure the maximum flexibility, adaptiveness, and responsiveness to the multifarious nature of social change. And all of this was put within the context of the next ten years. It is true that the Commission did not expect any radical rupture in the pace of technological change

> (We do not expect output per man-hour . . . to rise during the next decade at a rate substantially faster than the 2.8 percent characteristic of the postwar period. . . . Most major technological discoveries which will have a significant economic impact within the next decade are already . . . in a readily identifiable style of commercial development.)

But the relevant point is that the policy recommendations were framed within a series of expectations about the future. In effect, what the National Commission on Technology had become was a "surmising forum."

All of this becomes more important in the face of what is surely the most important change in the character of government today—the attitude of being future-oriented. No government today can be passive in the face of the rapid changes which erode older social forms, or indifferent to the linked nature of economic change which now so quickly ties together all parts of the society. The concern of the Administration with health, education, poverty, and urban affairs all indicate that the government necessarily has to become an active agent to design new policies and to implement them. But, as some of the studies of the Commission on the Year 2000 (of the American Academy of Arts and Sciences) have shown, many of these problems have to be looked at in terms of 20 and 30 year cycles, and ways have to be found to build these perspectives into some capital budgetary process.

Yet in this respect we are sadly deficient. The government today does not have any single agency which seeks to "forecast" social and technological change (though an individual agency, such as the Census Bureau, may be concerned with population trends, and the Council of Economic Advisors with short-run economic projections). There is no agency which seeks to link up current and possible future changes in a comprehensive way so as to trace out the linked effects on different aspects of government policy. And perhaps most importantly, at a time when we must begin consciously to choose among "alternative futures," to establish priorities about what has to be done—for it is only an illusion that we are affluent enough to take care of all our economic problems at once—we have no "forum" which seeks to articulate different national goals and to clarify the implications and consequences of different choices. The Congress is not such a forum. As Roscoe Drummond pointed out in a review of the legislation passed during the Johnson administration: "Congress does not resolve national controversies; it can only act after most of the controversy has been removed. This is what happened on all of this once controversial legislative program on which the Administration won such comfortable votes."

In his characteristically witty way, Bertrand de Jouvenal has summed up the problem as a choice between "Seraglio or Forum." In the one, decisions are taken in secluded rooms by small groups of men; in the other, decisions take shape by the process of open discussion. The contrast arises most sharply because of the altered nature of government. It is no accident, that, throughout the world, political power has passed increasingly to a strong executive and that we have witnessed the decline of parliamentary, legislative, and Congressional government. Efforts to "mobilize" a society—for war or for social change—necessarily gives the executive an active and interventionist role, and reduces the importance of the legislature. Therefore, one of the major problems for the political process in a democracy is the question, as de Jouvenal has put it: *"How can the future become a matter for public opinion?"* This is where the study of the future and a "surmising forum" join hands. And this is where government by Commission makes, perhaps, its most useful contribution.

$\approx$ 4

Policy
Formulation
in the Institutionalized
Presidency:
The Johnson Task Forces

NORMAN C. THOMAS
and
HAROLD L. WOLMAN

Every modern President since Franklin D. Roosevelt has made important contributions to the Presidency and Lyndon B. Johnson is no exception. Our purpose here is to examine a set of highly important changes in the institutionalized Presidency which occurred in the process of formulating presidential legislative programs in domestic policy areas singled out by President Johnson for special emphasis and attention. While not revolutionary, the changes constitute a substantial departure from past practices. They involve the extensive use of White House task forces as a formal means of policy formulation. We will analyze the nature of these changes and their consequences for na-

Reprinted by permission from a paper written in Summer, 1968. The authors wish to acknowledge financial support received during the conduct of research for this paper from the Relm Foundation, the National Woodrow Wilson Fellowship Foundation, and the Institute of Public Administration of The University of Michigan.

tional domestic policy-making focusing on the policy areas of education and housing. We have based our findings on data obtained through interviews with participants in the policy process in those areas.[1]

The Pre-Johnson Pattern

Almost every student of American government is familiar with the pre-Johnson pattern of presidential policy formulation and especially with the development of the President's legislative program. This pattern normally involved the formulation of the legislative program almost exclusively on the basis of proposals developed by the departments and agencies and submitted to the President through the Bureau of the Budget.[2] The Bureau and the White House staff then analyzed these proposals and from their analysis the legislative program emerged. The departments and agencies carried most of the burden of policy innovation.[3] Presumably the experience and expertise which they possessed in their special areas along with a steady input from their clientele groups would insure an adequate flow of new ideas. Although a few scholars have expressed uneasiness about the dependence of the President, the White House staff and the Bureau of the Budget on the agencies for ideas and information,[4] most political scientists have paid little attention to the operational consequences of this

---

[1] The interviews covered a wide array of subjects including policy formulation in the executive branch. A comparison of our initial findings suggested further examination of the process of formulating the President's legislative program and we conducted follow-up interviews. Our respondents included five members of the White House staff, seven Bureau of the Budget officials, and 32 department and agency officials and task force participants.

[2] The best description of this process and its development to the point of almost total dependence on agency submission of proposals by the early years of the Eisenhower Administration is Richard E. Neustadt, "The Presidency and Legislation: Planning the President's Program," *American Political Science Review,* Vol. 49 (1955), pp. 980–1018.

The classic studies of the Presidency have not examined in any detail the process of policy formulation within the institutionalized Presidency. See, for example, Edward S. Corwin, *The President: Office and Powers,* 4th ed. (New York: New York University Press, 1957) Chapter VII; and, E. Pendleton Herring, *Presidential Leadership* (New York: Farrar and Rinehart, Inc., 1940). However, more recent institutional analyses have begun to do so. See Joseph E. Kallenbach, *The American Chief Executive* (New York: Harper & Row, Inc., 1966), pp. 341–344; and, Louis W. Koenig, *The Chief Executive* (New York: Harcourt, Brace & World, 1964), pp. 166–183.

[3] See J. Lieper Freeman, "The Bureaucracy in Pressure Politics," *The Annals of the American Academy of Political and Social Science* Vol. 319 (1958), pp. 11–19.

[4] Arthur W. Maass, "In Accord with the Program of the President," in Carl J. Friedrich, ed., *Public Policy,* Vol. 4 (1953) pp. 79–93. Maass stated that the President needed staff in addition to the Bureau of the Budget "to meet the 'need for positive origination at the center of broad . . . objectives' and policies so that adequate 'leadership and direction' are given to the development of [his] program."

pattern. Some participants in the policy process within the institutionalized Presidency have contended, however, that this traditional pattern has resulted in the adulteration of new ideas by internal bureaucratic considerations and clientele pressures exerted through the agencies. The result they argue, has been a tendency to repeat proposals until they eventually are adopted or until the rationale for them has long disappeared. This has meant a dearth of imagination in agency-oriented proposals which tend to be remedial and incremental rather than broadly innovative. As Phillip S. Hughes of the Bureau of the Budget summarized this point of view:

> . . . The routine way to develop a legislative program has been to ask the departments to generate proposals. Each agency sends its ideas through channels, which means that the ideas are limited by the imagination of the old-line agencies. They tend to the repetitive—the same proposals year after year. When the ideas of the different agencies reach the departmental level, all kinds of objections are raised, especially objections that new notions may somehow infringe on the rights of some other agency in the department. By the time a legislative proposal from a department reaches the President, it's a pretty well-compromised product.[5]

The Johnson Pattern

Soon after President Johnson assumed office, he faced the necessity of developing a legislative program which could be identified as his own. There apparently was a feeling within the White House and in the Bureau of the Budget that such a program was not likely to be developed on the basis of proposals submitted by the departments and agencies. The need to obtain outside advice and suggestions was especially critical in an Administration where most key personnel and the basic values and goals remained unchanged from those of its predecessor.

Early in 1964, a number of President Johnson's close advisers including Budget Director Kermit Gordon, presidential assistants Bill Moyers and Richard Goodwin and Chairman Walter Heller of the Council of Economic Advisers, all of whom were familiar with the pre-inaugural Kennedy task forces,[6] suggested that the President commission a series of task forces to

---

[5] Quoted in William E. Leuchtenberg, "The Genesis of the Great Society," *The Reporter,* April 21, 1966, pp. 36–39.

[6] Upon returning his party to office after eight years of Republican rule, President Kennedy moved quickly to establish a legislative program and set the main policy directions for his Administration. By the time he was inaugurated, Kennedy had commissioned 29 task forces in various areas of foreign and domestic policy and 24 of them had reported back to him. See Arthur M. Schlesinger, Jr., *A Thousand Days: John F. Kennedy in the White House* (New York: Fawcett World Library, 1967), pp. 148–154. The task force reports served to collate for the new Administration some of the nation's best

study specific policy areas. In order to avoid the pitfalls encountered in the Kennedy task force operation, e.g., charges of overrepresentation of intellectuals in their membership and of a consequent lack of realism in their proposals which forced the Administration to defend their reports even before they had become the basis for action, the Johnson task forces operated under a cloak of secrecy. The members agreed not to reveal their assignments to the press or to professional associates and not to disclose the substance of their deliberations or reports. The Administration promised to reciprocate.[7]

The 1964 experience with task force operations was deemed successful and was refined and developed in the following years. Under the direction of Special Assistant Joseph A. Califano, the White House staff assumed the paramount role in setting the framework for legislative and administrative policy-making. As we have observed, policy planning prior to the Johnson Administration was primarily a function of the departments and agencies with review by the White House staff and the Bureau of the Budget. President Johnson brought that function more effectively under his control through the integration of the task force operation with legislative submissions and budget review and the creation of a small policy-planning staff under one of his key assistants.[8] The impact of the departments and agencies in the development of the presidential legislative program may still have been considerable, but it tended to come more through the participation of their policy-level personnel in White House meetings where task force reports were evaluated. A high-ranking official in the United States Office of Education (USOE) acknowledged that in the past few years "much policy development in education has moved from here to the White House." Similarly, a career official in the Bureau of the Budget observed that "at the stage of developing the presidential legislative program, the task force reports play a more significant role than any documents or proposals emanating from the agencies."

The agencies proposed a substantial amount of technical legislation which corrected defects and filled gaps in existing statutes but the most important substantive contributions came from elsewhere. "The task forces presented us with meaty propositions to which we could react," recalled a former Budget

---

thinking on the critical problems confronting it. They functioned primarily to aid the new President in formulating his program. Subsequent publication of the reports enabled them to provide a ready reference for policy proposals for individuals and groups inside and outside of the government. Texts of the reports appear in *New Frontiers of the Kennedy Administration* (Washington: Public Affairs Press, 1961).

[7] For an account of the establishment of the task forces in 1964 and their role in developing the legislative program of the Great Society, see W. E. Leuchtenberg, *op. cit.*

[8] A sharp differentiation of the functions of policy-planning and legislative liaison has occurred on the White House staff with the policy-planners enjoying greater influence and status. *See* Thomas E. Cronin, "The Presidency and Education," *Phi Delta Kappan*, February, 1968, pp. 295–299. (See this book pp. 220–229.)

Bureau official, "not the nuts and bolts stuff which we usually got from the agencies." The agencies also made major contributions to public policy in the course of drafting bills and implementing programs, but their participation in the formulative stages was somewhat reduced during the Johnson Administration.[9]

The processes of policy formulation in the institutionalized Presidency varied widely in the period from 1964 through 1968, but a general pattern appears to have emerged in the cycle of the task force operation as it developed under Califano and his staff.[10] Each year in late spring, Califano and his assistants visited a number of major university centers throughout the country in order to glean ideas for new programs. At the same time, the White House canvassed the Administration for new ideas. Various officials who were regarded as "idea men" were invited to submit proposals on any subject directly to the White House. This permitted them to by-pass normal bureaucratic channels and departmental and agency hierarchies. For example, according to a White House staff member, former Secretary of Defense McNamara submitted over 50 proposals on various domestic problems in one year.

After receiving them, Califano's assistants prepared written one-page descriptions of all the ideas. These "write-ups" included a "proposal" section which briefly explained the idea, a description of the problem and its relationship to on-going programs and a recommendation for action. Next, these papers were categorized and a high-level group within the institutionalized Presidency reviewed them. This group also reviewed the reports of previous task forces, presidential commissions and other advisory bodies which were filed during the course of the previous year. In 1967 this group included Califano, Budget Director Charles Schultze, his deputy Phillip S. Hughes, Chairman Gardner Ackley of the Council of Economic Advisers, Special Counsel to the President Harry McPherson and Califano's staff. Following the review, Califano and his assistants compiled a loose leaf book in which the remaining ideas were grouped by substantive policy areas. The screening group then reconvened for a second examination after which it sent the book to the President with a cover letter indicating the areas which it felt required further study. The President and Califano then reviewed the proposals deciding either to abandon them, study them further or mark them for additional study if time and staff were available.

---

[9] Louis Koenig's prediction, made in 1964 at the outset of the Johnson Presidency, that the White House staff would play a reduced and the old-line departments a greater role in policy formulation has not proved correct. The reverse has occurred. *Op cit.,* pp. 182–183.

[10] This description is based on our interviews. See also the description of the preparation of the 1968 State of the Union Message in "Formulating Presidential Program is Long Process," *Congressional Quarterly Weekly Report,* January 26, 1968, pp. 111–114.

Further development of the ideas which were not abandoned occurred through referral to individual consultants or formal advisory councils, study by departments and agencies, or examination by task forces. Reports of individual consultants are not often made public and their impact is difficult to assess. Advisory council reports usually are public documents. Their influence appears to vary with the reputations of their members, the quality of their content, and the current political significance of the subject matter. Agency studies also vary greatly in impact, but generally they can be regarded as contributing to internal bureaucratic thinking and policy development.

The assignment of a task force to examine an idea or a set of related ideas signified that the President and his top advisors regarded the problem as one of considerable significance. Although task forces did not routinely operate in all of the Great Society areas, they did function fairly frequently. In 1967 a total of 50 separate task forces were operating in various domestic policy areas. Task force assignments, which varied in scope and purpose, determined whether their members would be drawn from people outside or inside the government or from both groups.

Outside task forces were the primary means of securing new ideas for the development of policy. According to participants on various task forces in education and housing, they received broad directives which accorded them maximum freedom to come forth with ideas. "The President," observed a high-ranking presidential staff member, "wants their judgment on substance—not political feasibility."

There was some adjustment in the functions of outside task forces after 1964. In the words of one participant, the 1964 task forces were "happenings." President Johnson used the 1964 task forces as *ad hoc* devices to develop proposals which almost immediately became part of his legislative program. By 1966, the task forces were a normal and rather elaborate aspect of the operations of the Presidency. The President began to use them to take a long-range view of major policy areas and problems as well as to develop immediate legislative proposals. He and his staff took steps to institutionalize the task force operation by integrating it with the highly structured and formal budget review process.

As compared to outside task forces, inside, or interagency task forces functioned more to coordinate agency approaches and to obtain some measure of interagency agreement in areas of dispute. Inside task forces also provided agencies with a vehicle for reacting to the reports of outside task forces. While interagency groups may have generated some new proposals, their major purpose was to provide the President with a coordinated overview of functional problems that cut across departmental and agency lines and to suggest alternative solutions to them. An important aspect of this coordinating function of the interagency task forces was to conduct a "detailed pricing out of all proposals." Members of inside task forces usually included representatives of the Bureau of the Budget and Califano's staff and agency heads or departmental assistant secretaries.

Task forces did not displace that older and more familiar advisory mechanism, the public study commission, some of which are actually authorized by Congress (e.g., the Douglas Commission on housing). President Johnson employed a number of public commissions including the Kaiser Committee, the Heineman Commission on income maintenance, the Crime Commission, and the Kerner Commission. Public commissions can, as cynics have suggested, give the illusion that something is being done to attack a problem. Establishing a commission is a safe response—it is action yet at the same time it disturbs none of the very real political opposition which would emerge if substantive action were attempted.[11] The impact of the report of a public commission is likely to be through its educational effect on public opinion rather than through direct translation into the Administration's policy proposals. Occasionally, when the President has complete confidence in the commission chairman and stays in close contact with him, the report may have a direct impact on Administration policy. This was the case with the Kaiser Committee (President's Committee on Urban Housing) in 1967–1968.

Public commissions can also function to develop support for the Administration. By establishing representative groups and then exposing their deliberations and their reports to public attention, it is possible to develop support for the recommendations. The consensus-building functions of public commissions are no doubt advantageous, but the problems associated with their use is that reports and recommendations which are at all innovative tend to be "controversial" and hence an embarrassment to the White House.[12] The noncommittal response of President Johnson to the report of the Kerner Commission (President's Commission on Civil Disorders) in March, 1968 and the open criticism of the report by Vice President Humphrey and Secretary of Health, Education and Welfare Cohen illustrate the risks involved in creating public commissions—they may file reports and make recommendations which place the Administration in a less than favorable light. Nor are public commissions likely to serve as sources of information or new ideas.

---

[11] See Elizabeth Brenner Drew, "On Giving Oneself a Hotfoot: Government by Commission," *Atlantic,* Vol. 221, May, 1968, pp. 45–49. In her barbed though highly perceptive article, she lists several uses of public commissions including: to postpone action, yet be justified in insisting that you are at work on the problem; to act as a lightning rod, drawing political heat away from the White House; and to investigate, lay to rest, rumors and convince the public of the validity of a particular set of facts.

A highly placed official on the White House staff commented that "there's a hell of a lot of truth to some of the things in Drew's article. However, in some cases we do expect new and important things to come out of public commissions."

[12] Cf. Daniel Bell, "Government by Commission," *The Public Interest,* Vol. I, No. 3 (1966), pp. 3–9. (Also see this book pp. 117–123.)

According to one of our respondents, "The basic ideas in the Kerner report came to us at least two years ago in various task force reports." Furthermore, most task force reports are likely to undergo more intensive scrutiny than that accorded the reports of public commissions.

Once the task forces had written their reports, they submitted them to the President and deposited them with the Bureau of the Budget. Usually, outside task forces reported during the fall.[13] The Bureau of the Budget and the revelant departments and agencies (if the latter were consulted as they frequently but not always were) forwarded their comments directly to the White House.

Following the initial evaluation, the White House staff, under Califano's direction, took the lead in winnowing down task force proposals. (If, in the case of an outside task force report, it appeared that an interagency task force should be created, that decision was made by Califano, the Budget Director, the Chairman of the Council of Economic Advisers and the appropriate department and agency heads). In a series of White House meetings, department and agency heads and their top assistants, representatives of the Bureau of the Budget's examining divisions and of the Council of Economic Advisers and members of Califano's staff examined all task force reports in detail. The purpose of these meetings was to secure agreement on major areas of concern and proposed courses of action. The participants received continuous direction from the President as to his priorities. After much discussion and bargaining, they developed a proposed legislative program which was presented to the President who then made tentative final decisions on it.

The process of developing presidential legislative programs in domestic policy areas established under the Johnson Administration occurred in a more or less orderly temporal sequence. (See Figure 1). It can best be described as an irregular but definite pattern which was fairly well systematized.

---

13 We say usually because the entire process of policy formulation is flexible and somewhat unstructured. What happens in any given case may be, and often is, dependent on idiosyncratic personal and situational variables. There is a great temptation for the political analyst to impose a more rational order on the patterns of the governmental process then may be empirically justified. See James M. Burns, *Presidential Government* (Boston· Houghton Mifflin Co., 1966), p. 143. Burns cites the highly relevant comments of Arthur M. Schlesinger, Jr., based on his experience in the White House during the Kennedy Administration: "Nothing in my recent experience has been more chastening than the attempt to penetrate into the process of decision. I shudder a little when I think how confidently I have analyzed decisions in the ages of Jackson and Roosevelt, traced influences, assigned motives, evaluated roles, allocated responsibilities and, in short, transformed a disheveled and murky evolution into a tidy and ordered transaction. The sad fact is that, in many cases, the basic evidence for the historian's reconstruction of the really hard cases does not exist—and the evidence that it does is often incomplete, misleading, or erroneous." From "The Historian and History," *Foreign Affairs,* Vol. 41 (April, 1963), pp. 491–497.

Figure 1. *Sequence of Events in Preparing the Legislative Program:*
The Johnson Administration

APRIL/MAY/JUNE	JULY	AUGUST	SEPT/OCT/NOV	DECEMBER	JAN/FEB/MAR
Idea Gathering: Visits to universities; contacts with outside experts and "idea men" in government	Internal discussions of ideas gathered	Appointment of outside task forces	Receipt and review of task-force reports	White House meetings	Preparation of messages
			Agency submissions	Final Presidential decisions on the program	Introduction of bills

Task Force Operations

In order to provide a more detailed picture of the task force operation, we have analyzed some of those which have operated in the areas of education and housing. We have been able to examine carefully certain aspects of the task forces including the selection of members, the methods of operation, staffing, and the evaluation of task force reports. We studied the major task forces and public commissions in housing and education from 1964 through mid-1968. These included:

In education;

1964 Gardner* Task Force
1966 Early Childhood Task Force
1967 Friday Task Force
1967 Interagency Task Force

And, in housing;

1964 Wood Task Force
1965 Wood Task Force
1966 Ylvisaker Task Force
1967 Interagency Task Force
1967–68 Kaiser Committee

MEMBERSHIP SELECTION.   The President and his top policy advisers usually selected the members of outside task forces. The selection process operated quite informally. The White House Staff, the Bureau of the Budget, the Council of Economic Advisers in the case of housing, and the Office of Science and Technology in the case of education, and in some cases the concerned department or agency, suggested prospective members. The White House staff, principally Califano and his assistants, took the lead in screening the initial nominations. Then the President approved the final choices, sometimes adding names and perhaps deleting others. In 1965, for example, President Johnson added the names of Senator Abraham Ribicoff and Edgar Kaiser to the Wood task force. The acceptance rate for invitations to serve was high, especially among academics. According to one White House staff member, "only three or four out of some 250 [academics] have refused to serve. In reality, academics are anxious to be able to report privately to the President their views in critical policy areas and to do so with no holds barred."

The criteria employed in selecting members of outside task forces tended to vary with the mission of the task force. Many of our respondents emphasized

---

* By popular convention, outside task forces and public commissions are usually referred to by the name of the chairman.

the importance of independence of viewpoint. In language resembling that which Neustadt uses in *Presidential Power,*[14] a White House staff member commented that "the President has to have advice from someone who knows the right answers and who has no political axe to grind." On the other hand, persons known to hold supposedly "radical" points of view were not likely to be included. A participant in the selection of members for some of the housing task forces recalled that, "The names were selected on the basis of a kind of common sense soundness. We would not have picked a Michael Harrington, for example. We looked for people who had written with perspective and reasonable freshness and who haven't been in the Government for several years."

The membership of outside task forces was not as carefully balanced as that of public commissions tends to be.[15] However, since task forces contributed to policy formulation and the President wanted politically saleable

Table 1. Representation on Outside Task Forces

Education

	STATE AND LOCAL OFFICIALS	COLLEGE ADMINIS-TRATORS	COLLEGE PROFESSORS	BUSINESS	FOUNDATION OFFICIALS	OTHER
1964	3	3	2	2	2	1
1967	2	6	3	0	1	1

Housing

	STATE AND LOCAL OFFICIALS	COLLEGE ADMINIS-TRATORS & PROFESSORS	BUSINESS	LABOR	CIVIL RIGHTS GROUPS	INTEREST GROUPS IN HOUSING	OTHER
1964	1	6	0	0	0	1	3
1965	2	2	1	1	1	0	2
1967	2	5	0	1	1	0	1
1967*	1	1	10	3	1	2	0

* Kaiser Committee.

[14] R. E. Neustadt, *Presidential Power* (New York: John Wiley & Sons, 1960) *passim.*

[15] Drew criticizes the balancing of interests on public commissions on the ground that it tends to immobilize them. *Op cit.,* p. 47. Bell is more sympathetic toward the representational aspects of commissions, *op. cit.,* p. 7.

policies, their representativeness became a factor in selecting members, especially when the objective was to survey a policy area and come up immediately with new legislative proposals. If a task force report was unanimous, a supporting coalition representing most of the major elements in American society would already have been constructed. Thus, the housing task forces in 1964 and 1965 and the 1964 education task force were more or less representative of interests in those areas. (See Table 1).

Occasionally a Federal official served on an otherwise outside task force. In 1964 the Commissioner of Education, Francis Keppel, was a member of the Gardner task force and in 1965 Budget Director Kermit Gordon and Senator Ribicoff served on the housing task force. Perhaps what is most striking about the outside task force is the extent to which academically based persons were over represented in their memberships. This is particularly apparent when the housing task forces are compared with the Kaiser Committee.

In selecting members of outside task forces a conscious attempt was made to avoid overrepresentation of traditional clientele groups such as the National Association of Housing and Redevelopment Officials, the National Education Association and the American Council on Education. These groups had traditionally worked with and through the departments and agencies in formulating and developing policy. Once the agency role in initiating policy began to decline as a consequence of the task force operation, the access of the clientele groups to the central policy-makers also began to fall. These groups responded to their loss of effective access by criticizing the task forces:

> The task forces represent the worst form of intellectual and educational elitism. They are based on the implicit assumption that the education associations are incapable of any sort of creative or innovative thought.
>
> *A representative of a higher*
> *education association*

While the education task forces carefully included representatives of the so-called "establishment," such as a chief state school officer and a big-city school superintendent, they were weighted in favor of academicians. Given their fundamental purpose, to generate new ideas, this was not surprising. Education is a policy area in which there is wide agreement that serious problems exist, but great uncertainty and disagreement over appropriate solutions to them. In housing, however, task forces tended to be more representative of the various interests involved. Unlike education, housing is an area in which the number of possible solutions is limited and disagreements are usually over matters of technique rather than fundamental differences of philosophy.

Representative task forces and particularly the public commissions also have the added benefit, for the Administration, of co-opting relatively powerful but essentially conservative elements of society for social problem-solving. As a key presidential adviser volunteered:

> We try to bring some of these elements in to, in effect, co-opt them. We rub their noses in the problem and bring them along with the solutions. Hell, some of them have never seen slums before. We take them to the ghettos and they are amazed that such things can exist. It's surprising how radical some of them become.

PROCEDURES AND STAFFING. The operating procedures of the outside task forces in education and housing followed a similar pattern. Generally, the task forces commenced with from one to three meetings[16] at which the members, in the course of reacting to one or two broad position papers, ranged over the entire subject. During the opening sessions, the task forces identified areas for future study and commissioned additional position papers. The significance of the papers is that they provided the basis for initial discussions at task force sessions. After a few more meetings, either the staff or a task force member, usually the chairman, prepared tentative drafts of various sections of the task force reports. Further discussions focused on these drafts and the task forces began to move toward a consensus regarding their recommendations and reports.

The task forces do not appear to have used formal votes to reach their decisions, but rather the mode of decision was to bargain back and forth until they reached agreement. When members raised strong objections, efforts were made to satisfy them. According to one participant, the prevailing decisional norm established was one of acquiescence—"[I]f the rest of you agree, then I won't make a fuss." In some cases, however, dissident members refused to yield as when Whitney Young of the Urban League opposed shifting community action programs from the Office of Economic Opportunity to HUD in 1965, because the Negro community was suspicious of HUD. As this example suggests, the members do represent their institutional bases during task force or commission deliberations. Indeed, a staff member of one task force commented, "The members not only actually do speak in terms of the interests of that sector of society from which they are appointed, but in many cases, they perceive their role on the task force as doing exactly that."

The secrecy of the task force operation was perhaps one of its most manifest characteristics. One task force staff member told us:

> Our task force was a C.I.A.-type operation. I felt very odd about it. We were not sure about what should be said and what shouldn't be said. There was no name on our door for the task force. The task force staff director simply had his own name on the door. Papers were put under lock and key every evening.

These remarks were not atypical of comments made by people who were intimately involved in the task force operation. In the eyes of the President

---

[16] These meetings, which usually lasted for one or two days, were held on a monthly or bimonthly basis.

and his staff secrecy was the *raison d'être* for the task force operation. Without secrecy, they felt, the task forces would merely have become a series of public commissions and study groups and have been subject to the problems associated with that form of advisory organization.[17] Secrecy also meant that precise representational balancing of task force membership was not required. The President could appoint members to maximize the range of available experts rather than to balance interests. (In practice, the task forces in education and housing were balanced to represent specific interests to a considerable extent). Secrecy also enabled the President to ignore those task force reports which did not fall within the limits of what he considered possible to accomplish. Recommendations could be adopted or rejected without having to expend energy and political resources defending the choices that were made. The range of options was not only maximized, it was kept open for a longer period of time and at very little political cost. Thus, the secrecy of the reports prevented opposition from developing to task force proposals until a much later stage in the policy process.

Perhaps the principal differences [among] task forces in their operations lie in the roles played by their staffs. We found almost unanimous agreement that a competent staff is essential to a successful task force operation. Generally, they were staffed with personnel from the Executive Office of the President, from various agencies, or from outside government. The Bureau of the Budget had primary responsibility for staffing the 1964 housing and the three education task forces. The education task forces also had staff assistance from the Office of Science and Technology, the National Science Foundation, the Office of Education, the Office of Economic Opportunity and the National Institutes of Health. Usually the executive director of the task force devoted full time to staff work and other individuals were "borrowed" on a part-time basis. The executive directors of the education task forces and the first housing task force were Budget Bureau officials. They assumed responsibility for recruiting other staff members who came from within the Executive Office and the agencies.

Starting in 1965, housing task forces operated with professional staffs more responsible to the White House. The exclusion of the Budget Bureau from a major staffing role in this area was apparently a consequence of the feeling in the White House that financial conservatism on the part of the staff of the 1964 task force was responsible for an overly cautious and somewhat unimaginative report. In contrast, the Budget Bureau officials who served as staff directors for education task forces tended to prod them to be more venturesome and innovative than they might have been otherwise.

The White House assigned a staff member to act as liaison to every task force. This liaison man played a major role if legislative proposals were ex-

[17] See Drew, *op. cit.*

pected from the task force. This occurred when Richard Goodwin sat with the 1964 education task force and in 1965 when Harry McPherson was a vigorous participant in the deliberations of the Wood task force. The function of the liaison man with subsequent task forces, however, was mainly to represent the task force to the President and to convey his wishes to it through Special Assistant Califano. The Bureau of the Budget also maintained liaison with the task forces, primarily to keep them advised of the existence and nature of ongoing Federal programs. When a Budget Bureau official served as a staff director, he automatically provided this liaison. Moreover, Budget Bureau liaison men assumed an important role in the operations of outside task forces. This occurred in 1967 when the task forces were asked to make projections at alternative budgetary levels, thus assigning priorities to their proposals.

The departments and agencies, HUD and its predecessor the Housing and Home Finance Agency (HHFA) and HEW and USOE played an ambiguous role in the operations of outside task forces. Since the manifest intent of outside task forces was to bypass the departments and agencies as major instruments of policy formulation, their officials tended to distrust task forces and to denigrate their significance. Thus, a HUD official disdainfully observed, "I think the task forces have done an editing job that hasn't been done elsewhere and little more," while an HEW executive remarked that "the reports are kept so secret that they don't really pollinate anything."

In 1964, USOE through the participation of Francis Keppel and HHFA through Morton Schussheim were actively involved in the work of the outside task forces. In spite of this liaison, however, both agencies reacted negatively to many portions of the respective task force reports. Apparently, this was not appreciated at the White House, for since then both agencies were almost completely excluded from the activities of outside task forces. By mid-1966 outside task forces operated within the framework of the Executive Office, but beyond the scope of direct bureaucratic influence. In interagency task forces, however, the principal department or agency was likely to dominate the proceedings. One participant in the work of the 1967 housing interagency task force remarked "[I]nteragency task forces often reflect the lead agency's legislative program. Last fall HUD did all the staff work and [Secretary] Weaver chaired. The report would have been about the same had it simply come out of HUD without the participation of other agencies."

EVALUATION OF REPORTS. The evaluation of the reports of outside task forces was a flexible and somewhat unstructured process. After being sent to the President and deposited with the Budget Bureau's Office of Legislative Reference, the reports went to the Bureau's examining divisions, other units in the Executive Office and the agencies for comment. The role of the agencies in evaluation was minor, however, when compared with that of the Bureau of the Budget and the White House staff. Significantly, the same personnel from the

Bureau and the White House who served on task force staffs and sat with them as liaison men were usually involved in evaluating the reports. One Budget Bureau official recalled that while "I leaned over backward to be fair, I did feel like I was meeting myself coming back."

This dual role of the Bureau of the Budget and the White House staff produced a measure of governmental, but nonagency, input to the task forces. It meant that their reports had an Executive Office bias which was not openly acknowledged. One departmental official charged that "There is an incestuous relationship between the task forces on the one hand and the Budget Bureau and the White House on the other." (Presumably the reports are the offspring of the incestuous unions!) The Bureau was aware of the duality of its role and the problems inherent in it. As one of its officials said, "We are involved at the Bureau with task forces as participants and as critics. We have to be a force for sifting out the most workable proposals." But the dual role was perplexing and frustrating for those outside the decisional process in the Executive Office who were affected by its actions.

The extent of the evaluation accorded the reports depended, at least in part, on the closeness with which the White House and the Bureau of the Budget followed the proceedings of the task force and the confidence which the President had in its members. The report of the 1965 Wood task force, for example, underwent relatively little review. In most cases, however, there was extensive review of the reports followed by a series of White House meetings.

When an outside task force report was found to be of little immediate value, the White House sometimes commissioned an interagency task force to develop legislative proposals. This apparently happened in 1967 when the Friday and Ylvisaker reports were followed by the creation of interagency task forces in education and housing, both of which had a major impact on the development of 1968 legislation in those areas.

AGENCY REACTIONS. We have observed that the reaction of departmental and agency officials to the role of outside task forces in policy formulation was substantially negative. The principal objection was to the secrecy which surrounded the work of the task forces and the substance of their reports. While most officials recognized the rationale for secrecy, they felt that it had consequences which were adverse to their interests. One frequent complaint was that the reports tended to become standards within the institutionalized Presidency for evaluating program performance, but that program administrators lacked access to them. According to a USOE program official:

> The task force reports are textual [exegeses] used by those who have access to them. It is assumed in the higher echelons that the task force position is correct. The problem for us is that our performance is evaluated in terms of the objectives set in the reports, but we do not have adequate access to them.

There is little question that the independent expert advice and suggestions obtained from the task forces proved highly valuable to the Johnson Administration. But the Administration also recognized, apparently, that there are limits to the degree to which the President can and should insulate himself from agency influence in policy formulation. The expanded use after 1964 of interagency task forces as vehicles for legislative program development represented an effort to involve the agencies more effectively in Executive Office policy development and to ease agency resentments toward the use of outside task forces. This form of participation enabled the Administration to secure agency support and commitment to its proposals without having to yield to agency domination of their substance.

IMPACT ON POLICY. It is, of course, impossible to measure directly the impact which task force reports have had on public policy. Our research suggests, however, that in many cases the substance of President Johnson's legislative program was in large part shaped by task force recommendations. It does not appear to be mere coincidence that a sizable number of task force proposals ultimately became a part of the Administration's program and were enacted, with amendments, by Congress. Specifically, the rent supplement program authorized by Congress in 1966 was the major recommendation of the 1964 Wood task force; and, the model cities program enacted in 1966 was the major recommendation of the 1965 Wood task force. The major innovative programs authorized in the Elementary and Secondary Education Act of 1965, Titles III and IV, originated with the 1964 Gardner task force; and, virtually all of the recommendations of the 1966 Early Childhood task force were adopted, although at lower funding levels than those the task force recommended, including the establishment of parent-child centers and of Headstart follow through.

Not all task force reports, however, automatically became a part of the President's legislative program. For example, only a few recommendations of the 1967 Friday task force appeared in President Johnson's 1968 education message or the Administration's 1968 education bills. The muted impact of the Friday task force report can be explained in part by its focus on long-range rather than immediate problems and by the constraints which the Vietnam war imposed on the political and budgetary situations. The 1966 Ylvisaker task force also had little direct impact on policy because its recommendations were "too radical" and because its predecessors had been quite productive in terms of legislative accomplishments. As one White House staff member remarked:

> The Ylvisaker report had little policy impact, partly because it was the third in a row and the first two had set policy. Actually it served as a basis for the Kerner Commission report in that it changed the framework from

urbanism to racism. But, I admit, that observation is mostly hindsight. We didn't see the report as terribly important when it came in.

Task force reports can also have a major impact through administrative actions as well as through incorporation in the President's legislative program. For example, the 1966 Early Childhood task force recommended changes in Federal welfare regulations which were subsequently adopted by the agencies involved. In addition, the possibility of task force recommendations becoming Administration policy is enhanced if a key task force participant becomes a member of the Administration.[18] As one agency official remarked:

> Because they wrote the reports they are more likely to take up the cudgels for the task force proposals than someone else would be. What they can't get through legislation, they are likely to push for through administrative changes.

Appraisal and Prospects

Through the employment of secret White House task forces, the Johnson Administration developed a substantially altered pattern of policy formulation and legislative program development within the institutionalized Presidency. The extensive, though selective, use of groups of outside experts to generate new ideas and approaches coupled with the frequent use of interagency task forces to temper the recommendations of the outsiders with pragmatic considerations were the basic changes. Through them the Administration sought to expand the process of policy formulation beyond traditional reliance on the bureaucracy to develop most new legislative proposals. The changes constitute another phase in the institutionalization of the Presidency,[19] but they were not so highly routinized [as to become] deeply embedded in White House routines. While manifesting distinctly identifiable patterns, the operations of the task forces were highly flexible and adaptable to presidential requirements. There are signs, however, that the flexibility and adaptability of the task forces, at least in housing and education, had begun to decline as their operations became increasingly systematized and that they were tending to become elaborate instruments of incremental adjustment rather than catalytic agents of change. The problem is that a leadership technique—and that is what the task force operation is—designed to produce policy innovation worked so well initially that overuse may have rendered it counterproductive through institutionalization. After all, the scope for creative policy leadership

---

[18] This occurred in the cases of John Gardner, who became Secretary of HEW and Robert Wood who became Undersecretary of HUD.

[19] Cf. Lester G. Seligman, "Presidential Leadership: The Inner Circle and Institutionalization," *Journal of Politics,* Vol. 18 (1956), pp. 410–426.

is limited by circumstantial factors and even the most effective techniques can work successfully only part of the time.

It also appears to us that although the task forces were an important *procedural* innovation, the substantive innovations[20] in policy for which they have been responsible are somewhat less than their advocates in the institutionalized Presidency have claimed. As a Budget Bureau official acknowledged, "Task forces fail as innovators. . . . All they do is pull together existing things instead of coming up with new ideas." A staff member of a housing task force agreed: "We didn't really come up with any innovations, nor were we particularly creative." It does seem that the task forces which had the greatest immediate impact on legislation recommended programs which could hardly be characterized as intellectual breakthroughs. For example, the rent supplement idea had been circulating for several years, the HHFA was experimenting with major elements of the model cities approach before the task force proposed it, and three of the five substantive titles of the Elementary and Secondary Education Act, including the all-important Title I providing for massive aid to disadvantaged children, were primarily the products of other forces in the education policy system.

Furthermore, to the extent that task forces were made representative through their membership, tendencies toward innovation may have been mitigated. This appears likely since consensus was the fundamental decision-making rule and final agreement tended to represent compromise rather than creative thinking. As one high-ranking official in the Executive Office admitted, "It is true that with so many interests involved the result is, in some sense, the lowest common denominator."

However, because task forces may not have been quite as innovative (in the sense that no one had thought of their recommendations before) as their proponents claimed does not mean that essentially the same courses of action would have been followed had they not been used. The idea which they promoted may not have been entirely new, but they were not yet embodied in presidential policies nor, in most cases, were they supported by the bureaucracy. Without outside task forces it is not likely that the supplementary educational centers and regional education laboratories or the rent supplements and model cities programs would have been pushed by the Administration and authorized by Congress at the time and [in the] form that they were. But more important than the immediate legislative consequences are the long-range effects of the task force process. They provide a means of maintaining

---

[20] The problem of defining innovation is a familiar one which does not lend itself to any easy solution. As we view it, policy innovation includes the conception of ideas as well as giving substance and form to them. Cf. Victor A. Thompson, "Bureaucracy and Innovation *Administrative Science Quarterly,* Vol. 10 (June, 1965), pp. 1–20. Thompson defines innovation as "the generation, acceptance, and implementation of new ideas, products or services."

a steady input of ideas new to the thought processes of high-level policy-makers. Unfortunately, the consequences of this phenomenon cannot be measured, but its significance is manifest.

On balance, we believe that the task force operation was a significant contribution to policy leadership in the intitutionalized Presidency. Many Johnson Administration officials who were members of the institutionalized Presidency view the task force operation as its major institutional contribution. Whether it will survive is an open question. Much depends on future Presidents; their personalities, their attitudes toward the necessity for policy innovation and the extent to which they employ secrecy and surprise as elements of their leadership styles. Given the still highly personalized nature of the Presidency, it is by no means certain that processes within the framework of presidential activity that involve policy formulation can be quickly and indelibly institutionalized. Rather, institutionalization is a continuous and gradual process.

The task force operation was peculiarly suited to the leadership style of Lyndon B. Johnson. It fitted nicely with the oft-repeated emphasis on the need for a partnership between the public and private sectors, his life-long instinct for decision-making on the basis of consensus, and his preoccupation with secrecy.[21] Viewed in another way, it was a good example of what Theodore Lowi has called "interest group liberalism," a phenomenon which Lowi feels has come increasingly to characterize American politics in the 1960's.[22] Interest group liberalism is a philosophy which specifies that leading societal interests should all be represented in the interior processes of policy formulation.

Future Presidents are likely to utilize those features of the task force operation which they find compatible with their own styles and to create such new forms and patterns of policy formulation as are appropriate to their own circumstances. However, it is certainly expected that they will consider carefully the positive uses of presidential task forces during the Johnson Presidency and that some elements of the task force operation will become permanently institutionalized.

[21] See Rowland Evans and Robert Novak, *Lyndon B. Johnson: The Exercise of Power* (New York: New American Library, 1966).

[22] T. J. Lowi, "The Public Philosophy: Interest–Group Liberalism," *American Political Science Review,* Vol. 61 (1967), pp. 5–24.

Government
by White House
Conference:
Two Views

HELP FROM OUTSIDE

By HENRY FAIRLIE

BLUEPRINT FOR PEACE: Being the Proposals of
Prominent Americans to the White House Conference on
International Cooperation. Edited and with an Introduction
by Richard N. Gardner. 404 pp. New York:
McGraw-Hill. $7.95.

A British journalist, as he left the Oval Room of the White House, noticed the President being approached by one of his Special Assistants. As President Johnson turned on his heels, he could be heard to say: "No more White House conferences. I'm having no more White House conferences."

Anyone who reads this book will sympathize. It is a bleak book, although its bleakness almost makes it interesting. It reveals, unintentionally, the absurdity of its own premise: that it is possible to collect, in committees, the expert and inexpert talent of a nation, and expect it, by consultation and report, to illuminate the political problems of the day. Machiavelli would have abruptly told his Prince not to bother with such fiddle-faddle.

The reports and proposals published in this volume are of little intrinsic

Reprinted by permission from a book review of Richard N. Gardner's *Blueprint for Peace* by Henry Fairlie entitled "Help from Outside," *The New York Times Book Review*, November 27, 1966, pp. 32, 34; and letters to the editor regarding the book review in "Letters to the Editor," *The New York Times Book Review*, December 18, 1966, pp. 14–15. Copyright © 1966 by the New York Times Company.

interest, but the origins and methods of the White House Conference on International Cooperation are, and it is on them that it is worth concentrating.

The whole idea began with a resolution of the United Nations which designated 1965 as International Cooperation Year—a fact hardly likely to reach even a footnote in the history books. President Johnson then designated 1965 as International Cooperation Year in the United States, and announced that it would culminate in a White House Conference; it was also, of course, Escalation in Vietnam Year, but no matter.

"To implement this Presidential call to action"—action, mind you—the Secretary of State asked the United Nations Association to take the lead in coordinating the White House Conference. "Armed with this mandate"— armed? mandate? The words are a little overexciting—"Robert S. Benjamin, Chairman of the Board of UNA, convened a National Citizens' Commission on International Cooperation." This Commission had 230 members, working in 30 committees.

These committees—to which "other persons were added for their special competence in the subject matter"—then worked in consultation with "groups of Government officials . . . designated to assist the citizen committees." It is the reports of these committees, presented to the White House Conference last December, which make up the body of this book. They covered world problems ranging from agriculture, communications, finance, population, to youth activities. Being the work of committees, they explore the lowest common denominators of their subjects.

Looking at the lists of the "prominent Americans"—some of them very prominent—who composed the committees, one wonders first how much time they gave to their work. Whether private individuals or government consultants, many of them are extremely busy men and women; it is impossible to believe that they ever came together often, or for any considerable length of time. In the absence of further evidence, therefore, one is tempted to call the whole thing a hoax.

The editor is candid enough to admit that some of the participants reached the same conclusion. One dismissed the whole affair as "primarily public relations." Another complained that possibly only a third of those involved took "a forward-looking view."

In these circumstances, one would expect a series of recommendations which, although sensible and useful, were so sensible and useful that the State Department and other Government agencies could accept or consider them without much demur. This, of course, is exactly what happened. Of the over 400 recommendations made by the Committees, the State Department reported this summer that 33 had already been implemented; 143 were in the process of implementation; 24 were scheduled to be implemented; 209 were under study; and 26 were considered impractical at this time and perhaps at any time. It is all quite a tribute to the influence of the Government consultants.

The editor is again candid enough to admit that "the Government might have done many of these things anyway." But this only slides over what, to an outsider at least, is one of the most disturbing features of American politics: the constant inveigling of private individuals, who should represent independent interests and independent opinions, into the web of government.

"Many of the individuals involved," says the editor, in another unguarded moment, "gained a new insight and a new sense of commitment as a result of sustained analysis of the subject matter in cooperation with their government counterparts." Anyone who has ever found himself momentarily on the government side knows what this "new insight" means. It means that he begins to accept the "practical" outlook of government, and lets it erode his independent imagination. The editor again makes this point incidentally, when he quotes a foreign diplomat: "The President of the United States actually assembled 5,000 Americans to "tell them off.' " But, of course, this is exactly what did not happen.

In a valuable article in last spring's issue of The Public Interest, Daniel Bell applauded the work of "blue ribbon Commissions"—the equivalent of Royal Commissions in Britain—because they help to make policy "a matter of public opinion." But there is a world of difference between a 14-member National Commission, able to meet regularly, with a million dollars to spend, and with an expert professional staff of its own, and the kind of committees we are considering here.

The unreality that pervades the reports in this volume is twofold. First, by the very nature of the whole dubious exercise, they cannot concern themselves with the supreme political decisions that are necessary, because they are, in a partisan or nationalist sense, controversial. Secondly, they happily assume that, without these supreme political decisions, important advances can be made towards "international cooperation."

Cooperation between America and the Soviet bloc has fitfully increased in recent years because of vital political developments and political decisions on both sides. The hope of cooperation between America and Communist China depends on similar developments and decisions, also on both sides. It is, therefore, more than a little pointless to present a series of reports concerned with the small arrangement that can only follow these large political movements.

It is not only pointless. It is a characteristic example of Establishment obfuscation. Given the origins, the membership, and the methods of the White House Conference on International Cooperation, it is exactly Establishment obfuscation one would expect.

LETTERS TO THE EDITOR

BLUEPRINT FOR PEACE

TO THE EDITOR:

I was surprised, to say the least, to read Henry Fairlie's review of Richard N. Gardner's "Blueprint for Peace" (Nov. 27). The White House Conference produced original and important ideas on how to further world peace and welfare. To have these collected in one volume, together with Gardner's introduction, is surely a valuable contribution to our literature.

The simple answer to Mr. Fairlie's proposition that the conference was a showpiece for the Administration is two-fold: first, the proven integrity of the independent American citizens who participated in the conference; second, the fact that the advanced and valuable ideas offered by the conferees have thus far not been translated into official policy.

ARTHUR J. GOLDBERG
New York City

TO THE EDITOR:

Henry Fairlie, in his review of Richard N. Gardner's "Blueprint for Peace," makes a statement that is central to his criticism of the book. After pointing out, quite properly, that many of the individuals and Government consultants who participated in the White House Conference on International Cooperation Year were "extremely busy men and women," he says it is "impossible to believe that they ever came together often, or for any considerable length of time. In the absence of further evidence, therefore, one is tempted to call the whole thing a hoax."

The evidence is not absent. There are records of the working sessions, names of attending members, what was said and done. The full reports by the individual committees are also available. Mr. Fairlie says he cannot believe that busy people were willing to give their time to the project. The assumption is wrong.

The undersigned were co-chairmen of the Committee on Culture and Intellectual Exchange for I.C.Y. Because of the wide range of our assignment, our committee was divided into 12 subcommittees, all of which were active. If members were unable to attend the work sessions, generally because of geography, a full-time staff assistant went to see them.

In all, there were six meetings of our full committee, alternating between New York and Washington, and 17 smaller meetings principally involving the co-chairmen and the representatives of the subcommittees. Most of the meetings ran a full day. Toward the end, we spent three full days bringing the materials together and going over the draft of the report. . . .

The book . . . brings together the ideas and work of more than a thousand persons from the fields of the arts, communications, science, industry, arms control and disarmament, health, education, social welfare, etc. These people took their work seriously in the expectation of bringing about a serious and constructive result. If Mr. Fairlie is critical of their efforts he has every right to say so; but to assume that they accepted an assignment and then did little or nothing about it is to question their purpose and their integrity.

LUTHER H. EVANS

NORMAN COUSINS

JOHN F. WHITE

New York City

TO THE EDITOR:

If Mr. Fairlie had inquired, he would have learned that the Arms Control and Disarmament Committee of which I was chairman, whose members were indeed busy and important men and women, met as a full committee four times and many more times in small working groups. Many hundreds of hours went into our report. Other committees took their work no less seriously; any one of us who served as chairman would have been glad to provide Mr. Fairlie with details. . . .

Now let us assume that someone other than Mr. Fairlie just may be interested in what some of America's leading experts think about all these subjects. Well, says Mr. Fairlie, let them beware! These reports and recommendations were "so sensible and useful that the State Department and other government agencies could accept or consider them without much demur. . . ."

The point Mr. Fairlie is trying to make is that the White House Conference only told the Administration what it wanted to hear. But if Mr. Fairlie would examine the very statistics he himself quotes on the implementation of these recommendations, he would see that a number of the reports, as the correspondents who covered the White House Conference were quick to point out, go well beyond official policy or criticize it in important respects—which is exactly what one would expect in a free conference held in a free society. . . .

Most Americans believe that a dialogue between private citizens and their government on urgent matters of public interest can be of enormous benefit to both. Indeed, most foreign observers have expressed admiration for the comparative ease with which our Government can recruit part-time or full-time talent from the universities, the professions, and the business community.

The White House Conference committees worked with their counterparts in the executive branch over a period of six months. Most of the persons involved believe that this collaboration gave the government officials a better understanding of public attitudes, provided access to expert knowledge not available in government, and forced officials to consider alternative policies—and that, at the same time, it gave private citizens a more complete picture of all the factors which must be taken into account by those with official responsibility. . . .

The most striking thing of all is that the reviewer does not offer a single substantive comment on any of the proposals contained in the book—neither the ten-point peace program set forth in Richard N. Gardner's thoughtful introduction nor on the recommendations of the various committees. . . .

JEROME B. WIESNER
Cambridge, Mass.

TO THE EDITOR:

. . . What of the proposals made by the various committees? (I was executive officer of the Committee on Arms Control.) Fairlie opines that they could not be realistic, but his own figures gathered from the State Department indicate that 200 of over 400 recommendations have been or are about to be implemented. Fairlie dismisses even this, however, saying that a citizens' conference could not concern itself with the supreme political decisions that must precede serious attempts at international cooperation. If we cannot have the millenium, he suggests, we should not settle for less. He is oblivious to the value of "functional" cooperation on technical grounds and to the possible impact it may have in paving the way for political cooperation on a larger scale. . . .

Fairlie, an English political commentator, seems to have missed what is one of the greatest sources of flexibility and strength in American democracy—the possibility of a meaningful dialogue between citizen and government official. This possibility he describes as the "constant inveigling of private individuals, who should represent independent . . . opinions, into the web of Government." Perhaps Fairlie would prefer the polarization in which Government and citizens do not talk with but *at* one another—a situation in which the masses could "tell off" their President. . . .

It would be tragic if his critique were widely accepted, because his approach—ranging between cynicism and all-or-nothing—would militate against new efforts to organize deeper exchanges between Government and people, between bureaucrat and expert. To the credit of the United States, it may be said that one of the least fortunate aspects of the International Cooperation Year was that, taken together, the other Governments of the world did not spend 5 per cent of the energy which Washington invested in reappraising the road to peace.

WALTER C. CLEMENS, JR.
Boston

6

The Washington
Lawyers

JOSEPH KRAFT

One of the few authentic traditions in American politics arises out of the well-known love affair between the Republican party and the Wall Street lawyers. From Theodore Roosevelt through Dwight Eisenhower, there has been no Republican Administration in which men from the big downtown firms did not play a major role. From their ranks came four of the eight Secretaries of State during the period—Elihu Root, Charles Evans Hughes, Henry Stimson, and John Foster Dulles. So fixed was the tradition that when-ever the Democrats felt obliged to look bipartisan, they automatically reached for a Wall Street lawyer. Mr. Dulles, for that reason, was called to negotiate the Japanese peace treaty in 1951; and when the Cuban missile crisis broke in the fall of 1962, John McCloy was dispatched to the United Nations to sit next to Adlai Stevenson.

With the advent of the Johnson Administration, however, another seg-ment of the American bar finds its place as a political institution. The Washington lawyers have come to constitute a pool of talent specially qualified for the highest posts in government—a Democratic counterpart to the Wall Street lawyers. A striking mark of their role lies in the President's kitchen cabinet of unofficial advisers. Virtually all its members—Dean Acheson, Abe

Fortas, before becoming a Supreme Court justice, James Rowe, Clark Clifford, Thomas Corcoran—are Washington lawyers.

To be sure, the term Washington lawyer covers a multitude of practices and at least a few sins. There are 12,600 lawyers in the metropolitan district of the capital—a ratio of one in every sixty persons, which is the highest by far in the country. Perhaps half the local lawyers engage in distinctly local practice. They handle the murders, rapes, real-estate negotiations, wills, divorces, and accident cases that abound in any large community. Their work is no different from lawyers' work in any one of a dozen towns, and about them there is nothing remarkable.

Several thousand more lawyers in Washington are specialists. Every area where government action impinges upon private interest is worked by at least one specialized firm in Washington. There are firms for communications law, labor law, transportation law, patent law, public-utilities law, atomic-energy law, taxes, antitrust proceedings, land claims, Indian affairs, and the negotiation of defense contracts. Generally, the specialized firms are made up of three or four lawyers who not very long ago worked the same field on the government side of the fence. The communications firm of Cohn & Marks, which has handled Lady Bird Johnson's TV interest, for example, used to count among its four partners three who came to Washington as attorneys for the Federal Communications Commission. One of them, Leonard Marks, has resigned to become director of the United States Information Agency.

Most of the specialist firms are undoubtedly reputable. But because of their government contacts, and even more, because they work in areas remote from the public gaze, some of them tend to harbor the lobbyists, fixers, five-percenters, and operators who have given the Washington lawyer a bad name. And even apart from the matter of reputation, the specialist firms concentrate too narrowly to be a major force in the nation's affairs.

That role is reserved for a third kind of Washington practice—a national practice carried on by perhaps a score of different firms. These firms can handle anything from estates through antitrust cases to international transactions. They argue both in the regulatory agencies and in the courts. In size, they range from giants to midgets. Perhaps the supreme example is Covington & Burling, with a hundred lawyers including Mr. Acheson—"a Wall Street firm," as a local saying goes, "in Washington." But there is also Clifford & Miller, with only four lawyers including Clark Clifford. As clients, the national firms have most of the large corporations and industry groupings. Their lawyers have served in a wide variety of government posts, sometimes at the very top levels, and they tend to come from the best schools. They could, in other words, practice anywhere. But because they have practices in Washington, they have acquired a special relation to the enormous force that fills out the background of everything that happens in the town—the government.

Most of the national firms, to begin with, are the residue of past administrations. Covington & Burling was put together by two attorneys who came to work for agencies set up during Woodrow Wilson's time. The second-biggest firm in town—Hogan & Hartson—was formed by lawyers who worked for the Justice Department and Treasury in the Republican years before the Great Depression. The Truman Administration finds expression in the firm of Mr. Clifford, who was Special Counsel in the White House. General Eisenhower's Counsel, Gerald Morgan, and his Attorney General, William P. Rogers, both head the Washington offices of New York firms. And the New Deal, with all the lawyers it brought down, yielded a crop of law offices—which is the reason why the bias is so heavily Democratic. Perhaps the best-known is the firm of Arnold, Fortas & Porter, put together by Roosevelt's Assistant Attorney General for antitrust, Thurman Arnold, Under Secretary of Interior Abe Fortas, and the head of the Office of Price Administration under Truman, Paul Porter. Almost as prominent is Corcoran, Foley, Youngman & Rowe, engrossing two former White House aides, Thomas Corcoran and James Rowe, and a former Under Secretary of the Treasury, Edward Foley.

Because they come from inside, the Washington lawyers start off by knowing the government intimately—not as a vast, amorphous, remote force, but as a grouping of individuals and offices. That kind of feel for the government is enriched every day by the firm's ordinary practice. To represent du Pont, as Covington & Burling does, is to know not only all the twists and turns of antitrust law but also the moods of those who enforce the law in the Justice Department and the Federal Trade Commission and their relations with the Congress and its committees. To represent the United Fruit Company, as the Corcoran firm does, is to know something about the State Department, in general, and a great deal about the desk officers in the Latin-American field.

Even the most obscure case tends to involve major organs and offices of the government. One Washington firm, for example, was recently handling a dispute between a commercial ranch and an aviation company over a piece of land in Nevada. Apart from knowing the Grazing Acts, the case demanded knowledge of the position of the Secretary of Interior, who administers the acts, and of the pressures that beat upon him from the Defense Department and the Congress. Moreover, every action taken by the government has a parallel in other actions. To represent one airline is to have to know what the government is doing with respect to most other airlines. The Washington lawyer has to keep up. As Gerhart Gesell, of the Covington firm, says, "We read the papers—not just for the headlines."

As much as the Washington lawyers seek out the government, the government seeks them out. Because of their ties to the major companies they are a prime contact with industry across the country. Consider, for example, what happened back in the fall of 1962, when the Justice Department wanted to accumulate, for free, a store of drugs and foodstuffs as ransom for the Cubans taken prisoner by Fidel Castro in the Bay of Pigs. The first move the Department made was to be in touch with Lloyd Cutler, partner in the firm of Wilmer, Cutler & Pickering and Washington counsel for the drug industry. Cutler was able at the outset to warn the Department of the questions—notably tax questions—the drug companies would raise before making theirs wares available. At a critical juncture, he had a hand in arranging for Democratic and Republican leaders to assure the industry that contributing to the ransom fund would not expose it to charges of political favoritism.

In the course of the exercise, moreover, the Justice Department called on three more Washington lawyers for help—John W. Douglas and E. Barrett Prettyman, Jr., of Covington, and John Nolan of the firm of Steptoe, Johnson. All three subsequently entered the government—a mark of the easy transition from the Washington law firms.

For discreet Presidential business, the Washington lawyers, because of their experience and outside contacts, are particularly important. President Kennedy used Clark Clifford to approach the steel companies in the midst of the angry fight over steel pricing in the spring of 1962. Through Dean Acheson he once conveyed word to the West German government that he would like a different German ambassador in Washington. Before Mr. Fortas moved to the Supreme Court, President Johnson made hardly any major moves without first having his judgment on the matter. The President has called on Dean Acheson for help on the Cyprus issue and the NATO crisis initiated by General de Gaulle. He has pressed Clark Clifford into part-time service in such diverse matters as White House staffing and Vietnamese policy.

A high intellectual content, as well as official contacts, distinguishes the work of the Washington lawyer. For one thing, there is the presence of the Supreme Court. Not that Washington lawyers argue cases before the Court with special frequency. Whether in New York or Oshkosh, a lawyer with a case to be heard by the Supreme Court wants to argue it himself. But a great many of the Washington lawyers came to town originally as clerks to the Supreme Court justices. Covington, for instance, has eleven former Supreme Court clerks among its thirty-six partners—a showing that probably no other firm in the country could even begin to match. Moreover, because the Court is in town, because lawyers are always brushing up against the justices, and talking about their work in social gatherings, interest is sustained. There is almost no lawyer in the national firms who does not follow closely the work of the Court. At Arnold, Fortas & Porter, the lawyers' luncheon takes place on Monday, which is also decision day for the Court. On days when decisions are being announced, the luncheon is interrupted for bulletins as each decision is handed down.

The Washington lawyers, furthermore, are not client-dominated. Leading lawyers in most towns tend to become adjuncts of the dominant business. They are auto men in Detroit, steel men in Cleveland and Pittsburgh, securities men in New York. In Washington, none of the leading lawyers lives in the world of business. They are constantly mixing with politicians, journalists, professors, economists, military men, and foreigners from the embassies. It is a mark of their breadth of interest that there is a steady flow between the Washington law firms and the leading law schools. The principal founding partners in Arnold, Fortas & Porter—Thurman Arnold and Abe Fortas—were both professors at the Yale Law School.

Probably most important of all, the Washington lawyer works at the frontiers of his profession. The New York lawyer dealing with a corporate securities issue undoubtedly faces intricate problems. But much of the work is routine—a repetition of work done on previous securities issues. The Washington lawyer, in contrast, generally deals with new problems thrown up to government by the interplay of forces that are beyond, or not yet under, social control. As representatives of foreign governments in the United States, for example, the Washington lawyers daily set sail on the uncharted seas of international law. It was a Washington lawyer representing Pakistan— John Laylin of Covington & Burling—who mainly put together the Indus River development scheme that made it possible for this country to support joint exploitation of the water resources by both India and Pakistan.

Equally important to the Washington lawyer, and equally without precedent, is the area of government-business relations in a mixed economy. The Washington lawyers for the drug companies regularly wrestle with the issue of private marketing of products developed by government research. Washington lawyers, including Lloyd Cutler and Clark Clifford, played a principal part in putting together the unique public-private corporation set up to manage the communications satellite.

The loyalty-security cases of the late Truman and early Eisenhower years presented a similar kind of challenge. The underlying elements in those cases— the presence of Communists in government, on the one hand, and the overriding public interest in security—were both new. It was the Washington lawyers, acting on behalf of government employees, often without compensation, who worked out the procedures whereby loyalty cases came to be handled. It was also the Washington lawyers who mainly pressed the courts to draw boundaries around the proper activities of Congressional investigating committees. And it was another Washington lawyer, Edward Bennett Williams, acting on behalf of Bobby Baker, who raised anew the question of whether the committees had the right to televise the investigation of witnesses.

The thorny issues growing out of the civil-rights dispute have equally commanded the attention of the Washington lawyers. Dean Acheson first came to work with Lyndon Johnson, not as a foreign-policy expert but in connection with the civil-rights bill of 1960. It was another Covington lawyer,

Burke Marshall, recently the Assistant Attorney General for Civil Rights, who first hit on the idea of using federal referees to judge voting lists rather than local officials who were prone to bias.

The capacity to handle new problems of great magnitude in a creative way is, of course, the special requirement for success at the top levels of government. Given the talents and training of the Washington lawyers, it is, if anything, remarkable that they have so far played so little a part in government. The explanation lies in an historic accident. The Washington lawyers tended to come to the capital in the New Deal days and to enter private practice after World War II. Except for Mr. Acheson, they were too new a factor to enter much into the Truman Administration. During the Eisenhower regime, they were necessarily out: Democrats in a Republican day. The Kennedy Administration gave high office to a few—George Ball and Henry Fowler were both Washington lawyers; so were four of the eight Assistant Attorneys General.

But many of the ex-New Dealers in the Washington law firms found themselves in poor rapport with the men of the New Frontier who had made their careers in the postwar era. They were, so to speak, a generation removed. Lyndon Johnson, who came to Washington contemporaneously with the New Deal, erased the difference in generation. For the Washington lawyers, an hour had come round at last.

=== 7

The Policymaker
and the Intellectual

HENRY A. KISSINGER

I. Administrative Stagnation

It would be comforting to believe that our foreign policy difficulties are
due to specific mistakes of policy which can be reversed more or less easily.
Unfortunately, the problem is more deep-seated. It is remarkable that during
a decade of crisis few fundamental criticisms of American policy have been
offered. We have not reached an impasse because the wrong alternative has
been chosen in a "Great Debate." The alternatives have rarely been properly
defined. The stagnation of our policy is often ascribed to the fact that our
best people are not in government service. But the more serious and pertinent
question is how qualified our eminent men are for the task of policymaking
in a revolutionary period.

One of the paradoxes of an increasingly specialized, bureaucratized society
is that the qualities rewarded in the rise to eminence are less and less the
qualities required once eminence is reached. Specialization encourages administrative and technical skills, which are not necessarily those needed for leadership.
Good administration depends on the ability to coordinate the specialized functions of a bureaucracy. The task of the executive is to infuse and occasionally

Reprinted by permission from Henry A. Kissinger, *The Necessity for Choice,* Garden
City, N. Y., Doubleday Anchor edition by arrangement with Harper & Row, 1962, pp.
352–368.

to transcend routine with purpose. Administration is concerned with execution. Policymaking must address itself also to developing a sense of direction.

Yet, while the head of an organization requires a different outlook from that of his administrative subordinates, he must generally be recruited from their ranks. Eminence thus is often reached for reasons and according to criteria which are irrelevant to the tasks which must be performed in the highest positions. Despite all personnel procedures, and perhaps because of them, superior performance at the apex of an organization is frequently in the deepest sense accidental.

This problem, which exists in all complex societies, is especially characteristic of the United States. In a society that has prided itself on its "business" character, it is inevitable that the qualities which are most esteemed in civilian pursuits should also be generally rewarded by high public office. As a result, the typical Cabinet or sub-Cabinet officer in America comes either from business or from the legal profession. But very little in the experience that forms these men produces the combination of political acumen, conceptual skill, persuasive power, and substantive knowledge required for the highest positions of government.

The American business executive (or the lawyer coming from a business background) who is placed in a high policymaking position is rarely familiar with the substance of the problems into which he finds himself projected largely because, in the rise through the administrative hierarchy, the executive is shaped by a style of life that inhibits reflectiveness. One of the characteristics of a society based on specialization is the enormous work load of its top personnel. More energies are absorbed in creating a smooth-functioning administrative apparatus than in defining the criteria on which decisions are to be based. Issues are reduced to their simplest terms. Decision-making is increasingly turned into a group effort. The executive's task is conceived as choosing among administrative proposals in the formulation of which he has no part and with the substance of which he is often unfamiliar. A premium is placed on "presentations" which take the least effort to grasp—in practice usually oral "briefing." (This accounts for the emergence of the specialist in "briefings" who prepares charts, one-page summaries, etc.) The result is that in our society the executive grows dependent to an increasing extent on his subordinates' conception of the essential elements of a problem.

In such an environment little opportunity exists for real creativity, or even for an understanding of it. Creativity is not consciously discouraged—indeed, lip service is always paid to it—but it often goes unrecognized. In the private sector of our society the debilitating tendency of this bureaucratization is not always apparent because most executives can substitute long experience in their line of endeavor for reflectiveness. The goals of the business effort are relatively limited; they involve less the creation of a policy framework than successful operation within one—in itself a conciliatory procedure. But when the same method is applied to national policymaking, its limitations become dramatically apparent. On entering government, the executive soon discovers that he must pay a price for his lack of familiarity with his new environment.

Many a high official has to start governmental service with extensive briefing on almost every aspect—and sometimes the most elementary aspects—of the subject matter for which he is responsible. He therefore can rarely benefit from the strong will which is often his outstanding trait. Great decisiveness in a familiar environment may become arbitrariness or at least erratic behavior when the criteria of judgment seem elusive. Consciously or not, our top policymakers often lack the assurance or the conceptual framework to impose a sense of direction on their administrative staffs. Their unfamiliarity with their subject matter reinforces the already powerful tendency to think that a compromise among administrative proposals is the same thing as a policy.

The bureaucratization of our society reflects not only a growing specialization but also deep-seated philosophical attitudes all the more pervasive for rarely being made explicit. Two generations of Americans have been shaped by the pragmatic conviction that inadequate performance is somehow the result of a failure to understand an "objective" environment properly and that group effort is valuable in itself. The interaction of several minds is supposed to broaden the range of "experience," and "experience" is believed to be the ultimate source of knowledge. Pragmatism, at least in its generally accepted forms, produces a tendency to identify a policy issue with the search for empirical data. It sees in consensus a test of validity. Pragmatism is more concerned with method than with judgment. Or, rather, it seeks to reduce judgment to methodology and value to knowledge.

The result is a greater concern with the collection of facts than with an interpretation of their significance. There occurs a multiplication of advisory staffs and a great reliance on study groups of all types, whose chief test is unanimity. Disagreement is considered a reflection on the objectivity or the judgment of the participants. Each difficulty calls into being new panels, which frequently act as if nothing had ever been done before, partly, at least, because the very existence of a problem is taken as an indication of the inadequacy of the previous advice.

The problem is magnified by the personal humility which is one of the most attractive American traits. Most Americans are convinced that no one is ever entirely "right," or, as the saying goes, that if there is disagreement each party is probably a little in error. The fear of dogmatism pervades the American scene. But the corollary of the tentativeness of most views is an incurable inner insecurity. Even very eminent people are reluctant to stand alone. Torn between the desire to be bold and the wish to be popular, they would like to see their boldness certified, as it were, by general approbation. Philosophical conviction and psychological bias thus combine to produce in and out of government a penchant for policymaking by committee. The obvious insurance against the possibility of error is to obtain as many opinions as possible. And unanimity is important, in that its absence is a standing reminder of the tentativeness of the course adopted. The committee approach to decision making is often less an organization device than a spiritual necessity.

This is not to say, of course, that committees are inherently pernicious or that policy should be conducted on the basis of personal intuition. Most contemporary problems are so complex that the interaction of several minds is necessary for a full consideration. Any attempt to conduct policy on a personal basis inhibits creative approaches just as surely as does the purely administrative approach—witness the conduct of foreign policy by Secretary Dulles, whose technical virtuosity could not obscure the underlying stagnation.

The difficulty is not the existence of the committee system but the lengths to which reliance on it is pushed because of the lack of substantive mastery by the highest officials. When policy becomes identified with the consensus of a committee, it is fragmented into a series of *ad hoc* decisions which make it difficult to achieve a sense of direction or even to profit from experience. Substantive problems are transformed into administrative ones. Innovation is subjected to "objective" tests which deprive it of spontaneity. "Policy planning" becomes the projection of familiar problems into the future. Momentum is confused with purpose. There is greater concern with how things are than with which things matter. The illusion is created that we can avoid recourse to personal judgment and responsibility as the final determinant of policy.

The impact on national policy is pernicious. Even our highest policy bodies, such as the National Security Council, are less concerned with developing measures in terms of a well-understood national purpose than with adjusting the varying approaches of semi-autonomous departments. A policy dilemma indicates that the advantages and disadvantages of alternative measures appear fairly evenly balanced. (This leaves aside the question to what extent the committee procedure encourages a neutral personality to whom the pros and cons of almost any course of action always seem fairly even and who therefore creates artificial dilemmas.) But in assessing these alternatives the risks always seem more certain than the opportunities. No one can ever prove that an opportunity existed, but failure to foresee a danger involves swift retribution. As a result, much of the committee procedure is designed to permit each participant or agency to register objections, and the system stresses avoidance of risk rather than boldness of conception. The committee system is concerned more with coordination and adjustment than with purpose.

The elaborateness of the process is magnified by the tendency of advisors to advise. For silence may not imply a judgment on the idea under discussion, it may mean rather that the advisor is inadequate. Thus, the committee member is under pressure to speak whether he wishes to or not—indeed, whether he has anything to say or not.

The committee system not only has a tendency to ask the wrong questions, it also puts a premium on the wrong qualities. The committee process is geared to the pace of conversation. Even where the agenda is composed of memoranda, these are prepared primarily as a background for discussion, and they stand or fall on the skill with which they are presented. Hence, quickness of comprehension is more important than reflectiveness, fluency more useful than creativeness. The ideal "committee man" does not make his associates uncomfortable. He does not operate with ideas too far outside of what is generally accepted. Thus the thrust of committees is toward a standard of average performance. Since a complicated idea cannot be easily absorbed by ear—particularly when it is new—committees lean toward what fits in with the most familiar experience of their members. They therefore produce great pressure in favor of the *status quo*. Committees are consumers and sometimes sterilizers of ideas, rarely creators of them.

Unfortunately, not everything that sounds plausible is important. And many important ideas do not seem plausible—at least at first glance, the only glance permitted by most committees. Rapidity of comprehension is not always equivalent to responsible assessment; it may even be contrary to it.

The attitudes of our high officials and their method of arriving at decisions inevitably distort the essence of policy. Effective policy depends not only on the skill of individual moves, but even more importantly on their relationship to each other. It requires a sense of proportion and a sense of style. All these intangibles are negated when problems become isolated cases, each of which is disposed of on its merits by experts or agencies in the special difficulties it involves. It is as if, in commissioning a painting, a patron would ask one artist to draw the face, another the body, another the hands, and still another the feet, simply because each artist was particularly good in one category. Such a procedure of stressing the components would sacrifice the meaning of the whole.

The result is a paradox. The more intense the effort to substitute administration for conception, the greater is the inner insecurity of the participants. The more they seek "objectivity," the more diffuse their efforts become. The insecurity of many of our policymakers sometimes leads to almost compulsive traits. Because of the lack of criteria on which to base judgments, work almost becomes an end in itself. Officials—and other executives as well—tend to work to the point of exhaustion, as one indication that nothing has been left undone. The insecurity is also shown by the fact that almost in direct proportion as advisory staffs multiply they are distrusted by those at the top. Officials increasingly feel the need for "outside"—and therefore unbiased—advice. Memoranda that are produced within the bureaucracy are taken less seriously than similar papers that are available to the general public. Crucial policy advice is increasingly requested from *ad hoc* committees of outside experts, as, for example, the Gaither Committee on national defense or the Draper Committee on economic assistance or the Coolidge Committee on arms control.

These committees are often extraordinarily useful. They provide a fresh point of view. They can focus public discussion. They make possible the tapping of talent that would otherwise be unavailable, particularly in the scientific field. They may even galvanize the bureaucracy. Nevertheless, they rarely touch the core of the problem: to challenge the existing assumptions or to define a new sense of direction. This is because the assumption which calls the *ad hoc* committees into being is frequently mistaken. The assumption is that the obstacle to decisive policy has been the inability to resolve available facts into specific recommendations. But the lack of subtlety and comprehension of the top leadership is not much more amenable to outside committees than to the governmental variety because in the absence of criteria of judgment, advice often adds simply another element of confusion.

The result is a vicious circle: As long as our high officials lack a framework of purpose, each problem becomes a special case. But the more fragmented the approach to policy becomes, the more difficult it is to act consistently and purposefully. The typical pattern of our governmental process is therefore endless debate about whether a given set of circumstances is in fact a problem, until a crisis removes all doubts but also the possibility of effective action. The committee system, which is an attempt to reduce the inner insecurity of our top personnel, has the paradoxical consequence of institutionalizing it.

This explains to a considerable extent why American policy has displayed such a combination of abstractness and rigidity. The method of arriving at decisions places a greater premium on form than on substance. Thus, on any given issue some paper will be produced for almost any eventuality. But because policy results from what are in effect adversary proceedings, proposals by the various departments or agencies are often overstated to permit compromise or phrased vaguely to allow freedom of interpretation. In any case, what is considered policy is usually the embodiment of a consensus within a committee. The very qualities which make the consensus possible tend to inhibit sustained and subtle application. The statement is frequently so general that it must be renegotiated when the situation to which it is supposed to apply arises.

The rigidity of American policy is therefore often a symptom of the psychological burden placed on our policymakers. Policies developed with great inner doubt become almost sacrosanct as soon as they are finally officially adopted. The reason is psychological. The *status quo* has at least the advantage of familiarity. An attempt to change course involves the prospect that the whole searing process of arriving at a decision will have to be repeated. By the same token, most of our initiatives tend to occur during crisis periods. When frustration becomes too great or a crisis brooks no further evasion, there arises the demand for innovation almost for its own sake.

Yet innovation cannot be achieved by fiat. Crisis conditions do not encourage calm consideration. They rarely permit anything except defensive moves. Many ideas are first rejected in tranquil times because they are too far ahead of the thinking of the bureaucracy and then are accepted when a crisis produces the demand for a new approach, though it is now too late. Or else, they may be still relevant but rejected again because in the interim they have become "old hat."

The combination of unreflectiveness produced by the style of life of our most eminent people in and out of government, faith in administrative processes, and the conversational approach to policy has accounted for much of the uncertainty of our policy. It has led to an enormous waste of intellectual resources. The price we have paid for the absence of a sense of direction is that we have appeared to the rest of the world as vacillating, confused, and sometimes irrelevant.

It is sometimes argued that the characteristics described here are inseparable from the democratic process. But it surely is not inherent in a democracy that its most eminent people are formed by an experience which positively discourages political thinking and perhaps reflectiveness of any kind. In Great Britain, for example, the ablest young people have traditionally been drawn into political life. They have been exposed throughout their careers to a concern with problems very similar to those faced when eminence is reached.

The balance between the private and public aspects of our life, which has been the subject of national debate with respect to our allocation of resources, may be even more important with regard to the conceptual priorities of our eminent men. If our ablest people cannot be brought to address themselves to problems of national policy throughout their lives, no organizational device will save them from mediocrity once they reach high office. Substantial policy cannot be improvised. A democracy cannot function without a leadership group which has assurance in relation to the issues confronting it. We face, in short, a test of attitudes even more than of policies.

2. *The Position of Intellectuals*

How about the role of individuals who *have* addressed themselves to acquiring substantive knowledge—the intellectuals? Is our problem, as is so often alleged, the lack of respect shown to the intellectual by our society?

The problem is more complicated than our refusal or inability to utilize this source of talent. Many organizations, governmental or private, rely on panels of experts. Political leaders have intellectuals as advisors. Throughout our society, policy-planning bodies proliferate. Research organizations multiply. The need for talent is a theme of countless reports. What, then, is the difficulty?

One problem is the demand for expertise itself. Every problem which our society becomes concerned about—leaving aside the question of whether these are always the most significant—calls into being panels, committees, or study groups supported by either private or governmental funds. Many organizations constantly call on intellectuals for advice. As a result, intellectuals with a reputation soon find themselves so burdened that their pace of life hardly differs from that of the executives whom they counsel. They cannot supply perspective because they are as harassed as the policymakers. All pressures on them tend to keep them at the level of the performance which gained them their reputation. In his desire to be helpful, the intellectual is too frequently compelled to sacrifice what should be his greatest contribution to society—his creativity.

Moreover, the pressure is not produced only by the organizations that ask for advice; some of it is generated by the image the intellectual has of himself. In a pragmatic society, it is almost inevitable that the pursuit of knowledge for its own sake should not only be lightly regarded by the community but also that it should engender feelings of insecurity or even guilt among some of those who have dedicated themselves to it. There are many who believe that their ultimate contribution as intellectuals depends on the degree of their participation in what is considered the "active" life. It is not a long step from the willingness to give advice to having one's self-esteem gratified by a consulting relationship with a large organization. And since individuals who challenge the presuppositions of the bureaucracy, governmental or private, rarely can keep their positions as advisers, great pressures are created to elaborate on familiar themes rather than risk new departures.

The great value our society places on expertise may be even more inimical to innovation than indifference. Not only the executive suffers from over-specialization. Panels of experts are deliberately assembled to contain representatives of particular approaches; a committee on military policy will have spokesmen for the "all-out war" as well as for the "limited war" concept. A committee on foreign policy will have spokesmen for the "uncommitted areas" as well as specialists on Europe. These are then expected to adjust their differences by analogy with the subcommittee procedure of the bureaucracy. Not surprisingly, the result is more often a common denominator than a well-rounded point of view.

This tendency is magnified by the conception of the intellectual held by the officials or organizations that call on him. The specialization of functions of a bureaucratized society delimits tasks and establishes categories of expectations. A person is considered suitable for assignments within certain classifications. But the classification of the intellectual is determined by the premium our society places on administrative skill. The intellectual is rarely found at the level where decisions are made. His role is commonly advisory. He is called in as a "specialist" in ideas whose advice is combined with that of others from different fields of endeavor on the assumption that the policymaker is able to choose intuitively the correct amalgam of "theoretical" and "practical" advice And even in this capacity the intellectual is not a free agent. It is the executive who determines in the first place whether he needs advice. He and the bureaucracy frame the question to be answered. The policymaker determines the standard of relevance. He decides who is consulted and thereby the definition of "expertness."

The fact that the need for excellence is constantly invoked is no guarantee that its nature will be understood. Excellence is more often thought to consist of the ability to perform the familiar as well as possible than of pushing back the frontiers of knowledge or insight. The search for talent more frequently takes the form of seeking personnel for familiar tasks than of an effort to discover individuals capable of new and not yet imagined types of performance. The "expert" not uncommonly is the person who elaborates the existing framework most ably, rather than the individual charting new paths.

The contribution of the intellectual to policy is therefore in terms of criteria that he has played only a minor role in establishing. He is rarely given the opportunity to point out that a query limits a range of possible solutions or that an issue is posed in irrelevant terms. He is asked to solve problems, not to contribute to the definition of goals. Where decisions are arrived at by negotiation, the intellectual—particularly if he is not himself part of the bureaucracy—is a useful weight in the scale. He can serve as a means of filtering ideas to the top outside of organizational channels or as one who legitimizes the viewpoint of contending factions within and among departments. This is why many organizations build up batteries of outside experts or create semi-independent research groups, and why articles or books become tools in the bureaucratic struggle. In short, all too often what the policymaker wants from the intellectual is not ideas but endorsement.

This is not to say that the motivation of the policymaker toward the intellectual is cynical. The policymaker sincerely wants help. His problem is that he does not know the nature of the help he requires. And he generally does not become aware of the need until the problem is already critical. He is subject to the misconception that he can make an effective choice among conflicting advisors on the basis of administrative rules of thumb and without being fully familiar with the subject matter. Of necessity the bureaucracy gears the intellectual effort to its own requirements and its own pace; the deadlines are inevitably those of the policymaker, and all too often they demand a premature disclosure of ideas which are then dissected before they are fully developed. The administrative approach to intellectual effort tends to destroy the environment from which innovation grows. Its insistence on "results" discourages the intellectual climate that might produce important ideas whether or not the bureaucracy feels it needs them.

Thus, though the intellectual participates in policymaking to an almost unprecedented degree, the result has not necessarily been salutary for him or of full benefit to the officials calling on him. In fact, the two have sometimes compounded each other's weaknesses. Nor has the present manner of utilizing outside experts and research institutes done more than reduce somewhat the dilemma of the policymakers. The production of so much research often simply adds another burden to already overworked officials. It tends to divert attention from the act of judgment on which policy ultimately depends to the assembly of facts which is relatively the easiest step in policy formation. Few if any of the recent crises of U.S. policy have been caused by the unavailability of data. Our policymakers do not lack advice; they are in many respects overwhelmed by it. They do lack criteria on which to base judgments. And in the absence of commonly understood and meaningful standards, all advice tends to become equivalent.

In seeking to help the bureaucracy out of this maze, the intellectual too frequently becomes an extension of the administrative machine, accepting its criteria and elaborating its problems. While this, too, is a necessary task and sometimes even an important one, it does not touch the heart of the problem. The dilemma of our policy is not so much that it cannot act on what it has defined as useful—though this, too, happens occasionally—but that the standards of utility are in need of redefinition. Neither the intellectual nor the policymaker performs his full responsibility if he shies away from this essential task.

This does not mean that the intellectual should remain aloof from policymaking. Nor have intellectuals who have chosen withdrawal necessarily helped the situation. There are intellectuals outside the bureaucracy who are not part of the maelstrom of committees and study groups but who have, nevertheless, contributed to the existing stagnation through a perfectionism that paralyzes action by posing unreal alternatives. There are intellectuals within the bureaucracy who have avoided the administrative approach but who must share the responsibility for the prevailing confusion because they refuse to acknowledge that all of policy involves an inevitable element of conjecture. It is always possible to escape difficult choices by making only the most favorable assessment of the intentions of other states or of political trends. The intellectuals of other countries in the free world where the influence of pragmatism is less pronounced and the demands of the bureaucracies less insatiable have not made a more significant contribution. The spiritual malaise described here may have other symptoms elsewhere. The fact remains that the entire free world suffers not only from administrative myopia but also from self-righteousness and the lack of a sense of direction.

Thus, if the intellectual is to make a contribution to national policy, he faces a delicate task. He must steer between the Scylla of letting the bureaucracy prescribe what is relevant or useful and the Charybdis of defining these criteria too abstractly. If he inclines too much toward the former, he will turn into a promoter of technical remedies; if he chooses the latter, he will run the risks of confusing dogmatism with morality and of courting martyrdom—of becoming, in short, as wrapped up in a cult of rejection as the activist is in a cult of success.

Where to draw the line between excessive commitment to the bureaucracy and paralyzing aloofness depends on so many intangibles of circumstance and personality that it is difficult to generalize. Perhaps the matter can be stated as follows: one of the challenges of the contemporary situation is to demonstrate the overwhelming importance of purpose over technique. The intellectual should therefore not refuse to participate in policymaking, for to do so confirms the stagnation of societies whose leadership groups have little substantive knowledge. But in co-operating the intellectual has two loyalties: to the organization that employs him and to values which transcend the bureaucratic framework and provide his basic motivation. It is important for him to remember that one of his contributions to the administrative process is his independence, and that one of his tasks is to seek to prevent routine from becoming an end in itself.

The intellectual must therefore decide not only whether to participate in the administrative process but also in what capacity: whether as an intellectual or as an administrator. If he assumes the former role, it is essential for him to retain the freedom to deal with the policymaker from a position of independence, and to reserve the right to assess the policymaker's demands in terms of his own standards. Paradoxically, this also may turn out to be most helpful to the policymaker. For the greater the bureaucratization and the more eminent the policymaker, the more difficult it is to obtain advice in which substantive considerations are not submerged by or at least identified with organizational requirements.

Such an attitude requires an occasional separation from administration. The intellectual must guard his distinctive and, in this particular context, most crucial qualities: the pursuit of knowledge rather than of administrative ends and the perspective supplied by a non-bureaucratic vantage point. It is therefore essential for him to return from time to time to his library or his laboratory to "recharge his batteries." If he fails to do this, he will turn into an administrator, distinguished from some of his colleagues only by having been recruited from the intellectual community. Such a relationship does not preclude a major contribution. But it will then have to be in terms of the organization's criteria, which can be changed from within only by those in the most pre-eminent positions.

3. The Highest of Stakes

Ultimately the problem is not the intellectual's alone or even primarily. There is no substitute for greater insight on the part of our executives, in or out of government. Advice, however excellent, is not a substitute for knowledge. Neither Churchill, nor Lincoln, nor Roosevelt was the product of a staff. As long as our executives conceive their special skill to be a kind of intuitive ability to choose among conflicting advice on the basis of administrative or psychological criteria, our policy will be without a sense of proportion and a feeling for nuance. As long as our eminent men lack a substantive grasp of the issues, they will be unable to develop long-range policy or act with subtlety and assurance in the face of our challenges. In these circumstances, the policy-maker's relation with the intellectual will produce frustration as often as mutual support. The executive, while making a ritual of consulting the intellectual, will consider him hopelessly abstract or judge him by his ability to achieve short-term ends. And the intellectual, while participating in the policymaking process, will always have the feeling that he never had a chance to present the most important considerations. The executives' lack of understanding of the nature of reflection and the administrative approach to policy cause them to place a premium on qualities in intellectuals which they can most easily duplicate in their own organization. It leads them to apply administrative criteria to the problems of creativity, thereby making it difficult to transcend the standards of the moment. The intellectuals' unfamiliarity with the management of men makes them overlook the fact that policymaking involves not only the clear conception of ideas but also their implementation.

The result is often a tendency on both sides to confuse policymaking with analysis—on the part of the policymaker as a means to defer difficult choices, on the part of the intellectual to acquire greater knowledge. However, policy-making, while based on knowledge, is not equivalent to analysis. Effective policy fits its measures to circumstances. Analysis strives to eliminate the accidental; it seeks principles of general validity. The policymaker is faced with situations where at some point discussion will be overtaken by events, where to delay for the sake of refinement of thought may invite disaster. Analysis, by contrast, can and must always sacrifice time to clarity; it is not completed until all avenues of research have been explored. The difference between the mode of policy and the mode of analysis is therefore one of perspective. Policy looks toward the future; its pace is dictated by the need for decision in a finite time. Analysis assumes an accomplished act or a given set of factors. Its pace is the pace of reflection.

The difficulty arises not from the analytic method but from the failure to relate it to the problems of the policymaker. The quest for certainty, essential for analysis, may be paralyzing when pushed to extremes with respect to policy. The search for universality, which has produced so much of the greatest intellectual effort, may lead to something close to dogmatism in national affairs. The result can be a tendency to recoil before the act of choosing among alternatives, which is inseparable from policymaking, and to ignore the tragic aspect of policymaking, which lies precisely in its unavoidable component of conjecture. There can come about a temptation to seek to combine the advantage of every course of action: to delay commitment until "all the facts are in," until, that is, the future has been reduced to an aspect of the past.

The solution is not to turn philosophers into kings or kings into philosophers. But it is essential that our most eminent men in all fields overcome the approach to national issues as an extra-curricular activity that does not touch the core of their concerns. The future course of our society is not a matter to be charted administratively. The specialization of functions turns into a caricature when decision making and the pursuit of knowledge on which it is based are treated as completely separate activities, by either executives or intellectuals. A way must be found to enable our oldest people to deal with problems of policy and to perform national service in their formative years. This is a challenge to our educational system, to the big administrative hierarchies, as well as to national policy.

—✐— III

Presidential
Policy
Politics:
Explorations
of Advisory
Roles

Parts I and II have dealt with the advisers and various advisory processes; this part treats the roles which advisers and outside experts play in some selected policy spheres. Policy specialists, both in and out of government, are constantly engaged in evaluating new proposals and searching for new legislative and managerial ideas. While these selections primarily treat the roles of consultants, task forces, and White House advisory councils, they are suggestive of comparative research that might be extended to examine university-government relations as well as the relations of both profit and non-profit corporations with various national public policy arenas.

1

The Two
Presidencies

AARON WILDAVSKY

The United States has one President, but it has two presidencies; one presidency is for domestic affairs, and the other is concerned with defense and foreign policy. Since World War II, Presidents have had much greater success in controlling the nation's defense and foreign policies than in dominating its domestic policies. Even Lyndon Johnson has seen his early record of victories in domestic legislation diminish as his concern with foreign affairs grows.

What powers does the President have to control defense and foreign policies and so completely overwhelm those who might wish to thwart him?

The President's normal problem with domestic policy is to get congressional support for policies that he believes will protect the nation—but his problem is to find a viable policy.

Whoever they are, whether they begin by caring about foreign policy like Eisenhower and Kennedy or about domestic policies like Truman and Johnson, Presidents soon discover they have more policy preferences in domestic matters than in foreign policy. The Republican and Democratic parties possess a traditional roster of policies, which can easily be adopted by a new President—for example, he can be either for or against Medicare and aid to education. Since existing domestic policy usually changes in only small steps, Presidents find it relatively simple to make minor adjustments. However, although any President knows he supports foreign aid and NATO, the world

Reprinted by permission from Aaron Wildavsky, "The Two Presidencies," *Trans-action*, December, 1966, pp. 7–14. Copyright © 1966 by *Trans-action*.

outside changes much more rapidly than the nation inside—Presidents and their parties have no prior policies on Argentina and the Congo. The world has become a highly intractable place with a whirl of forces we cannot or do not know how to alter.

The Record of Presidential Control

It takes great crises, such as Roosevelt's hundred days in the midst of the depression, or the extraordinary majorities that Barry Goldwater's candidacy willed to Lyndon Johnson, for Presidents to succeed in controlling domestic policy. From the end of the 1930's to the present (what may roughly be called the modern era) Presidents have often been frustrated in their domestic programs. From 1938, when conservatives regrouped their forces, to the time of his death, Franklin Roosevelt did not get a single piece of significant domestic legislation passed. Truman lost out on most of his intense domestic preferences, except perhaps for housing. Since Eisenhower did not ask for much domestic legislation, he did not meet consistent defeat, yet he failed in his general policy of curtailing governmental commitments. Kennedy, of course, faced great difficulties with domestic legislation.

In the realm of foreign policy there has not been a single major issue on which Presidents, when they were serious and determined, have failed. The list of their victories is impressive: entry into the United Nations, the Marshall Plan, NATO, the Truman Doctrine, the decisions to stay out of Indochina in 1954 and to intervene in Vietnam in the 1960's, aid to Poland and Yugoslavia, the test-ban treaty, and many more. Serious setbacks to the President in controlling foreign policy are extraordinary and unusual.

Table I, compiled from the Congressional Quarterly Service tabulation of presidential initiative and congressional response from 1948 through 1964, shows that Presidents have significantly better records in foreign and defense matters than in domestic policies. When refugees and immigration—which Congress considers primarily a domestic concern—are removed from the general foreign policy area, it is clear that Presidents prevail about 70 percent of the time in defense and foreign policy, compared with 40 percent in the domestic sphere.

World Events and Presidential Resources

Power in politics is control over governmental decisions. How does the President manage his control of foreign and defense policy? The answer does not reside in the greater constitutional power in foreign affairs that Presidents have possessed since the founding of the Republic. The answer lies in the changes that have taken place since 1945.

The number of nations with which the United States has diplomatic relations has increased from 53 in 1939 to 113 in 1966. But sheer numbers do not tell enough; the world has also become a much more dangerous place. However remote it may seem at times, our government must always be aware of the possibility of nuclear war.

Table I. Congressional Action on Presidential Proposals from 1948–1964

POLICY AREA	CONGRESSIONAL ACTION		NUMBER OF PROPOSALS
	% PASS	% FAIL	
Domestic policy (natural resources, labor, agriculture, taxes, etc.)	40.2	59.8	2499
Defense policy (defense, disarmament, manpower, misc.)	73.3	26.7	90
Foreign policy	58.5	41.5	655
Immigration, refugees	13.2	86.0	129
Treaties, general foreign relations, State Department, foreign aid	70.8	29.2	445

SOURCE: Congressional Quarterly Service, *Congress and the Nation,* 1945–1964 (Washington, 1965).

Yet the mere existence of great powers with effective thermonuclear weapons would not, in and of itself, vastly increase our rate of interaction with most other nations. We see events in Assam or Burundi as important because they are also part of a larger worldwide contest, called the cold war, in which great powers are rivals for the control or support of other nations. Moreover, the reaction against the blatant isolationism of the 1930's has led to a concern with foreign policy that is worldwide in scope. We are interested in what happens everywhere because we see these events as connected with larger interests involving, at the worst, the possibility of ultimate destruction.

Given the overriding fact that the world is dangerous and that small causes are perceived to have potentially great effects in an unstable world, it follows that Presidents must be interested in relatively "small" matters. So they give Azerbaijan or Lebanon or Vietnam huge amounts of their time. Arthur Schlesinger, Jr., wrote of Kennedy that "in the first two months of his administration he probably spent more time on Laos than on anything else." Few failures in domestic policy, Presidents soon realize, could have as disastrous consequences as any one of dozens of mistakes in the international arena.

The result is that foreign policy concerns tend to drive out domestic policy. Except for occasional questions of domestic prosperity and for civil rights, foreign affairs have consistently higher priority for Presidents. Once, when trying to talk to President Kennedy about natural resources, Secretary of the Interior Stewart Udall remarked, "He's imprisoned by Berlin."

The importance of foreign affairs to Presidents is intensified by the increasing speed of events in the international arena. The event and its consequences follow closely on top of one another. The blunder at the Bay of Pigs is swiftly followed by the near castastrophe of the Cuban missile crisis. Presidents can no longer count on passing along their most difficult problems to their successors. They must expect to face the consequences of their actions—or failure to act—while still in office.

Domestic policy-making is usually based on experimental adjustments to an existing situation. Only a few decisions, such as those involving large dams, irretrievably commit future generations. Decisions in foreign affairs, however, are often perceived to be irreversible. This is expressed, for example, in the fear of escalation or the various "spiral" or "domino" theories of international conflict.

If decisions are perceived to be both important and irreversible, there is every reason for Presidents to devote a great deal of resources to them. Presidents have to be oriented toward the future in the use of their resources. They serve a fixed term in office, and they cannot automatically count on support from the populace, Congress or the administrative apparatus. They have to be careful, therefore, to husband their resources for pressing future needs. But because the consequences of events in foreign affairs are potentially more grave, faster to manifest themselves, and less easily reversible than in domestic affairs, Presidents are more willing to use up their resources.

The Power to Act

Their formal powers to commit resources in foreign affairs and defense are vast. Particularly important is their power as Commander-in-Chief to move troops. Faced with situations like the invasion of South Korea or the emplacement of missiles in Cuba, fast action is required. Presidents possess both the formal power to act and the knowledge that elites and the general public expect them to act. Once they have committed American forces, it is difficult for Congress or anyone else to alter the course of events. The Dominican venture is a recent case in point.

Presidential discretion in foreign affairs also makes it difficult (though not impossible) for Congress to restrict their actions. Presidents can use executive agreements instead of treaties, enter into tacit agreements instead of written ones, and otherwise help create *de facto* situations not easily reversed. Presidents also have far greater ability than anyone else to obtain information on developments abroad through the Departments of State and Defense. The need for secrecy in some aspects of foreign and defense policy further restricts the ability of others to compete with Presidents. These things are all well known. What is not so generally appreciated is the growing presidential ability to *use* information to achieve goals.

In the past Presidents were amateurs in military strategy. They could not even get much useful advice outside of the military. As late as the 1930's the number of people outside the military establishment who were professionally engaged in the study of defense policy could be numbered on the fingers. Today there are hundreds of such men. The rise of the defense intellectuals has given the President of the United States enhanced ability to control defense policy. He is no longer dependent on the military for advice. He can choose among defense intellectuals from the research corporations and the academies for alternative sources of advice. He can install these men in his own office. He can play them off against each other or use them to extend spheres of coordination.

Even with these advisers, however, Presidents and Secretaries of Defense might still be too bewildered by the complexity of nuclear situations to take action—unless they had an understanding of the doctrine and concepts of deterrence. But knowledge of doctrine about deterrence has been widely diffused; it can be picked up by any intelligent person who will read books or listen to enough hours of conversation. Whether or not the doctrine is good is a separate question; the point is that civilians can feel they understand what is going on in defense policy. Perhaps the most extraordinary feature of presidential action during the Cuban missile crisis was the degree to which the Commander-in-Chief of the Armed Forces insisted on controlling even the smallest moves. From the positioning of ships to the methods of boarding, to the precise words and actions to be taken by individual soldiers and sailors, the President and his civilian advisers were in control.

Although Presidents have rivals for power in foreign affairs, the rivals do not usually succeed. Presidents prevail not only because they may have superior resources but because their potential opponents are weak, divided, or believe that they should not control foreign policy. Let us consider the potential rivals—the general citizenry, special interest groups, the Congress, the military, the so-called military-industrial complex, and the State Department.

Competitors for Control of Policy

THE PUBLIC.   The general public is much more dependent on Presidents in foreign affairs than in domestic matters. While many people know about the impact of social security and Medicare, few know about politics in Malawi. So it is not surprising that people expect the President to act in foreign affairs and reward him with their confidence. Gallup Polls consistently show that presidential popularity rises after he takes action in a crisis—whether the action is disastrous as in the Bay of Pigs or successful as in the Cuban missile crisis. Decisive action, such as the bombing of oil fields near Haiphong, resulted in a sharp (though temporary) increase in Johnson's popularity.

The Vietnam situation illustrates another problem of public opinion in foreign affairs: it is extremely difficult to get operational policy directions from the general public. It took a long time before any sizable public interest in the subject developed. Nothing short of the large scale involvement of American troops under fire probably could have brought about the current high level of concern. Yet this relatively well developed popular opinion is difficult to interpret. While a majority appear to support President Johnson's policy, it appears that they could easily be persuaded to withdraw from Vietnam if the administration changed its line. Although a sizable majority would support various initiatives to end the war, they would seemingly be appalled if this action led to Communist encroachments elsewhere in Southeast Asia. (See "The President, the Polls, and Vietnam" by Seymour Martin Lipset, *Transaction*, Sept./Oct. 1966.)

Although Presidents lead opinion in foreign affairs, they know they will be held accountable for the consequences of their actions. President Johnson has maintained a large commitment in Vietnam. His popularity shoots up now and again in the midst of some imposing action. But the fact that a body of citizens do not like the war comes back to damage his overall popularity. We will support your initiatives, the people seem to say, but we will reserve the right to punish you (or your party) if we do not like the results.

SPECIAL INTEREST GROUP. Opinions are easier to gauge in domestic affairs because, for one thing, there is a stable structure of interest groups that covers virtually all matters of concern. The farm, labor, business, conservation, veteran, civil rights, and other interest groups provide cues when a proposed policy affects them. Thus people who identify with these groups may adopt their views. But in foreign policy matters the interest group structure is weak, unstable, and thin rather than dense. In many matters affecting Africa and Asia, for example, it is hard to think of well-known interest groups. While ephemeral groups arise from time to time to support or protest particular policies, they usually disappear when the immediate problem is resolved. In contrast, longer-lasting elite groups like the Foreign Policy Association and Council on Foreign Relations are composed of people of diverse views; refusal to take strong positions on controversial matters is a condition of their continued viability.

The strongest interest groups are probably the ethnic associations whose members have strong ties with a homeland, as in Poland or Cuba, so they are rarely activated simultaneously on any specific issue. They are most effective when most narrowly and intensely focused—as in the fierce pressure from Jews to recognize the state of Israel. But their relatively small numbers limits their significance to Presidents in the vastly more important general foreign policy picture—as continued aid to the Arab countries shows. Moreover, some ethnic groups may conflict on significant issues such as American acceptance of the Oder-Neisse line separating Poland from what is now East Germany.

THE CONGRESS. Congressmen also exercise power in foreign affairs. Yet they are ordinarily not serious competitors with the President because they follow a self-defining ordinance. They do not think it is their job to determine the nation's defense policies. Lewis A. Dexter's extensive interviews with members of the Senate Armed Service Committee, who might be expected to want a voice in defense policy, reveal that they do not desire for men like themselves to run the nation's defense establishment. Aside from a few specific conflicts among the armed servies which allow both the possibility and desirability of direct intervention, the Armed Services Committee constitutes a sort of real estate committee dealing with the regional economic consequences of the location of military facilities.

The congressional appropriations power is potentially a significant resource, but circumstances since the end of World War II have tended to reduce its effectiveness. The appropriations committees and Congress itself might make their will felt by refusing to allot funds unless basic policies were altered. But this has not happened. While Congress makes its traditional small cuts in the military budget, Presidents have mostly found themselves warding off congressional attempts to increase specific items still further .

Most of the time, the administration's refusal to spend has not been seriously challenged. However, there have been occasions when individual legislators or committees have been influential. Senator Henry Jackson in his campaign (with the aid of colleagues on the Joint Committee on Atomic Energy) was able to gain acceptance for the Polaris weapons system and Senator Arthur H. Vandenberg played a part in determining the shape of the Marshall Plan and so on. The few congressmen who are expert in defense policy act, as Samuel P. Huntington says, largely as lobbyists with the executive branch. It is apparently more fruitful for these congressional experts to use their resources in order to get a hearing from the executive than to work on other congressmen.

When an issue involves the actual use or threat of violence, it takes a great deal to convince congressmen not to follow the President's lead. James Robinson's tabulation of foreign and defense policy issues from the late 1930's to 1961 (Table II) shows dominant influence by Congress in only one case out of seven—the 1954 decision not to intervene with armed force in Indochina. In that instance, President Eisenhower deliberately sounded out congressional opinion and, finding it negative, decided not to intervene—against the advice of Admiral Radford, chairman of the Joint Chiefs of Staff. This attempt to abandon responsibility did not succeed, as the years of American involvement demonstrate.

THE MILITARY. The outstanding feature of the military's participation in making defense policy is their amazing weakness. Whether the policy decisions involve the size of the armed forces, the choice of weapons systems, the total defense budget, or its division into components, the military have not prevailed. Let us take budgetary decisions as representative of the key choices to be made in defense policy. Since the end of World War II, the military has not been able to achieve significant (billion dollar) increases in appropriations by their own efforts. Under Truman and Eisenhower defense budgets were determined by what Huntington calls the remainder method: the two Presidents estimated revenues, decided what they could spend on domestic matters, and the remainder was assigned to defense. The usual controversy was between some military and congressional groups supporting much larger expenditures while the President and his executive allies refused. A typical case, involving the desire of the Air Force to increase the number of groups of planes is described by Huntington in *The Common Defense:*

> The FY [fiscal year] 1949 budget provided 48 groups. After the Czech coup, the Administration yielded and backed an Air Force of 55 groups in its spring rearmament program. Congress added additional funds to aid Air Force expansion to 70 groups. The Administration refused to utilize them, however, and in the gathering economy wave of the summer and fall of 1948, the Air Force goal was cut back again to 48 groups. In 1949, the House of Representatives picked up the challenge and appropriated funds for 58 groups. The President impounded the money. In June, 1950, the Air Force had 48 groups.

The great increases in the defense budget were due far more to Stalin and modern technology than to the military. The Korean War resulted in an increase from 12 to 44 billions and much of the rest followed Sputnik and the huge costs of missile programs. Thus modern technology and international conflict put an end to the one major effort to subordinate foreign affairs to domestic policies through the budget.

It could be argued that the President merely ratifies the decisions made by the military and their allies. If the military and/or Congress were united and insistent on defense policy, it would certainly be difficult for Presidents to resist these forces. But it is precisely the disunity of the military that has characterized the entire postwar period. Indeed, the military have not been united on any major matter of defense policy. The apparent unity of the Joint Chiefs of Staff turns out to be illusory. The vast majority of their recommendations appear to be unanimous and are accepted by the Secretary of Defense and the President. But this facade of unity can only be achieved by methods that vitiate the impact of the recommendations. Genuine disagreements are hidden by vague language that commits no one to anything. Mutually contradictory plans are strung together so everyone appears to get something, but nothing is decided. Since it is impossible to agree on really important matters, all sorts of trivia are brought in to make a record of agreement. While it may be true, as Admiral Denfield, a former Chief of Naval Operations, said, that "On nine-tenths of the matters that come before them the Joint Chiefs of Staff reach agreement themselves," the vastly more important truth is that "normally the *only* disputes are on strategic concepts, the size and composition of forces, and budget matters."

Table II. *Congressional Involvement in Foreign and Defense Policy Decisions*

ISSUE	CONGRESSIONAL INVOLVEMENT (HIGH, LOW, NONE)	INITIATOR (CONGRESS OR EXECUTIVE)	PREDOMINANT INFLUENCE (CONGRESS OR EXECUTIVE)	LEGISLATION OR RESOLUTION (YES OR NO)	VIOLENCE AT STAKE (YES OR NO)	DECISION TIME (LONG OR SHORT)
Neutrality Legislation, the 1930's	High	Exec	Cong	Yes	No	Long
Lend-Lease, 1941	High	Exec	Exec	Yes	Yes	Long
Aid to Russia, 1941	Low	Exec	Exec	No	No	Long
Repeal of Chinese Exclusion, 1943	High	Cong	Cong	Yes	No	Long
Fulbright Resolution, 1943	High	Cong	Cong	Yes	No	Long
Building the Atomic Bomb, 1944	Low	Exec	Exec	Yes	Yes	Long
Foreign Services Act of 1946	High	Exec	Exec	Yes	No	Long
Truman Doctrine, 1947	High	Exec	Exec	Yes	No	Long
The Marshall Plan, 1947–48	High	Exec	Exec	Yes	No	Long
Berlin Airlift, 1948	None	Exec	Exec	No	Yes	Long
Vandenberg Resolution, 1948	High	Exec	Cong	Yes	No	Long
North Atlantic Treaty, 1947–49	High	Exec	Exec	Yes	No	Long
Korean Decision, 1950	None	Exec	Exec	No	Yes	Short
Japanese Peace Treaty, 1952	High	Exec	Exec	Yes	No	Long
Bohlen Nomination, 1953	High	Exec	Exec	Yes	No	Long
Indo-China, 1954	High	Exec	Cong	No	Yes	Short
Formosan Resolution, 1955	High	Exec	Exec	Yes	Yes	Long
International Finance Corporation, 1956	Low	Exec	Exec	Yes	No	Long
Foreign Aid, 1957	High	Exec	Exec	Yes	No	Long
Reciprocal Trade Agreements, 1958	High	Exec	Exec	Yes	No	Long
Monroney Resolution, 1958	High	Cong	Cong	Yes	No	Long
Cuban Decision, 1961	Low	Exec	Exec	No	Yes	Long

SOURCE: James A. Robinson, *Congress and Foreign Policy-Making* (Homewood, Illinois, 1962).

MILITARY-INDUSTRIAL.   But what about the fabled military-industrial complex? If the military alone is divided and weak, perhaps the giant industrial firms that are so dependent on defense contracts play a large part in making policy.

First, there is an important distinction between the questions "Who will get a given contract?" and "What will our defense policy be?" It is apparent that different answers may be given to these quite different questions. There are literally tens of thousands of defense contractors. They may compete vigorously for business. In the course of this competition, they may wine and dine military officers, use retired generals, seek intervention by their congressmen, place ads in trade journals, and even contribute to political campaigns. The famous TFX controversy—should General Dynamics or Boeing get the expensive contract?—is a larger than life example of the pressures brought to bear in search of lucrative contracts.

But neither the TFX case nor the usual vigorous competition for contracts is involved with the making of substantive defense policy. Vital questions like the size of the defense budget, the choice of strategic programs, massive retaliation versus a counter-city strategy, and the like were far beyond the policy aims of any company. Industrial firms, then, do not control such decisions, nor is there much evidence that they actually try. No doubt a precipitous and drastic rush to disarmament would meet with opposition from industrial firms among other interests. However, there has never been a time when any significant element in the government considered a disarmament policy to be feasible.

It may appear that industrial firms had no special reason to concern themselves with the government's stance on defense because they agree with the national consensus on resisting communism, maintaining a large defense establishment, and rejecting isolationism. However, this hypothesis about the climate of opinion explains everything and nothing. For every policy that is adopted or rejected can be explained away on the grounds that the cold war climate of opinion dictated what happened. Did the United States fail to intervene with armed force in Vietnam in 1954? That must be because the climate of opinion was against it. Did the United States send troops to Vietnam in the 1960's? That must be because the cold war climate demanded it. If the United States builds more missiles, negotiates a test-ban treaty, intervenes in the Dominican Republic, fails to intervene in a dozen other situations, all these actions fit the hypothesis by definition. The argument is reminiscent of those who defined the Soviet Union as permanently hostile and therefore interpreted increases of Soviet troops as menacing and decreases of troop strength as equally sinister.

If the growth of the military establishment is not directly equated with increasing military control of defense policy, the extraordinary weakness of the professional soldier still requires explanation. Huntington has written about how major military leaders were seduced in the Truman and Eisenhower years into believing that they should bow to the judgment of civilians that the economy could not stand much larger military expenditures. Once the size of the military pie was accepted as a fixed constraint, the military services were compelled to put their major energies into quarreling with one another over who should get the larger share. Given the natural rivalries of the military and their traditional acceptance of civilian rule, the President and his advisers— who could claim responsibility for the broader picture of reconciling defense and domestic policies—had the upper hand. There are, however, additional explanations to be considered.

The dominant role of the congressional appropriations committee is to be guardian of the treasury. This is manifested in the pride of its members in cutting the President's budget. Thus it was difficult to get this crucial committee to recommend even a few hundred million increase in defense; it was practically impossible to get them to consider the several billion jump that might really have made a difference. A related budgetary matter concerned the planning, programming, and budgeting system introduced by Secretary of Defense McNamara. For if the defense budget contained major categories that crisscrossed the services, only the Secretary of Defense could put it together. Whatever the other debatable consequences of program budgeting, its major consequence was to grant power to the secretary and his civilian advisers.

The subordination of the military through program budgeting is just one symptom of a more general weakness of the military. In the past decade the military has suffered a lack of intellectual skills appropriate to the nuclear age. For no one has (and no one wants) direct experience with nuclear war. So the usual military talk about being the only people to have combat experience is not very impressive. Instead, the imaginative creation of possible future wars— in order to avoid them—requires people with a high capacity for abstract thought combined with the ability to manipulate symbols using quantitative methods. West Point has not produced many such men.

THE STATE DEPARTMENT. Modern Presidents expect the State Department to carry out their policies. John F. Kennedy felt that State was "in some particular sense 'his' department." If a Secretary of State forgets this, as was apparently the case with James Byrnes under Truman, a President may find another man. But the State Department, especially the Foreign Service, is also a highly professional organization with a life and momentum of its own. If a President does not push hard, he may find his preferences somehow dissipated in time. Arthur Schlesinger fills his book on Kennedy with laments about the bureaucratic inertia and recalcitrance of the State Department.

Yet Schlesinger's own account suggests that State could not ordinarily resist the President. At one point, he writes of "the President, himself, increasingly the day-to-day director of American foreign policy." On the next page, we learn that "Kennedy dealt personally with almost every aspect of policy around the globe. He knew more about certain areas than the senior officials at State and probably called as many issues to their attention as they did to his." The President insisted on his way in Laos. He pushed through his policy on the Congo against strong opposition [from] the State Department. Had Kennedy wanted to get a great deal more initiative out of the State Department, as Schlesinger insists, he could have replaced the Secretary of State, a man who did not command special support in the Democratic party or in Congress. It may be that Kennedy wanted too strongly to run his own foreign policy. Dean Rusk may have known far better than Schlesinger that the one thing Kennedy did not want was a man who might rival him in the field of foreign affairs.

Schlesinger comes closest to the truth when he writes that "the White House could always win any battle it chose over the [Foreign] Service; but the prestige and proficiency of the Service limited the number of battles any White House would find it profitable to fight." When the President knew what he wanted, he got it. When he was doubtful and perplexed, he sought good advice and frequently did not get that. But there is no evidence that the people on his staff came up with better ideas. The real problem may have been a lack of good ideas anywhere. Kennedy undoubtedly encouraged his staff to prod the State Department. But the President was sufficiently cautious not to push so hard that he got his way when he was not certain what that way should be. In this context Kennedy appears to have played his staff off against elements in the State Department.

The growth of a special White House staff to help Presidents in foreign affairs expresses their need for assistance, their refusal to rely completely on the regular executive agencies, and their ability to find competent men. The deployment of this staff must remain a presidential prerogative, however, if its members are to serve Presidents and not their opponents. Whenever critics do not like existing foreign and defense policies, they are likely to complain that the White House staff is screening out divergent views from the President's attention. Naturally, the critics recommend introducing many more different view-points. If the critics could maneuver the President into counting hands all day ("on the one hand and on the other"), they would make it impossible for him to act. Such a viewpoint is also congenial to those who believe that action rather than inaction is the greatest present danger in foreign policy. But Presidents resolutely refuse to become prisoners of their advisers by using them as other people would like. Presidents remain in control of their staff as well as of major foreign policy decisions.

How Complete Is the Control?

Some analysts say that the success of Presidents in controlling foreign policy decisions is largely illusory. It is achieved, they say, by anticipating the reactions of others, and eliminating proposals that would run into severe opposition. There is some truth in this objection. In politics, where transactions are based on a high degree of mutual interdependence, what others may do has to be taken into account. But basing presidential success in foreign and defense policy on anticipated reactions suggests a static situation which does not exist. For if Presidents propose only those policies that would get support in Congress, and Congress opposes them only when it knows that it can muster overwhelming strength, there would never be any conflict. Indeed, there might never be any action.

How can "anticipated reaction" explain the conflict over policies like the Marshall Plan and the test-ban treaty in which severe opposition was overcome only by strenuous efforts? Furthermore, why doesn't "anticipated reaction" work in domestic affairs? One would have to argue that for some reason presidential perception of what would be successful is consistently confused on domestic issues and most always accurate on major foreign policy issues. But the role of "anticipated reactions" should be greater in the more familiar domestic situations, which provide a backlog of experience for forecasting, than in foreign policy with many novel situations such as the Suez crisis or the Rhodesian affair.

Are there significant historical examples which might refute the thesis of presidential control of foreign policy? Foreign aid may be a case in point. For many years, Presidents have struggled to get foreign aid appropriations because of hostility from public and congressional opinion. Yet several billion dollars a year are appropriated regularly despite the evident unpopularity of the program. In the aid programs to Communist countries like Poland and Yugoslavia, the Congress attaches all sorts of restrictions to the aid, but Presidents find ways of getting around them.

What about the example of recognition of Communist China? The sentiment of the country always has been against recognizing Red China or admitting it to the United Nations. But have Presidents wanted to recognize Red China and been hamstrung by opposition? The answer, I suggest, is a qualified "no." By the time recognition of Red China might have become a serious issue for the Truman administration, the war in Korea effectively precluded its consideration. There is no evidence that President Eisenhower or Secretary Dulles ever thought it wise to recognize Red China or help admit her to the United Nations. The Kennedy administration viewed the matter as not of major importance and, considering the opposition, moved cautiously in suggesting change. Then came the war in Vietnam. If the advantages for foreign policy had been perceived to be much higher, then Kennedy or Johnson might have proposed changing American policy toward recognition of Red China.

One possible exception, in the case of Red China, however, does not seem sufficient to invalidate the general thesis that Presidents do considerably better in getting their way in foreign and defense policy than in domestic policies.

The World Influence

The forces impelling Presidents to be concerned with the widest range of foreign and defense policies also affect the ways in which they calculate their power stakes. As Kennedy used to say, "Domestic policy . . . can only defeat us; foreign policy can kill us."

It no longer makes sense for Presidents to "play politics" with foreign and defense policies. In the past, Presidents might have thought that they could gain by prolonged delay or by not acting at all. The problem might disappear or be passed on to their successors. Presidents must now expect to pay the high costs themselves if the world situation deteriorates. The advantages of pursuing a policy that is viable in the world, that will not blow up on Presidents or their fellow citizens, far outweigh any temporary political disadvantages accrued in supporting an initially unpopular policy. Compared with domestic affairs, Presidents engaged in world politics are immensely more concerned with meeting problems on their own terms. Who supports and opposes a policy, though a matter of considerable interest, does not assume the crucial importance that it does in domestic affairs. The best policy Presidents can find is also the best politics.

The fact that there are numerous foreign and defense policy situations competing for a President's attention means that it is worthwhile to organize political activity in order to affect his agenda. For if a President pays more attention to certain problems he may develop different preferences; he may seek and receive different advice; his new calculations may lead him to devote greater resources to seeking a solution. Interested congressmen may exert influence, not by directly determining a presidential decision, but indirectly by making it costly for a President to avoid reconsidering the basis for his action. For example, citizen groups, such as those concerned with a change in China policy, may have an impact simply by keeping their proposals on the public agenda. A President may be compelled to reconsider a problem even though he could not overtly be forced to alter the prevailing policy.

In foreign affairs we may be approaching the stage where knowledge is power. There is a tremendous receptivity to good ideas in Washington. Most anyone who can present a convincing rationale for dealing with a hard world finds a ready audience. The best way to convince Presidents to follow a desired policy is to show that it might work. A man like McNamara thrives because he performs; he comes up with answers he can defend. It is, to be sure, extremely difficult to devise good policies or to predict their consequences accurately. Nor is it easy to convince others that a given policy is superior to other alternatives. But it is the way to influence with Presidents. For if they are convinced that the current policy is best, the likelihood of gaining sufficient force to compel a change is quite small. The man who can build better foreign policies will find Presidents beating a path to his door.

$\equiv\!\!\!\!\!\!\!\!\!\sim 2$

The Gaither
Committee
and the Policy
Process

MORTON H. HALPERIN

Despite the extensive government apparatus for policy-making on problems of national security, the American President in the postwar period has, from time to time, appointed groups of private citizens to investigate particular problems and report to the National Security Council.[1] Some of these groups have performed their task without the public's ever becoming aware of their existence; others have in one way or another come to public attention. Among the latter are those which have become known under the names of their chairmen: Finletter, Gray, Paley, Sarnoff, Gaither, Boechenstein, and Killian. President Truman made use of such groups, and the variety of tasks

Reprinted by permission from Morton H. Halperin, "The Gaither Committee and the Policy Process," *World Politics,* No. 3, April, 1961, pp. 360–384. The author is indebted to the following for comments and criticisms: Gabriel Almond, Paul Hammond, Paul Nitze, Harry Ransom, Henry Rowen, Thomas Schelling, Warner Schilling, and H. Bradford Westerfield.

[1] The first such Presidential Commission was appointed by President Truman in January 1948 to make a general survey of foreign intelligence activities (see U.S. Senate, Subcommittee on National Policy Machinery, Committee on Government Operations, *Organizational History of the National Security Council,* 86th Congress, 2nd Session, Washington, D.C., 1960, p. 10).

for which they were appointed grew steadily during the Eisenhower Administration.[2]

Some analysts have seen in this development an indication that the government is exploiting all possible sources of policy recommendations, and have praised the use of such private groups.[3] Others have argued that their use reflects the bankruptcy of the NSC procedure.[4] There is agreement that the committees have often made imaginative and valuable recommendations, but the degree to which such advice can and should be fitted into the Executive decision-making process has been the subject of some dispute.

Perhaps the most publicized and controversial of such groups was the Gaither Committee, which, in 1957, presented a report on the nation's defense requirements. The Report remains a classified document but the effects of the Committee and its work continue to be mentioned in the nation's press. The Gaither Report was probably the most general study of the nation's defense effort to be undertaken by an *ad hoc* civilian group. Much of its contents and the events surrounding its drafting and presentation have become public, shedding a good deal of light on the national security decision-making process.

In this article I will attempt to trace and analyze the series of events connected with the Gaither Report. While explicating an important political incident, I will use the Gaither episode to generate hypotheses about the use of civilian study groups, about the Executive decision-making process, and about the role of information in the public debate about national security policy.

I. Drafting the Report

In the spring of 1957 the Federal Civilian Defense Administration (FCDA) submitted a report to President Eisenhower recommending that the government spend 40 billion dollars over a period of several years to erect shelters which would provide protection against the blast-effect of nuclear weapons.[5]

---

[2] See the following articles by former NSC staff members reprinted in U.S. Senate, Subcommittee on National Policy Machinery, Committee on Government Operations, *Organizing for National Security, Selected Materials* 86th Congress, 2nd Session, Washington, D.C., 1960 (cited hereinafter as *Selected Materials*): Sidney W. Souers, "Policy Formation for National Security," p. 32; Robert Cutler, "The Development of the National Security Council," p. 58; and Gordon Gray, "Role of the National Security Council in the Formation of National Policy," p. 65.

[3] See the articles by Bowie, Cutler, and Gray in *ibid*.

[4] See the articles by Kissinger, Nitze, and Jackson in *ibid*.

[5] *New York Times,* December 21, 1957, p. 8:4; Chalmers M. Roberts' article in the *Washington Post and Times Herald,* December 20, 1957, reprinted in the *Congressional Quarterly Weekly Report,* xv (December 27, 1957), pp. 1328–30, and in the *Congressional Record,* 85th Congress, 2nd Session, Washington, D.C., 1958, p. 858 (Roberts citations hereinafter refer to the *Congressional Quarterly Weekly Report*).

The FCDA proposal was discussed by the National Security Council, and the President ordered a study to be made by an *ad hoc* committee of private citizens. The sense of the NSC meeting had been that before the Administration considered spending a sum equal to its annual military expenditure, it should investigate other possible uses of the 40 billion dollars. It was argued that if the government were prepared to increase spending for defense, it should explore the advantages of increasing its active defense effort.

The Eisenhower Administration had come to rely on the use of private consultants and this was the type of situation in which an *ad hoc* group was likely to be most helpful. An alternative would have been to set up a committee of the interested Executive agencies, but such a group would either have been unable to agree or would have drafted a "compromise" split of the proposed 40 billion-dollar expenditure. A committee of private citizens might be expected to take an unbiased look at the situation. The FCDA proposal was too serious to be rejected out of hand and it was too expensive to be adopted. Formation of an expert committee was an effective way of handling the proposal.

Reflecting the NSC discussions, the directive asked the committee to evaluate the shelter-building proposal as part of a study of American active and passive defense capability. It anticipated that the committee would find it necessary to explore other aspects of national security as they impinged on the nation's defense effort. The committee was titled the Security Resources Panel of the Science Advisory Committee to the FCDA, but, in fact, it was directly subordinate to the NSC and its members were considered NSC consultants.

The President, acting with the advice of his Special Assistant for National Security Affairs, Robert Cutler, called in H. Rowan Gaither, Jr., a West Coast lawyer and chairman of the boards of the Ford Foundation and The RAND Corporation, and asked him to head the Committee. Robert C. Sprague, an industrialist and an expert on continental defense, was asked to serve as co-director of the study. Together they recruited an eleven-man panel which included experts on various aspects of military policy.[6] In addition to Gaither and Sprague, it included William C. Foster, a former Deputy Secretary of Defense organization; James A. Perkins and William Webster, who had studied civil defense extensively; and, as staff director, Jerome Wiesner, an expert on weapons systems evaluation who is now [1961] President Kennedy's science advisor. Supplying additional technical competence for the panel were Robert C. Prim and Hector R. Skifter, and rounding out the group were Robert Calkins, John J. Corson, and James Baxter, who provided some of the expertise of the social scientist, particularly in economics and history.

The panel met briefly in the spring of 1957 and set in motion a series of

---

[6] The membership of the Gaither Committee and its advisory panel was released by the White House and printed in the *Congressional Record, loc.cit.*

technical studies by the large scientific staff which it had brought together.[7]
Much of this work was completed over the summer and the Committee mem-
bers arrived in Washington in the fall to devote full time to a study of defense
policy. At this point the Committee appointed as special advisors Colonel
George A. Lincoln of West Point and Paul H. Nitze, a former head of the
State Department Policy Planning Staff and now Assistant Secretary of Defense
(International Security Affairs).[8]

No public announcement had been made of the existence of the Committee
as it set to work in the old State-War-Navy Building on the study which was,
in a few months, to come to public attention as the Gaither Report.[9] The first
decision taken by the group was to broaden the scope of its inquiry to cover the
whole range of defense problems facing the country.[10] This is a phenomenon
which seems to typify such *ad hoc* studies. In the absence of agreed American
policy on most aspects of national security, it is difficult for any group to evaluate a proposal in any one area without considering other problems. In this case
the panel had been asked in effect how the United States could best spend an
additional sum for continental defense. But clearly defense is only one part of
the deterrence strategy and hinges on how well other parts function. It might
very well be true that the greatest payoff for continental defense would come,
for example, for investing in ballistic missiles. In the absence of any priority
plans for spending additional sums for various systems, the Committee was
forced to study the whole problem. In addition, the members were so prominent and had such definite opinions on the problems of American military
policy that it was natural for them to decide to use the rare opportunity of drafting a paper for the NSC to present their views on a wide range of topics.

Just as the Committee was beginning its study, Gaither was taken ill and
was hospitalized for several weeks.[11] Direction of the study fell to Sprague and
Foster, who became co-directors.[12] Each member of the Committee took responsibility for a particular section of the Report, but they all met frequently as a
group to discuss each other's work. The Committee drew on the technical studies
which had been prepared for it and had clearance to reports of the Defense

---

[7] A part of this staff was supplied by the Institute for Defense Analyses (IDA).
See *IDA Annual Report II,* March 18, 1958, pp. 6–7.

[8] Also serving as advisors to the panel were Albert C. Hill, General James Mc-
Cormack, and Edward P. Oliver of The RAND Corporation.

[9] The only leak regarding the Gaither study had come in August when Stewart
Alsop reported that the President had asked Gaither to study the possibility of employing new technological means of defense against atomic attack. He noted that the
Committee was attracting "top level" talents, but he warned that "it remains to be seen
whether anything solid comes of Gaither's assignment, in the present national mood of
complacency" (*New York Herald Tribune,* August 26, 1957, p. 12:7).

[10] Interview with Gaither, *New York Times,* December 25, 1957, p. 24:6.

[11] *Ibid.,* p. 24:5.

[12] *Ibid.,* December 21, 1957, p. 8:4.

Department and other agencies concerned with national security.[13] It also held frequent sessions with high military officials, including the Joint Chiefs of Staff. In addition, it consulted with a number of private experts on national security policy and with quasi-public experts, including members of The RAND Corporation.

An advisory panel for the Gaither Committee, appointed by the President, met periodically with the Committee members to fill in gaps in their expertise. Among the panel's eleven members were retired military officers; Frank Stanton, the president of CBS; two prominent Republican financiers, Robert Lovett and John J. McCloy, now head of the United States Disarmament Agency; and I. I. Rabi and Ernest O. Lawrence, two of the nation's top scientists.[14]

As the Committee members sifted through this mass of material, it became clear to them that the top echelons of the government did not fully appreciate the extent of the Soviet threat as it was described by the Pentagon and the CIA.[15] With a real sense of urgency, the Committee set to work to draft a summary report based on the individual studies prepared on various aspects of military policy. Just as the Report was being completed, the nation was shaken out of its complacency by the Soviet Union's announcement on October 4, 1957, that it had launched Sputnik. This event gave the Committee greater hope that the Administration would accept its recommendations.[16] A week later the Report was finished and presented to the President for discussion at an NSC meeting.[17]

II. Presenting the Report

On November 7, 1957, the President presided over one of the largest NSC meetings in history. Over forty people gathered in the White House for the presentation and discussion of the Gaither Report. In addition to the dozen top officials who regularly attended, the civilian secretaries of the services and the Joint Chiefs of Staff joined members of the Committee and its advisory panel and other top government officials. Almost everyone present had read the Report in the three weeks between its completion and the meeting, and chief interest was focused on what the reaction of the President would be.

The briefing on the contents of the Gaither Report was opened by Sprague,

13 Press release by Presidential Press Secretary James Hagerty, *ibid.,* December 22, 1957, p. 4:1.

14 The other members of the advisory panel were Admiral Robert C. Carney, General James H. Doolittle, James B. Fisk, General John E. Hull, Mervin J. Kelly, and James R. Killian.

15 Testimony of Dr. James R. Perkins in U.S. Senate, Subcommittee on National Policy Machinery, Committee on Government Operations, *Hearings,* Part II, 86th Congress, 2nd Session, Washington, D.C., 1960, p. 293 (cited hereinafter as *Jackson Hearings,* Part II).

16 Roberts, *loc.cit.,* p. 1328.

17 Perkins testimony, *Jackson Hearings,* Part II, p. 294.

and in turn Wiesner, Foster, Corson, and Webster came up to the podium to discuss different sections of the Report. Graphs and charts were used extensively to illustrate the points that it made.

The report presented to the NSC was in many ways not a typical NSC document. Unlike most NSC papers, the Gaither Report did not result from a compromise of the views of a number of departments and agencies. It did not represent an amalgam of considerations, including those of domestic finance. Furthermore, it was not bound by previous government policy decisions and specifically was not within the framework of budgetary limitations laid down by the President. The Report was thus able to call for measures which the Committee thought to be necessary and to present them in a dramatic fashion to the President and his top advisors. It deviated from government policy in a number of ways, but most fundamentally in the estimation of the danger facing the country and the amount of money which the United States should spend for defense.[18]

The report began with an analysis of Soviet and American capabilities. It compared the economic situation in the two countries, pointing out that the Soviets devoted 25 per cent of their GNP to defense, while the United States invested only 10 per cent. This meant that both countries were spending the same absolute amount and suggested that, given the faster Soviet growth rate, Russia would soon be devoting much larger sums to defense.[19] Tables were presented comparing Soviet and American industrial capability and military forces, and projecting relative strength into the future on the basis of present growth rates.[20] The report contrasted America's armed forces of two and one-half million men equipped and trained only for general nuclear war with the larger Russian army supplied with weapons for both nuclear and conventional warfare.

After drawing this rather grim picture of comparative capabilities, the briefing moved on to an analysis of the situation and a series of policy proposals. The major danger facing the country, according to the Committee, was the

---

[18] The text of the Gaither Report has not been made public. This account relies entirely on published sources. It draws heavily on Roberts' article (see note 5 above), about which Senator Clark declared on the Senate floor: "The importance of the article arises from the fact that it is well known by many Members of this body, including myself, that this newspaper account accurately and clearly states the major findings and conclusions of the Gaither Report" (*Congressional Record, loc.cit.,* p. 859). The information in the Roberts article has been supplemented and checked with news and news analysis articles in the *New York Times* and *Herald Tribune,* as well as columns by Arthur Krock, James Reston, Drew Pearson, and Stewart Alsop, and various magazine articles. In addition, speeches by members of the Committee and its Advisory Panel after the Gaither Report was presented, and their testimony at the Jackson Hearings, provided confirmation of the major points made in the Report.

[19] Cf. testimony by Robert Sprague, *Jackson Hearings,* Part I, p. 50.

[20] Roberts, *loc. cit.,* p. 1329.

vulnerability of the American strategic force.[21] The briefing dwelt at length on the problems of maintaining an effective second-strike force. It was pointed out that what must deter the Russians was not the force which the United States had, but the force which was capable of surviving an all-out Russian attack. The vulnerability of SAC was stressed. The planes of America's strategic force were exposed and concentrated in a way that made it extremely unlikely that they could survive a nuclear attack. The Committee warned that by the early 1960's, when Russia had an operational ICBM, she would be capable of destroying the American retaliatory force.[22]

The Gaither Report argued that the United States must give overriding priority to the development of an invulnerable second-strike force. It urged that for the short run everything possible be done to enable SAC to survive an attack.[23] It also called for an acceleration of the IRBM program.[24] For the longer run the Report urged that the missile production program be greatly accelerated. It warned that there was little value in acquiring missiles which were difficult to fire and which were exposed to enemy bombing. It urged therefore that American missiles be hardened and dispersed.

The Report laid the greatest stress on this point, reflecting the feeling of the Committee members that top Administration officials did not have a complete understanding of the problem of effectively deterring a Russian strategic strike.[25] The Report stressed the need to look at the problem in terms of the vulnerability of the force rather than its initial destructive capacity.[26] This was the problem which most bothered the Committee and gave its members the feeling that the government was dangerously underestimating the gravity of the Russian threat.

The Committee Report reflected the feeling that the vulnerability of the American strategic striking force was *the* great danger facing the country, but it also indicated that this was not the only military danger. The Report advised that, once the United States had recovered its full retaliatory capacity, the mili-

[21] The Committee's proposals on strategic vulnerability were heavily influenced by a classified RAND report prepared under the direction of Albert Wohlstetter. For a discussion of the RAND report, see Joseph Kraft, "RAND: Arsenal for Ideas," *Harper's*, CCXXI (July 1960), pp. 71–73.

[22] Alsop, *New York Herald Tribune*, November 25, 1957, p. 18:7, and *ibid.*, November 23, 1957, p. 1:8; Claude Witze, "Classified Report Says Soviets Can Neutralize SAC by 1960," *Aviation Week*, LXVII, (December 2, 1957), p. 28.

[23] Such a program would presumably include dispersal of SAC, some planes in the air, and a ready alert for the rest of the command.

[24] Drew Pearson, "Gaither Report Release Sought," *Washington Post and Times Herald*, December 18, 1957, p. 11:5.

[25] Cf. the testimony by Sprague, Baxter, and Perkins in *Jackson Hearings, passim.*

[26] For an unclassified but well-informed discussion of the problem of maintaining a stable strategic balance, see Albert Wohlstetter, "The Delicate Balance of Terror," *Foreign Affairs*, XXXVII (January 1959), pp. 211–34.

tary develop a capacity to fight limited wars.[27] The establishment of a nuclear balance would mean that local aggression would be the likely form of warfare. The Committee found that the American military force was unprepared to engage in limited wars. The Report suggested that the Middle East and Asia were the most likely areas in which local wars might erupt and it discussed the importance and the problems of keeping a war limited.[28] The second recommendation of the Committee was therefore that the United States train and equip its forces for conventional local warfare.

The Gaither Committee had considered the FCDA proposal to spend 40 billion dollars for blast shelters, and while conceding that such shelters would save some lives in the event of war, it assigned a very low priority to such construction. In making policy proposals to the NSC, the Committee ranked its suggestions, giving top priority to the need to revitalize the strategic force and improve America's limited-war capability. In the civil defense field, the Report gave first priority only to a comparatively modest proposal to spend several hundred million dollars in the following few years for research on various aspects of shelter construction and other non-military defense measures.[29] The Committee assigned secondary priority to a proposal to spend approximately 22 billion dollars for the construction of radiation (rather than blast) shelters. It was anticipated that any construction program would follow the research phase.

Foster briefed the NSC gathering on the defense reorganization proposals contained in the Gaither Report. He urged that the military command structure be organized to place primary reliance on joint and specified commands. The Report urged that a joint limited-war command be established. It suggested that most planning and research be carried on directly under the Joint Chiefs of Staff. Orders, it was argued, should go from the Secretary of Defense through the Joint Chiefs to the commands, and the services should concentrate on logistics and training operations. The Report also urged that the layers of Pentagon committees be eliminated and the Secretary of Defense be given his own military staff.[30]

---

[27] "Leak—and a Flood," *Newsweek*, L (December 30, 1957), p. 14; *New York Times*, November 23, 1957, p. 8:3; *New York Herald Tribune* November 23, 1957, p. 1:8.

[28] Krock, *New York Times*, December 22, 1957, IV, p. 3:2.

[29] The Committee's analysis of the civil defense problem reflected the influence of Herman Kahn of The RAND Corporation. The alternative civil defense proposals sketched here are elaborated in *Report on a Study of Non-Military Defense*, RAND, R-322-RC, July 1, 1958.

[30] That the Gaither Report included proposals on defense reorganization was indicated by Defense Secretary McElroy (*New York Times*, January 22, 1958, p. 15:4). The proposals were spelled out by Foster in a speech before the Student Conference on United States Affairs (SCUSA), IX, printed in *Proceedings of the Conferences*, West Point, N. Y., 1957, p. 9.

Although it was only forty pages long,[31] the Gaither Report also touched briefly on other subjects. It urged the government to increase spending for basic scientific research and stressed the importance to military policy of other areas of foreign policy. It also discussed the potential immediate impact on the American economy of the proposed increase in defense spending. The Report did not provide an exact estimate of the cost of all of its recommendations, but in indicated the need for rapid increases in the military budget to about 48 billion dollars per year in the 1960's.[32]

The entire NSC paid close attention during the presentation of the Report. The President had a copy of the writers text balanced on his knee and alternated between following along in the Report and watching the speaker.[33] When the briefing was concluded, a general discussion followed. The President thanked the group and indicated that he was impressed with the arguments contained in the Report and wanted to implement them. However, he expressed a nagging fear that the American people would not be willing to pay the bill.[34] For reasons which I shall explore in the next section, none of the department heads present was willing to give support to the proposals as a whole. In fact, Secretary of State John Foster Dulles spoke out strongly in opposition to the Report's recommendations. Support came from some members of the Committee's advisory panel. John J. McCloy and Robert A. Lovett, both prominent members of the American financial community as well as former Defense Department officials and active Republicans, argued that the American economy could afford to pay for the vitally needed measures outlined in the Report. They predicted that the people as a whole and the business community in particular would support the President if he urged increased spending for defense.[35]

The session broke up without any sense of the meeting having been arrived at. According to standard NSC procedure, the Report was formally sent to the departments concerned for their information and comments. In general, with reports of this nature nothing further happens. The reports are either used or rejected at the departmental level and the consultants return to their civilian jobs. However, in the case of the Gaither Report, there were significant further developments which throw considerable light on the policy process. Some of the Committee members made a determined effort to have their proposals implemented and at the same time they joined with others in seeking to have the Gaither Report made public.[36]

[31] Cutler testimony in *Jackson Hearings,* Part IV, p. 594.

[32] *New York Times,* December 21, 1957, p. 8:4.

[33] Charles J. V. Murphy, "The White House Since Sputnik," *Fortune,* LVII (January 1958), p. 230.

[34] Roberts, *loc. cit.,* p. 1328; *Newsweek,* L (December 30, 1957), p. 14.

[35] Roberts, *loc. cit.,* p. 1328.

[36] Some of the Committee members, including Gaither, returned to their civilian jobs and took no part in the campaign discussed below.

III. The Effect of the Report

Even in the early stages of their work on the Gaither Report, the members of the Committee were aware of the great discrepancy between the danger which was being described to them by the CIA and the military, and the sense of complacency at the top levels of the government. At least some of the Committee members became convinced that they had an obligation to make a strenuous effort to obtain the implementation of their proposals. Even as they worked on the Report, they were concerned with how best to proceed to secure its adoption by the Administration. In discussion with top civilian and military leaders, the Committee sought support for the types of recommendations it was considering. In the office of the President it attempted to make clear the nature of the problem facing the country.[37]

In seeking to influence national security policy-making at the Executive level, the Committee was dealing with a complex and bewildering decision-making process. It was clear, however, that in seeking to influence policy in a number of agencies, the most direct route was through the President. Some days before the NSC presentation, several of the most prominent members of the Committee and its advisory panel, including Gaither (who had just rejoined the group), Sprague, and Foster, met with President Eisenhower to discuss the content of the Report.[38] Again, at the NSC meeting, the Committee members had several hours in which to present him with their views.

The difference in tone of two speeches delivered by the President suggests that these briefings had at least a momentary impact on his thinking. On the evening of the NSC meeting of November 7, he gave the first of two scheduled addresses on the state of the nation's security.[39] The tone of this speech was one of reassurance. President Eisenhower stressed the present military strength of the United States:

> It is my conviction [he declared], supported by trusted scientific and military advisers, that . . . as of today the over-all military strength of the free world is distinctly greater than that of the Communist countries.
>
> •   •   •
>
> It misses the whole point to say that we must now increase our expenditures on all kinds of military hardware and defense. . . .[40]

The President recognized the need "to feel a sense of urgency," but he was determined that the United States not "try to ride off in all directions at once."

---

[37] Sprague testimony, *Jackson Hearings,* Part I, pp. 49–51.
[38] Murphy, *op. cit.,* p. 230; Cutler testimony, *Jackson Hearings,* Part IV, p. 594.
[39] Reprinted in *New York Times,* November 8, 1957, p. 10.
[40] *Ibid.,* p. 10:3, 8.

The speech stressed the need to support a sound economy and to keep down the level of defense expenditure.

A week later in Oklahoma City the President delivered the second part of his talk, entitled "Future Security."[41] While this speech did not directly contradict the first, its tone was completely different. He discussed again the problems of balancing expenditures and receipts and keeping the budget low, but this time he asserted: ". . . now, by whatever amount savings fail to equal the additional costs of security, our total expenditures will go up. Our people will rightly demand it. They will not sacrifice security to worship a balanced budget."[42] The President recalled one of his statements of the previous week, but made a significant addition:

> I assure you, as I did last week, that for the conditions existing today they [U.S. military forces] are both efficient and adequate. But if they are to remain so for the future, their design and power must keep pace with the increasing capabilities that science gives both to the aggressor and the defender.[43]

In spelling out the strategic requirements for the future, the President showed most clearly the effect which the Gaither Report was having, at least momentarily, on his thinking. He seemed to be recognizing that the country *did* have to ride off in many directions at once. The first requirement was, he declared, to maintain a nuclear retaliatory force such that an attack by the Soviets "would result, regardless of damage to us, in their own national destruction." In addition, forces were needed to deal with any form of local aggression, and home defense had to be improved. And, the President continued, more money must be spent on SAC dispersal and an acceleration of the missile program. "The answer," President Eisenhower asserted, "does not lie in any misguided attempt to eliminate conventional forces and rely solely upon retaliation. Such a course would be completely self-defeating."[44]

The members of the Gaither Committee quickly realized that the incorporation of some of their ideas into a Presidential speech did not mean that their proposals were about to be adopted by the Administration. The President might forward the Report to his writers with the suggestion that they use some of its ideas, but he was not likely to impose policy decisions on the operating agencies. Under the staff system used by President Eisenhower, policy proposals had to come up through the regular channels before he would act upon them. The Gaither Report had not sufficiently impressed or convinced the President for him to seize the initiative. He was not only reluctant to upset routine staff procedures, but also not eager to embark on the

[41] Reprinted in *ibid.,* November 14, 1957, p. 14.
[42] *Ibid.,* p. 14:6.
[43] *Ibid.,* p. 14:2.
[44] *Ibid.*

large-scale spending programs urged in the Report. The President was anxious to maintain his image as a man of peace and had no wish to approve a major expansion in the American military forces. He sought from his advisors assurance that the problems were being met rather than programs for new action.

After the failure of the initial attempt to alter Administration policy, the Gaither Committee, led by Foster, considered, and to some extent implemented three courses of action. These were: further attempts to reach the President directly, efforts to enlist the support of operating agencies, and measures to arouse the American public and elite groups to the dangers facing the country. The operating agencies were perhaps the most likely allies of the Gaither Committee, and the failure to gain the support of a single department suggests the built-in forces for stability in the process.

The Gaither Report had recommended across-the-board increases in spending. While assigning some priorities, it had not made any really hard choices among weapons systems. Here was seemingly a document which might have been acceptable to everyone. Why then was no support forthcoming?

The Gaither Committee had taken seriously the question which, in effect, had been put to it: how the government should spend vastly increased sums of money. It was clear, however, to the operating agencies who were at the same time wrestling with limitations imposed by the Budget Bureau that the "pie" was, in fact, not going to get bigger. The military services, the AEC, and the FCDA could only look upon the Report as a proposal to redivide the pie.[45] As such, they were naturally highly suspicious of its recommendations. The civil defense proposals caused the most difficulty. The FCDA was unwilling to accept a report which rejected its major proposal for blast shelters and which accepted implicitly the notion that civil defense spending should be weighed against possible military uses of the same funds. The military services were unwilling to support a plan which recommended a further splitting of the military-spending pie by including civil defense spending. The Report had given secondary priority to a 20-billion-dollar spending program within the next few years. The military could not have been expected to advocate such spending when their assumption was that it would come out of their funds.

In terms of individual proposals, the Committee members found some support within the services.[46] The Army, for example, was eager to endorse the proposals for a limited-war force. However, the individual recommendations were not new and only provided some additional leverage for the service

[45] In considering the reaction of Executive agencies, it should be kept in mind that the Administration placed very tight restrictions on access to the Report. For example, NATO Supreme Commander General Lauris Norstad did not see it (*New York Herald Tribune,* January 8, 1958, p. 2:2).

[46] The recommendations of the Gaither Committee were broken down into groups. The agencies concerned prepared papers on these proposals and they were discussed at a series of NSC meetings. See Cutler testimony, *Jackson Hearings,* Part IV, p. 594.

viewpoint.[47] In addition, the services were reluctant to endorse a paper which suggested that they had been derelict in their duty of keeping the country militarily strong. Although the Army would continue to argue for larger limited-war forces, it would never be ready to agree that it was not in a position to win a limited war. Similarly the Air Force was not willing to concede that its forces were as vulnerable as suggested by the Gaither Report. The military services could not admit the extensive deficiencies outlined by the Report. The formal comment of the Joint Chiefs was reportedly that the study did not contain any new proposals, but was "largely a summation and endorsement of steps under way or under consideration."[48]

The military services were also reluctant to commit themselves to what was in effect a new, more "rational" method of splitting up the defense pie. Under the "political" method the services could pretty well predict what their percent of the defense budget would be. There was no way to tell just what budget-making by outside experts would look like. There is a general distrust among operating officials of this type of advice. In discussing the weakness of private expert committees, Nitze explicated one of the problems facing the Gaither group:

> The most serious of these disadvantages is the possibility that the committee may be too far removed from executive branch responsibility to be fully effective. Those members of the executive branch who are actually responsible for carrying out policy . . . feel, perhaps rightly, that such groups are out of touch with the real problems with which the officials, in the end, must always deal. In any case, it is obvious that the committee, once its report has been presented, is in a poor position to help fight its recommendation through the decision stage. *Both of these difficulties characterized the reception of the Gaither Report* two years ago. . . .[49]

This fear of civilian expertise and the inability of the Gaither group to put any influence back of its recommendations combined with the motives dis-

---

[47] Cf. General Maxwell Taylor, *The Uncertain Trumpet*, New York, 1959, *passim*. Taylor, in discussing policy papers drafted for the NSC while he was Army Chief of Staff, makes it clear that most of the strategic concepts and recommendations of the Gaither Report were discussed frequently by the Joint Chiefs and the NSC before and after the Gaither Report was presented, although he does not mention the Report itself.

[48] *New York Times*, December 21, 1957, p. 8:3. This phenomenon clearly needs greater study. The strait jacket which has confined the military chiefs, preventing them from admitting extensive weakness even while pressing for more funds, has surely been an important restraint on the flow of information to the White House and to Congress. A comparison of the statements to Congress made by Army Chiefs of Staff on, for example, the adequacy of our capability for limited war and the statements they make after retiring indicates vividly the reality of this phenomenon. (I am indebted to Paul Hammond and Louis Kushnick for bringing this point to my attention.)

[49] Paul H. Nitze, "Organization for National Policy Planning in the United States," *Selected Materials*, p. 168 (italics added).

cussed above to explain the failure of administrative agencies to support the Gaither proposals. There were, however, two men in the government who might have been expected to take the over-all view necessary to endorse the recommendations of the Report. For vastly different reasons, however, neither the Secretary of State nor the Secretary of Defense was prepared to do so. Defense Secretary Neil McElroy viewed his job as that of an administrator. He refused to be drawn into strategic discussions or debates about the level of defense spending. He felt that he had been appointed because of his ability to run an organization efficiently and refused to deal with subjects about which he had no expertise.

Secretary of State John Foster Dulles was in no sense reluctant to discuss military matters. He had in fact become closely associated with the policy of massive retaliation which the Report indirectly, but clearly, challenged. Dulles was not prepared to endorse a program which called for large-scale spending and which committed the United States to local defense in the peripheral areas. In addition he felt that a shelter program would frighten America's allies. He feared that the Gaither proposals would use funds that otherwise could be used to increase foreign aid.[50] Dulles' influence with the President on foreign affairs suggests that his opposition must have been a major stumbling block in the efforts to convince the President to implement the Gaither proposals. Both the Treasury and the Budget Bureau were of course opposed to the Gaither recommendations because of the large-scale increase in spending proposed. With the Secretaries of State and Treasury and the Director of the Budget opposed to them and the Secretary of Defense refusing to express an opinion, the Gaither group members had to try either to influence the President directly[51] or to arouse American public opinion.

Following the presentation of their Report, the members of the Gaither Committee discussed possible courses of action among themselves and with experts on American foreign policy and defense. Following these weeks of informal discussion, a dinner meeting was held in Foster's Washington home in mid-December. Joining Foster were Frank Stanton and Paul Nitze, who had worked on the Gaither Report, and others, including Laurance Rockefeller and Elmo Roper.[52] Vice-President Richard Nixon attended on his own initiative but,[52] according to one report, with the approval of the President.[53] Part of the evening was taken up with a further briefing of the Vice-President. In

[50] Cf. Dulles' testimony before the Senate Foreign Relations Committee, *New York Times,* January 10, 1958, p. 1:5.

[51] For an excellent discussion of the kinds of problems that President Eisenhower would have faced in seeking to impose the recommendations of the Gaither Report on the operating agencies, see Richard Neustadt, *Presidential Power,* New York, 1960, *passim.*

[52] *New York Times,* December 11, 1957, p. 8:6; *New York Herald Tribune,* December 11, 1957, p. 1:3.

[53] *New York Times,* December 12, 1957, p. 11:1.

addition, Foster made two proposals to the group. He suggested that it aim at publication of a "sanitized" version of the Gaither Report.[54] He also urged the formation of a committee which would seek to convince the American people of the need for greater sacrifices in light of the grave Soviet threat. Foster argued that the release of the Report was essential to mobilize public opinion to support new programs. At the same time that it was trying to arouse public opinion, Foster suggested that his proposed committee continue the fight within the Executive for the implementation of the Gaither proposals.

In the discussion that followed, a general feeling was expressed of the need to do whatever was possible to alert the Administration and the people. Although Foster's proposal to set up a committee was received with much sympathy, the consensus was that the crucial problem lay with the President. If President Eisenhower could be convinced of the need to take bold action, he would have no difficulty arousing the American people. On the other hand, without the leadership of the President, it was felt that no group, whatever its composition, could reach the public.[55] Other members of the Gaither Committee shared this viewpoint. In testifying before the Jackson Committee, Sprague expressed his own opinion and in effect summed up the feeling of the meeting at Foster's home. In answer to a question as to what could be done to arouse the public, Sprague replied: "Senator, a citizen like myself, *or a group of citizens,* can do very little about this. I think there is one man in the United States that [*sic*] can do this effectively, and that is the President. I do not think there is anybody else."[56] Sprague's testimony reflected the bewilderment of the Foster group as to the position of the President. The Gaither Committee members were not sure whether the problem was to convince the President that their analysis was correct, or to get him to act on the basis of the information which he now had. As Sprague explained it:

I believe . . . that the danger is more serious than the President has expressed himself to the American public. I do not know whether he feels this or

54 Krock, *ibid.,* December 13, 1957, p. 26:5.

55 This feeling that the President constituted the key to the problem was reflected in a report by Samuel Lubell on a field trip made soon after Sputnik II. Lubell reported that "one thing I found especially striking was how closely the public's reactions corresponded to the explanatory 'line' which was coming from the White House. Relatively few persons repeated the criticisms which were being printed in newspaper editorials or were being made by members of Congress or by scientists. In talking about [S]putnik, most people tended to paraphrase what Eisenhower himself had said. . . . The public generally tended to follow the President's lead. In no community did I find any tendency on the part of the public to look for leadership to anyone else—to their newspapers or radio commentators, to Congressmen or to men of science. Nor, with some exceptions, could people be said to be in advance of the President, or to be demanding more action than he was." (Samuel Lubell, "Sputnik and American Public Opinion," *Columbia University Forum,* I, Winter 1957, p. 18.)

56 *Jackson Hearings,* Part I, p. 55 (italics added).

whether he does not. But I do not believe that the concern that I personally feel has as yet been expressed by the President to the American public. This is a complicated matter.[57]

The gathering at Foster's home broke up without a firm decision on whether or not to form a committee, but with a commitment on the part of those present to work for release of the Gaither Report to the public.[58] The efforts of members of the Gaither Committee[59] to have their Report released coincided with the demand of other groups.

IV. The Public Debate

The Gaither Committee had drafted its Report for the President without Congress' or the public's being aware of its existence. When the Report was presented to the NSC on November 7, 1957, the *New York Times* simply stated that an extraordinary meeting of the Council had been held and that members of the President's Science Advisory Committee were in attendance.[60] On November 9, the *New York Times* indicated that a special committee headed by Rowan Gaither had presented a report.[61] The contents of the Report leaked out slowly to the press. On November 23, 1967, the *Herald Tribune* published a fairly complete account of the contents of the Gaither study[62] and on December 20 the *Washington Post and Times Herald* ran a story by Chalmers Roberts which contained the most accurate report of the study's contents that had appeared to date.[63] As the nature of the Report and its sober conclusions came to the attention of the public,[64] a number of groups called for release of the official text. Thus, when the group meeting in Foster's home decided to press for publication of the Report, they were echoing the demand of others.

The group's desire to have the Report released coincided with a similar request from Congressional Democrats and some Republican Senators, includ-

---

[57] *Ibid.*

[58] Ultimately no committee was set up reflecting the view expressed by Sprague. A leak to the press about the gathering and its purpose made further action by the group more complicated and, in addition, embarrassed the Vice-President.

[59] Not all of the Gaither Committee joined in this effort. Gaither, for example, told a news conference that "a report like this to the Security Council and to the President is never made public. If all or part of it is made public, it would be an exception, and the first time such a thing was ever done." (*New York Herald Tribune,* December 25, 1957, p. 31.)

[60] *New York Times,* November 8, 1957, p. 10:8.

[61] *Ibid.,* November 9, 1957, p. 11:6.

[62] *New York Herald Tribune,* November 23, 1957, p. 1:8.

[63] See note 5 above.

[64] The leaks apparently came both from within the Administration and from members of the Gaither Committee.

ing Styles Bridges.[65] The debate over making the Report public attracted wide interest in the press and among the attentive elites. As Senator Clark made clear on the Senate floor, those demanding release of the Report were not concerned with learning its contents. Anyone with this goal had only to turn to one of several newspaper and magazine accounts. To make this task easier, Clark inserted in the *Congressional Record* the Roberts article and assured the readers of the *Daily Record* that it was accurate.[66]

Congressional Democrats, particularly those Senators who had been advocating higher defense spending, viewed the Report as a vindication of their views. The declaration by a group of distinguished citizens, including a number of prominent Republicans that the Eisenhower Administration had failed to act in the face of a grave danger to the survival of the country was excellent political ammunition. The Democrats had been trying to paint a picture of an inactive President failing to respond to the challenges of the time. Since it would be difficult to publish the Report without creating the impression that its findings were valid, release of the Report by the Administration itself could not fail to bolster this image, with important political advantages for the Democratic Party in the next Congressional election. Apart from the partisan political advantage which they saw in publication of the Report, the Senate Democrats were concerned about the state of the nation's defenses. The Preparedness Subcommittee was conducting extensive hearings and an official request for the Report came from Senator Lyndon Johnson, the majority leader and chairman of the subcommittee. The Johnson Subcommittee was briefed on the substance of the Report[67] but nevertheless pressed for its publication, apparently feeling that it would aid its case regarding the need for the nation to make greater sacrifices.

The Senate debate over release of the Gaither Report followed the presentation to Congress of the President's budget message. The proposed spending for national defense had greatly disappointed those who held the views outlined in the Report. In his State of the Union address on January 9 the President had declared that the United States must act "wisely and promptly" to maintain the capacity to deter attack or defend itself, and he had added: "My profoundest conviction is that the American people will say, as one man: No matter what the exertions or sacrifices, we shall maintain that necessary strength."[68] But while the budget message had called for some increase in spending, it was not enough in the opinion of those demanding release of the Gaither Report. The budget called for modest acceleration of the missile

[65] *New York Herald Tribune,* December 13, 1957, p. 1:3; *Washington Post and Times Herald,* December 21, 1957, p. 1:6.

[66] *Congressional Record, loc. cit.,* p. 858.

[67] *New York Times,* December 23, 1957, p. 6:4.

[68] Paul Zinner, ed., *Documents on American Foreign Relations, 1958,* New York, 1959, p. 2.

and SAC dispersal programs but, while recognizing the need for conventional forces and civilian defense, it called for a curtailment of these programs to save part of the amount needed for the expanded activities.[69]

Once again there was a sharp contrast between what was included in the President's speech and the actual policy position of the Administration. Any possibility that the President would have overruled his subordinates on this issue was eliminated by Eisenhower's stroke. He was not working during most of the period between presentation of the Gaither Report and the submitting of his budget to Congress.

Senators and Representatives urging release of the Report felt it would strengthen their hand in trying to convince the Congress to increase defense expenditures substantially and to generate pressures on the Administration to spend the money which was appropriated. As Senator Clark declared on the Senate floor: "That [Gaither] Report should have caused this Administration to have a far greater sense of urgency than it presently gives any indication of having."[70] He urged a reading of the Roberts article in order to "have an understanding of the very critical situation which confronts our country, and which I must say in all good conscience the President's budget does so little to remedy."[71]

Echoing this Congressional demand for release of the Report were newspapers and magazines which argued that the public was entitled to read this study by a group of distinguished citizens.[72] It was pointed out that various distortions had appeared in print, including one that suggested that the Committee had advocated preventive war.[73] Only the full publication of the Report

[69] Portions of the budget message relating to national security are printed in *ibid.,* pp. 15–23.

[70] *Congressional Record, loc. cit.,* p. 860.

[71] *Ibid.*

[72] See, for example, the editorials in the *New York Times,* December 13, 1957, p. 26:2; *New York Herald Tribune,* December 23, 1957, p. 16:1; and *Washington Post and Times Herald,* December 30, 1957, p. 14:1.

[73] In his column in the *New York Times* on December 20, 1957 (p. 26:5), Arthur Krock inferred from what he knew about the Gaither Report that it recommended a "first strike" strategy and speculated that this was why the Report was being kept secret. Two days later he was able to write that "it is authoritatively stated that this point was not included in the report" (*ibid.,* IV, p. 3:2).

The Communists sought to exploit this and other distortions of the Gaither Report. On December 26, Moscow and Peking broadcasts monitored in London charged that the "authors of the report are proponents of a limited war which would be fought with all types of modern nuclear weapons" (*New York Times,* December 27, 1957. p. 4:5). Then Soviet Premier Bulganin in a note to President Eisenhower on March 7, 1958, wrote that "the American press has been discussing for the past few weeks the idea of 'preventive war' against the U.S.S.R. which, according to such well-known American commentators as Hanson Baldwin, Arthur Krock and Drew Pearson, was advanced in a secret report to the National Council of Security [*sic*] by the so-called Gaither Committee" (*ibid.,* March 8, 1958, p. 2:8).

would stop the rumors and give the people an opportunity to evaluate this Report which, it was stressed, had been written by an extremely able group of private citizens. Members of the Gaither Committee pressed for publication of the "sanitized" version of the Report which Foster had offered to prepare. Publication would indicate that the Administration took the Report seriously and was prepared to implement it. It also would be an effective first step in what they hoped would be a Presidential campaign to arouse the American people to meet the crisis facing the nation. Those within the Administration who favored more spending for defense were pressing for release of the Report for the same reasons and leaked its contents. Private citizens concerned about the nation's defense effort were also seeking publication of the Report.

Despite these intense efforts, the President refused to yield. The official Administration position was set forth in a letter to Senator Johnson:

> . . . From time to time the President invites groups of specially qualified citizens to advise him on complex problems. These groups give this advice after intensive study, with the understanding that their advice will be kept confidential. Only by preserving the confidential nature of such advice is it possible to assemble such groups or for the President to avail himself of such advice.[74]

To publish this Report, the letter concluded, would violate the privacy of this relation and also the standing rule that NSC documents are not made public.[75] Earlier, at a press conference, the President had made it clear that he considered the Report confidential and had no intention of making it public.[76] A Presidential press release noted simply that "the report is, of course, a highly classified document."[77] James Reston, analyzing the Eisenhower Administration's refusal to publish the study, termed the Report an indictment of Eisenhower's policy and noted that publication would have weakened the President as well as the Republican Party.[78] The desire to withhold political ammunition from the Democrats undoubtedly played a part in the decision not to release the Report, as did the need to maintain the tradition of privacy for such reports. Probably more important, however, was the President's oft-repeated fear that the American people, if panicked, would

---

[74] *Ibid.*, January 23, 1958, p. 10:4.

[75] This was not an unimportant consideration. It undoubtedly heavily influenced the President's Special Assistant for National Security Affairs, Robert Cutler, who argued against the release of the Report. Cf. Robert Cutler, "Organization at the Policy Level," *General Electric Defense Quarterly*, II (January–March 1959) pp. 12–13. For a general discussion of this problem, see Francis E. Rourke, "Administrative Secrecy: A Congressional Dilemma," *American Political Science Review*, LIV, (September 1960) pp. 691–93.

[76] *New York Times*, January 16, 1958, p. 14:6.

[77] *Ibid.*, December 22, 1957, p. 4:1.

[78] *Ibid.*, January 22, 1958, p. 10:5.

ride off in all directions and demand spending which would be unwise and would damage the economy.[79] Thus, after Sputnik the President moved to calm the nation and ultimately rejected the fundamental assumption of the Gaither Report that the country was in grave danger. To take the unusual course of releasing the Report would imply that it presented an accurate picture and would increase pressures, which the Administration was fighting, to step up defense spending substantially.

The Eisenhower Administration continually denied that the Gaither Report showed the United States to be weak at the time the document was being written. It asserted that the government was already dealing with the problems outlined in the Report and that adequate measures were being taken on the basis of this and other reports to assure the nation's survival.[80]

Although they failed to have their Report released, many of the Gaither Committee members spoke out in an effort to alert the nation to the imminent dangers. Foster, in particular, appeared before numerous groups to argue the need for greater sacrifices. Sprague told the Jackson Committee that he had spoken to thirty or forty groups since serving on the Gaither panel, but, he continued, "I do not think this is very effective. I have done all that I can."[81] After a while the Committee members gave up the effort to arouse the public, with the realization that they could not compete against the President's words of reassurance.

V. *Conclusion*

The dispute about releasing the Gaither Report was a short episode in the continuing political debate over American defense strategy and the level of military spending necessary to implement the foreign and military policies of the United States. While the Report did not substantially alter the course of the struggle, it helped to bring some of the issues and pressures more sharply into focus. The fight over the release of the Report reflected almost exactly the larger dispute over defense spending. The American political process may be viewed as a struggle between clusters cutting across governmental structure, political parties, and interest groups and forming and reforming around various causes or specific proposals.[82] The defense debate which followed the launching of the Russian earth satellites brought into action two groups. One, which included the President, members of his Cabinet, some Congressional leaders, and members of the attentive elite, reacted to

---

[79] Krock, *ibid,* December 22, 1957, IV, p. 3:1.

[80] *Ibid.,* December 29, 1957, p. 1:3.

[81] *Jackson Hearings,* Part I, p. 56.

[82] For a similar model spelled out see Roger Hilsman, "The Foreign Policy Consensus: An Interim Research Report," *Journal of Conflict Resolution,* III (December 1959) pp. 361–82. I am indebted to H. Bradford Westerfield for the model used here.

Sputnik with programs for modest increases in national security spending but continued to assert that no large increase in spending or re-evaluation of strategy or governmental structure was needed. The other group, which included members of the Gaither Committee, Congressional Democrats, and some Republicans, directors of mass media, and national security experts, saw in the Sputniks an affirmation of its belief that the United States was faced with a grave threat to its survival and an opportunity to have its views prevail. Its members urged substantial increases in government spending and an awakening to the serious military, economic, and political challenge facing the United States and its allies. The Gaither Committee included a number of men who even before Sputnik had been arguing for substantial increases in defense spending. The other members of the Committee were won over to this view by the intellectual climate of the Committee as well as their review of the military situation. The Gaither Report provided a guide for the "pro-spending cluster,"[83] presenting a rationale for its position and a blueprint for the expenditure of the additional sums which were to be made available. It hoped that the Administration could be pressed to accept the Report drawn up by a committee of NSC as a guide for a substantially increased military effort.[84]

The Gaither Report was valuable to the pro-spending cluster in a number of ways. Within the Administration it provided an excuse for a further review of the American defense position, and brought before the President and his top advisors in a dramatic fashion the arguments for spending substantially larger sums of money. It contributed to an awareness, on the part of the President and his top advisors, of the vulnerability problem and of the crucial importance of the dispersal of SAC and the development of mobile, hardened missile systems. The Report was instrumental in convincing the

[83] The term "pro-spending cluster" is not meant to imply that its members favored spending for its own sake. While some people supporting the Gaither proposals were willing to back any plan for larger government spending, others (notably Sprague) were reluctant to endorse any spending programs; most of this cluster supported the Gaither proposals without being influenced by the spending implications.

[84] NSC 68 provides some interesting parallels to the Gaither Report and suggests the role it might have played if Sputnik had led to an Administration decision to increase the defense budget substantially. NSC 68 was drafted by a joint State Department-Defense Department committee, but it was, like the Gaither Report, prepared without considering domestic economic or political factors and without regard to the budget level set by the President. It included a complete review of the national security situation and called for a large increase in defense spending—providing a blueprint for the use of the funds. The Report was presented to the NSC just prior to the outbreak of the Korean War. It was initialed by President Truman just after the war started and served as the government's rationale for the expanded defense effort. It enabled the Administration to assert that spending was being guided by a long-range plan drafted prior to the war. See Paul Hammond, "NSC 68: Prologue to Rearmament," to be published in a volume sponsored by the Institute of War and Peace Studies of Columbia University.

Air Force of the need to develop invulnerable second-strike forces. In the longer run it was probably partly responsible for the acceptance by both the Eisenhower Administration and the Air Force of programs for SAC dispersal and missile hardening. It also undoubtedly contributed to the growing acceptance by the Administration of the need to have forces for limited war (although it did not alter the failure to implement this decision in the military budget). It contributed to the pressure which raised military spending slightly.

By leaking the Report, those in the Administration arguing for higher spending aided those with similar views in the legislature and the attentive public. For these groups the Report provided substantiation from a source with access to all government intelligence of the arguments frequently offered by critics outside the government.[85] The Report made it clear that Executive optimism was based not on additional information but on a different reading of the facts available to the public. The data and reasoning of the Gaither Report could be used to bolster the case for increased spending, the need to overcome the missile gap and to develop a limited-war force. In addition, the struggle over publishing the Report was dramatic and helped to publicize the somewhat technical arguments over military strategy and the demands for greater expenditure on defense. Their service on the Gaither Committee substantially increased the prestige and influence of its members. Some continued in advisory capacities in the Eisenhower Administration, and all are looked to as experts on national security problems.

The Report had a significant influence on the analysis of strategic problems by national security experts. The recent emphasis in the military policy literature on the problems of vulnerability and second-strike forces stems partly from the impact of the Gaither Report and the members of the Committee and its advisory panel.

While the Gaither Report served temporarily as a rallying point for those favoring increased spending, the anti-spending cluster was quick to recognize the danger which the Report posed. The President, battling the pressure for greater military expenditures, refused to make the Report public and stressed that it was just one of a number of reports made to him. Senate Republicans opposed to large spending urged that the Report be kept secret, noting with alarm the influence it had already had in increasing the pressures on the Administration. Had the Report been made public, it would have represented a significant victory for the pro-spending cluster and would have probably indicated that that group was gaining the upper hand in the Administration.

[85] For example, in the Rockefeller Brothers study on defense problems, whose recommendations closely parallel those of the Gaither Report; see Special Studies Report II, Rockefeller Brothers Fund, *International Security: The Military Aspect,* Garden City, N. Y., 1958 (reprinted in *Prospect for America: The Rockefeller Panel Reports,* Garden City, N. Y., 1961, pp. 93–155).

The complexities of military planning and strategy are such that public debate (and even the Congressional appropriations process) plays a limited role in making critical decisions. The failure of Congress to have the Gaither Report published indicated the ability of the Executive to limit Congress' role by cutting off vital information. Insofar as Congressional and public debate play a role in the process of national strategy, the Gaither incident was of some value. The public debate had an important educational function in bringing to the attention of the Administration an analysis of the situation different from that provided by operating agencies. By calling attention to problems of vulnerability and limited war, the Gaither Report increased public understanding of these crucial questions.

In part, Congressional activity on defense matters can be viewed as a massive lobbying effort to influence the political decision-making process of the Executive branch.[86] The analysis of the Gaither Committee added to the ability of Congress to influence the process and to press for increased and more rational spending. If the public dispute over the Gaither Report contributed to the political climate which has influenced President Kennedy, it may well have made a vital contribution to the nation's security.

Although when the contents of their reports are leaked or released, the work of civilian *ad hoc* NSC committees is of value to Congressmen and private citizens, such groups are primarily instruments of the President and need to be evaluated in terms of their possible contribution to the Executive decision-making process. Within the Executive the Gaither Report provided a fresh look at the nation's defense posture. It served as an effective communication procedure to bring before the attention of the President and his principle advisors concerns which were being felt at the middle and upper levels of the operating agencies but which had not filtered through to the White House.

The Committee Report provided clear, well-reasoned statements of the problems of vulnerability and limited war, of the role of dispersal and hardening, and of the problems and opportunities of civil defense. It undoubtedly made a major contribution to the understanding of these problems by top officials. The panel was able to point out serious deficiencies where it found them because it was not responsible for past policy action, and the President could receive such advice because he anticipated being able to keep it private. The Committee also advanced a number of new policy proposals, particularly in the field of defense reorganization, which were not likely to come from the armed services themselves.[87]

Having made its proposals, the Gaither Committee found that it lacked

[86]Cf. Samuel P. Huntington, "Strategic Planning and the Political Process," *Foreign Affairs*, xxxvii (January 1960), pp. 285–99.

[87] Some of its proposals were adopted in the 1958 reorganization of the Defense Department.

the power base to fight for their implementation. But clearly the value and activity of such a group are not measurable in terms of its political influence on the decision process. The Committee furnished the President with a program, which, while perhaps not very precise or well thought-out in detail, could have served as a guide for action. The Committee thus fulfilled its primary purpose of providing an additional source of information for the President, unencumbered by future and past policy responsibility. The operating agencies can only view such committees as threats to their prerogative. But to a strong, vigorous President they could prove to be a powerful tool for overcoming bureaucratic and political opposition to the implementation of new, vitally needed programs.

3

A President's
War
on Poverty

JOHN C. DONOVAN

Once the President [Lyndon B. Johnson] made the decision to declare war on poverty and to bring forth a new legislative proposal which would encompass a set of programs bearing a distinctly LBJ brand, the actual preparation of the antipoverty bill became a major, all-consuming effort on the part of high-level executive staff people, most of whom were several layers removed from the President.

The Council of Economic Advisers . . . had been at work for some time preparing a staff analysis which was to provide a profile of poverty in the United States. The Bureau of the Budget, which has the central responsibility for preparing the president's budget and his legislative program, had already received from the executive departments scores of specific suggestions either for new programs or for means of implementing existing activities. In addition, there were certain legislative proposals which had been introduced in Congress as part of the Kennedy program still on the Hill awaiting action. The Youth Employment Act, for example, introduced in the Eighty-eighth Congress as S1, proposed a two-pronged attack on the problems of jobless youth between the ages of sixteen and twenty-one. Title I of the act would establish a youth conservation corps, and Title II would authorize

Reprinted by permission from John C. Donovan, *The Politics of Poverty*, New York, Pegasus Press, a division of Western Publishing Company, 1967, pp. 27–38.

the secretary of labor to assist states and cities, by means of grants, to develop local community service occupations. There was also the possibility of establishing a national service corps—often referred to as a "domestic" peace corps—although this had been so much a special Kennedy family project that a new president might find it difficult to impose his imprint.

These is reason to think that the White House at first inclined in the direction of using these legislative items from the Kennedy past as vehicles for the new Johnson program. The January 5 presidential statement endorsing the "One-Third of a Nation" report, for example, specifically called for the enactment of the Youth Employment Act. There were also words of praise for the national service corps concept. In fact, the President went on to say: "I will include funds for them in the forthcoming budget."

Thus, as late as January 5, 1964, the presumption would have been that President Johnson was about to place the weight of his office and his own legislative skill behind two more Kennedy measures, the Youth Employment Act and the domestic peace corps, which were bogged down on the Hill, just as he was to do for civil rights legislation, the tax cut, aid to education, and Medicare. The need for a brand new omnibus antipoverty bill was neither obvious nor certain in the first days of January, when it was not yet clear that the President wished to have a major new program which he could call his own.

It now seems reasonably clear that President Johnson decided shortly after January 5 that he wanted a new legislative proposal to support the declaration of the war on poverty which was announced in his State of the Union message on January 8, and that the new approach was to provide for a broader attack on the causes of poverty than would have been possible under the Youth Employment Act and domestic peace corps proposals.

Shriver's Task Force

On January 31 President Johnson announced that he had asked Sargent Shriver, director of the Peace Corps, to serve as his special assistant in developing strategy for the war on poverty. Shriver brought to his new assignment the aura of Peace Corps success, a quality of creative imagination, a talent for public relations and salesmanship, and a solid reputation on Capitol Hill. He was a dramatic personality, a man with a reputation as a practical idealist who "gets things done." Shriver in turn immediately obtained the services of Adam Yarmolinsky from the Defense Department, Daniel P. ("Pat") Moynihan from the Labor Department, and James Sundquist from Agriculture to serve as his task force in preparing the new bill.

The choices are interesting. Yarmolinsky was special assistant to Secretary Robert McNamara; a brilliant young lawyer, Yarmolinsky was considered an authentic "whiz kid." He had worked before for Shriver, in the period prior to the Kennedy inauguration, as a key member of the talent search team. During the six months in which the poverty program moved through the legislative labyrinth, Yarmolinsky was to become Shriver's principal deputy, in fact if not in name. Pat Moynihan, a liberal New York intellectual-politician, had first worked as an Averell Harriman staff man in Albany, later served as assistant secretary of labor upon the recommendation of Willard Wirtz shortly after Mr. Wirtz succeeded Goldberg in the Cabinet chair. Sundquist came to the Shriver task force from the Office of the Undersecretary of Agriculture, where he served as the principal deputy. This might be slightly misleading inasmuch as Sundquist was also a former Governor Harriman aide who had served in the White House during the Truman years and who had also served most recently as administrative assistant to Senator Joseph Clark, the Senate's leading spokesman on manpower and employment issues.

When President Johnson decided to initiate a major new domestic program of his own, it was a team of Eastern liberal intellectual-politicians under the leadership of a member of the Kennedy family establishment which was given responsibility for formulating it. No one from Texas played a key staff role in the formulation of the antipoverty legislation with the possible exception of Bill Moyers, who was presumed to be close to Mr. Shriver as well as to Lyndon Johnson.

There is by this time a legend in the making which grossly oversimplifies reality. The legend suggests that Yarmolinsky, Moynihan, and Sundquist, presumably with Sargent Shriver looking over their shoulders, wrote the Economic Opportunity Act all by themselves. There were other important participants in the process, one may be sure. Among them: Wilbur Cohen, the peripatetic assistant secretary for legislation in the Department of Health, Education, and Welfare. Cohen was not only one of the nation's leading academic experts on social security legislation, he was also a skilled lobbyist with a reputation for looking after HEW's bureaucratic empire; he was not likely to sit quietly in a corner when a significant new education and welfare program was in the making. The professional staff of the President's Committee on Juvenile Delinquency was a key group. It was true that it tended to be composed of men who had been selected by Attorney-General Robert Kennedy, and that the juvenile delinquency committee was considered a Robert Kennedy special activity; on the other hand, the committee's professional staff collectively represented most of the expertise in the federal government in what was to become "community action," a significant concept in the new program. Inevitably, there also were important, though often publicly anonymous, men from the Bureau of the Budget, that all-powerful, elite presidential staff agency which was not likely to let an *ad hoc* Shriver-led team take over completely a Bureau of the Budget function, the development of new legislation for the President. After all, the Bureau of the Budget had a new boss, and it was anxious to show Mr. Johnson what *it* could do.

There were other agencies and departments which had bureaucratic interests to protect as well as ideas to offer. Chief among them were Labor and HEW, whose views presumably were represented by Moynihan and Cohen, respectively. The others: the Council of Economic Advisers, Interior, Commerce, Agriculture, Justice, the Small Business Administration, and the Housing and Home Finance Agency.

But Mr. Shriver alone had the presidential mandate, and he was in charge. No one ever doubted that important fact. Since Mr. Shriver was known to have no great receptivity toward old-line bureaucrats, even old-line agencies soon learned to keep that type away from him. To an exceptional degree, then, the forces Shriver represented in this operation were those of the presidential-Cabinet policy-making group, which at this time was still overwhelming Kennedy in style, inclination, tempo, and mood.

In typical "Kennedy" fashion, the men of the Shriver task force lost no time in turning to idea men outside government for specific program concepts, especially as they soon discovered that the ideas emanating from the executive department reflected a great deal of conventional wisdom and more than a little bureaucratic self-interest.

The most influential program concepts came from economist Robert Lampman, foundation executive Paul Ylvisaker, Mitchell Sviridoff, a community leader from New Haven, Connecticut, and the techincal experts on the staff of the President's Committee on Juvenile Delinquency. It was Lampman's studies of the incidence of poverty which Walter Heller used to document his original brief in May and which also led the way to the chapter on poverty which appeared in the President's 1964 Economic Report. Ylvisaker, who was in charge of the public affairs program for the Ford Foundation, pioneered the development of the "gray areas" program which in turn helped pave the way for the community action program in the Johnson war on poverty.[1] It was Ford Foundation money which underwrote the successful series of pilot projects in New Haven, and it was in New Haven that a talented group of people, led by Mayor Richard Lee and Mitchell Sviridoff, put together what is perhaps the best local community action program in the nation. In addition, there was the small staff working for the President's Committee on Juvenile Delinquency, which had developed relationships with nearly every significant program of social experimentation in the leading cities. This was the intellectual and professional "bank" whose resources Sargent Shriver was to draw upon most heavily in drafting the Economic Opportunity Act of 1964.[2]

---

[1] See Charles Silberman, *Crisis in Black and White* (New York, 1964), for more detail on the Ford Foundation gray areas program. Silberman is critical of Ylvisaker's approach and, in fact, defends Saul Alinsky's direct action methods.

[2] A great deal has been made at one time or another about the contribution of Michael Harrington to the war on poverty. There can be no doubt that Harrington's brilliant book, *The Other America* (New York, 1962), touched the national conscience.

During the search for ideas which could be translated into program concepts, Shriver and his small team of assistants also heard, as one might expect, from church, labor, business, farm, and academic and civil rights spokesmen.[3] In view of what was to become a difficult issue later, it is worth noting now that the American poor themselves did *not* participate in the process which led to the creation of the act. (It goes almost without saying, of course, that it is in no way rare that the poor did not participate in the design of a major administrative proposal for legislation.)

The men who wrote the draft bill in the executive branch worked against awesome time pressures. Shriver was given the assignment on January 31; the bill went to the Hill on March 16. The discussion and negotiation process in bill-drafting is inherently time-consuming. The Shriver style of work encouraged sessions which typically ran into the late evening hours. The remarkable fact is that in about six weeks the task force, aided by a group of legal draftsmen from various executive departments headed by Assistant Attorney-General Norbert Schlei, were able to put together a bill which was ready to go to the Hill. Ordinarily, a routine updating of an established department's legislation might be expected to take six months in the drafting.

The Economic Opportunity Act of 1964 represented an interesting mixture of old and new. Although the bill in its original form carried six titles, only two are of major importance to an analysis of the political potential of the war on poverty. Title I established three youth programs, two of which differed only slightly from similar provisions in the Kennedy youth employment opportunities bill which had been passed by the Senate and reported by the House committee before languishing in the House Rules Committee. The third youth program, a work-study program for college students, had been considered earlier as a possible amendment to the National Defense Education Act. Title II, on the other hand, bearing the label "Urban and Rural Community Action Programs," was without precedent as a legislative matter. Under ordinary circumstances, a new multimillion-dollar proposal coming to Capitol Hill for the first time would be certain to receive careful scrutiny by appropriate congressional committees, regardless of program content. . . . [I]t is worth noting now that the idea [of community action] came from the staff of the President's Committee on Juvenile Delinquency.[4]

We are told that President Kennedy read Harrington's book. We know that Harrington is one of the "experts" Shriver called to Washington. Harrington is both an attractive and energetic evangelist for social reform, but the precise nature of his influence on any program idea in the Economic Opportunity Act has not been identified

[3] At the time the bill went to Capitol Hill, the administration released a list of 137 names, described as "a partial list of people Mr. Shriver consulted in developing the poverty program."

[4] See Brian Smith, "The Role of the Poor in the Poverty Program: the Origin and Development of Maximum Feasible Participation" (unpublished Master's thesis, Department of Public Law and Government, Columbia University, 1966). Smith convincingly

If it is difficult to understand the influences of professionals in the formulation of a key legislative concept with such an obvious political potential, it may be that Mr. Shriver found this particular group easy and natural to work with because of the close ties to Robert Kennedy's office. But it is additionally significant that key people in the Bureau of the Budget, after looking over all of the program suggestions from the various executive departments, were disappointed to find little that was strikingly new—until they hit upon community action which was being actively propagated by the juvenile delinquency committee staff. At least part of the responsibility for community action and "maximum feasible participation of the poor" should be assigned to the Bureau of the Budget, without whose support these new ideas might not have found their way into the Economic Opportunity Act, certainly not in the form of a $315 million allocation during the first year. This may help explain the firm parental interest which the Bureau of the Budget later displayed in community action, even in public, an unusual posture for this non-publicity-seeking presidential staff agency. Bibby and Davidson, in their study, go further; they suggest that Bureau of the Budget and juvenile delinquency staff people encouraged Robert Kennedy to get in touch with a somewhat skeptical Shriver. According to this version, the Attorney-General ". . . persuaded [Shriver] to emphasize the Community Action programs as Title II of the new bill."[5]

Congress Ratifies LBJ's Program

The first opportunity for congressional influence to be felt in the development of the Johnson administration's antipoverty program came in the House of Representatives where the Ad Hoc Subcommittee on the Poverty Program, a subcommittee of the House Education and Labor Committee, opened hearings on March 17 under the chairmanship of Congressman Adam Clayton Powell. The committee made relatively few changes in the bill. In part this can be accounted for by the way in which Republican committee members were turned aside. Republicans on the House committee, led by Representative Peter Frelinghuysen of New Jersey and Representative Charles Goodell of New York, who had often been able to offer suggestions for amendments to similar proposals in the past and occasionally win committee acceptance,

---

shows that community action and "participation of the poor" came directly from the juvenile delinquency committee staff. Smith, who interviewed several key government officials, identifies Richard Boone of the committee staff as the person who was most directly responsible. I am convinced on the basis of my own research and many informal conversations with knowledgeable individuals, including members of the Shriver task force, that this is an accurate assessment.

[5] John Bibby and Roger Davidson, *On Capitol Hill,* (New York, 1967), p. 236.

now learned that Mr. Shriver was not interested in Republican-sponsored amendments to the administration bill. Mr. Shriver was more than ever the President's spokesman inasmuch as the President had announced the day the bill went to Congress that Shriver was to be his chief-of-staff in directing the war on poverty.

Since nothing had occurred to alter the basic arithmetic of voting on domestic issues in the House (except the advent of Mr. Johnson to the presidency), the blunt turning aside of Representative Goodell and his group seemed unusually provocative. Further intensifying anxieties was the announcement that Congressman Phil Landrum of Georgia was to be the chief sponsor of the bill in the House. Landrum seemed hardly the ideal choice from the viewpoint of civil rights leaders. Organized labor remembered that Landrum had played a key role in the Landrum-Griffin Labor Reform Bill in 1959, a bill generally thought to be antilabor.

Although there were muffled groans from a few professional liberals, Andrew Biemiller, chief lobbyist for the AFL-CIO, made no public protest. The tactical plan seemed clear. Northern administration loyalists would obviously vote for a bill so close to the President's heart. Landrum was to help line up a sufficient number of Southern votes to make this a Democratic program. If ambitious young Republicans wanted to oppose a war on poverty in a presidential election year, so be it. This was the strategy pattern within which the Economic Opportunity Act was sent to the Congress. It is hard to imagine that such a daring strategy was set by anyone other than the President himself.

The House Ad Hoc Subcommittee heard testimony from a long parade of witnesses, most of whom favored the bill. From the President's official family came Shriver, Heller, McNamara, Celebrezze, Wirtz, Hodges, Freeman, Kennedy, Weaver, Foley and Udall. Their testimony was largely in terms of generalities; the questioning by and large, was anything but probing. If this was the program the President wanted, the Democratic majority on the committee was not interested in creating any special obstacles in the spring of 1964.

Seventy-nine witnesses appeared during twenty days of House committee hearings, seventy of them speaking in favor of the bill. The Chamber of Commerce, the National Association of Manufacturers, and the American Farm Bureau Federation predictably found little merit in another welfare "spending" proposal. In view of later developments, there is some irony in the fact that five mayors, including Mayor Richard Daley of Chicago, urged prompt passage of the Economic Opportunity Act.

Although it would be almost impossible to imagine a legislative proposal with a greater potential for arousing congressional anxiety than community action, Title II came through the Congress intact in 1964. Attorney-General Robert Kennedy, administration spokesman for Title II, testified before the

House committee. He had this to say about the "maximum feasible participation" requirement:

> The institutions which affect the poor—education, welfare, recreation, busi-
> ness, labor—are huge, complex structures, operating far outside their con-
> trol. They plan programs for the poor, not with them. Part of the sense
> of helplessness and futility comes from the feeling of powerlessness to affect
> the operation of these organizations.
>
> The community action programs basically change these organizations by
> building into the program real representation for the poor. This bill calls for
> maximum feasible participation of residents. This means the involvement of
> the poor in planning and implementing programs: giving them a real voice
> in their institutions.[6]

Community action provided a direct financial relationship between the
federal government and the local community. The federal funds might even
go to non-governmental groups, including those at the neighborhood level.
Community action encouraged the development of local projects whose purpose might well include the stimulation of fundamental change in urban
ghettos and in slum schools. Title II explicitly proposed that this was to be
carried on with "maximum feasible participation" of poor people in local
neighborhoods. (Congressmen might have been expected to read this "in
local *precincts.*") In community action the revolutionary aspects of the war
on poverty came to a focus; power was to be given to those not included
in any establishment.

Oddly enough, Congress did not probe the potentially explosive Title
II. Congress in 1964 either did not understand community action or it did not
bother to take a close look.[7]

This is not to suggest that the Congress did nothing. It was Congress
which added two new programs—aid for adult literacy education and assistance for migrant farm workers. Representative Edith Green (Democrat of
Oregon) insisted that the Job Corps be open to women as well as to men.
The House committee came dangerously close to reviving the church-state
controversy when a compromise was reached under which parochial schools
could receive aid for non-sectarian "remedial non-curricular" programs. The
House committee Democrats had no difficulty voting down a Republican
alternative bill sponsored by Representative Frelinghuysen. The House committee also eliminated a program of incentive loans to businessmen.

---

[6] *Hearings Before the Subcommittee on the War on Poverty Program: The Economic
Opportunity Act of 1964,* Part 1, 1964, p. 305.

[7] Daniel P. Moynihan has reported that community action as a concept was not
changed at all from the first task-force draft through the enactment of the bill in final
form. See his article "What is Community Action?" (*The Public Interest,* Vol. 5, Fall
1966), pp. 3–8.

The portion of the bill which drew the greatest congressional resistance had to do with alleviating *rural* poverty, and the greatest pressure to amend that portion (Title III) was felt not in the House where the voting was thought to be close, but in the Senate where the Administration's strength was great. The Senate leadership agreed to delete a provision authorizing outright grants to impoverished farmers, and substituted a loan program. The Senate also accepted an amendment sponsored by Senator Frank Lausche (Democrat of Ohio) which deleted a plan to set up farm development corporations to buy blocks of land to be sold at lower prices for family farms.

Shriver and the Southern Critics

The Senate passed the Economic Opportunity Act (S.2642) in a 61–34 roll call vote on July 23 [1964]. The House passed the bill in amended form on August 8 by a roll call vote of 226–185, a wider victory margin than the White House expected. Representative Landrum, powerfully aided by White House muscle, converted a good many Southern members to the cause of social reform and community action as 60 Southern Democrats joined 22 Republicans and 144 Northern Democrats to form the House majority. Only 40 Southern representatives voted "nay." They were joined by 145 Republicans.

The administration paid a price for some of this Southern support. There was, first, the matter of a gubernatorial veto which originally appeared as a Senate amendment and was later incorporated by Representative Landrum in the House version. In its final form, the veto applied to Titles I and II, giving the governor thirty days to review any proposed projects within his state.

Sargent Shriver paid an even higher price for Southern support. Adam Yarmolinsky who was slated to become the deputy director of the new Office of Economic Opportunity somehow had attracted the active animosity of several Democratic congressmen. The so-called case against Yarmolinsky will probably never be known, but it is a fair guess that it resulted from a mixture of labels—"leftist," "abrasive," "intellectual," and "whiz kid" among them. The terms of the deal upon which the Southern congressional critics insisted were simple; the price of their support in the House was that Yarmolinsky was to have no part in the administration of the new program.[8]

As time went on, there was reason to believe that Shriver may have paid a higher price than, perhaps, he had originally realized. Yarmolinsky was almost the only man in the embryonic Office of Economic Opportunity who knew where all the pieces in the jigsaw puzzle were located. Time and again, Yarmolinsky alone had represented Shriver in complex high-level negotiations

---

[8] Rowland Evans and Robert Novak, *Lyndon B. Johnson: The Exercise of Power* (New York, 1966), pp. 432–433.

with federal departments and with the Bureau of the Budget; only he knew the precise terms of a number of detailed administrative arrangements which went to the heart of the operations of an enormously complicated new program. Indeed, Yarmolinsky sometimes appeared to responsible operating officials in other agencies to be the only Shriver subordinate who could speak for his boss with any real authority and make it stick. In any event, from that day forward, Mr. Shriver evidently has had great difficulty finding a deputy with whom he could work. . . . Mr. Shriver appears to be the kind of inspirational leader who needs a strong deputy.

The congressional role in developing the Economic Opportunity Act was essentially a minor one. The evidence supports the judgment that ". . . Congress was asked not to draft the war on poverty, but rather, to ratify a fully prepared Administration program, and invited, though hardly encouraged, to propose marginal changes."[9] The Economic Opportunity Act moved from drawing board to enactment in just about six months. It is doubtful that any single piece of domestic legislation of similar importance and scope had moved so rapidly and easily through the Congress in a quarter of a century. One would have to go back to FDR's one hundred days in 1933, that classic time of executive dominance over Congress, to find a clear precedent.

The Economic Opportunity Act is a prime example of executive legislation; it was written in the executive branch and subsequently endorsed by the Congress. It is part of a twentieth-century development in which the president's role as "chief legislator" has been "institutionalized" not only in the sense of establishing the congressional agenda, but also for proposing the specific content of bills. One result is that "the classic legislature function—bringing political combatants together to hear their claims, and then resolving these claims—is becoming, in the complex modern polity, less and less the exclusive domain of Congress."[10]

What does this portend for the vitality of the legislative branch? We have tended to believe that political bargains are struck in the Congress; the executive, according to this view, ratifies the bargains when the president signs them into law and when the bureaucrats begin to administer the programs. Is the tendency now to reverse the traditional institutional roles? If the pattern we have seen at work in the origins of the Johnson war on poverty were to prevail, what would the congressional role become?

Perhaps it would be wise not to bury Congress prematurely. The congressional role in writing the antipoverty program was indeed a minor one in 1964, but the circumstances were highly unusual. Congress did add two programs and emasculate another; it did provide for a gubernatorial veto— of sorts. Likewise, Congress, through the work of its appropriations com-

[9] Bibby and Davidson, *op. cit.,* p. 238.
[10] *Ibid.,* pp. 249–250.

mittees, cut back the funds for the first year from $962.5 million to $800 million. Furthermore, Title I of the Economic Opportunity Act borrowed heavily from a Kennedy youth bill which had passed the Senate and moved as far as the Rules Committee in the House before Mr. Johnson assumed the presidency.

Only Title II was strikingly new, and it *was* the creature of the executive branch. Its unprecedented use of federal funds and federal encouragement to arouse the poor against established political organization and established welfare and educational bureaucracies scarcely received a glance from the Congress in 1964.

The important question raised by the example of the Economic Opportunity Act is: What is the congressional attitude in the long run likely to be toward a program it did not help create, once that program stirs "controversy"?

$$\rightleftharpoons 4$$

The Presidency
and Education

THOMAS E. CRONIN

When Lyndon Johnson assumed the presidency, education was both a major political item and the source of cleavage and tension among congressmen and the education lobbies. Kennedy's stand on the issue had attracted understanding, support, and unprecedented public attention, and Johnson lost little time in invoking Kennedy's dreams in his effort to continue and enlarge the federal program. In 1964, Johnson campaigned actively in support of education measures. Behind the scenes, Francis Keppel, S. Douglass Cater, and task force chairman John Gardner were forging alternative strategies for building the necessary political coalitions to pass major education bills.

Johnson demonstrated continually that he deeply cared about maximizing educational opportunities, particularly for the disadvantaged. As a young elementary and secondary school teacher, and later as a regional administrator of the National Youth Administration, he had seen at first-hand the difficulties of teaching in poverty areas with inadequate facilities. Lyndon Johnson, making no secret of his desire to be remembered as an "Education President," looks to his education program as an important, as well as popular, policy area in which to make a major personal contribution. Occupants of the White House frequently seize upon selected key issues, not only for political motives but to satisfy personal ambition.[1] It is as if Johnson in his commitment to education

Reprinted by permission from Thomas E. Cronin, "The Presidency and Education," *Phi Delta Kappan,* vol. XLIX, No. 6, February, 1968, pp. 295–299.

[1] For an analytical discussion of ambition theories of politics see Joseph A. Schlesinger, *Ambition and Politics.* Chicago: Rand McNally, 1967.

were seeking to disprove that informal advice given to a young Franklin Roosevelt by that celebrated descendent of Presidents, Henry Adams:

> Young man, I have lived in this house many years and seen the occupants of that White House across the square come and go, and nothing that you minor officials or occupants of that house can do will affect the history of the world for long.[2]

Machinery of Advice

No President since Franklin Roosevelt can complain about a dearth of advice; opinions from the most celebrated specialists pour in along with advice from many an earnest if ill-informed citizen. Counsel comes through the mail, in editorials and columns, via electronic media, from cabinet members, from bureau memoranda, and increasingly from the frequently cited but seldom seen presidential advisory councils, commissions, and consultants. Of course an abundance of advice and prescription also emanates from Congress, although rarely do new ideas make their debut on Capitol Hill. Few tasks, however, are more fruitless than trying to trace the original parentage of the more significant new ideas in public policy. To say new legislation comes from the Executive Branch is far too simplistic. As Adam Yarmolinsky has recently suggested: "One observes that the theory of simultaneous—and seemingly spontaneous—invention applies here."[3]

The entire Washington political community now turns to the presidency for articulation of new directions in public policy.[4] Post-World War II administrations have witnessed vast expansion in the President's Executive Office, to include, for example, a Council of Economic Advisors, an Office of Science and Technology, an enlarged Bureau of the Budget, staff assistants for minority affairs, and a special assistant for health, education, and welfare concerns. From May to December, the White House domestic staff is engaged in developing the President's legislative program. This process culminates in the January State of the Union address, Budget and Economic messages, and a series of major legislative messages (recently numbering at least a dozen, e.g.: Education, Children and Youth, Older Americans, Crimes, etc.).

One of the frequently exercised prerogatives of the President is the calling of national conferences on major policy topics. Examples are the White House Conferences on Children and Youth, begun by Theodore Roosevelt,

[2] Cited in Richard Hofstadter, *American Political Tradition*, New York: Vintage Books, 1960, p. 315.

[3] Adam Yarmolinsky, "Ideas into Programs," *The Public Interest*, No. 2, Winter, 1966, p. 73. (See also this book, pp. 91–100.)

[4] Richard E. Neustadt, "Presidency and Legislation: Planning the President's Program," *American Political Science Review*, December, 1955; and Louis W. Koenig, *The Chief Executive*. New York: Harcourt, Brace & World, 1964, pp. 126–85.

and the more recent White House Conferences on Education. Such convocations are the focus of much publicity—but celebration rather than cerebration usually predominates. Then, too, there can be embarrassing liabilities. See, for example, the charges and countercharges which surrounded the selection of delegates at Eisenhower's White House Conference on Education or the critical retrospective assessment of Johnson's White House Conferences on Civil Rights and International Cooperation Year.[5] Amid the fanfare and rising expectations involved in these gala affairs, Presidents have frequently and understandably paused to wonder whether there are not other means for attracting support and giving legitimacy to new directions in public policy.

In his search for new proposals, the President looks to many sources: the cabinet, the Bureau of the Budget, the bureacracy, foundations, the business community, and to the White House–recruited "thought brigades" and task forces, who are charged with reviewing what policy needs remain unmet and what other problems need resolution.[6] In the past two years, several key White House staffers have conducted "brainstorming" sessions at major university communities across the country, while others, at presidential urging, have spent several days living in some of the most depressing inner-city ghettoes in order to acquire a first-hand appreciation of employment, health, welfare, and education policy problems. But the time resources of the permanent presidential staff are severely limited by their day-to-day political, legislative, press, and writing assignments. Inevitably, the White House leans on intra- and extra-governmental task forces for a review, ranking, and recommendation of measures worthy of incorporation into the President's program.

On the average of several times a day, the White House will telephone or write to university presidents, foundations and business executives, union leaders, university or nonprofit institutional researchers, and other hosts of public officials and professionals, asking these prominent individuals to serve on a presidential task force or advisory commission. At any given time, a handful of different advisory bodies exist to deal with education. At one point last year [1967] 15 different advisory councils were studying aspects of the President's war on poverty. There are task forces or temporary study groups examining higher education, vocational education, urban education, research and educational development in the biological sciences, and so forth. An

[5] See *Federal Role in Education.* Washington: *Congressional Quarterly,* 1967, p. 24; Henry Fairlie, "Help from Outside," *The New York Times Book Review,* November 27, 1966, pp. 32, 34; and Lee Rainwater and William L. Yancey, *The Moynihan Report and the Politics of Controversy.* Cambridge, MIT Press, 1967.

[6] The term "thought brigade" has been used by one author who raises considerable concern about the use of outside experts: "Backstairs government of any kind is dangerous." See Roger W. Stuart, *The Thought Brigade.* New York: Ivan Obolansky, 1963. For a more balanced view see Daniel Bell, "Government by Commission," *The Public Interest,* No. 3, Spring, 1966, pp. 3–9.

increasing number of advisory bodies serve on a continuing basis: a National Council on the Education of Disadvantaged Children, National Advisory Council on Education Professions Development, Panel on Educational Innovation, National Advisory Commission on Selective Service, and many others. Their policy assessments and proposals literally pour into the west wing of the White House. In the area of education alone, hundreds of "outside" specialists contribute to the legislative program development process yearly. Customarily, these consultants journey to Washington for a few days each month, although use of time-saving conference telephones and detailed memoranda are likely to ease the travel burdens in the future.

It is not to the advantage of the White House to misuse outside advisors and consultants. Task force and commission members quickly recognize when they are being "manipulated" for purely political reasons. Most advisors are aware of the support-building for the President's program which occurs when prominent citizens make personal investments in the preparation of the program. Occasionally, this process backfires. If, for example, after repeatedly proposing certain directions in public policy one of these advisors feels that his proposals are falling on deaf ears at the White House, he may become discouraged with lending his further support to the President. Such sequences of events kindle the stand once taken by John Kenneth Galbraith:

> To those who feel they can best serve by endowing the scene with their presence rather than pursuing their convictions, let me simply say that I agree it is a good life, but also a bit like being one of the warriors in the Washington parks. The posture is heroic, the sword is being waved, but alas, movement is nil.[7]

Another risk is that despite the usually sincere intentions of both the appointer and appointee, appointment to advisory bodies is considered, by some, a form of patronage. Major organizations are greatly offended if they do not have "proper" representation on bodies relating to their spheres of interest. However, from balanced councils it is impossible for any but the most compromised version of a proposal to emerge. This simulation in miniature of the congressional political system inhibits any innovative functions of these task forces. It also lends credibility to charges of "window dressing." To avoid these liabilities, the White House can rely on nonpublicized task forces which need not suffer the burdens of political balancing—but secrecy on these matters is hard to maintain for sustained periods.

The White House is often accused of using advisory positions to pay off political debts. Not surprisingly, some long-time friends of the President, or members of the well-heeled President's Club (persons contributing $1,000

7 John Kenneth Galbraith, in a speech to the National Committee on Pockets of Poverty, quoted in *Time*, December 20, 1963, p. 10.

annually to presidential campaign coffers), are sprinkled among his appointments to such panels. Similar problems are the over-reliance on the same prominent advisors (some of whom serve on as many as six or seven councils) and the temptation to appoint only the well-known, well-established specialists. Failure to establish a highly professional identification and recruitment system, especially one which attracts talented young professionals, is likely to result in an inert and stagnant advisory system.

Another frequent criticism is that the White House uses task forces and commissions for dilatory purposes such as "ducking" direct confrontation with political controversy. A President proposing a controversial measure often goes out of his way to stress that the measure has been "under careful study" and is "the recommendation of the best minds and specialists in the country." Such criticisms fail to appreciate that advisory bodies are reasonable political resources, when used wisely. But Presidents and presidential staffs can ill afford to become casual in the exercise of the presidential prerogative of calling upon outside advisors.

Perpetual Bargaining

Presidents who deliberately adopt the role of policy advocates must, if they wish to be successful, constantly negotiate and bargain. Eisenhower, despite limited experience with Congress, quickly learned the strategic importance of having a skilled staff of congressional relations men. This staff function is now firmly institutionalized at the White House and has taken on the major responsibilities of maneuvering the President's program through the congressional system.

When John Kennedy was elected President, he gave detailed consideration to the kind of presidential-congressional rapport he wished to establish. Kennedy as congressman and senator had rarely heard from the White House: *"I recall my 14 years on the Hill, and I cannot recall during that 14-year period having any direct or meaningful contact with a member of the White House staff."*[8]

Kennedy, as President, with talented assistance from Larry O'Brien, extended the influence of the White House far beyond the circle of congressional leadership and committee chairmen to virtually every congressman, and, in doing so, significantly refined the strategies of presidential lobbying. Favors and patronage were selectively dispensed; birthdays and pet interests were recognized and remembered; files were kept of requests and voting records; and congressmen were entertained and consulted with calculated frequency. Paradoxically, members of Congress are frequently more covetous of

[8] See the interview of Larry O'Brien, *Legislators and the Lobbyists*. Washington: *Congressional Quarterly*, 1965, p. 15.

presidential invitations to White House bill-signing, pen-awarding, picture-taking ceremonies and of the privilege of placing key constituents on early morning special tours of the White House than of the widely heralded "pork-barrel" forms of patronage.

Lyndon Johnson brought to the White House more accumulated mastery of congressional procedure and wisdom about the congressional political subculture than any previous occupant of the White House. For eight years during the Eisenhower Administration, he was known as the "leader" in the Senate and was recognized by many as second only to the President in political influence.[9] Assisted by daily contact with every Democratic member of the Senate and a widely dispersed network of assistants, Johnson developed an uncanny ability to manipulate the role perceptions of many of his Senate colleagues.[10] The overwhelming success of the Johnson education program in the 89th Congress is testimony to his skill as a legislative broker. The 1964 Goldwater backlash is frequently and correctly credited with giving Johnson added legislative leeway; but it still fell to the President and his staff to develop the legislative program, to forge the needed coalitions (always sensitive to formulas which would benefit as many congressional districts as possible), and to perfect the timing sequences of the legislative program. These were no small tasks.

With the establishment of a highly specialized legislative liaison staff has come a separation of the policy planning functions from the overt lobbying functions. This new manner of organizing the White House "inner circle" has prompted at least one observer to fear that the President's program will be argued less on its policy merits than according to political reasons hinged to patronage.[11] Others find that it is difficult to know with whom to deal at the White House (e.g., is a policy amendment a matter for the President's legislative or policy aides?). The confusion raised by staff differentiation at the White House is compounded by the same differentiation in the departments and agencies. Indeed, the Department of Health, Education, and Welfare is differentiated not only according to policy staff and legislative liaison staffs, but additionally the functions of the latter are operationally separated according to the legislative authorization and appropriations processes. There is occasional chaos when the parties concerned are unable to engage in the necessary collaboration on last-minute changes. Not infrequently, the special assistant for HEW matters at the White House will call an "eleventh-

[9] See Rowland Evans and Robert Novak, *Lyndon Johnson: The Exercise of Power.* New York: The New American Library, 1966, pp. 50–194.

[10] Ralph K. Huitt, "Democratic Party Leadership in the Senate," *American Political Science Review,* June, 1961, pp. 333–44.

[11] This concern was raised by Joseph Kraft, "Kennedy's Working Staff," *Harper's Magazine,* December, 1962, pp. 29–36.

hour" strategy session to which the legislative and policy officials from both HEW and the White House will come to iron out the Administration's plan of action and to prepare last minute advice for the Chief Executive.

Prizes, Programs, Performance

In the aftermath of President Johnson's legislative victories with the 89th Congress, some major administrative questions for education have arisen, many of which still stand in need of attention: the problem of institution building, personnel recruitment and training, long-range policy planning and evaluation relations with the states and local school systems. These problems have occasioned changing relations between the President and the agencies administering domestic programs. Both Kennedy and Johnson have had to allocate most of their time resources first to the task of overseeing national security matters and secondly to steering legislative programs through Congress. Not surprisingly, project directors at the Office of Education occasionally complain of White House indifference once a new program has been passed:

> I wish those people over at the White House and the Bureau of the Budget would hold back for a while on all these new programs and give just a little attention to this program which we're still trying to get off the ground. They start all these new programs, but never follow through—we'll never accomplish anything until somebody helps us get adequate funding for this undertaking. I am convinced those people over there are going about this matter in the wrong way![12]

Even without international responsibilities, HEW Secretary Abraham Ribicoff (1961–1962) viewed the department as unwieldy and unsusceptible of reasonable administration. He called for the creation of separate departments at the time he announced his resignation.[13]

President Johnson has acknowledged many of these difficulties and has responded in several ways. For the first time, a top special assistant to the President has been charged with overseeing and thinking ahead on education and health matters.[14] In previous administrations, public policy for education, along with practically all domestic policy matters, had usually been delegated to the Special Counsel. From May, 1964 until October, 1968, S. Douglass Cater, a Harvard-educated author, journalist, and sometime government consultant and speech-writer, was among the "inner circle" in the Johnson White House, pri-

[12] This is a paraphrasing and combination of two similar statements made to me by Office of Education officials.

[13] See David T. Stanley, *Changing Administrations*. Washington: The Brookings Institution, 1965, p. 106.

[14] Charles Roberts, *LBJ's Inner Circle*. New York: Delacorte Press, 1965, pp. 103–05.

marily performing strategy and broker roles in conjunction with the formulation and bargaining stages of the President's education and health programs.

Cater's assignment has evolved informally since he joined the staff just prior to the 1964 campaign, initially involving speech-writing and editing functions, but soon including responsibility for acting as the "eyes and ears" for the President in education and health matters—with other specialized interests such as international education, public television, and student affairs. Generally acknowledged as the White House liaison with HEW, he is especially charged with trying to keep the President's program from bogging down at key points where congressional or bureaucratic resistance threatens. Cater and his staff of two are constantly in communication with HEW officials, Budget Bureau staff, and consultants and representatives from the major education organizations.

Johnson has won praise for recruiting Carnegie Foundation President John Gardner as Secretary of HEW, along with Harold Howe as Commissioner of Education, and for promoting long-time professional Wilbur Cohen to HEW's undersecretary post. Gardner's impressive background of professional concern for innovation in education results in his being considered by the educational community as the first genuine educator to occupy this strategic cabinet post. By these appointments President Johnson has secured the most effective leadership to date [1968] to head up the major aspect of the federal government's role in education. While HEW's Office of Education and National Institutes of Health oversee less than half of total federal expenditures in education, most of the 20-odd other federal agencies playing a role in education are usually involved only as contractors for supportive research, e.g., Defense, AEC, Transportation. In theory, at least, HEW is expected to play a government-wide coordinating role for federal education programs.

Secretary Gardner strengthened HEW's management capabilities and facilitated the establishment of planning and evaluation staffs throughout the department. Key to this latter effort was his creation of an Office of Planning and Evaluation under Assistant Secretary William Gorham, a one-time Rand economist and formerly deputy assistant secretary at the Department of Defense. Another Gardner-created post, that of the assistant secretary for education, is explicitly charged with the task of coordinating interdepartmental education matters, an incredibly difficult task.

The White House, HEW, and the Office of Education continue to rely heavily on interagency task forces and increasingly on outside advisory councils. Despite the uncertainties of a complex election year [1968], the search for new ideas, new programs, and new managerial techniques goes on. Currently under study are the following questions: How can education for the disadvantaged be improved? How can the federal government assist in upgrading teacher and school administrator education? What incentives can be used to lure more universities and private enterprise to tackle the problems of urban education?

How can vocational education and manpower development programs be linked? What can help ease the rapidly rising burdens of financing higher education? The answers are not easy and the processes of seeking them is not without its critics. Not a few HEW civil servants have voiced impatience and even resentment to the incremental tendency of relying on outside consultants.[15]

It has become fashionable to call for the creation of new structures staffed by policy scientists who would integrate research efforts and priority setting throughout federal domestic programs. Increasing support has recently been given to a number of proposals. Senator Walter F. Mondale (D., Minn.) has called for a Council of Social Advisers which would advise the President and Congress on education and welfare matters.[16] Daniel P. Moynihan of Harvard and Senator Ribicoff have argued for an Office of Policy Evaluation to assist the members of Congress in evaluating new social inventions.[17] Senator Edmund S. Muskie (D., Maine) has held widely publicized Senate hearings on a bill to establish a White House–level National Council for Intergovernmental Affairs.[18] Senator Fred Harris (D., Oklahoma) has held inquiry sessions and endorsed the motion to establish a National Social Science Foundation to accomplish for the social sciences what the National Science Foundation has been doing for the "hard" sciences.[19] The once-popular proposal to create a National Board of Education is only rarely mentioned now,[20] but proposals to establish a Council of Education Advisors, a Department of Education and Manpower, or a Department of Education and Technology are heard almost monthly in Washington political circles.[21] More plausible is the proposal, favored by [former] Secretary John Gardner, to elevate the Office of Education to subdepartment status at HEW under an under-secretary for education.

Thus far President Johnson has postponed closure on these proposals.[22]

[15] Illustrative of this sentiment is the assessment of advisory councils in Homer D. Babbidge, Jr., and Robert M. Rosenswig, *The Federal Interest in Higher Education.* New York: McGraw Hill, 1962, pp. 82–84.

[16] See "Council of Social Advisors: New Approach to Welfare Priorities," *Science,* July 7, 1967, pp. 49–50.

[17] Daniel P. Moynihan, "A Crisis of Confidence?" *The Public Interest,* No. 7, Spring, 1967, pp. 3–11.

[18] Senator Edmund Muskie, "The Challenge of Creative Federalism," *Congressional Record,* March 25, 1966.

[19] Fred R. Harris, "The Case for a National Social Science Foundation," *Science,* August 4, 1967, pp. 507–09.

[20] See Hollis P. Allen, *The Federal Government and Education.* New York: McGraw-Hill, 1950, pp. 299–305.

[21] A recent restatement of the cabinet status proposal was made by Congresswoman Edith Green, *Study of the United States Office of Education.* Washington, D.C.: Government Printing Office, 1967, pp. 451–54.

[22] Subsequent to the first publication of this article, President Richard Nixon established a Cabinet level Council on Urban Affairs with Daniel P. Moynihan as its first chairman.

He seldom fails, however, to urge his departments to emulate the Defense Department model of using cost effectiveness analysis and the much talked about Planning, Programming, and Budgeting System (PPBS). Around the President in the White House offices, barely a handful of professionals, those associated currently with special assistants S. Douglass Cater and Joseph A. Califano, as well as a few Budget Bureau staff members, have the perspective and capability required for long-range thinking and priority-setting in education. But, as noted earlier, these presidential assistants rarely have much time for "in-depth" analysis of new research results and the incoming flow of advisory reports.

A President committed to excellence in education and seeking to strengthen his leadership in the educational policy system has many resources, but none is more important than attracting the highest qualified people for top government posts and key advisory spots. Looking to the future, Presidents desiring effective long-range planning processes for education should consider 1) further strengthening the role of the special assistant for education policy and politics, 2) establishing some type of "station look-out" at or near the White House Office, for long-range planning in domestic programs, 3) creating a talent bank of prospective professional education advisors, 4) making better use of Budget Bureau and Office of Science and Technology staffs for evaluating education programs, and very importantly, 5) elevating the Office of Education to subcabinet status at HEW to be headed by an undersecretary for education.

$\underset{\sim}{\sim}$ 5

The Moynihan Report and a White House Civil Rights Conference

LEE RAINWATER
and
WILLIAM L. YANCEY

The Man

Daniel Patrick Moynihan joined the New Frontier in 1961 as special assistant to Secretary of Labor Goldberg and by 1963 was appointed Assistant Secretary of Labor in charge of the Office of Policy Planning and Research. He was one of a new breed of public servants, the social scientist-politicos, who combine in their background both social science training and experience and full-time involvement in political activity. He had attended the City College of New York and Tufts University and received a Ph.D. in political science from the Fletcher School of Law and Diplomacy in 1961. He had attended the London School of Economics on a Fulbright fellowship. From 1955 to 1959 he had worked as an assistant to Governor Harriman of New York. From 1959 to 1961 he had been the director of the New York State Government Research Project at Syracuse University. His particular interests in political

Reprinted by permission from Lee Rainwater and William L. Yancey, *The Moynihan Report and the Politics of Controversy,* Cambridge, The M.I.T. Press, 1967, pp. 17–19, 25–36, 274–278, 286–291.

science, coupled with his experience in New York politics, had moved him in the direction of an increasing emphasis on the sociological study of urban life; his work in the Department of Labor was to sharpen further his sociological bent.

The Office

An Assistant Secretary of Labor and Director of the Office of Policy Planning and Research, with an additional over-all responsibility for the work of the Bureau of Labor Statistics, Moynihan was concerned with the development of information from which the effectiveness of the Department's activities could be assessed and with the development of programmatic ideas and policy goals in line with the Department's responsibilities. As an assistant secretary, his constituency involved most naturally the higher level members of the Department of Labor and the White House staff. Cabinet officers and their assistants stand between the Presidential Government of each administration and the Permanent Government of civil servants and appointed officials who serve for longer periods of time than the elected administration. Moynihan's political experience and personal conception of public service pointed him very strongly in the direction of the Presidential Government. He clearly defined himself over the years of his service in Washington as a member of the "Presidential party." In addition to the normal privileges of his office, Moynihan had close personal relationships with the White House staff, relations that grew out of the Kennedy period and antedated his appointment as Assistant Secretary.

He had conceived President Kennedy's study of selective service rejectees (the Task Force on Manpower Conservation), that had been part of the groundwork for planning the War on Poverty. The Task Force had produced a report, "One-Third of a Nation," which provided Moynihan a model as he began to work on his Negro family report. Moynihan had been a member of the four-man team that developed the War on Poverty legislative proposals [the others were Sargent Shriver, Adam Yarmolinsky, and James Sundquist]. In his effort, he had been particularly concerned to strengthen the employment aspects of the poverty program.

The office that Moynihan held is of crucial importance in understanding the report and the controversy. The report itself was written from the standpoint of a member of the Presidential Government who has the right to suggest policy of the sweeping nature that Moynihan had in mind. Only a person in this position would have been able to write a report relatively free of the long review process typical of government reports or to ensure that it received high-level distribution. Only a person in this position would have been able to speak directly and on a relatively equal footing with the White House staff. Finally, only a person who was defined as solidly part of the Presidential Government would have a chance of resisting the counter-pressures that would come from other departments who might feel the report had policy implications inimicable to their programs.

Once the existence of the report became public knowledge, the fact that its author occupied such a high position meant that it must be taken seriously. The government produces thousands of reports every year, many of which have implications that considered on their merits alone deserve consideration by the public and by representatives of organizations and interest groups likely to be affected. However, very seldom are such reports given the kind of public notoriety and serious attention that was given the Moynihan Report. The attention reflected the seriousness implicit in its authorship as much or more than it derived from the content of the report itself. This is, of course, one of the reasons why "nothing new" caused a controversy.

•　•　•

The Strategy

. . . Moynihan mulled the question of Negro poverty and the family and began to examine some of the data already in his office on unemployment rates and rates of marital disruption over a fifteen year period. At the same time, he thought he sensed in Washington a tendency on the part of some administration officials to think that the Civil Rights Act of 1964 had solved a good part of the civil rights problem. He was concerned with the credence given public opinion polls that showed that a majority of Negroes in Harlem felt that the Civil Rights Act would make a "very great difference" in their lives. The sharp contrast between this optimistic mood and the depressing figures on social and economic status disturbed him. Late in November of 1964, he decided to write a report on the Negro family for internal use in the government:

> I woke up a couple of nights later [that is, after one such conversation with a highly placed optimist] at four o'clock in the morning and felt I had to write a paper about the Negro family to explain to the fellows how there was a problem more difficult than they knew and also to explain some of the issues of unemployment and housing in terms that would be new enough and shocking enough that they would say, "Well, we can't let this sort of thing go on. We've got to do something about it."

He organized a small working staff and through them began to collect government statistics that in one way or another had bearing on the problem. He had available to him not only the vast range of published and indexed government statistics but also the services of Labor Department economists and of the Bureau of Labor Statistics to pull together information that was not already in published form. The basic paradigm he worked with was that of the social and economic analysis that had laid the ground work for the poverty program, except that he was doing this on his own and on a much smaller scale. From December through March, then, Moynihan and his staff put together the document and in the process worked out a strategy of placement and presentation. At the same time, he laid the groundwork for the reception of the report by speaking from time to time to those he wished in the end to persuade. In March, the document was formally cleared by Secretary of Labor Wirtz and one hundred nicely printed and bound copies run off in the basement of the Department of Labor. Despite its small audience, he wanted a handsome, finished-looking document. No more than eighty of the numbered copies of the report were distributed by July, when it was decided to make the document public and turn it over to the Government Printing Office.

Moynihan was writing for a very small audience. His concern was to have adopted at the highest levels of the administration the view that family welfare provided a central point of reference in evaluating the effectiveness of programs to deal with disadvantaged groups. He sought to achieve a basic redefinition of the civil rights problem at the highest level of the administration as a preliminary to a broader redefinition by the government as a whole. In order to do this, he wanted to formulate a clear diagnosis of the problem, to acquaint officials with facts that he felt they either did not know or of which they did not see the full implications.

While the document was to be an unusual one for government policy papers, it must at least have some kinship with them. Therefore, there was heavy emphasis on government statistics, since these are the "authoritative data" with which high level officials are accustomed to working. Though it sought to present a complex argument, the document must be short and sharply focused. Although early in his planning Moynihan had thought of suggesting solutions as well as defining a problem, he finally determined not to include any reference to solutions in the report itself in order to force his readers to focus their attention on understanding the problem qua problem.

Thus, the report was distributed to only a few persons within the Department of Labor and the White House. As time went on, particularly as the reputation of the report spread within the Administration and demands for it increased, the circle of distribution grew wider. But at least from April through most of June only a handful of persons outside the White House and the Department of Labor had seen copies. During April and May, with the report as the formal basis for his views, Moynihan pursued his goal in personal conversations and with briefer memoranda. The events of the first week of June provided the first indication that his report had found its target.

In the meantime, Moynihan had completed a slightly different version of the same ideas for publication in *Daedalus;* the draft of this paper was discussed at a *Daedalus* conference on May 14th and 15th. Though the essential points contained in the report are also found in the article prepared for publication, some of the issues that were to prove sensitive when the report made its way into the press are much subdued in the paper—there are a scant two sentences dealing with illegitimacy and no discussion of slavery and other historical factors.

On May 4th [1964] Secretary Wirtz forwarded to the White House a memorandum for the President that summarized the report and added several recommendations. Secretary Wirtz indicated that the memorandum had been prepared by Moynihan but that he agreed with the analysis and concurred in the recommendations. The memorandum was sent to Presidential Assistant Bill Moyers; it is not clear whether the President [Lyndon B. Johnson] in fact ever read it (apparently he did not read the report), but the effect of the memorandum was to place the report and several recommendations on the White House agenda.

Moynihan sought to present a sharply focused argument leading to the conclusion that the government's economic and social welfare programs, existing and prospective ones, should be systematically designed to encourage the stability of the Negro family. He sought to show, first, that the Negro family was highly unstable (female-headed households produced by marital breakup and illegitimacy). This instability resulted from the systematic weakening of the position of the Negro male. Slavery, reconstruction, urbanization, and unemployment had produced a problem as old as America and as new as the April unemployment rate. This problem of unstable families in turn was a central feature of the tangle of pathology of the urban ghetto, involving problems of delinquency, crime, school dropouts, unemployment, and poverty. Finally, Moynihan wanted the Administration to understand that some evidence supported the conclusion that these problems fed on themselves and that matters were rapidly getting worse.

In the report, in conversations, and in memorandums, Assistant Secretary of Labor Moynihan sought to persuade his peers and his superiors in the Presidential Government that they were confronted with a crisis situation no less dangerous than that of Birmingham, Selma, or Mississippi for all that it might be somewhat drawn out. Though he did not deal with the summer riots of 1964 in the report, he was quite willing to point out to anyone who was interested that these riots had at their core Negro youth who knew how bad off they were and that there would be more such riots.

In the May 4th memorandum to the President, he sought to emphasize the necessity for planning. The first step in the solution of these problems was simply that the government must acknowledge the problem and its urgency—agencies and key individuals must be brought together, focus on the problem, and agree that the basic strategy must be to strengthen the family. There must be a stop to decision-making processes in which policy makers rush off after solutions before really agreeing on what the problem is. Once the focus was on the stability of the family, the government would have an absolute measure of whether or not its efforts were producing any results. The government would not be able to tell itself that it had changed anything until it really had; that is, until the proportion of Negro marriages that break up begins to decline and the proportion of Negro families with male heads begins to increase. Moynihan believed that should the government be able to create the conditions in which this would happen, other indices of disorganization would also show improvement—more children would complete school and they would do better in school; there would be less crime and delinquency, less dope addiction, and so forth. In short, the mutually reinforcing tangle of pathology would begin to unravel.

Though he had decided not to include recommendations in his report—for fear that all of the attention would go to the recommended programs rather than to the definition of the problem and also that there would be premature budget estimates of the cost of the recommended programs in the memorandum he suggested several steps as a start. These reflected two kinds of concerns, one administrative and the other programmatic.

The first had to do with institutionalizing the kind of policy-assessment approach he had sought to essay in his report. He felt a group should be appointed to review all the programs of the federal government with a view to determining whether they were helping to strengthen the Negro family or simply perpetuating its weaknesses. In line with this, the government should establish a place at which relevant data on the changing situation of Negroes could be brought together, organized, and made available to other agencies. Such an information center would provide a better means of measuring the success or failure of programs than the present widely dispersed source of information allowed.

In the area of concrete programs, Moynihan felt that jobs had primacy and that the government should not rest until every able-bodied Negro man was working even if this meant that some women's jobs had to be redesigned to enable men to fulfill them. He felt that housing programs should be initiated that provide decent family housing and, in particular, that the housing in suburbs must be planned so that families could escape the ghetto.

In addition, birth control programs were sorely needed so that Negroes could limit their families in line with their needs and desires and the illegitimacy rate could be reduced. Then, finally, Negro youth should be given a greater opportunity to serve in the Armed Forces. It would be possible to set up training programs to allow more Negroes who volunteer for the services but are rejected to qualify on the standard tests and thus be accepted.

In short, though he felt that the general direction of solutions to the problems he had posed—employment, income maintenance (in the form of family allowances perhaps), better housing and family planning—were clear, he did not formulate specific program proposals. Rather, he hoped that if he were successful in persuading the Administration to adopt his view of the nature and urgency of the situation, working groups would be set up to develop such specific programs.

Moynihan's principal immediate goal was to stimulate a commitment by the Administration to engage in long-range policy-planning. At the time he formulated his strategy there were many senior career men in the government (and others outside) who were desperately trying to elicit from the Administration this kind of commitment and who were trying to put together social science materials of various kinds to demonstrate the value of such policy planning. Moynihan's position as Assistant Secretary and his personal relations with the White House staff allowed him a kind of access that the career men did not have (some had had such access under Kennedy). He had the ear of the White House and the political status and skill to make use of it. One career planner credited him with "making the one main inroad into the White House" to get action, though he noted that Moynihan's goal and ability to use social science data in its services were not unique to him.

That Moynihan was not very successful in his efforts to win White House aides over to the philosophy of careful policy planning before program development and something of the nature of the resistance to such an approach are suggested by the following experience related by one of the nation's best informed experts on ghetto problems. This man had been called to the White House in the summer of 1965 to meet with the President's top aides to discuss what should be accomplished in the fall conference. He found the senior man at the meeting "terribly impatient":

> He kept demanding specific proposals for specific programs and specific legislation: "Our job is to legislate." I tangled with him because I saw my function as trying to suggest the complexity of the problem and the need for co-ordination between programs and community organization or social action from within the Negro community. I was terribly conscious of the enormous obstacles in the way of any attempt by government to stimulate authentic social action within a community. I was also terribly aware of what seemed to me then—and still seems—the serious failures of many of the governmental programs that had already been established. I was trying to suggest that we might come closer to a solution of the problem if the government tried to do a few things well instead of doing a great many things badly. He was extremely impatient with any discussion of complexity and disinterested in any critique of weakness of the existing programs. His orientation—stemming, I assume, from the fact that he had to report directly to the President—was "what do we do next?" He just was not interested in anything that did not lead directly to a specific proposal which he could place before the President—and before the Congress.

Other experts have made similar observations about White House aides in the meetings of that summer.

There is an interesting contrast between the internal policy statement that the report represents and the political statement which the Howard

University speech [June 4, 1965] represents. The report is addressed to the concerns of those who manage the nation. That is, it presents a problem rather than an argument about rights and justice. It says that things are going badly in one segment of the society and will continue to go badly until the government sets them right. The argument rests less on moral considerations than it does on a certain kind of high-level administrative rationality. If the nation is to be *governed* properly, or indeed be governable, national social and economic policy must operate in such a way that Negroes have different life experiences than they now have. The Howard University speech, on the other hand, places the same views in the context of justice and morality and thereby lacks the highly impersonal and detached tone that the report brings to bear. While this latter tone is appropriate and desirable for an internal document, it can seem almost heartless if considered outside of that context.

One other aspect of the tone of the report deserves mention. Moynihan was concerned to demonstrate the extent of family disorganization among poor Negroes and the relation of family disorganization to various social problems in the ghetto. In line with this goal, he emphasized very strongly the destructive potential of disorganized family life much as Frazier, Clark and others before him had done. However, there is another way of looking at Negro lower-class family forms—one concerns oneself with how particular family patterns function to enable individuals to adapt to their depriving lower-class existence and to maintain themselves biologically, psychically, and socially in the one world in which they must live. From this perspective some of the same behaviors that appear pathological (in terms of ability to function in line with the demands of stable working or middle-class norms and institutions) are functional in terms of the ability to make as gratifying a life as possible in a ghetto milieu. Had Moynihan dealt with this aspect of the situation he might have avoided some of the criticism of the report—but problably would have earned other kinds of criticism. As many sociologists have noted, functional analysis tends to appear as rather conservative; bowdlerized versions of the adaptive quality of "pathological" lower-class patterns could undoubtedly be made to appear to support the view that lower-class Negroes are really not so dissatisfied with their situation. In any case, this line of argument would hardly be persuasive with high officials for the federal initiatives Moynihan hoped to stimulate. For that purpose, he needed to point to what poor Negroes were deprived of, not to how they managed to make out despite their deprivations.

The Results

The report had sought to establish in the Presidential Government a new view of the situation of Negro Americans and to set in motion program planning in line with that new view. (This, despite the fact that there was nothing at all new to a wide group of social scientists and citizens well-informed in the civil rights area about the views Moynihan advanced.) The strategy seemed to have paid off handsomely. Moynihan's White House constituency was already concerned as to the direction the government should move after the 1965 Civil Rights Bill, and they seemed to understand his contention that purely antidiscrimination programs would not alone solve the problems of the northern ghettos. They were sympathetic to the notion that the family provided a worthwhile focus for evaluating the effectiveness of programs and some of them developed a fairly thorough intellectual sophistication in what all of this implied. Finally, the President decided to use Moynihan's work as the basis for his speech at Howard University. (The facts are unclear to us, but there is some reason to believe that the President [Lyndon B. Johnson] decided to accept the invitation from Howard *because* he wanted a forum at which to test out these ideas concerning "the next more profound stage of the battle for civil rights.") In line with this thinking, the White House decided to call a conference to discuss the problems that would now be confronted in this next stage.

While those in the government who were privy to Moynihan's views saw in them a powerful tool for understanding and planning, they also recognized considerable danger should the report's ideas be communicated to the public in the wrong way. Interestingly enough, some persons in the Administration saw the dangers not so much in a negative reaction from persons concerned with civil rights but rather in the unpleasant prospect of Southern newsmen and public figures seeking to twist the argument to substantiate their views of the inferiority of Negroes. As knowledge of the main ideas in the report became more widespread within the government, however, some individuals began to warn of the backlash from Negro leaders who would be concerned about the discussion of such sensitive issues as family instability, illegitimacy, and the like.

In any case, when Moynihan left the country on June 4th to attend a conference in Yugoslavia on multiethnic societies, he had every reason to believe that the initial goals of his strategy had been achieved and that the road was open to the ultimate goal of a revised national strategy for Negro equality. Though he was to be involved in the conference planning that followed the speech, his central role was ended. The staff job of "preplanning" was turned over to an ad hoc group, which used the staff facilities of the President's Council on Equal Opportunity headed by Vice-President Humphrey and staffed by men primarily identified with him. Moynihan returned to Washington late in June and left on July 18th to run in the New York Democratic Primary for the office of President of the City Council.

The Follow-Up

A series of preparatory meetings for the conference were held in a White House conference room during the month of July. At these meetings, social experts presented their views to a group of about ten White House assistants and staff members of the "preplanning" group. The experts came in one at a time so that each man gave his own views but without an opportunity for exchange of views with any of the other experts. Several of the experts found this arrangement a rather uncomfortable one since they felt very much on the spot vis-à-vis the government people; they found it difficult to present their arguments as vigorously or as broadly as they would have liked or as would have been possible working in concert with other experts. From the point of view of the government, of course, this arrangement was desirable since it did not want to be lobbied or instructed but simply informed and left free to decide what to do with the knowledge. It was, of course, also in a very good position to see the extent of spontaneous consensus among the experts since no expert knew what the others were saying.

Those called to the White House for these meetings included a distinguished list of social scientists—Professors Talcott Parsons, Eric Erikson, Kenneth Clark, Robert Coles, Thomas Pettigrew, Urie Bronfenbrenner, and James Wilson. During this period no civil rights leaders attended the preparatory meetings; the staff had wished to invite John Turner, Professor of Social Work at Western Reserve University and consultant to the National Urban League, and Bayard Rustin, but they were out of the country at the time the schedule was arranged.

The experts scheduled for these meetings could be expected to deepen considerably the officials' understanding of the problems of the Negro family and of ghetto pathology. With the exception of Erikson and Parsons, all of them were men who had devoted a considerable part of their professional careers to studying the impact on individuals and group of living in a lower-class environment. Almost all of the academicians had also participated in the *Daedalus* conferences and reflected its "Eastern Establishment" cast; five were Harvard professors.

It is important to note that these preparatory meetings and the staff work connected with them did not involve an officially appointed planning group for the conference but a preplanning group which was beginning to work out tentative ideas as to what the conference might be like. For a number of reasons the planning staff was not appointed until early October. Nevertheless this preplanning group worked out an over-all design that was to persist through the actual planning conference held in November.

Much of the later controversy about the conference and the Moynihan Report had to do with whether or not the conference was going to be "about the family." As best we can determine the answer to this question can be yes or no depending on what "about the family" is taken to mean. It is clear that at no time and in no way was the conference planned as a conference on the Negro family (that is, as a conference that would deal solely with the subject of the Negro family even in the relatively broad way it had been treated in Moynihan's work of Spring 1965). On the other hand, it seems quite reasonable to believe that the White House had in mind that the main overarching theme of the conference would be the welfare of Negro families in the sense in which Moynihan used the idea: as the basis from which to evaluate the effectiveness of programs designed to cope with the next stage of the civil rights struggle. From this point of view, then, the discussions in the prospective conference dealing with employment, education, health and welfare programs, and the like would have been subjected to the standard of whether or not they seemed to be likely to pay off in greater family stability and well-being. However, some of the other areas of persisting concern in civil rights—voting, the administration of justice, protection of civil rights workers—could not be so directly related to this concern.

In any case, quite early in the July discussions, government officials in the preplanning group pointed out that the family emphasis would prove a very sensitive and touchy issue with people involved in civil rights activity and argued against heavy emphasis on the subject, even in the form of an over-arching standard of program effectiveness. In late July, therefore, an outline of panels for the conference was developed, using a traditional subgrouping around topics that had long been dealt with by the U.S. Civil Rights Commission in its hearings—jobs, education, voting, protection of persons, and so on. In addition, it was obvious that some new areas needed to be introduced to cope with northern and urban problems. At one point, it was thought that there should be a panel on "the dynamics of the ghetto" that would consider both the family and the community, but in the end this was broken up into two sessions—one on family and one on community. From this time, late July, until the planning conference there were frequent expressions of concern both within the government and from outside about the existence of even one session dealing specifically with the family—for reasons that we trust will become apparent in the sections that follow.

One final point can be raised concerning the connection between the conference and Moynihan's thesis. This has to do with why there should have been a conference at all. The White House decision to call a conference was apparently not subjected to a great deal of discussion and consideration; it just seemed a good idea in the context of the President's speech, the new issues that he raised, and the Administration's continuing concern about where to go next in civil rights. (Apparently while drafting the speech, Richard Goodwin conceived the idea of the conference and included it in the draft sent to the President, who adopted the idea.) Since the new theme was clearly aimed at a significant departure from previous ways of dealing with the problem (although in line with the War on Poverty philosophy), it seemed a good idea to call together experts, civil rights leaders, and government officials to map out the new territory.

However, White House conferences do not generally serve this function.

In the past most, but not all, conferences had served primarily to ratify programs already on the drawing board and to build public support for them. Most of the questions and answers are known in rough line and the conference provides a stage on which they can be made public in a context that symbolizes their importance. Yet here a conference was going to take on the task of solving the most sensitive domestic issue confronting the country and do so in the full light of publicity. It was this disparity between the goal of the conference and the administrative and political realities of a sensitive issue that caused the fall meeting to be scaled down to a planning conference; nor was the spring meeting able to overcome these obstacles. In a very real sense, it seems that the White House did not understand what it was getting into.

• • •

We have suggested that the Moynihan Report fitted almost perfectly into the government's needs to "leapfrog" the movement and to rechannel the civil rights movement away from the mere passage and implementation of legislation into the area of social and economic change, thereby reducing the conflict with the movement by co-optation. But ideological movements do not change so readily. The focus on the family as the government's policy base in the area of civil rights obviously did not work. Not only was it found that the civil rights movement did not want to focus efforts on the Negro family but it was also seen that the money required to ensure family stability was more than the government was willing to spend. Yet what was learned in 1965— that the next stage of the movement would involve social and economic changes and that if Johnson was to reach a consensus he needed to co-opt the civil rights movement—remained true in the spring of 1966. The problem then was one of the government asserting an "independent" policy in the area of civil rights that would be accepted by the movement and would therefore take the lead away from the movement's leaders. How could it assert itself and co-opt the movement at the same time?

In February, the President announced the appointment of Mr. Benjamin Heineman, Chairman of the Chicago and Northwestern Railway, as the chairman of the [White House] conference. Prior to this, Mr. Heineman had little to do with civil rights. Also appointed were A. Phillip Randolph as Honorary Chairman of the conference and a Conference Council of some thirty persons. Eight of the council were associated with industry and big business; seven were leaders of the civil rights movement; the remaining half were government men, lawyers, judges, labor leaders, and scholars.

The small social science representation on the council and among the delegates to the final conference indicates another change away from the President's Howard University speech. There Johnson had said that the delegates would be "scholars, and experts, and outstanding Negro leaders— men of both races—and officials of the government at every level." (There was no mention of the businessmen who came later to dominate the council.) The fall planning session was attended by scholars, civil rights leaders, and government officials; indeed, the panel discussions were dominated by scholars and experts.

This cannot be said of the final conference. Delegates were primarily local civil rights leaders, a few national Negro leaders and even fewer scholars and experts. There were several rather well-known social scientists and writers who were strikingly absent. Social scientists such as Frank Riessman, Urie Bronfenbrenner, Herbert Gans, Arnold Rose, Marvin Wolfgang, Nathan Glazer, Charles Grigg, and Lewis Killian and authors such as Michael Harrington and Charles Silberman were not present. All were present at the fall planning conference.

The conference had changed in character from one dominated by scholars and experts to one which was supposedly "representative of American civil rights interests." This change of character of the delegates is only one indication of the entire redefinition of the White House Conference. The fall planning session was designed to study the problems carefully and to begin to suggest solutions. Six months later, the government felt it knew enough about the problems and that the conference did "not have to spend a great amount of time defining the problems with which we must deal; they have been described, analyzed, and discussed at length in many forums and in the preparatory stages of this conference."

Thus the government seemed to have backed away from its earlier practice of using social science consultants in developing a meaningful and effective strategy against the Northern slums. In a very real sense, the social scientists had already served their purpose insofar as they had legitimated the government's stance in this area. Social scientists had dominated the fall planning conference, and some of them were listed as consultants to the council for the spring conference. If the heated debates of the fall planning conference were any indication, their presence at the spring conference would only threaten the peace of the meeting. Social science had legitimized the "Council's Report and Recommendations to the Conference," and a social science attack on the report would be quite embarrassing.

The council's principal job was the production of the central document for the conference, the "Council's Report and Recommendations to the Conference." This 104-page document contained a wide range of recommendations focusing on the areas of Economic Security and Welfare, Education, Housing, and Administration of Justice. (Of course there was no mention of the Negro family.) It was further legitimated, based on the fall planning conference, by the consultation of social scientists and leaders of the civil rights movement who were members of the council and [it] was the principal tool in using the White House Conference to reach the goal of consensus politics.

The recommendations were to be read by the delegates to the Conference prior to the meeting, and the business of the conference was to be the discussions, criticisms, and additions to these recommendations. Then, after the conference was over, the council, with the aid of government staff people, was to study the transcripts of the conference discussions and rewrite the recommendations. The final document would then be presented to the President. This group, behind closed doors, away from the press and critics of the government, would be able to assess which of the recommendations would be the best, and the government would not have to take the risk it had taken in 1965. The Administration would have "feedback" on all its recommendations, and Johnson would know the kind of policy that would be acceptable and could further co-opt the movement.

This plan for the White House Conference was defended by Mr. Heineman as the most democratic format that was possible, given the meeting of 2,400 persons for two days. Heineman said in defending the council's decision not to allow resolutions to be voted on during the conference:

> After considerable discussion by the Presidentially appointed council consisting of a broad representation of persons interested in civil rights, it was concluded at that time that taking of formal votes would not be in the best interest of this conference. This was true for several reasons. The report consisted of broad, complex and numerous recommendations. The conference was open to suggestions, proposals and comments by any conferee. Everyone should be given an opportunity to speak. To establish this session with 2,400 persons on a parliamentary basis would be undemocratic in itself. This is true because it would not allow people to make their views known.
>
> A fair and desirable substitute is to make a complete stenotype transcript of the proceedings, all of which would be considered in the draft of recommendations to the President.
>
> With such an arrangement persons who are not familiar with parliamentary procedures and are unskilled in competitive debate would have an opportunity to participate in the conference.

With such an arrangement it is true that everyone at the conference would have a chance to speak and that the government would get feedback on its recommendations. But there is a real question of how "democratic" the conference was, particularly with respect to decision making. If one makes the (incorrect) assumption that the Administration called the conference so persons interested in civil rights would have a determining part in the formation of national policy in civil rights, the format of the conference was hardly democratic.

Floyd McKissick of CORE said that the conference had been rigged and later changed his mind and said it was a hoax. Delegates told reporters, "We came for a dialogue and we are going to get a monologue."

It was suggested by many of the delegates that the list of delegates had been carefully screened so as to eliminate any "bomb throwers" from attendance at the conference. Many said that no grass roots activists were invited to the conference. Southern grass roots were represented, and a number of "grass roots" people were there from the North—the most verbal from Watts and Harlem. Activists such as Julius Hobson of Washington ACT or Jesse Gray, organizer of the New York Rent Strikes, were not invited. But Lawrence Landry, leader of Chicago ACT, was. There were several delegates who came to the conference without invitations and after some pressure on the conference staff were able to pay the $25 registration fee, and obtain delegate badges.

The conference staff must be seen as walking a very thin line between maintaining reasonable order and control over the conference and at the same time not meeting objections with direct conflict. Conflict would itself produce additional conflict. The organizers had to compromise to maintain control. Allowing persons who had come to Washington on their own into the conference is one example of this strategy. Perhaps a clear example is the change in the resolution policy. Floyd McKissick had let it be known he was going to present a motion at the first general meeting of the conference that resolutions be made and voted upon in the conference committee. The National Council of Churches passed out a mimeographed sheet supporting such a move immediately before the opening session. The [conference] council, hearing McKissick's demands, had moved after a night of deliberation to compromise and allowed resolutions to be made during the last committee meetings. By changing the rules, the council avoided direct conflict with the more militant delegates and therefore maintained control over the convention.

Resolutions were made only during the last part of the last session. (It should be pointed out that several delegates objected to taking up the entire time of the last committee meeting to make resolutions. They wanted to talk about the scheduled subject.) Some of the committees required their members to draw up the resolutions and turn in a written copy to a "Resolutions Committee." These committees then reviewed the resolutions and selected those that were finally presented before the committee. One resolution on preferential treatment was rejected by such a committee and not presented to the group. The delegate who had turned in this resolution was not recognized by the committee chairman when he discovered that his resolutions were not going to be presented. Later, when talking to the chairman, he was unable to find any reason for its rejection other than "You didn't start your paragraph with 'Whereas be it resolved!' "

There are many ways in which one can say that the conference was open and free, and likewise there are ways that the conference was tightly controlled. It is true that anyone could stand up and say anything in the committee meetings. Also, the council did back down on the policy of "no resolutions from the floor" and allowed resolutions to be made during the last meeting of the panel. But perhaps most important is the fact that control over the federal policies that result from the White House Conference are at least two steps away from the delegates of the conference. First the transcript from the committee meetings will be screened and then a set of recommendations will be sent to the President. The President still has the alternative of rejecting any proposal he wishes. As one member of the conference staff said, "The President doesn't have to do a thing that they recommend unless he wants to."

• • •

"Spin Off"—Get the Heat Out of the White House

No amount of legislation, no degree of commitment on the part of the national government, can by itself bring equal opportunity and achievement to Negro Americans. It must be joined by a massive effort on the part of the States and local government, of industry, and of all citizens, white and Negro.

From the President's [Johnson's]
Message to Congress
April 28, 1966

This statement by the President provided a major guideline for the White House Conference. In addition to suggestions for action on the federal level the council's report contains many recommendations indicative of a developing governmental policy. News columnist Joseph Kraft has labeled the decentralization of government's domestic efforts as "spin-off." He observed that the "mere composition of the council [dominated by businessmen and industrialists] suggested that, if the Federal Government had a role in securing civil rights, the main burden fell on the private and semi-private sectors of the economy."

The "Introduction" to the council's report made the direction of this policy of emphasizing the efforts of the private sector quite clear. The council wrote:

The need for additional legislation, administrative changes, and executive leadership at all three levels of government has been extensively treated; the proposals in this category and the Conference reactions to them will be transmitted to the President and will be made available to state and local public officials.

But the Conference would fail in its purpose if it did no more than that. Governmental action, however forceful and creative, can not succeed unless it is accompanied by a mobilization of effort by private citizens and the organizations and institutions through which they express their will. In deed, the role of government itself is in large part determined by the presence or absence of such citizen efforts. *That is why the major emphasis of this Conference must be on immediate, practical steps to enlist in this cause the great mass of uncommitted, uninvolved Americans* [emphasis ours].

While there are few specific recommendations on how to enlist "the great mass of uncommitted, uninvolved Americans," the Council's Report does contain a number of suggestions which clearly indicate that the developing federal policy in civil rights, as in other domestic problem areas, would be that of decentralization, if not withdrawal of federal efforts.

Running through the document was a strong emphasis on local co-ordination of government and private civil rights efforts. This was most notable in the largest section of the report, "Economic Security and Welfare," which begins with a proposal to "Establish Metropolitan Jobs Councils in All Major Urban Areas, to Plan, Co-ordinate, and Implement Local Programs to Increase Jobs."

The local orientation of this first recommendation by the Conference Council was quite explicit. The report stated that

> Membership of the Councils should include representatives of business, organized labor, metropolitan governments, education and training institutions and other appropriate community organizations. Each Council should be free to develop its own organization and sources of funds, including foundations, business and labor contributions and government grants.

The section on "Education" which contained very extensive recommendations for federal action, began with the "warning" that

> State and local governments, if they are to preserve control and development of education in their own hands, must take a new approach to revenue needs. *States must commit themselves to a public policy of equalization, educate their citizens on revenue needs, and devise formulas in allocation of financial and human resources that will remedy past inequities.*

Also:

> *Individual local school districts must also take the initiative in achieving equality of educational opportunity.*

The "spin-off" policy could also be seen in the conclusion of the "Education" section where the council wrote:

> The only truly viable solutions will arise from communities which treat the issue as a whole, and devise connecting and continuous plans to carry them towards the goals simultaneously—in short, "workable programs."
>
> State administrative and financial reforms are crucial. Federal sanctions against unconstitutional and inhumane conditions, federal investment, and experimental leadership are equally vital. *But the heart of the educational change, as with its social and economic framework, lies in the commitment of each community to higher goals* [emphasis ours].
>
> And the community commitment involves much more than modification of policy and program by government and school systems. It depends on a broad base of cooperation, and the active participation of religious in-

stitutions, business and labor organizations, civic and community groups, social and fraternal society, private foundations, and individual families and citizens.

Perhaps the best example of "spin-off" is contained in the section of the report covering "Housing." There the Council outlined four goals: (1) freedom of choice; (2) an adequate and expanding supply of new housing for low- and moderate-income families; (3) racially inclusive suburban communities and new towns; and (4) revitalization and integration of existing ghetto areas. In each of these areas, the Council's Report delineated the responsibilities of the federal government, the state government, local government, private groups, and individual citizens. The "Housing" section stated in its concluding pages,

> The recommendations in this report include many examples of the type of local initiative which might be undertaken. However, taken separately they do not constitute a program. Before significant change is likely to occur, it will be necessary to develop a broadly based community effort through which many groups can be persuaded, assisted, and guided in carrying out specific projects which collectively would constitute a program.
> While it will take time to develop the organizational machinery for achieving the four housing goals listed in this report, a start can be made in any community at any time. Outlined below is a broadly sketched model for a metropolitan area program to work toward the goals set forth in the report.

Only the section of the report on Administration of Justice can be characterized as directing primary responsibility to the federal government in the protection of Negroes and civil rights workers from intimidation, obtaining equal justice for Negroes, and improving police-minority-group relations.

The Council was very much aware of this strategy of "spin-off." The "Conclusion" that began with the remarks of the President just quoted included the statement:

> We will need new Federal legislation and more executive action. Every section of this Report deals with these needs as well as the necessity for better enforcement of present laws and more realistic funding.
> There is no question that much remains to be accomplished by our national government.
> But these recommendations should not blind us to a central issue. It is that the national government's response to the compelling cry of the Negro American for justice and true equality has not been matched by state and local government, by business and labor, the housing industry, educational institutions, and the wide spectrum of voluntary organizations who, through united effort, have the power to improve our society.

It remains to be seen whether or not the White House Conference will generate the support and action from previously unmotivated, inactive or reactive, groups. The Administration must have been aware of the history of previous failure to change inaction by local government through exhortation. Yet it seemed to assume that now that there had been a White House Conference, local, state, and private efforts would begin on a full scale. We doubt it.

There is little question that Joseph Kraft was accurate in maintaining that the federal government had recently discovered that the American system was too complicated and diverse to be managed solely from the top. Johnson's waning popularity on the Gallup ratings could also have contributed to this subtle republicanism.

Though Joseph Califano, a White House aide, had sought to justify the "spin-off" policy by asserting that under modern conditions the federal system required "joint action at the local level through groups of governmental units and of citizens," one expert on the civil rights movement was probably more accurate about White House motivations when he observed of the conference:

> It seems to me that the move away from the position of the Howard speech is now complete. The "Council's Report and Recommendations to the White House Conference" strikes me as an incredible hodgepodge of every idea that has been advanced so far, with no analytic structure underlying it. I have the feeling that the White House has now lost its desire to legislate, too: the report recommends so much, in such vague terms, that it strikes me as a prescription for inaction. Certainly the White House has moved away from any position that might arouse criticism from or by the civil rights movement—which means moving away from an attempt to develop bold or new approaches.

It will be remembered that from the time of the Howard speech on, and particularly after the "disaster" of the planning conference, some Administration spokesmen had complained that the movement "knows only how to put its hand out to Uncle Sam." The stage management of the spring conference was sufficiently expert to prevent this issue from being too much out into the open; rather than attack the movement, the Administration strategy was to ignore anything that contradicted the emphasis on "spin-off," and to maintain that the delegates shared the belief that the federal government does not have the lion's share of responsibility for programs to solve civil rights problems. Thus, by the middle of the first day of the conference, a newsman could report the following conversation with Berl Bernhard, general counsel of the conference:

> Most heartening, Bernhard said, was his feeling that the delegates seemed to have become convinced that the federal government cannot be saddled with the whole task of solving all the nation's civil rights problems, but that the solutions can come only from a sharing of the responsibility by all segments of society.

Yet, in fact, the major refrain of the conference delegates was that the federal government should take more and more responsibility for civil rights problems; the dominant form of delegate comments involved simply the explication of specific problems and the request or demand that the government do something about them.

The Johnson Administration is not noted for its attachment to a philosophy, as opposed to strategy, of government. The idea of "spin-off," of local responsibility, and of the importance of coordination (which may well be a bowdlerized version of the long-range policy planning which Moynihan and others in the government had argued for) should probably be viewed more as a political tactic than as a new-found White House philosophy. So long as the Vietnam war, or other intense and expensive foreign adventures last, the White House will find attractive ideas about domestic society that direct responsibility away from the Administration, and ones that privatize domestic social problems. There was little in the actions of the President before the summer of 1965 that would lead one to believe that he was so little interested in federal initiative and involvement as this new view would suggest. In any case, it became clear at the spring conference that the White House had mastered the rhetoric and tactics of encircling and leapfrogging the civil rights movement as a national force, though it had lost its will, and probably its ability, to use its new position to begin any major domestic reform that might significantly improve the situation of Negro Americans.

⚶ 6

Advisory
Councils
and National
Social Welfare
Policy

GILBERT STEINER

Tripartite advisory bodies representative of employers, employees, and the public have been a favored official technique for the development of new policies in social security. The first such group, the Advisory Council on Economic Security, was created to advise the small Committee on Economic Security appointed by Franklin Roosevelt to produce a social security program. That Advisory Council was less than a great success because it actually was a kind of competitor of the committee it served, itself a *de facto* advisory body to the President and to the appropriate committees of Congress. Thereafter, the technique has been successful in establishing a focal point for policy proposals, partly because the advisory bodies subsequently created have had no competition from any official agency. Social security advisory bodies have taken on both the specialized subcommittee and the social security staffing jobs that the congressional committees have not developed. In addition, because they are advisory bodies of private citizens, and because their original conception

Reprinted by permission from Gilbert Steiner, *Social Insecurity: The Politics of Welfare,* Chicago, Rand McNally & Company, 1966, pp. 169–175.

involved a balanced representation of the interest groups concerned, advisory bodies are presumed to be uncommitted.

Before 1958, public assistance and social security were fused for advisory council purposes in accordance with the still prevailing myth that assistance was a residual aspect of social insurance. Tripartite councils on social security worked in 1937–1938 and in 1947–1948 with the understanding that both problems were within their scope. Enactment of two important public assistance improvements—the caretaker grant in ADC [Aid to Dependent Children] and separate medical vendor payments—"was immeasurably aided," according to Wilbur Cohen, by the support given these proposals by "a distinguished advisory council. . . . The contribution of the advisory council [of 1947–1948] was of great significance."[1] Ten years later, public assistance and child welfare were split off from social security and made the subject of separate advisory council inquiry. President Eisenhower hoped that one result of the work of the public assistance advisory council created in 1958 would be a recommendation for increased state and local financial responsibility in the categorical assistance program, that the council would put a break on the prevalent congressional disposition to add to the federal grant over administration opposition.

Creation of a separate public assistance advisory council posed a unique kind of problem in the selection of members. The earlier advisory councils concerned with social security could, by their tripartite character, represent the principal beneficiaries, the principal benefactors, and the general public. Social insurance, after all, involved special tax levies against employees and employers and the creation of a trust fund for the benefit of contributors whose views would understandably be solicited in the governance of the program. Tripartitism allowed for participation of the major groups directly involved—employers and employees—while protecting the interests of groups only peripherally involved by including public members. Resulting activity can range from free collective bargaining to mediation to arbitration, depending on whether public members sit silent, work for an agreement satisfactory to both the employer and employee groups, or impose an agreement by siding with one of the groups against the other. To achieve this tripartite character, the earlier social security councils were drawn from organized labor and from the organized business community with most public members holding government or university attachments.

An advisory council on public assistance alone required either a new theory of tripartitism or a complete substitute for tripartitism to govern the designation of members. Public assistance is not a contributory program; it is

[1] Wilbur J. Cohen, "Factors Influencing the Content of Federal Public Welfare Legislation," *The Social Welfare Forum, 1954* (New York: Columbia University Press, 1954), p. 212.

supported by general revenue. No special trust fund is established; the program competes with all other public causes for public funds. No organized group can be said to be even remotely representative of the beneficiaries; no employer organization can be said to have a particular stake in the program directly comparable to that established by the social security tax on employers. An advisory council in the established tradition would be a case of using an old model for a new purpose.

The statute creating the council in 1958, however, was part of the sweetening used to produce presidential approval for a bill increasing public assistance benefits after the President had specifically requested a reduction in the federal share. There was neither time nor disposition to theorize about the niceties of the applicability or inapplicability of tripartite councils in view of the new, separate emphasis on public assistance. On signing the bill, Eisenhower warned that "increases in the proportion of the public assistance which are financed by the Federal Government can lead only to a weakening of the responsibility of the states and communities."[2] Charged with worrying over the presumably frightful consequences of spending more federal money on public assistance was a council of 12 "who shall, to the extent possible, represent employers and employees in equal numbers, persons concerned with the administration or financing of the State and Federal programs, other persons with special knowledge, experience, or qualifications with respect to the program, and the public." That the job of the council was to worry about the distribution of costs between governments was made clear in its assignment: to review the status of the public assistance program in relation to OASDI [old age, survivors and disability insurance] (where there is no state money), in relation to "the fiscal capacities of the States and the Federal Government, and [to review] any other factors bearing on the amount and proportion of the Federal and State shares in the public assistance program."[3]

Whether by chance or design, the Health, Education, and Welfare advisory council appointed under the 1958 act lacked a single obvious spokesman for the Eisenhower position, but included a minimum of eight persons either already on record or otherwise certain to support increased federal funds, however they might divide on the issue of federal control. The eight included four state or local officials who could certainly not be against unrestricted federal funds (among them a state welfare commissioner, a state legislator who was also a professional social worker, a liberal southern governor, and the manager of a county supervisors' association), two welfare "professionals" whose views were well know (Wilbur Cohen, then of the University of Michigan Social Welfare faculty, and Loula Dunn, then finishing her tenth year as Director of the American Public Welfare Association), the Assistant

2 *Congressional Quarterly,* XIV (1958), 159.
3 Title VII, Sec. 704 (B), Public Law 840, 85th Cong., 1958.

Director of the AFL-CIO Department of Social Security, and the Executive Director of the Division of Christian Life and Work of the National Council of Churches of Christ in the United States. Previous public positions of the National Council and of the AFL-CIO left little doubt about the stand of their spokesmen. Nor were all of the four doubtful cases really very doubtful. They were the Secretary of the New York State Catholic Welfare Commission, a Hunter College sociologist who had written on the relationship of juvenile delinquency to various sociological variables, a Cornell University Vice-President for Business who had, however, served as New York State Budget Director for seven years, and the Chairman of the Board of General Mills.

The council made short shrift of Eisenhower's expressed concern about increased federal funds weakening state and community responsibility. "We have considered the concern expressed in some quarters," said its report, euphemistically passing over the opportunity directly to challenge the President of the United States, "that the present degree of Federal responsibility assumed for public assistance endangers the authority or responsibility of State-local governments. We have found no convincing evidence to support this viewpoint."[4] The 19 other points made by the council all went to liberalization of the program; they included federal grants for general assistance; extension of ADC benefits to a second parent, thereby covering unemployment; elimination of state residence requirements by federal legislative action; equalization of ADC grants with those of the adult categories; federal support for training of public assistance workers and federal grants to schools of social work for training of potential workers; development of more comprehensive medical care programs; and appropriations for research and demonstration grants in the strengthening of family life. After the council's report was filed in January, 1960, no more talk was heard in the remaining year of the Eisenhower administration about increasing state and local responsibility.

Another opportunity to get advisory assistance came in preparing for the 1962 Public Welfare Amendments. An Ad Hoc Committee on Public Welfare was named by Secretary Ribicoff in 1961 and charged to "undertake a careful and thorough review of the Federal welfare laws" in accord with President Kennedy's assertion that in the quarter century since passage of the Social Security Act, "The times, the conditions, the problems have changed—and the nature and objectives of our public assistance and child welfare programs must be changed, also, if they are to meet our human needs."[5] Recognition of the importance of change evaporated when it came to naming members of the Ad Hoc Committee. Members of the closed society were invited to reassemble and again to assure each other that all the old truths had lost none of their validity, that patience and statesmanship would finally

---

[4] *Senate Document 93,* 86th Cong., 2d Sess., 1960.
[5] Ways and Means, Hearings, 1962, p. 64.

overcome partisan political, selfish interests, and that noneconomic services were needed. Committee members were not drawn from a broad spectrum as had been the case in 1937 and in 1947 in choosing social security advisory groups. Instead, like the composition of the 1958 council, that of 1961 could have doubled as the Board of Directors of the American Public Welfare Association. There was overlapping between the 1958 group, the group assembled by Elizabeth Wickenden in 1960, and the 1961 group—and there was to be further overlapping in 1963 when an ADC Audit Advisory Committee was named to help guide the national audit of the ADC program demanded by Senate Appropriations. But there was little diversity within any of the groups. What this meant was that the Ad Hoc Committee could take on faith as matters of agreement the very kinds of questions that most require reexamination and inquiry. The people whose professional lives were dedicated to services as a necessary element of welfare could neither fail to stress services nor be expected to think it necessary to wipe the slate clean and build a new empirical theory of public assistance.

As it developed, the committee report was no more informative than the charge to it had been. After acknowledging differences between conditions of 1935 and those of 1961, but not mentioning technological change, race tensions, urban slum ghettos, and changed patterns of sex behavior other than by the simple assertions that "there have been sweeping social and cultural changes" and "large numbers of people have changed geographic location, often moving to a totally new kind of community (rural to urban, urban to suburban)," the Ad Hoc Committee went on—without documentation—to assert the importance, as its primary recommendation, of increasing federal grants for rehabilitative and preventive services and for the training of social work personnel. Relying on its own members' experience, the committee had no public hearings, reported only conclusions. For information on which to base its conclusions, the committee substituted platitudinous summary statements. The report included no data, an omission that apparently did not disturb Ribicoff, but provoked one congressman to ask: "How about some of the raw material? . . . I am interested in conclusions, but I am interested in finding out the reasons and what data they have."[6]

The report did not, for example, include an analysis of the ADC case load by way of separating out the percentage of cases that might realistically be involved in a rehabilitation program. Rehabilitation became the keystone of the program of services proposed by the committee; the rehabilitation recommendation, however, was not based on the identification of a new situation in public assistance. If most of the client group did not lend itself to rehabilitation, there would not be much innovation. It didn't; and there hasn't been.

[6] *Ibid.,* p. 175.

. . . [I]t is important that, like the members of the earlier advisory council, the Ad Hoc Committee members were not really free to consider the problem of public assistance *de novo*. By virtue of professional attachments, they were to a man committed to liberalization of existing policy which is a different animal—and may actually be less liberal—from creation of a policy adequate to the current problem. No one would know from the 1961 Ad Hoc Committee report any more than from the 1960 advisory council report that 67 percent of ADC cases are families with an absent parent; that the costs of public assistance are deeply resented by numerous northern governors and state legislators who allege that migrants from the south are an important burden on their states; that if provision of minimum standards for the needy is the goal of public assistance, variation in benefits between jurisdictions over a protracted period raises some doubt about the validity of the federal-state cooperative arrangement; that race, illegitimacy, and birth control are critical public assistance problems now, while they scarcely existed as issues in 1935. Most important, if release from economic dependency is the test of success, there is little evidence that services to lead to rehabilitation are a solution to the ADC problem. The specific remedy for the ailment is not at hand in present policy.

Advisory councils in public assistance are now built into the system since provision was made in the 1962 amendments for a council to report in 1966 and for subsequent councils to be named by the Secretary of Health, Education, and Welfare. The first such council was appointed by Secretary Celebrezze in July, 1964. It is unlikely that any fair-minded person would question the competence of the 12 appointees, but surely there is a certain futility involved in Wilbur Cohen formally and officially soliciting public assistance advice from Fedele Fauri, who is chairman of the council, and from Elizabeth Wickenden—friends, colleagues, coarchitects of current policy. The council chosen in 1964 is composed of the same kinds of excellent people whose impressions have dominated national policy in the field for three decades, this very circumstance makes it unlikely that they can undertake the kind of "independent review" that the Ways and Means Committee regarded as important.

There can be no drive for innovation as long as an elaborate facade exists which obscures the need for innovation. A critical part of that facade is the advisory or *ad hoc* committee which, to be useful, should be representative of widely divergent groups, uncommitted to any existing way of meeting the problem, committed to assembling information. The recent councils and committees are not broadly representative; neither are they uncommitted, nor have they substituted inquiry for impressions. It is not certain, of course, that there is a better way to meet the problem of public assistance; it is certain that before the question of a better way will even be asked about, it will be necessary to broaden subsequent advisory groups to include a goodly number of those who neither created nor administered the existing policy, nor are bonded to it by faith in professional colleagues. There are critics of present public assistance policy who are neither in favor of antediluvian standards nor ill-informed; none of them has been attracted to one of the advisory groups. Before the philosophers of innovation in public assistance can appear in the advisory groups, the company union must first be dissolved.

══✐═ IV

Contemporary Perspectives on Presidential Advisory Systems

The Hoover Commissions on Administrative Management have long served as the focal point of Presidential reforms; many of the Commissions' suggested reorganizations have, at one time, and in one manner or another, been put into practice. In recent years, it has proved more practical to reform through executive orders and to alter institutions incrementally (and often discreetly) rather than to urge major reorganizations upon Congress. As Harvey Mansfield has pointed out:

> The Johnson Administration in four years accomplished more reorganization than had been transacted in the previous decades. Given the supporting staff resources now available in or to the Executive Office and the supply of unofficial consultative talent among experienced former political executives, in academic quarters, and elsewhere, the advantages of confidentiality in getting advice and preparing reorganization proposals appear overwhelming from the President's viewpoint.[1]

[1] Harvey Mansfield, "Federal Executive Reorganization: Thirty Years After the President's Committee On Administrative Management," paper delivered at the 1968 Annual Meeting, American Political Science Association, Washington, D.C., September 2–7, p. 9.

But many critics still decry the lack of high-level planning and policy evaluation. Some speak of a growing "intelligence gap," while others believe that recent Presidents have become overwhelmed by too much information and too many policy responsibilities.[2] Soon after leaving his Cabinet post, John Gardner, the distinguished former Secretary of Health, Education, and Welfare, stressed the need for a major overhaul of national domestic program management:

> I believe that the Federal Government cannot go on much longer with its present organization of agencies on the domestic side of Government. It is not the fault of any one Administration, but for the past 20 years the problems of overlap and conflict of mission have grown steadily worse. I have reason to believe that if Lyndon Johnson had served another term he would have undertaken a major reorganization—and believe me, it is needed.[3]

Recent years have witnessed an unending stream of new proposals for creating a more effective Presidency and fashioning a more responsive White House advisory system. It would be impossible to do justice to the diversity and imagination of these proposals. Here we offer only a few examples of the quest for better White House intelligence and of the use of such intelligence. The reader interested in pursuing a number of other discussions about reorganization and institution-building at the White House level is referred to the lengthy bibliography at the end of the book.

[2] For examples of these two viewpoints, see Bertram Gross, ed., *A Great Society?*, New York, Basic Books, 1968, and Rexford Tugwell, "The President and His Helpers," *Political Science Quarterly,* June, 1967, pp. 253–267.

[3] See the interview with John Gardner, reported by Peter Kihss, "Gardner Wants President to Appoint an Executive to Coordinate Agencies on Domestic Matters," *New York Times,* July 18, 1968, p. 21.

1

Toward Improving Presidential Level Policy Planning

MICHAEL D. REAGAN

This is an essay around a single theme: how to construct a more tightly organized policy planning system at the national level. While it stays within the existing formal limits of the Constitution, I do not pretend to advocate only what might be put through Congress now. Rather, the intent is to set forth the direction which improvement of our political institutions seems likely to take, and to prove our ideas in that direction as a first step toward more concrete institutional change.

Reprinted by permission from Michael D. Reagan, "Toward Improving Presidential Level Policy Planning," *Public Administration Review,* vol. XXIII, March, 1963, pp. 177–186. The author wishes to express his appreciation to the Conference on the Public Service for underwriting an earlier version of this article and for granting permission to publish the revision, which has not been reviewed by the Conference and does not necessarily represent the views of the organization or its members.

The Meaning of Policy Planning

The privilege of using words as we wish to use them entails a corresponding obligation to make clear to the reader what use we are making of crucial terms. The crucial term here, obviously, is *planning*. By this I do not mean simply projection of existing trends or prediction of what will happen if certain assumptions are granted. Projection and prediction are a part of planning, but a part only. Two other elements are equally essential: the choice of goals, and the devising of programs to achieve the chosen goals.

Planning will therefore be used here to refer to a four-factor process:

Establishing goals, and priorities among them, in relation to resources (those currently available plus those whose future availability may itself be a planning goal);

The measurement of the distance and difficulties between the present situation and the desired objectives (including projections of how far and fast already existing programs would go toward accomplishment of the objectives);

The formulation of programs (timing, assignment of specific tasks to specific agencies, estimating required resources in detail, budgeting yearly increments, etc.) by which it is hoped the objectives can be reached; and,

Periodic modification of both objectives and programs in the light of experience with incremental actions.

By *policy* planning, I mean to indicate an emphasis on central planning at the presidential-congressional level, where the choice of goals involves not just competitive techniques, but competitive values, and where, in consequence, the resolution of conflicting interests and the establishment of a solid base of political support is an essential part of the planning process.

Assumptions

The initial assumption is that we cannot as a nation afford to cross bridges as we come to them—rather, we must anticipate the needs of the future and plan for them today. Townsend Hoopes put the point well when he wrote that:

> Our difficulty is that, as a nation of short-term pragmatists accustomed to dealing with the future only when it has become the present, we find it hard to regard future trends as serious realities. We have not achieved the capacity to treat as real and urgent—as demanding action today—problems which appear in critical dimension only at some future date. Yet failure to achieve this new habit of mind is likely to prove fatal.[1]

[1] Townsend Hoopes, "The Persistence of Illusion," *Yale Review* (Spring, 1960), pp. 321–37.

Secondly, I assume that the most fundamental structural obstacle to effective planning lies in the scatteration and fragmentation of power and responsibility in American national government. The division of labor between President and Congress is uncertain and the difference in the character of their respective constituencies encourages goal-setting on a least-common-denominator basis. The fragmentation of power within Congress unfits that body for unified, consistent legislative action. On the Executive side, too, the textbook unity of the presidency is too often belied by centrifugal forces operating on the departments and agencies.

Finally, I assume that while the quality of planning will be affected by the total organization of government at the top levels, only the President can provide the initiative and the coherent view of national priorities that must underlie effective planning. An editorial in the *New York Times* commented regarding the Report of the President's Commission on National Goals that:

> Perhaps the chief lesson to be learned from this experience is the irreplaceable role of creative, elected political leadership in our democracy. No unofficial committee of distinguished leaders having differing views can do the job of articulating and implementing national goals. That responsibility falls most heavily upon the President of the United States.[2]

The flabbiness of a report by a "committee of distinguished leaders" is a result of the need to compromise too many viewpoints; Congress has the same characteristic, hence, effective planning must be presidential planning.

Given these assumptions regarding the need for planning and the inadequacies of the existing organizational pattern at the top levels of American national government, what constructive suggestions can be made, within the broad limits of the Constitution, for sharpening the goal-setting process, providing the necessary political support for more rational planning, and improving the policy-planning capacity of the President, as both Chief Executive and Chief Legislator? In answering this question illustrations will be drawn predominantly from the area of planning for economic growth and stability.

The President and Presidency in the Planning Process

PROBLEMS:

1. The State Department has had a policy-planning staff since the late 'forties. The Budget Bureau has recently encouraged the development of equivalents in other departments. Yet the President has no such staff. He needs one.

The "program of the President" is arrived at now primarily by Budget

[2] Editorial, *New York Times,* November 28, 1960.

Bureau review of proposals welling up from the agencies. This review is programmatic (legislative clearance) as well as financial—or do fiscal considerations inevitably intrude even at the stage of program clearance—and competent observers[3] give the Bureau high marks for coordination of on-going programs. But coordination of existing programs, difficult and important as it is, does not obviate the need for integrated policy initiation and development. This job is one the Budget Bureau may not be well suited for. Thus, Maass and Radway have written that:

> . . . negative and piecemeal review of individual proposals flowing up from agencies to the chief executive cannot produce an integrated governmental program at the time it is required. It is becoming clear that top level executives require policy staff organs to formulate general programs which subordinate units cannot evolve because of limited terms of reference, inertia, organizational or professional bias, or inadequate factual information. Such a policy general staff, *by supplying common premises for action,* can help insure coordination "before the event," that is, by prior indoctrination.[4]

Similar sentiments have been expressed by others.

Also, while the Budget Bureau's jurisdiction covers all *agencies*, it does not cover all *functions:* its primary concern is with expenditure only. Yet national economic policy also embraces monetary policy, taxation, loan policy and debt management—all of which lie outside the Bureau's jurisdiction, thus making it less suitable than the Council of Economic Advisers for the task of integrating national economic policy.

Perhaps, then, *the* next step in supporting the President in his personal task of national goal setting and policy planning would be to build a presidential policy-planning staff, to supply the common premises of which Maass and Radway wrote, to develop alternative sets of goals (related closely to economic resources analysis) to facilitate rational presidential choice, and then to ensure that programs-in-being service presidential priorities.

2. Leon Keyserling tells a story of Napoleon's reported preference for one bad general over two good ones to illustrate the need for unified planning. Our economic policy planning today may all be in the hands of "good generals," but there are too many of them. The Secretary of the Treasury, the Council of Economic Advisors (CEA), Budget Director, Federal Reserve Board and a number of lending agencies are all heavily involved in the determination of pieces of economic policy, but no one is in a position to *insist* that they operate on common premises. Not even the President can do so, because of the statutory "independence" of the Federal Reserve and

---

[3] Jesse Burkhead, *Government Budgeting* (New York, 1956), p. 300.

[4] Arthur Maass and Lawrence Radway, "Gauging Administrative Responsibility," in Dwight Waldo, *Ideas and Issues in Public Administration* (New York, 1953), p. 451 (italics added).

of independent regulatory agencies whose functions importantly affect the nation's economic performance and structure (e.g., ICC, CAB, FPC, FTC). An interdepartmental coordinating device—the Advisory Board on Economic Growth and Stability—was created in 1953 to alleviate this problem, but its record was less than impressive. Coordination of transportation, communications, energy resources and regulatory agencies generally by Executive Office staff was proposed by James M. Landis in 1960, but the President did not pass the recommendation on to Congress.

3. The directly political problem of presidential policy planning relates to the President's *personal* role as articulator of policy goals and *Chief Support Builder.*

As Neustadt has noted,[5] the President cannot rely on sheer command very often or very much. His power is only the power to persuade. This is where constructs of planning mechanisms (especially in the milieu of public administration thinking) tend to go astray: they assume that the internal job is the whole job. It is not. The President must first make clear to Congress and the public what his policy goals are; then he must seek their support. Neither job has been or is being done adequately.

The articulation of goals suffers the same defects as their formulation: lack of over-all integration, lack of long-range planning. Consider the annual State of the Union address, which could be an excellent vehicle for educating Congress and the public about planning needs, yet is generally on the order of abstract exhortation and/or a listing, without priority or relationships indicated, of short-run legislative goals.

President Kennedy, it should be added, has sent to Congress a steady stream of special messages on a wide variety of problems, including conservation and recreation, consumer protection, public works, and federal pay. In fact, the stream has inundated the legislators. Individually, many of these are excellent statements of national needs and objectives; as a group they lack coherence and an indication of their relative contributions to an improved "State of the Union."

RECOMMENDATIONS:

1. *The three annual presidential messages should be reoriented and reconstituted so that (1) the State of the Union message becomes a statement of goals for an extended period of years, and (2) the Economic Report and Budget messages are combined into a single National Economic Budget statement.*

The State of the Union address could express the President's view of the state of the union as he envisages it five or more years ahead. It should

---

[5] Richard Neustadt, *Presidential Power* (New York, 1960), p. 26 and, generally, Ch. 2.

present goals and assess prospects, as well as reviewing the past year. It should be a message of candor, setting forth the nation's problems as the President sees them, stating alternative policies with the expected consequences of each, and explaining the case for the specific set of goals to which the President is committing himself. Such a message, while avoiding the rigidity of a detailed "five-year plan," would force the President to think through long-range priorities and relationships among competing objectives. It would focus public attention on the basic value choices of future national development. And it would foster a shift in public attitude toward realization of the necessity for long-range, conscious anticipation of problems, if Americans are to continue to be masters, not puppets, of their fate. A day or two of congressional debate of this message, perhaps under out-party control, should serve further to quicken public engagement and aid in the development of a majority consensus on the broad outlines of policy, thus in turn giving guidance to the President regarding what he can expect the public to support when his long-range goals are translated into short-run incremental legislation.

A single National Economic Budget message should go far toward compelling close correlation of the larger economic considerations with particular programs, of long- and short-run plans, and of the governmental and private sector relationships. Projection for several years ahead of the resource requirements implied by the goals enunciated in the State of the Union message would be a powerful tool of public education.[6] The long-range projection, plus a spelling out of the governmental policies designed to achieve the needed rate, composition and allocation of production would form a basis for assumption of responsibility toward national economic needs by the decision makers of business and labor in the private sector. The short-run budget section of the message would be placed in its proper perspective a the one-year steps toward multi-year objectives.

2. *There should be created an Office of Policy Planning (OPP), using the Council of Economic Advisers as its core, to provide the common premises upon which integrated planning must be based, and to give the President an overall planning staff for the preparation of his annual messages.*

By taking over the legislative clearance function from the Budget Bureau (thus emphasizing substantive program content apart from money-cost), filling the policy gaps left by problems that fall between agencies, and emphasizing the development of new policies to meet problems that lie too far over the horizon for the operating departments to encompass in their necessary orientation toward on-going programs, the OPP would centralize primary responsi-

---

[6] Long-range budget projection made an unheralded entrance on the scene at the very end of the Eisenhower Administration when the Bureau of the Budget published its *Ten-Year Projection of Federal Budget Expenditures* (Washington, 1961).

bility for development of "the President's program." Transfer of legislative clearance is needed to mesh agency plans with the independent policy-goals planning done for the President; it would also give OPP the degree of involvement in executive operations which it needs for leverage with the agencies and to keep it tied to "reality."

Spelling out the functions of the proposed OPP a bit further, it would include the following:

a. devising alternative sets of policy goals for consideration by the President in the course of preparing the reoriented State of the Union message;

b. resources and requirements analysis (a somewhat expanded version of the CEA is envisaged here) to accompany the goal-sets;

c. preparation of the National Economic Budget, under the clauses of the Employment Act which call for the President to specify the levels of employment and production needed to achieve the Act's goals and to offer a program for achieving those levels. (Sections 3(a) (1) and 3(a) (4) of the Employment Act provide an adequate legislative base for a national economic budget, even though the more specific mandate for governmental investment contained in the original Full Employment bill of 1945 was eliminated in the final version). And,

d. coordination of on-going programs with Presidential objectives and priorities.

3. The President should strongly support, and urge the Office of Policy Planning (the CEA, in the absence of OPP) to use vigorously, the authority contained in Section 4(c) (3) of the Employment Act for CEA to "appraise the various programs and activities of the federal government" from the viewpoint of their contribution to the larger economic goals.

The Chairman of the CEA would thus provide the single focus of responsibility for economic policy that President Kennedy appears to desire in every major policy area. This would be an alternative mode of coordination to replace the unlamented Advisory Board on Economic Growth and Stability.

4. The President should seek from Congress a degree of authority over the now independent regulatory bodies adequate to permit action rather than mere exhortation, when it is necessary to bring their policies into line with the larger economic needs. This would be a logical corollary to the appraisal developed under the preceding recommendation.

The purpose of this pair of recommendations is to strengthen the ability of presidential staff to exert a coordinating influence against the centrifugal tendencies of the departments, agencies, and independent commissions. Even within the regular executive branch hierarchy, coordination is difficult and often deficient. The existence of the CEA and the discipline of the President's Economic Report have perhaps made each agency a bit self-conscious about the relationship of its own program to stabilization policy; yet the full potential of the CEA's authority to appraise agency programs and recommend to the President ways to improve their fit with overall economic policy appears not to have been achieved.

At the minimum, a new President should be granted authority to name the chairman of each regulatory commission from among the hold-over members or by replacement with a new appointee, and to change the chairman when he wills. Abandonment of the bipartisan characteristic of these boards would also enhance presidential authority—and accountability. James Madison wrote quite enough checks and balances into our political system without our adding additional impediments to effective action.

The combination of more vigorous staff appraisal of agency programs from a presidential perspective and with strong presidential backing, plus a strengthening of the President's legal authority over agencies having important economic functions, should noticeably improve the integrative capacity of the presidency. Should these measures be tried and prove insufficient over a period of years, the alternative of a super-department of economic affairs may have to be explored. But the staff approach appears to be the more promising and the more consistent with recent trends.

• • •

Presidential–Congressional Relations

PROBLEMS.   Because of divergence of constituencies between the President and congressmen and the absence of compensating unifying factors such as a disciplined party system, an inherent difference often amounting to direct conflict exists between the viewpoints of the two branches. The President, because elected nationally, thinks of national problems; senators and representatives, elected locally, think locally. To the congressmen, the national interest is most frequently the sum of local interests. But the President's concern, in domestic as well as more obviously perhaps in foreign policy, must be with the interests common to the national community. These differences are reflected in the goal-setting process, for the goals of localities and partial interests will not entirely coincide with the goals the President seeks for the nation.

In fact, the legislative view tends toward distrust of national objectives as such, toward faith that self-adjustment of divergent groups will obviate the need for any goal-setting. And when congressmen do see a need for national goals—as probably a majority of them do in the educational field today—the legislative process is such that goals set by Congress are likely to be either extremely vague or internally inconsistent and bland.

At present, the burden of proof is on the President and the national interest. Partial and local interests represented in Congress have the upper hand. The basic problem in the Legislative-Executive relationship may be expressed (in an admitted oversimplification) as the President's need to build a positive majority for his proposals by compromising with divergent interests wanting either no action or each a different kind of action. Can the burden of proof be shifted, while remaining within the present constitutional framework?

RECOMMENDATIONS:

1. *By mutual agreement, the President and Congress should extend the logic of the Reorganization Act procedure to the area of substantive policy making.*

The Reorganization Act reverses the normal legislative procedure. That is, the President does not just *propose* a statutory change in administrative organization, but he *declares* that change and his declaration becomes law without further legislative approval. Only if Congress (currently, a majority of either house of Congress) disapproves and "vetoes" the President's action does it fail to become law. Thus, the burden of proof is shifted: instead of the President having to form a positive majority for his proposal, it becomes law unless the opposition is able to form a majority against it. Granting that the opposition was able to do this in 1961 against Kennedy's initial reorganization plans for the independent regulatory commission and in 1962 against the Urban Affairs Department, this is simply to say that nothing can be done without adequate political support. In the long run, because Congress would be more hesitant to veto legislation of substantive importance than it is to throw out administrative changes that lack public appeal or understanding, the chances for action would be increased by this shift in the burden of proof to those who would deny the need for action or the appropriateness of the President's particular action. Action obtained under the legislative veto system is likely to be more coherent than that for which positive congressional assent is required because the scheme, as embodied in the Reorganization Act, permits approval or disapproval, but not amendments. It is in the process of amendment that legislation originally coherent often becomes a hodgepodge of contradictory crumbs for every interest. If Congress disciplines itself to accept or reject, but not amend, presidential legislation, the legislators themselves would have some protection from the log-rolling they now, find as necessary as it may be distasteful. And because Congress would retain a veto, it would retain final legislative authority in accord with constitutional requirements.

Use of the device of delegated law-making authority in the President's hands, subject to legislative veto, would also go a considerable distance toward resolving the problems of irresponsibility and stalemate in American political structure, and without requiring constitutional amendment. Harold Laski persuasively argued that the Chief Executive cannot rationally be held responsible for policies that are not of his own design; yet that is what the separated powers system requires. Under the legislative veto arrangement, however, the plans he used would be his own and Executive responsibility would be clear. Similarly, Congress would be acting more responsibly if its refusal to go along with Presidential actions were the express judgment of a majority rather than the result of minority obstruction in the House Rules or Ways and Means Committee or a Senate filibuster.

It seems clear that we *are* moving in this direction. The Reciprocal Trade Agreements acts have, since 1934, delegated to the President an area of discretionary lawmaking, and the 1958 revision embodies the legislative veto principle in permitting a two-thirds vote of Congress to override Presidential action under the escape clause. In 1961, President Kennedy proposed a farm plan employing the same principle: each commodity group would, with Department of Agriculture participation, develop its own program, subject to congressional veto.[7] The Commission on Money and Credit proposed that the President be granted authority to vary the personal income tax rate counter-cyclically, subject to congressional veto,[8] and President Kennedy adopted a modification of this proposal in his 1962 Economic Report.[9] While the immediate reaction has been generally negative on Capitol Hill, I believe that these proposals constitute the handwriting on the wall.

Effective government, it might be said, requires that what the Founding Fathers separated—President and Congress—we must put together. This recommendation would institutionalize the Presidential role of chief legislator and would thus be a major step toward the avoidance of stalemate. But change in the legal structure can only create an opportunity; the opportunity must be fulfilled through more vigorous efforts in the directly political arena. As J. S. Mill said, "in politics, as in mechanics, the power which is to keep the engine going must be sought for outside the machinery." The next two recommendations concern the motive power.

2. *The President, as party leader, should more intensively woo the rank and file of congressmen, toward the end of building a solid, lasting phalanx of support.*

What James M. Burns wrote of FDR's second-term congressional difficulties perhaps applies to most Presidents:

> Roosevelt had led Congress during his first term by his adroit and highly personal handling of congressional leaders and by exploiting the sense of crisis; but, intent on immediate tactical gains on Capitol Hill, he had neglected to build up a position of strength with the rank and file of Congress.[10]

[7] *New York Times,* March 17, 1961.

[8] Commission on Money and Credit, *Money and Credit* (New York, 1961), pp. 136–37.

[9] *1962 Economic Report of the President,* pp. 18–19.

[10] James M. Burns, *Roosevelt: The Lion and the Fox* (New York, 1956), p. 348.

Since neither a parliamentary system nor tightly disciplined parties on the British model are on the immediate horizon, the best chance of closer cooperation between President and Congress lies in incremental changes in the informal relationships. Since one of the larger weaknesses of the existing relationship —from the viewpoint of achieving sustained support for long-range planning— lies in a presidential tendency to work through committee leaders almost exclusively, this is one of the crucial informal relationships, and gains await only a more sustained Presidential effort to reach out to the rank and file.

3. *The President and national committee of the party in power, and the national committee chairman of the out-party, should organize continuing local discussion of the President's program and work toward selection of congressional candidates oriented toward national issues.*[11]

Every major interest group now recognizes two ways of influencing Congress: by representation to the legislators directly, and by molding "grass roots" opinion among the lawmakers' constituents. The latter is in the long run the surer type of influence. The President of the United States—through his State of the Union Message, special messages addressed ostensibly to Congress but really to the electorate, press conferences, and fireside chats—tries to put across his conception of the national interest in the same way. But, unlike the AFL-CIO or the Chamber of Commerce, his attempt to communicate with his constituency, the national electorate, lacks the nexus of *organization*. It is, therefore, less effective by far than it could be.

During each presidential election year the state-and-local oriented party structure is supplemented by various "Citizens for X" groups: volunteer participants in the political process whose concern is with national issues and national candidates. Between elections, these groups generally disappear— and with them the chance for a President to build a grass-roots organizational base of continuing support. In recent years, however, the club movement, most notably in New York and California, has brought into being for the first time a type of local political organization whose members' interests are keyed to national concerns. The national committees should use and support, financially and by moral encouragement, these local organizations. These local organizations should recruit talent for local congressional nominations, endorsing in each district a man who promises vigorous support for his party's national platform. In return, the national committees must give campaign funds, research help, and publicity to such candidates, to orient them in a practical way toward national interest thinking by lessening their dependence on local, partial interests.

Card-carrying membership in the *national* parties should be extended beyond the experimental stage it reached during Paul Butler's tenure as

[11] The above two paragraphs draw heavily upon a series of three articles by James M. Burns in *Atlantic Monthly,* February, March, April, 1960.

Democratic national chairman. This will help promote a continuing psychological tie between a President and the voters who put him in office.

To make the tie more effective, to link it to immediate legislative issues, and to increase voter engagement in public policy making—all of which would constitute a big step toward the sustained support required by viable long-range planning—the national committees should experiment with the promotion of national policy discussion at the local level, by supplying speakers, literature, and a prod to local party organizations and clubs, as well as to non-party voluntary groups, like the Foreign Policy Association.[12]

Presidential Planning and the National Style

Except during the wars of the twentieth century, our national style has been one of looseness, of pursuing private goals in the faith that God would watch over children, drunkards, and the United States of America.

This is not good enough. Instead of a system which suspends the normal workings of centrifugal forces in favor of "constitutional dictatorship" whenever an obvious crisis occurs, we need now and for the future a process that will provide sustained strength for effective government even when crises are not obvious.

A reorientation of our system in the direction of Presidential planning is the way to strengthen our capacity to govern. Informally, we have been moving in this direction for some time. But, we have tried to do so without directly challenging the loose national style inherited from the nineteenth century. It is time to make that challenge, time to institutionalize and push further with the logic of presidential planning.

---

[12] Since these paragraphs were written, a development along these lines has occurred, in the form of White House Regional Conferences, held in several cities in November, 1961.

2

Improving
the Foreign
Policy
"Machinery"

ROGER HILSMAN

Foreign policy is politics, and politics is a "slow boring of hard boards." There is probably no quick or easy way of making improvements. Certainly tinkering with the organizational "machinery" is not going to help very much. The debate about how to "organize for national security" that preceded the Kennedy administration reached the conclusion described, that the problems of national security policy were not going to be solved by reorganizing the government. "Super-Staffs and super-secretaries" were no way out, it was clear, and neither was strengthening the National Security Council or creating a "vice-president for foreign affairs." And certainly nothing happened in the Kennedy administration that would alter that conclusion. In fact, the major recommendation that came out of the debate about organizing for national security—that the prime voice and co-ordinating power should center in the Department of State—in practice only proved the validity of the conclusion that reorganizing was no solution. Merely assigning power to the State Department did not guarantee that the Secretary and the Department would use it.

Reprinted by permission from Roger Hilsman, *To Move a Nation*, Garden City, N. Y., Doubleday, 1967, pp. 564–576.

All this, of course, does not mean that changes in organization do not affect policy. Organizational changes usually follow a shift in power, as for example, the changes in the way intelligence problems were handled in the State Department followed CIA's loss of power in the aftermath of the Bay of Pigs. But changes in organization can in themselves bring about an increase or decrease of power and alter the weight that one set of considerations will have over another in policy deliberations. But whether the result is better or worse policy depends on your point of view, on whose interests are being given additional weight. What is an "improvement" in this sense to one person may not be to another.

Some improvements are undoubtedly possible in organizational structure that everyone would agree were improvements. Ways might be found, for example, to make the communications process among participants in the making of policy quicker and easier. There might also be organizational changes that could bring more precision in assigning the flow of work, or in the effectiveness of applying the proper expertise at the proper stage. But these are not of fundamental importance and would result in only marginal improvement in the foreign policies that came out the other end.

Prediction and Knowledge

Effective foreign policy depends on the capacity to predict events in the social affairs of men, and a better capacity to predict would mean better and more effective foreign policy. But more is required than simple factual information. Predicting the outcome of alternative policies requires knowledge in the sense of an ability to identify and weigh the different factors bearing on the particular situation and an understanding of the dynamism by which those different factors interact.[1] In the Middle Ages, for example, no one foresaw the Black Death, the great plague that swept Europe, or knew what to do about it after it came. Yet when men learned that germs cause disease and the means by which germs are transmitted, they could not only treat individual cases of the plague, but could foresee that an increase in filth in the cities and the rats that live on it would create the conditions for an outbreak of the plague and indicate the measures needed to head it off.

There is no doubt that knowledge in this sense of the ability to make sound predictions is the crux of the matter. The debate in the Kennedy administration over Vietnam policy, for example, revolved around rival analyses about the nature of guerrilla warfare and predictions about the effects of alternative ways of dealing with it. In China policy, the debate centered on the analysis of the nature of Chinese Communism, its capacity to change

---

[1] For discussions of the role of facts and the role of theory, see Morris R. Cohen, *Reason and Nature,* 1959, and my own *Strategic Intelligence and National Decisions,* 1956.

Chinese society, and whether or not it was a "passing phase" as well as on predictions about the effects of the rival policies of "isolating" Communist China or maintaining an "open door" for a lessening of hostility and eventual accommodation. And so it was through all the other cases—the Cuban missile crisis, the Congo, Laos, and Indonesia. The crux of the debate in each instance turned on an analysis of the factors bearing on the problem and on predictions about the consequences of alternative ways of dealing with it.

More and better knowledge of the kind that permits accurate prediction is undoubtedly the most important single thing that is needed for the improvement of foreign policy. But here again, there is no quick or easy solution. If there was a wide and obvious gap between the pool of basic knowledge available in the universities, say, and what was actually used in informing governmental decisions, something dramatic might be done. But this particular gap, the gap between the knowledge of experts in government and experts outside, is infinitesimal. Take, for example, the field of "Sovietology." The great body of what is known about the Soviet Union and the workings of Soviet society is shared—and subscribed to—by Soviet specialists within and outside the government. By and large, in fact, the personnel themselves are interchangeable and frequently do shift back and forth. What disagreements there are in the field of "Sovietology" are not between government experts and academic experts but between one group of specialists cutting across both government and academia and another, also cutting across both government and academia. And what is really remarkable is how small the area of disagreement is, how accurate are their judgments about Soviet reactions and behavior, and how few are their failures at prediction—no matter how harshly their role in the Cuban missile crisis is judged.

New and better knowledge is needed, but how can it be developed? Certainly the attempts to institutionalize the effort within government have not been very fruitful. It was this need for knowledge and foresight, according to Dean Acheson, that led General Marshall when he was Secretary of State to establish in 1947 the Policy Planning Staff, a group of about a dozen top-level specialists under an assistant secretary.[2] But, in practice, the Policy Planning Staff did not work out to be the panacea some had hoped for. It proved to be a useful pool of talent that could be tapped in time of crisis— as its second chief, Paul Nitze, for example, was pulled out for the negotiations after Mossadegh and his government nationalized oil in Iran. Its members have also contributed "think-piece" memoranda, which have been neither better nor worse, on the average, than similar thoughtful memoranda written in the action bureaus, in the intelligence agencies, or by outside scholars and writers. But none of this, no matter how well done, fulfills the concept

[2] Dean Acheson, "The President and the Secretary of State," in *The Secretary of State,* edited by Don K. Price for the *American Assembly,* 1960, p. 48.

of a "planning" staff, and yet beyond this the Policy Planning Staff has done very little.

What is "planning"? Men building a dam or a bridge can plan in a long-range and very precise sense. They can predict the forces that the dam or bridge must withstand and determine with great accuracy the materials and strength needed for each part of the structure. In building a dam or a bridge, men can also draw blueprints and develop a schedule for the work to be done that will permit them to specify months in advance the exact dates on which cement, for example, should be ordered and delivered. Some military planning is also of this nature, such as providing port facilities and hospitals and stockpiles of ammunition and so on. But beyond the field of logistics, military planning is limited—for the fundamental reason that there is an enemy who has some choice in the matter too. In war, the only long-range "planning" that can be done apart from logistics is the making of very broad strategic choices.

Long-range planning in foreign affairs is more similar to this kind of military planning than it is to either logistics planning or the kind of planning used to build a dam or a bridge. It is, essentially, analyzing the nature of the problem and making broad strategic choices for dealing with it. Secretary Dulles in his 1957 speech about Communist China, for example, which argued for a strategy of isolating the Chinese Communists was one strategic choice. The "open door" speech of 1963, which argued for an alternative strategy of "firmness and flexibility" leading toward an eventual accommodation, was another strategic choice. The choice in dealing with Indonesia and Sukarno was the United States posture toward the "new nationalism," whether it could be brought into constructive channels or would respond only to firmness. In Vietnam, the problem was how to treat guerrilla warfare, as we have said—as fundamentally a political problem or as fundamentally a war.

Short-range planning in foreign affairs is working out the moves and countermoves in the midst of an ongoing situation, of developing instructions for an ambassador or orders for the fleet. Should the United States move troops into Thailand in response to the Communists' violation of the cease-fire in Laos, and if so what will the Communists then do? Should the United States use an air strike to take out the Soviet missiles in Cuba, confine its action to diplomatic moves, or begin with a blockade? In China policy, should the United States lift travel restrictions on Americans, push for Chinese participation in disarmament talks, and recognize Mongolia, and if so, what will be the Chinese response?

But both the making of broad strategic choices in foreign affairs and this short-range form of making contingency calculations of move and countermove are at the political heart of policy-making. Consequently, the truth of the matter is that both of these kinds of "planning" are done at several places at once—by the advocates of the rival policies and their allies. In the Laos crisis of 1962, for example, one set of "plans" of what the United States should do if the Communist side continued to violate the cease-fire in spite of our having put troops in Thailand was prepared in the Pentagon and another was prepared by the Bureau of Far Eastern Affairs and their allies in the State Department's Intelligence Bureau. In the struggle over Vietnam policy, one strategic concept for fighting the guerrillas was developed out of the work of Thompson in Saigon, people in the Intelligence Bureau at the State Department and in the White House, and military people at the Special Forces center at Fort Bragg—but all this "planning" was overridden by the "planning" for traditional warfare that took place in the military headquarters at Saigon. In the Congo crisis, "planning" took place most of the time in the Bureau of African Affairs, but every now and again it was done elsewhere—in the bureau responsible for UN affairs, in the Intelligence Bureau, and occasionally, to be completely accurate, in the office of Senator Dodd.

At one time or another, the Policy Planning Staff "planned" in this sense as the ally of one or another set of advocates, but it succeeded in being the *principal* advocate and planner in very few cases. The Multilateral Force for NATO and the earlier Developmental Loan Fund are two outstanding examples, and it is instructive of the politics of statecraft that both of these problems were bureaucratic orphans, matters that cut across the regular responsibilities of both the regional and the functional offices of the State Department.

Policy is made in a political process for good and sufficient reasons, and, so long as these basic reasons persist, attempts at institutionalizing "planning" or "foresight" or "wisdom" are likely to fail. Some improvements, of course, can be made. A climate of receptivity to new ideas and knowledge can be created rather easily, for example, and creating such a climate of receptivity can have important consequences as people are encouraged to experiment with new ideas and to put them forward. Although it was partly nullified in the State Department by the attitude at the top, President Kennedy established this climate of receptivity at the beginning of his administration very quickly. His actions showed that he was reading people's memos, and he called up "little" men on the phone, all of which created an excitement that the bureaucracy had not known for many years. Government can also do more to encourage research and the development of new knowledge in political and social affairs. The Defense Department, for example spends billions of dollars supporting research in the physical sciences but it was not until the Kennedy administration that the State Department obtained money for supporting research in foreign affairs and as it was, Congress appropriated less than one hundred thousand dollars for the purpose. Something might also be done to direct research and the work of increasing basic knowledge to questions that are more immediately relevant to the issues of foreign policy. Much of the work in the universities on social, political, and economic matters, for example, would benefit from a better understanding of the issues as the policy-maker must view them. Not only would the results be of more utility to governmental decisions, but the research itself would benefit in a purely scholarly sense by a sharpening of its perspectives.

But important though the results of these kinds of effort might be in the long run, the immediate results would not be any very dramatic improvement in United States foreign policy. The making of foreign policy is a groping effort at understanding the nature of the evolving world around us. It is a painful sorting out of our own goals and purposes. It is a tentative, incremental experimentation with various means for achieving these purposes. It is an unremitting argument and debate among various constituencies about all of those questions and an attempt to build a consensus on how the United States as the United States should decide on these questions and what action it should take. And none of these several activities is the kind that will yield to organizational or institutional gimmicks.

Personnel

One other possible area for improvement in United States foreign policy is people. Other things being equal, good people make good foreign policy and better people make better foreign policy.

There is a wide variety of people who make foreign policy, as we have seen—the press, interest groups, attentive publics, congressmen—but within the Executive Branch itself, where something concrete could be done, the "people who make foreign policy" fall into two general groups. One group is made up of career officials in the foreign service, the civil service, and the military services. The other group are presidential appointees and the people they bring with them—the group of officials who make up an "administration."

There was a time when the quality and training of people in the career group were undoubtedly not as good as they should have been. But much has been done in the years since World War II, not only to broaden the foreign service and the career civil service, but to improve the knowledge and training of everyone concerned with foreign affairs and national security, civilian and military. Pay, retirement, and other benefits have made a government career more attractive. Qualifications have been raised. Mid-career training is provided, not only at the Foreign Service Institute and the service war colleges, but also by new legislation that permits agencies to send officials to private universities for special training. The task of maintaining high standards in the career services and of seeking new ways to improve training is never completely ended, but by and large the United States can be proud

No, what would be revolutionary is that somebody or some agency has to do this, and it has to be decided who or which agency would do it. (It also has to be decided whether the Congress wants this done; and that may depend on who does it.)

Who should do it? An easy answer is that the Budget Bureau should do it; the Budget Bureau is the centralized agency that brings consistency and compatibility to the claims of diverse governmental programs, foreign and domestic. But what I said earlier about the relation of budgeting to control commits me to the belief that we are talking about the question, "Who coordinates foreign policy?" I do not believe the answer should be the Bureau of the Budget.

Maybe the answer is "nobody." Maybe, as a practical matter, the answer is that the coordination will be fragmented, and the Budget Bureau will exercise a good part of the coordination. But if both the President and the Congress want this responsibility fixed unambiguously, in the absence of a drastic reorganization of the Executive Branch, it would be hard to identify any formal locus of responsibility except the Office of the Secretary of State.

But to put this responsibility on the Secretary of State is to give him both a means and an obligation to assume the kind of executive authority that has never, in spite of executive orders and the logic of ideal government, either been wholly acceptable to the Department of State or freely offered to it. This is to put the purse strings directly into the hands of the Secretary of State with encouragement to use them in the executive management of foreign policy.

I think it makes sense, but I am not sure that this is what the Congress wants nor sure that this is what Secretaries of State and their senior staffs want. But this is where we are led by the philosophy of PPBS; and we are led there not by fancy analytical techniques but by the simple logic of "program packages" and the need to develop policies, as well as budgets, in a coherent process that recognizes the country as the primary unit of budgeting and policy-making.

I am not trying to lead the reader, through any line of reasoning or casuistry, to a particular conclusion. If we were concerned exclusively with bureaucratic architecture, we would end up with a good case for demanding of the Secretary of State that his office do this kind of budgeting and do it with the impartiality that would estrange the Foreign Service from the Office of the Secretary of State. But these issues cannot be settled by reference to the aesthetics of organization charts. These are pragmatic questions. Do we want coordination at the price of centralization? Can we split the Department of State into an executive foreign-affairs office and a foreign service? Does coordinated, centralized programming undermine the decentralized initiative and responsibility of such programs as the Peace Corps, AID, or cultural exchanges? Does the Congress itself lose bargaining power when the Executive Branch gets better organized for foreign affairs, and is the Congress willing to encourage this?

I should like to see the Office of the Secretary of State accept the philosophy according to which it becomes the executive arm of the President for foreign affairs, and is emancipated from the Foreign Service. I should like to see it use the budget process to clinch its authority and to rationalize its decision processes. I should like to see all overseas programs and activities brought under the purview of an "Office of the Secretary of State," streamlined to provide executive direction. And I should like to see the Department of State enjoy the benefits of modern analytical techniques of the kind that Secretary Enthoven has brought to the Department of Defense, as well as other kinds. But I cannot—I wish I could, but I cannot—declare with any confidence that this can be done. I come back to the remarks with which I began. Foreign affairs is complicated and disorderly; its conduct depends mainly on the quality and mutual confidence of the people who have responsibility; decisions have to be based on judgments, often too suddenly to permit orderly analytical processes to determine those decisions. The best—the very best—performance that is humanly possible is likely to look pretty unsatisfactory to the Congress, to Washington correspondents, to the electorate, even to the President who presides over the arrangement. The system can be improved, but not to anybody's complete satisfaction. In this improvement, PPBS will eventually have a significant role.

4

Major
Proposals
for the Science
Advisory
"Machinery"

DON K. PRICE

A Department of Science?

. . . Since the late nineteenth century many have believed that scientific activities should not be scattered among various departments but centralized in a Department of Science,[1] partly to get additional status for science, and partly to keep it from being subordinated to departmental purposes. In the mid-twentieth century, however, the idea that it would really be possible to separate the big research programs from their parent departments has come to seem highly unrealistic, and undesirable even in theory. Leading scientists, with few exceptions, have come to rely instead on more effective

Reprinted by permission from Don K. Price, *The Scientific Estate*, Cambridge, Harvard University Press, 1965, pp. 257–269.

[1] A. Hunter Dupree, *Science in the Federal Government* (Cambridge, Mass., Harvard University Press, 1957). See Chap. XI, "The Allison Commission and the Department of Science, 1884–1886."

and flexible coordinating arrangements, including both interagency collaboration and guidance from the President's Executive Office.

There is a more limited, and more attractive, version of the Department of Science proposal: to bring together in a new department those agencies of applied research that, by the very nature of their programs, are not tied mainly to the purposes of a single operating agency. If, so the proposal runs, the Bureau of Standards, the Weather Bureau, the Geological Survey, the Naval Observatory, and several others were brought together, the total collection would get more support and attract better scientists. It could also prepare a more balanced program for each of its constituent units—more balanced in terms of its contribution to the national policy as a whole and to the programs of the government's operating agencies.[2]

There is a great deal of merit in this argument. In a government of completely centralized legislative responsibility, it should be feasible to set up such a Department of Science, and to decide on purely pragmatic grounds whether or not a particular applied research bureau should be included in it. Would the Geological Survey, for example, benefit more from a closer association with other research bureaus, and a better balanced relationship with various operating agencies, than from its present connection with the Department of the Interior? But under the Congressional system, which is far from centralized, that cannot be the only criterion. Programs of applied research get their legislative support, and their funds, because of their apparent connection with the programs of operating agencies, and the political support of those agencies and of their constituencies. It is highly doubtful that a group of research bureaus, if taken out of the operating agencies and put in a Department of Science, would continue to get as much support from the operating agencies and as much money from the Congress as they do under the present system.

Basic research, of course, is a different matter. It commands a certain amount of political support in its own right, quite apart from the fact that the universities of the country provide it with a constituency of considerable influence. Should it be made into an executive department? Would the status of a Secretaryship and a post in the cabinet help basic science either to get more funds, or to be administered on a more rational basis with less obligation to the operating agencies? In the past, a few half-hearted efforts have been made to take responsibility for the support of basic research away from the operating agencies and give it to the National Science Foundation. The results have been generally disappointing; the appropriations system does not yet operate in quite so rationalized a manner. It seems clear, on the basis of experience, that more money will be provided for basic research if each

---

[2] This and other proposals are analyzed in Dael Wolfle, "Government Organization of Science," *Science,* May 13, 1960, pp. 1407–1417.

operating agency will, in effect, tax itself to contribute to the basic science that is linked to its applied sciences, than if the total basic research program were handled in a single budget and defended before a single appropriations sub-committee. If practical policitians ever agree to centralize all support for basic research in a single department, it will probably be from the same motive that leads business corporations in many cities to support the creation of a united Community Chest: it would lead to a more rigorous centralized review of applications, tighter controls, and a smaller total budget. It is partly for this reason, but even more because the plurality of sources of support keeps any one agency from dominating them, that the universities and research labora-tories do not generally advocate the creation of a centralized federal department for basic research.

But if the idea of centralization were to be forgotten, the case for strengthening the present arrangements for the support of basic research would be a strong one. A more important agency than the National Science Founda-tion might well be created. The support of basic research, as the National Science Foundation demonstrated in the oceanography story, carries few im-plications for particular policies or programs. The National Science Foundation and the National Institutes of Health would obviously provide the nucleus of such an agency. But to propose to raise it to departmental status would bring up two questions that should be faced: [H]ow is federal support for scientific research to be related to support for research on other subjects, and how are all kinds of research to be related to general educational policy? There is no question that present federal activities tend to distort the programs of the universities, which are able to keep a proper balance between the sciences and the humanities, and between research and teaching, only by great ingenuity in finding and juggling funds from other than federal sources. A department of basic research and education could help to bring about a better balance. It would need to build into its grant-making procedures enough scholarly advisory committees to satisfy even the academic world without doing any damage to Congressional or Presidential responsibility. If this could be managed, such a department might be an appropriate instrumentality for dealing with the new importance of the scholarly estate in our constitutional system.

An Operations Research Corporation for the President?

The privately incorporated agencies for operations research have been extra-ordinarily useful to the military services. Hence it was inevitable that from time to time scientists in Washington would suggest that what is good for the Army or Navy or Air Force ought to be even better for the President. Why should not the Executive Office have a private subsidiary corporation to study issues involving the application of science to policy?

There are three main reasons for the success of the operations research corporations. The first and least important is money—they can pay their professional staff members higher salaries than would be possible in the civil service, though much less than comparable persons are paid by industrial corporations. The second is that they can offer an environment that is attractive to the scientist or professional, who tends to be repelled by either the routines of the civil service or the constraints of working in an atmosphere dominated by military rank, tradition, and conformity. Third and most significant for our question, they provide a basis of independence from which scientists and professionals can criticize, on a confidential basis, the technological and operational doctrines of the moment and make alternative suggestions to military leaders. This is not a matter of applying pure science to military problems, but of seeking to find better ways to blend scientific and professional and economic and psychological thinking in accomplishing the mission of a service.

This all works well at the level of a particular military service, where an operations research corporation can take the service's mission for granted. As you go up in the hierarchy, however, the problems get further away from those in which the scientific and professional issues are crucial, and take you into more conflicts of departmental purpose. It has been much harder to make a success of the Institute for Defense Analyses (IDA), set up to serve the Secretary of Defense and the Joint Chiefs, than of the operations research corporations attached to the several services. For the IDA's recommendations are not presented to a unified and strongly disciplined system of authority which can take them or leave them but which finds them useful as stimuli to thought even when it rejects them. They go instead to an arena of competing purposes, in which there is considerable danger that the professional recommendations will be misinterpreted by higher political authority. Hence, the Joint Chiefs must give the IDA far less leeway in setting the assumptions on which it bases its studies, and in choosing the subjects on which to report, than a military service may permit its particular private subsidiary.

. . . the President needs little help from his Executive Office in thinking of new scientific programs that may be needed; he can get that from the operating agencies, from the National Academy of Sciences, or from a multitude of willing volunteers. He needs scientific advisers who can help him evaluate proposals from operating agencies, identifying proposals that are based on scientific and professional certainty and those for which equally attractive alternatives are available. These advisers must be able to work with others in the Executive Office to blend scientific advice with advice on the financial, diplomatic, legal, and many other aspects of policy. Above all they must protect him from being presented with advice, ostensibly based on scientific considerations, that will really represent an invasion of his general policy by a special interest. The purpose of his scientific and professional advisers should not be merely to enable him to rely on science in making his policy decisions, but, even more, to protect him from having to adopt special-interest programs that pretend to be based on scientific necessity.

The President does not need a single operations research corporation, though he might usefully employ the services of several. He should not entrust his staff work to the control of any single private agency, and he can use a variety of private agencies only if he has the protection of adequate technical advice that is fully responsible to him.

A Science Advisory Staff for Congress?

Bills were introduced in both houses of Congress in 1963 to establish a Congressional Science Advisory Staff, or a Congressional Office of Science and Technology (H.R. 6866, H.R. 8066, and S. 2038).

To the question whether Congress should have at its disposal any scientific advice that it needs, there can be only one answer: it should. But there remain questions as to whether Congress really wants a central office for this purpose, and how it would use such an office.

The need of Congress for scientific advice is roughly the same as that of the President. On public policy it wishes not only to consider the ends but to understand the proposed means and it wishes to understand not only the current programs of operating agencies, but the ways in which current research may offer promise of future developments. Unlike the President, however, the Congress, being made up of two equal houses, each of which includes many equal members, has to subdivide itself in order to get its work done, and this process of subdivision into committees creates problems quite different from those of organizing the staff divisions within the Executive Office.

The President can keep the lines of responsibility within the executive branch at least tolerably clear by distinguishing sharply between his operating agencies, which he holds responsible for running their programs, and his staff agencies, which he holds responsible for advising him on national policy as a whole and helping him to control the means used by the operating agencies. Political responsibility can be enforced only in a single line of operations. And the staff agencies are subject to two types of discipline, both of which serve to prevent scientists from exaggerating their competence to help determine policy: first, the staff agency has less status in executive councils, and less political claim on the President, than the responsible heads of the operating agencies; second, the science advisers' opinions are checked by others within the Executive Office. Their opinions are checked by criticism and competing opinions, not only of others within the same field of science, but by experts in other fields, and also by the various types of administrative staff work by which the President makes sure that all aspects of any particular policy are considered. Moreover, the discipline of the Executive Office prevents a scientific adviser from making a public issue of one of his dissenting opinions.

The main potential danger in the creation of a single Congressional office or advisory staff for science and technology is that it would be subject to none of these restraints. If a particular committee should choose to rely on the advice of that office, and to publicize it in committee hearings without reconciling it with the opinions of other committees and the judgments of other types of experts, the Congress and the public would be presented with an issue which laymen are not competent to judge, and ought not to be asked to judge. It is all too likely that the creation of such an office in the Congress might have the opposite effect from the one intended; it might give a few scientists who have no responsibility for the conduct of government business, and are under no disciplined compulsion to submit their opinions to the criticism of other experts (and especially of experts from other fields) an opportunity to push their personal views on policy beyond the extent which their scientific knowledge would justify.

There are three alternative ways by which Congress has obtained independent scientific advice in the past. One is to employ scientific members of committee staffs; this has the advantage of relating the professional staff member closely to the policies and programs on which he is advising, and giving the members of Congress a chance to understand his limitations as well as his competence. The second, which was adopted late in 1964, is to employ scientific staff members in the Legislative Reference Service; this has the advantage of putting them in a staff together with experts of other types of background, and within some framework of general responsibility. The third is the original plan of a century ago, which may yet prove the best of all: to make use of the advisory services of the National Academy of Sciences. This enables Congress to get, at any time and on any problem, advice from scientists of the highest order of competence in the particular field in question, and the very fact that they are chosen for particular assignments, rather than kept on retainer, is a guarantee of their objectivity and freshness of point of view.

Some combination of all three of these methods would seem preferable to the creation of an institution that would put scientists in the position of commenting with authority on political issues without subjecting their science to expert appraisal of its limitations. And all three methods put together are much less important to Congress than the way in which its senior members understand that the most important issues are not determined by scientific considerations at all, and that they can get at them more effectively by close questioning of responsible administrators and professionals than by any amount of expert staff work. If, as politicians, they have an eye first on who is to have authority and how much are we to trust him, and second on what are the main purposes he proposes to pursue, they can safely leave most of the technical issues to be determined by the consensus of the scientific and professional estates.[3]

Divide the Roles of the President's Science Adviser

Scientists greeted President Eisenhower's appointment of a Special Assistant for Science and Technology, and a Science Advisory Committee of scientists from private institutions, with a chorus of enthusiasm. But the unanimity of that enthusiasm was no more enduring than the unanimity of any other political opinion among scientists. Among the Science Advisory Committee's panel members themselves there was occasional grumbling that their scientific advice did not get to the President undiluted, and that the committee's chairman was too responsive to nonscientific considerations in dealing with major issues. And when some scientists on the outside naturally became dissatisfied with various aspects of science policy—for example, with the extent to which research grants were concentrated in a comparatively few universities—they reacted in the best Jeffersonian tradition and proposed to break up what seemed to them too great a concentration of power at the center. They did not like a single individual to be presidential adviser, chairman of the Science Advisory Committee, and chairman of the Federal Council on Science and Technology. And when Dr. Jerome B. Wiesner resigned from those jobs in 1963 the editor of *Science,* Dr. Philip H. Abelson, charged that the combination of functions had led to an undesirable concentration of power that was exercised arrogantly and in secret, and proposed that the several positions be separated.[4]

The critics are concerned, of course, not merely with the actions taken in person by the science adviser, but with what his subordinate staff members do in his name and the President's. It is inevitable that scientists and engineers in operating agencies will not like to have their plans interfered with by professional staff members in the Executive Office, especially by men who are junior to them in rank and professional eminence. It is even likely that some of the actions of staff members are the result of the itch of any

[3] Arguments in favor of a special staff of science advisers for Congress may be found in *Establishment of a Congressional Science Advisory Staff,* Hearing before the Subcommittee on Accounts of the Committee on House Administration, House of Representatives, 88th Cong., 1st Sess., December 4, 1963. The negative point of view may be found in Senator Clinton Anderson, "Scientific Advice For Congress—Need Is Clear But Solution Isn't," *Science,* April 3, 1964. The opposition of the House Appropriations Committee is reported in *Chemical and Engineering News,* December 30, 1963, pp. 24–26. An excellent summary of the problem appears in *Government and Science No. 3, Scientific–Technical Advice for Congress—Needs and Sources,* Staff Study for the Subcommittee on Science, Research and Development of the Committee on Science and Astronautics, House of Representatives, 88th Cong., 2nd Sess., 1964.

[4] Editorial, *Science,* Number twenty-two, 1963.

aggressive staff member to interfere more than he should with the operating agency's plans. But the remedy for this type of meddling (which is very hard for anyone to distinguish from the desirable type of staff work) is not to break up the staff, but rather for the head of the operating agency either to refuse to accept the views of the President's staff man, or appeal to the President against him.

For example, *Science* has cited an illustration of the type of problem on which it is right for Executive Office staff to raise issues, and on which it may be equally right for the operating agency to refuse the recommendations and be sustained by the President. The Office of Science and Technology considered the plans of the National Aeronautics and Space Administration for landing on the moon. Those plans called for sending a space vehicle directly into an orbit around the moon. The OST thought it would be better to have an intermediate stage in the operation—to put into orbit around the earth a vehicle from which a smaller moon vehicle could be launched. The OST "contended that, since the military potential for space appears to be in the near-earth regions, an earth orbit in the lunar program would help develop techniques that could be adapted for military purposes." NASA argued instead that it was cheaper and faster to employ a lunar orbit, and NASA won.[5]

Whether or not this is an accurate summary of the technical considerations involved in the OST argument, the story illustrates the key administrative issue. An operating agency may properly propose to do a major job in a way that best suits its own particular purpose. If a staff agency can then discover a way in which the operating agency can do the same job in a way that will also contribute to the purposes of other parts of the government, it should speak up. If it can get the agency's voluntary agreement to such a course of action, all the better; if not, it may recommend it to the President. And the President may take the advice, or he may prefer to support the judgment of his operating agency. It is by deciding which to support—his staff agency or an operating agency—that he makes some of his most crucial decisions.

What is essential is that the staff advice on which the President acts must not be partial and fragmentary. On any major problem, the staff advice which comes to him may need to be a blend of technology, economics, diplomacy, and domestic politics; it must be put together by collaboration among specialists of various types in the Executive Office, all of whom must do their best to become generalists. Personally, the President could never deal with the myriad of problems on his desk by trying to puzzle out for himself how, with respect to each one, a great many competing types of expert knowledge fit together.

---

[5] Daniel S. Greenberg, "Science and Government: A Survey of Some of the Major Elements in a Growing, Troubled Relationship," *Science*, July 26, 1963, p. 340.

A single principal science adviser may bring together advice from outside experts and from scientific administrators inside the government, and help blend that advice with the views of the Bureau of the Budget and other staff in the Executive Office. He can do so most effectively if, as director of the Office of Science and Technology, he also remains the chairman of both the Science Advisory Committee and the Federal Council on Science and Technology. If he were replaced in these jobs by three scientists, equal in status, the odds are heavy that none of them would ever get the ear of the President, because to the rest of the Executive Office it would simply become too complicated to deal with all three of them on any difficult issue.

To consider the members of the Executive Office staff publicly accountable for their advice seems, at first glance, a democratic idea. But it ignores the fact that the electorate and the Congress, even more than an executive, have to focus and concentrate responsibility in order to enforce it. It ignores the further fact that political responsibility is most efficiently enforced with respect to operating responsibility for major purposes, not with respect to the technological means to accomplish those purposes. And it ignores, even more, the need that any responsible executive has for staff advisers who will be motivated to operate as members of a team, adjusting their several specialized interests to his common policy objectives, and who cannot be called to account by anyone for their failure to defend a special professional point of view within the executive's confidential councils.

Congress must not give up its right to review the scientific and technological aspects of policy from time to time, just as the President must not give up his right to intervene in details of departmental administration. These are the ways by which democratic political authority may purge the government of the ills of bureaucracy, and of the pretensions of professional subordinates to extend their authority beyond its proper limits into policy decisions. But a purgative is not to be confused with a healthy diet; no one should think that the quality of democratic responsibility is measured by the extent to which professionals take part in political controversy, or politicians preoccupy themselves with technology, even though a little of both may be a good thing.

In our system of constitutional relativity, it is impossible to prescribe precisely the proper balance between special professional interests and the public interest as defined by responsible political authority. The balance must be maintained in the actual conduct of public business. But it cannot be maintained unless the Congress permits the President to use scientific advisers, and other staff advisers, who are not forced to acquire political influence in their own right to maintain their positions, or obliged to represent any special professional interest within the Executive Office. The President ought not to be given the authority to make the final decisions on the big policy issues; that can be done only by the processes of legislation. But he ought to be given a chance to formulate the questions, and to propose answers for consideration by the Congress.

The technical ideas of scientists and professional men can be judged most effectively in the councils of their peers. On the other hand voters can best judge those types of general issues on which they are as wise, or at least as entitled to a preference, as any expert. The reconciliation of these two types of judgment is the most difficult responsibility of political leadership and administrative staff work.

5

Royal
Commissions
for the U.S.?

CHARLES J. HANSER

There is . . . certainly no lack of variety in American advisory bodies. However, though some in each category have had beneficial results, none of these devices really approximates the British Royal Commission or has even established any priority in respect or effectiveness. Indeed, there are serious criticisms of all of them.

It is virtually impossible for private advisory bodies to match the prestige of public bodies. Departmental committees, Congressional Select and Special Committees all deal with minor or more specialized short-range problems and hence are of secondary rank even if they operate properly. There remain the Congressional Investigating Committees (or subcommittees), the Presidential Commissions, and the Commissions created by some joint effort of Congress and the President, as the chief American mechanisms for investigation and advice.

Confusion and contradiction mark most Congressional Investigating Committees. The legitimate purpose of appointment—to determine if some problem requires remedial legislation and, if so, what kind, or to probe executive agencies—is often mixed with the desire of Congressmen for public attention. This is no mere whim. The relative lack of solidarity of American political

Reprinted by permission from Charles J. Hanser, *Guide to Decision: The Royal Commission,* Totowa, N.J., The Bedminster Press, 1965, pp. 225–234.

parties, the uncertainties of party support for individual senators or representatives, make headline-seeking almost a political necessity. And few opportunities for national attention equal the hearings of an investigating committee. Also, the legitimate purpose is often mixed with the partisan desire to damage political opponents. These influences invariably distort membership, procedure, and findings.

The membership of Congressional Investigating Committees, confined as it is to members of Congress, is hopelessly partisan and unbalanced. The members do not have the time to study problems adequately. They bring the single perspective of a party organization man, accustomed to look at problems in the light of political expediency and conditioned by the threat of elections. Absent are the perspectives of laymen, specialists, the impartial academic mind, and many others. The consequence is a structural incapacity to handle involved problems.

Criticism of the procedure of Congressional Investigating Committees has been very severe. Due process, constitutional and civil rights of witnesses, long-standing norms—such as the right not to incriminate oneself, the right of privacy, the presumption of innocence—have been repeatedly violated. Conduct in the hearings has sometimes been a national disgrace. The committees also frequently go on fishing expeditions outside their legitimate area of investigation. The consequence is that they tend to assume functions for which they are not fitted: the exposure of wrong-doing and the development of evidence for use in criminal prosecutions, which is the proper function of the police; and the punishment of wrong-doers, which is the proper function of the courts. Their paid counsel and staff, not being civil servants on loan, tend to develop a vested interest in prolonging the inquiry. Findings and recommendations are usually split, reflecting the partisanship of the members.

Many Congressional Investigating Committees have, without doubt been useful in educating both Congress and the public on important societal problems. This could be done far more effectively, however, by another kind of structure and without the excesses, the corroding side-effects, the unsavory spectacles, the weakening of norms, the damage to respect for governmental processes which have also been the consequences of many of these committees. Even as they now stand, it would certainly be possible to correct these grossly improper procedures. There is no need to deny a legitimate place to these committees. But their unbalanced membership and their political party perspective make it quite impossible for them ever to achieve the competence and hence the prestige of the Royal Commission.

Presidential Commissions have no crippling inherent defects (except perhaps Congressional attitudes) that would prevent their approximating Royal Commissions. There have, however, been serious and persistent errors in their use, membership, and procedure.

At different periods, for example during President Hoover's tenure, they have been used so frequently, and unfruitfully, that the mechanism has almost been scorned. In far too many instances the terms of reference have been unconscionably broad, inviting recommendations so general as to be completely untranslatable into statutes or regulations. So, for instance, President Hoover's Committee on Social Trends in 1933 was asked "to inquire into social trends," which the Committee interpreted to mean, "to examine . . . recent social trends in the United States with a view to providing such a review as might supply a basis for the formulation of large national policies looking to the next phase in the nation's development." President Eisenhower's Commission on National Goals in 1960 had a similarly vague mandate.

Membership is usually bipartisan and has rarely been properly balanced. Where impartiality has been particularly sought, Commissions have often been over-weighted with persons from the academic world. Sometimes critics of the administration have been appointed in a clumsy effort to gain their support. Far too often, again, Commissions are characterized less by members willing to sacrifice time to the Commission's work than by those willing to accept the publicity of appointment in return for a minimum of effort.

Such memberships, as a consequence, tend to rely on their technical staffs to do most of the work, and the various studies by these staff members or consultants are published without any corporate responsibility. Rightly or wrongly, citizens have the feeling that the Commissioners just meet from time to time to frame their final and usually very general report—and the "bigger" the names of the Commissioners the stronger this impression. The President, moreover, has the right to keep the report secret if, for instance, its findings would be politically damaging to his administration.

Advisory bodies appointed in some collaborative effort of Congress and the President have probably been the most successful. Though too many of them are bipartisan in character, some have one or more independent members, for instance the Civil Rights Commission set up by the Civil Rights Act of 1957 to make recommendations in this field. The two Hoover Commissions on Organization of the Executive Branch of the Government have seen over half their recommendations implemented, and had the Commissions had more public attention there might be even more pressure to secure implementation of the rest.

It is these mixed Presidential-Congressional Commissions, then, that have most promise of development into American equivalents to the Royal Commission—if this mechanism were to be used in the United States.

Creation of American Equivalent to the Royal Commission

There are several problems that must be overcome before this is possible, and the first and probably most serious relates to Congress. With the constitutional separation of powers between legislative and executive branches there is a built-in tension and rivalry between the two. Congress has the function of legislating, and to do that properly it must be informed on problems. And Congressmen are unable to rely on enough support in elections from their parties because of their loose structure; hence they take every possible chance to bring themselves to favorable public attention.

These facts of American political life form the basis for several attitudes of Congress. These attitudes need not follow, but as long as they persist they will be fatal to the development of any reasonable facsimile of the Royal Commission.

The first attitude is that Congress has the right, and need, to make its own investigations and that the best advice comes from its own members. The second is that unless any advisory body includes members of Congress its findings will probably be deficient or at least untrustworthy for legislative purposes. The third is that appointment by the President of advisory bodies on which Congress is not represented probably is an attempt to encroach on the legislative prerogative of Congress; that findings and recommendations by a genuinely impartial body somehow may impair Congressional responsibility for legislation—this last possibly inspired by some unspoken fear that their influence might be so great the public would demand implementation and Congress would then be just a rubber stamp. The fourth attitude is that investigations provide a legitimate (though never openly avowed) opportunity for building up individual Congressional reputations.

A second set of problems centers in the President. If Congress were willing to accept a Commission appointed by the President in place of one of its own investigating committees it would impose on the President a responsibility for understanding the nature of an effective advisory body and for meeting its standards. He must, first, use the device with discrimination, not too frequently and only on suitable occasions. It is no more possible to define a suitable occasion than to define due process. But there should be some element of controversy or uncertainty and a need for definitive findings on a subject of major importance—and a reasonable likelihood of action. The mechanism should never be used just to expose or punish wrong-doing.

The President must frame terms of reference that permit a sufficiently comprehensive inquiry but also call for recommendations specific enough to form the basis for legislative or administrative action. He must select members who are genuinely distinguished in intellect, sensibly balanced in their different perspectives, and willing to devote whatever time is necessary to make the Commission's findings *their* collaborative effort, not the work of a staff to which they merely lend their names. They must, in short, be able to inspire the confidence of citizens.

Any attempt by the President to use a Commission for political advantage, any attempt to slant its terms or to pack its members with biased or mediocre persons to secure a pre-desired end, would be fatal. An American President can never match the above-politics character of the British Monarch. But this does not mean that in creating a Commission he cannot subordinate partisanship to the standards of the structure, reserving exercise of his function as leader of his party to the disposition of the recommendations of the Commission. This is what a British Prime Minister does.

The President should also be willing to release on loan any administrative official or civil servant who would be capable of serving as the executive secretary of the Commission. If there is no one suitable from that source, he should be co-opted from among those already having an established position, so that the Commission does not have to hire someone who might benefit from prolonging the Commission.

Both the President and Congress should trust the discretion of the Commission as to the funds and time it needs, and not set limits on either. The Commission should report to the President and Congress co-equally (or to the President, who would in turn transmit to Congress), and, except for some situation clearly dangerous to the country's security, neither should be able to withhold a Commission's report from the public. Both these prescriptions apply also to any succeeding administration, which should not be able to dismiss or curtail the work of any already-existing Commission. A Commission, that is to say, for the length of its existence should be accorded a rank co-ordinate with the legislative, executive, and judicial branches of the government.

This is not to propose any constitutional changes. The act of creating the Commission and the right of final decision on implementation of any recommendations amply preserve the sovereignty of the legislative and executive branches. From this position of unchallenged supremacy Congress and the President could well afford to grant this temporary or acting equality to the Commission as an important element in its authority. If the President cannot be trusted to name competent persons of integrity to a Commission, he certainly cannot be trusted with the life-and-death powers he exercises, say in military affairs. And if the best brains and balanced consciences in the country cannot, as Commissioners, be trusted not to squander time or money, who *could* be trusted?

The President should not ask Congress to give a Commission subpoena powers unless there is close to certainty that information necessary for the Commission's work would not be given except under compulsion. Commissions must rather build up a prestige which will ensure voluntary co-operation. Reliance on the genuine respect of blocs and public will also help the Commission avoid any violation of due process.

A third set of problems centers in the public, the press, and special-interest groups. The more understanding all three have of the requirements for effective operation of a supreme advisory body, the greater the likelihood of successful initiation; and, once established, maintenance of its standards should ensure its successful continuance.

It is on the President that the chief burden of initial education would rest. Citizens should give the first Commissions a chance to prove the usefulness of the mechanism and not apply to them any sense of futility or disrespect engendered from past experience with inadequately structured bodies. The press should give maximum, nonpartisan coverage to the hearings and reports of Commissions in news columns, and should accept the responsibilities of segmental criticism in editorial columns.

There are two ways in which an American equivalent to the Royal Commission might be created. Congress might pass a single Enabling Act (something like the New York State Moreland Act of 1909), which would permit the President to set up a Commission at his discretion, to name its members, and to frame its terms of reference. The Act would provide funds for the operation of any Commission but would not give it subpoena powers. These could be granted on request of the President any time he was convinced a particular Commission needed them.

This method would oblige the President, as he ought in any event, to consult unofficially with Congressional leaders to avoid opposition to the creation, membership, or terms of any Commission.

A second possible method would involve creation of each Commission by Congressional statute. The Act would be initiated by Presidential request for a Commission. Again, the Act would provide funds but no subpoena powers unless specifically requested. The President would select the Commission members and frame their terms (again in informal consultation with Congressional and other leaders), and the Act would then include the terms but not necessarily the names. This method would oblige Congress to accede to Presidential request on the same presumptive basis that it presently accepts his choice of cabinet members. That is, it should approve except in the face of the very strongest opposition.

Neither single Enabling Act nor separate Act for each Commission should impose any restrictions on membership—for instance, that it be bipartisan or include members of Congress. Though the President might well include a senator or representative on any given Commission, his must be the responsibility for selecting the best persons regardless of source.

Neither method would remove Congressional right to create its own investigating committees, but where the President chose to create a Commission both methods would call for Congress to defer its own investigation at least until after the Commission reported. And both would require Congress to accord debate and serious attention to the Commission's findings. The fact that the findings would be entirely advisory and, even with Presidential endorsement if they secured it, would require Congressional approval for any legislative implementation would preserve the ultimate authority of Congress.

Responsibility for creation, selection of members, and framing their terms of reference would, however, be centered in one person, the President, and criticism of any violations of standards could then home unerringly on him.

To mark out these Commissions, especially from the permanent executive or semi-judicial regulatory agencies, such as the Interstate Commerce Commission or the Federal Trade Commission, they should be given a distinguishing title, perhaps "The United States Commission on . . ." whatever the subject. The "United States" in the title should indicate acting equivalence in rank to the Senate, the House of Representatives, the President, or the Supreme Court of the United States.

It should be unnecessary to add one further requirement for the successful development of any American equivalent to the Royal Commission. All would be in vain if the national leadership, whether from inertia, intellectual incompetence, or inability to stand up to vested interests, were consistently to ignore its recommendations. The dismal record of disregard of the rare advisory groups that have really performed well is ominous. It may be that only some disaster can overcome this habit. But it would not seem unreasonable to regard the challenges that already face the country as sufficiently stimulating to muster the best possible attack. And not many improvements in problem-solving could match the development of an equivalent Royal Commission mechanism—if, then, its findings guide decision and action.

6

Citizen
Advice
and a Domestic
Policy
Council

HUBERT H. HUMPHREY

The distinguishing characteristic of American democracy has been its capacity for dynamic—but at the same time orderly—change.

We have always been impatient with the status quo.

Restless . . . rarely satisfied . . . always demanding more of ourselves—raising our standards: These characteristics have kept America young—even as we approach our 200th anniversary.

We have invited controversy of ideas, and used disagreement and dissent as testing, tempering forces.

But there has been the other side to it.

Self-criticism, as Adlai Stevenson once said, has been democracy's secret weapon.

But so has self-respect.

So has self-confidence.

This balance has given American democracy an uncommon degree of responsiveness and stability.

Reprinted by permission from an address delivered by Vice-President Hubert Humphrey at Town Hall Luncheon, Los Angeles, Calif., July 11, 1968.

Today this balance is challenged.

Established institutions—public and private—are being tested by the rush of events and the demands of a new day—and a new generation.

But the reasoned dialogue which democracy requires is too often interrupted by the shouters and the walkers-out. Confrontations and ultimata can never substitute for free-swinging debate—however spirited.

Our political debate is too much focused on personalities and not enough on the critical issues which confront America.

It is time to restore this balance between self-criticism and self-confidence . . . between dissent and dialogue.

This does not permit any closing of democracy's processes.

It requires, on the contrary, increased vigor in assuring even fuller opportunity for participation in those processes.

It requires open government—with maximum opportunity for the citizen to take part in the affairs of his government.

It requires the candidates for the Presidency to speak precisely of their plans for the conduct of this high office and how, as President, they would take account of our present circumstances in America.

Whoever becomes President next January will discharge the traditional demands upon that office: To build consent . . . to magnify the people's conscience . . . to cause them to see what they might otherwise avoid . . . to recommend to the Congress measures for the redress of grievances and injustices . . . and then fight for their passage . . . to conduct international discussions directed toward a more peaceful world . . . to counter threats to domestic tranquility and national security.

He will face, as have few before him, the insistent demand *now* for one citizenship for all Americans—one birthright of freedom and opportunity to which all may claim equal inheritance.

We shall know in our time whether this democratic ideal can be won—or whether America, despite her momentous achievements and her promise, will become another of history's false starts.

Realizing the fullness of our democracy will depend, first and foremost, *upon our ability to extend the promise of American society to every citizen in an environment where the rights of all are preserved—peacefully and without violence.*

The next President will strive particularly to reach the people whose disappointment over America is keenest—including the most idealistic of our young people—because their basic hope for America is perhaps deepest.

The next President must be America's teacher and leader—expressing our highest aspirations for justice and peace, at home or abroad. He must simultaneously be student and follower—learning from the people of their most profound hopes and their deepest concerns.

Teacher and student . . . leader and follower: The Presidency demands that both sides of the equation be kept in balance. To gravitate toward either extreme for any period of time invites either tyranny or chaos—oppression or license.

Our circumstances today call increasingly for an Open Presidency.

> . . . open in the sense of assuring the fullest possible use of that office to inform the American people of the problems and, even more, the prospects we face.

> . . . open in the sense of stimulating the frankest and widest possible discussion and ventilation of America's problems—both inside and outside government.

> . . . open in the sense of marshalling the spirit and mobilizing the energies of America to complete the attack on urban decay . . . illiteracy . . . unemployment . . . disease . . . hunger.

> . . . open in the sense of a readiness to use the Presidency as the instrument not for the enlargement of the federal executive function, but for the distribution of such responsibility to states and localities ready to accept it.

> . . . open in the sense of greater access to all the people.

An Open Presidency must be a *strong* Presidency . . . one that draws its strength from direct and daily closeness to the people.

And part of that strength will be found in reshaping the Executive Department to make it more responsive to individual—as well as "national"—needs.

I suggest these more specific courses of action to develop the concept of the Open Presidency:

First. There must be new channels of communication with the President for those persons previously excluded from meaningful participation in our national life because of race, poverty, geography, or modern technology and industrialization.

This is especially needed in the Executive branch of government. Today the Presidency provides principal initiative in drawing up America's agenda of action;—Congress then responds and reviews the President's proposals.

It is vitally important that popular involvement occur *before* governmental programs reach the legislature. And there is need for greater popular participation once the executive departments come to administer acts of Congress.

We should consider establishing *Councils of Citizens* in the Executive Office of the President and in each major executive department—to promote the broadest range of public discussion, debate and popular consultation.

Members of these Councils could solicit ideas, reactions, and grievances from all segments of the general public.

Prior to any major departmental decision, such as the promulgation of administrative guidelines, persons affected by [the] decision could be fully consulted.

In like manner, Neighborhood Councils of Citizens could be established in metropolitan and rural areas. Local decisions have national dimensions. Citizens need a place near their home to speak up, sound-off, or simply register their opinions.

Neighborhood Councils can dispel fears. They can start people talking . . . and knowing each other better. Some form of financial incentive or assistance to encourage the formation of local councils should be considered.

Second. We must encourage new and imaginative combinations of governments, groups, and individuals committed to solving our critical domestic problems—combinations of power and interest which go far beyond the traditional interest groups of American life.

The past decade has taught us how the challenges of urban life . . . of poverty . . . of mass education . . . of employment . . . are insufficiently met by governments acting alone, or by private action if its immediate interests are pursued in isolation from society's broader goals.

These problems demand the commitment of society's *full* resources applied in ways which produce maximum impact—and often these combinations will occur outside the established channels of "government" or "business."

We are only beginning to understand the new institutions and procedures which can do the job.

The National Alliance of Businessmen—private business leaders who are carrying forward a major part of the federal government's assault on hard-core unemployment—not only illustrates a partnership of *public* and *private* members, but also one which operates on national, regional and local levels.

The Urban Coalition represents a different but equally creative approach to marshalling society's resources in the struggle to rebuild and renew the American city—a common front of concerned private citizens polling their energies and talent on the national and local levels.

The Presidency should continue to develop as a forum for the private groups and individuals whose talents are essential to success. Boards, commissions, task forces, or advisory panels: These and similiar devices help the President take the nation's pulse, and then prescribe necessary remedies.

The Presidency must be a distribution point for the new forces of constructive change—whatever their origins or specific areas of interest. And [the President] must take special pains to relate these forces constructively to the more established institutions of government, particularly [to] the Congress.

Whoever our next President may be, he will soon realize the crucial importance of his dealing effectively with the Congress. These are not the times for stalemate between the White House and Capitol Hill.

Third. The President must encourage the new spirit of localism already at work in this country . . . combined with a new openness of government to the concerns of the people.

The paradox of the contemporary Presidency is precisely this need to build local initiative and responsibility through the creative and judicious use of national power.

We know that federal funds must be used increasingly to stimulate state, local and private energies to develop new and indigenous responses to our unsolved domestic issues.

We know, too, that local, state, and federal structures for administering programs of human development must be reordered and simplified.

Fourth. A National Domestic Policy Council should be established to provide the same comprehensive, systematic, and reliable analyses of domestic problems which the National Security Council and its staff produce on foreign policy and national defense issues.

The National Domestic Policy Council would include the heads of Cabinet and other agencies dealing primarily with domestic concerns.

The Vice President might be designated to act for the President in chairing the National Domestic Policy Council.

The establishment of such a Council would expand in a real way the President's capacity to foresee and deal rationally with the crush of domestic problems . . . to sharpen priorities and identify the full implications of alternative domestic policy decisions . . . to determine how federal programs interrelate, support, or diminish the effectiveness of other programs . . . to develop a system of *Social Indicators* leading annually to a President's *Social Report,* such as today we have a system of Economic Indicators leading to an Economic Report.

The establishment of a National Domestic Policy Council is centrally important to the idea of an Open Presidency.

Today, there is an almost hopeless cobweb of relationships that have developed between some ten or a dozen federal agencies on the one hand, and fifty states, thousands of cities, and tens of thousands of private organizations, on the other.

There won't be effective federal-state-local relationships until there is a fuller integration of federal domestic activities.

There won't be an effective mobilization of private resources for government as long as so many different federal agencies are making separate demands on those resources.

Conversely, once there is this integration and coordination of federal domestic agencies, there can be an effective demand on state and local governments to take those administrative actions at *their* end which permit coordination of the total government effort.

John F. Kennedy said: "The history of this nation . . . has been written largely in terms of the different views our Presidents have had of the Presidency itself."

The proposals I have made today bear upon the Presidency in the same way that the restless mood of social change bears upon the nation.

For a nation in search of an Open Society, the Chief Executive must be committed to an Open Presidency.

In an Open Presidency, one question is paramount: Do existing institutions or traditions help the individual lead to a freer and more meaningful life?

If they do not, they must be changed.

The Open Presidency demands the exposure of ideas—*all* ideas which relate to the fundamental working of our society—exposed to the maximum number of people.

The Open Presidency means broader responsibilities upon every American . . . and the broadest demands of morality upon those chosen to lead.

The American Presidency is the prize possession of all the people.

And the Open Presidency is a ceaseless reminder of their domain.

7

An Office
of Executive
Management
for the Presidency

NELSON A. ROCKEFELLER

The future life of our Republic—and the working of our whole Federal system of government—critically depend on a Presidential leadership that is dedicated in principle and effective in practice.

I have spoken in recent days of certain and essential qualities of this leadership. It must have the courage to make firm decisions and tough choices. It must act with keen sense of the history of these times of headlong revolutionary change. And it must excite and enlist a sense of unity in the nation, based on trust in its purposes and its word.

We have not, over recent years, seen such popular trust or such national unity.

Yet there is another dimension to the problem. The Presidency means not only a man: it means an institution—the *Executive Branch* of our government. And this Branch is precisely named: it is meant to *execute*—translating purposes into programs and programs into action.

We all know that the Presidency today must meet a range of challenge

Reprinted by permission from a statement made by Governor Nelson A. Rockefeller May 27, 1968.

on two great fronts: those in the world at large and those at home in the nation. On the foreign front, there exists the National Security Council to serve the President in planning and in execution— although . . . there is much more to be done here, both in anticipating and confronting foreign crises. On the domestic front, there exists no such office to assure coherent planning and effective execution.

We cannot risk a national leadership that—even with high intentions—*fails* to *execute,* fails to follow through, and fails to reach the people and to serve the nation.

I know no lesson more deeply impressed on me by more than 20 years of my own experience in government at both the national and state levels. For ten of these years, I have served as the Chief Executive of a great State. And all of these years have taught me this law of the democratic process: to conceive great programs is not enough. They must be intelligently and efficiently *executed.*

We are not today respecting this law of democratic action at the national level. We are living from crisis to crisis and from problem to problem—coping as we can. This pattern of passive response—not acting but reacting—only breeds more problems, more crises. And this is no longer rational or tolerable.

Within the national government—and particularly within the Executive Office of the President—there must be profoundly new approaches and new mechanisms. These must do three things:

(1) They must discern and meet national needs before these grow to crisis-size.

(2) They must use all the devices of modern technology and modern administration in the full and fast assembling of all pertinent information for the President as he shapes answers to these needs.

(3) They must integrate all programs of government action finally set in motion to resolve these problems.

All this is imperative to help close one of the greatest gaps in our national life—the gap between political *promise* and political *performance.*

For these reasons, I am proposing the creation of an *Office of Executive Management* within the Executive Office of the President. The essential mission of this Office would be to serve the President directly in formulating, coordinating, and executing all domestic programs.

This Office would operate on the same level as the Bureau of the Budget and the National Security Council.

So vast and complex are the challenges to modern government today that the *absence* of such an Office of Executive Management is almost incredible. And it is an absence that explains much of the disorder and the disarray of Federal programs, the popular resentment of their cost and confusion, and their often dismal failure to achieve their purposes.

The size of national government and the range of its activities are equally staggering.

The President today directs a complex of 2.8 million employees—a workforce that has grown by almost 20% in only the last six years. And this total *exceeds* by more than 20% the sum of all persons employed in the automobile and steel and telephone industries combined.

By official reckoning, the huge number is dispersed among 12 Departments, 31 Independent Offices and Establishments, and nine offices and bureaus in the Executive Office. And these scattered authorities are responsible for hundreds of major domestic programs. In the area of federal grants alone, there are more than 400 confusing and often conflicting programs.

Without effective leadership and direction, all such Federal activity cannot mount a serious attack on our great national problems. It can only carry on a kind of sporadic guerilla warfare against them.

In the biting words of the Riot Commission Report, after surveying all Federal actions to meet the needs of our cities:

> The Federal Government has not yet been able to join talent, funds and programs for concentrated impact in the field. Few agencies are able to put together a comprehensive package of related programs to meet priority needs. There is a *clear and compelling requirement* for better coordination of federally funded programs.

It is to meet this urgent requirement that I stress the importance of a new Office of Executive Management. Its key responsibilities would include:

(a) to anticipate national needs on a broad front and prepare programs to deal with them;

(b) to play a continuing role in domestic policy planning within the White House;

(c) to exercise general oversight to assure the most efficient management of federal programs;

(d) to focus these programs more sharply by simplifying or combining the essential, eliminating the nonessential; and

(e) to help introduce into government the most qualified personnel, efficient technology, and modern techniques of management.

All this is vital to the supreme political task before us: *making free government work.*

Under our political system, this can happen only if the Executive Branch and the Executive Office of the President themselves work—with full efficiency and full effect.

This kind of execution is the decisive test of the Presidential leadership that our people demand and deserve.

8

Political Science and Executive Advisory Systems

THOMAS E. CRONIN

In the past few years, the empirical focus in political analysis has discouraged political scientists from making broad generalizations about such concepts as "power," "authority," "executive leadership," and the like. It has prompted instead a greater concentration on systematic and cumulative studies of individual political behavior or of small units of government. Not accidentally, then, has there been major research attention to how people vote and why people develop their particular brand of political opinion and ideology. Similarly, the community or urban political system has received substantial research scrutiny: Who participates in community decision making? How pluralistic or elitist is the representative process? The past few years have also witnessed an increased interest in the study of state politics and state public policy outcomes. A very rich accumulation of studies is now available on Congressional and state legislative processes and behavior. In contrast to these recent emphases, relatively little attention has been given to the study of chief executives at any level of government. Indeed, it would not be inaccurate to say that the study of executives has been more the province of those in the business and administration schools than of those in political science departments or research institutions.

The state of the political science discipline with regard to the study of executive politics has been accurately depicted by the following criticism:

> The study of political leadership has been the orphan of contemporary political science. Empirical studies of political life have focused on the behavior of groups rather than on the statecraft of leaders; efforts at theory have produced a glut of typologies and models of political systems, often at a level of abstraction that squeezes out the role and impact of political leaders. Only political philosophy has continued to be concerned with the phenomenon of statecraft—under such headings as authority and legitimacy —but all too frequently without regard for empirical data.[1]

As this complaint suggests, our methodological and theoretical efforts have so far been inadequate for the very difficult task of comprehending the consequences and implications of executive political leadership. It is quite obvious that we will not be able to study governors or presidents with the systematic rigor with which we have been able to examine, for instance, Congressional subcommittees or city councils, but comparative study will offer some advantages as will be discussed later. The imperative of relevance and significance encourages anew the exploration of all facets and dimensions of executive politics. It is very likely that considerably more attention soon will be paid to what might logically be called the field of comparative executive politics.

While it would be much too involved to outline here the variety of substantive and theoretical concerns likely to be subsumed within this new "field" of comparative executive politics, the study of executive advisory systems and the analysis of policy intelligence and recommendation functions will certainly be an important subfield. The following research notes will discuss relevant concerns in this subfield which appear to merit our particular professional attention. Illustrations will be selected at the level of the Presidential advisory system, although we could just as easily call upon examples of mayors, county chief executives, governors, or other executive roles and positions. Four general dimensions of advisory politics should be included on an agenda of comparative executive advisory politics:

1. Role analysis and advisory system participation
2. Advisory systems and comparative political analysis
3. Future planning and executive politics
4. Social scientists and executive intelligence

Role Analysis and Advisory System Participation

Our cumulative and comparative understanding of executive advisory system processes is so limited that it would be profitable to start by examining and exploring the roles and perspectives adopted and the role behavior exhibited by the participants in these processes. Role analysis has been increasingly

---

[1] Stanley Hoffmann, "Heroic Leadership: The Case of Modern France" in Lewis Edinger, ed., *Political Leadership in Industrialized Societies,* New York, Wiley, 1967, p. 108.

useful in the study of strategic political participants.[2] (By "role," we mean the coherent set of norms, expectations, and perspectives which a Presidential adviser holds with respect to his performance.[3]) Role analysis is concerned with such questions as: Who or what helps to shape the roles of this Presidential adviser? What are the cues or influences from superiors, colleagues, or others which facilitate the adoption of one role as opposed to another? What helps us to understand intensity of preference for a given role or a certain set of roles? One can imagine a great variety of possible advisory roles ranging from, for instance, expert to layman, trustee to delegate, critic to lobbyist, inventor to ritualist, localist to internationalist. Admittedly, some clarification of the variety of roles commonly held and exhibited is necessary prior to large-scale research efforts along these lines.

The concept of "role" is generally considered to include a normative implication, for example, What *should* I do? What is *expected* of me as an adviser? How am I being *evaluated* and viewed by my chairman, by my professional or interest group organization, or by the President, Congress, the press, and so forth? An adviser's behavior may not necessarily be a consequence of his view of his role, but role perception is just about the best approximation to behavior that we have. As Fenno notes in his study of Congressional committee processes, we can learn a great deal about political behavior by examining the congruence or lack thereof between role and role behavior:

> To talk in terms of role is to describe how an individual in certain position should act. But if one wants to describe how individuals in those positions do act, we must talk in terms of role behavior. In some instances role and role behavior may correspond. In other cases they may not. One could, of course, find out how the Committee behaves simply by observing its behavior and dispensing altogether with the examination of the structure of expectations. But one could not explain the behavior nor base any predictions upon it. If, however, one knows whether or not observed behavior meets or does not meet expectations, explanation and prediction are advanced. If the observed behavior meets expectations, then behavior represents a normal, stable, explainable, predictable pattern of behavior. If lack of congruence shows up between behavior and expectations, then the behavior is recognized as deviant. It can then be accorded special attention, in order to determine what expectations were not met and why, how the Committee prevents deviant behavior from recurring, or how, if it does recur, the Committee adjusts its expectations to accommodate change.[4]

[2] See especially Neal Gross, Ward S. Mason, and Alexander W. McEachern, *Explorations in Role Analysis,* New York, Wiley, 1958; John Wahlke, Heinz Eulau, William Buchanan, and Leroy Ferguson, *The Legislative System,* New York, Wiley, 1962; and Lewis Edinger, *Kurt Schumacher: A Study in Personality and Political Behavior,* Stanford, Stanford University Press, 1965.

[3] See Wahlke *et al., op. cit.,* chap. 1.

[4] Richard F. Fenno, Jr., *The Power of the Purse,* Boston, Little Brown, 1966, pp. 128–129.

These same distinctions can be used in examining the way in which advisers perform their jobs and how they relate to the President, the Cabinet, the Congress, and so forth.

Knowledge about advisory system politics can be measurably increased simply by exploring the different ways Presidential advisers view their assignment and the purpose of their contributions. Illustrative of the purposive roles which advisers hold are the two following interview responses from Presidential commission members:

> A. It is really very much like a Visiting Committee at a university: sometimes these reports result in the overhaul of a Department. In other cases the ideas are solid, but because of Congressional opposition, the report's ideas are, for the time being, not translated into legislative programs. . . . I think the main task for the members of these advisory groups is to state the arguments with sufficient clarity and convincing style so it can never be dropped.
> B. Congress won't pay much attention to our report. They never do. They like to get individual advice on their own, rather than formal advice like this. But what we do will be a standard to which to repair.[5]

Obviously, our long-range interest is to understand the implications and the effects of differentiated roles. How does the adoption of a certain role affect the performance of advisory functions? What roles are most "appropriate" to the nurturing of new and inventive policy proposals? What relationships exist between certain roles and the exercise of special strategies and bargaining styles? What are some of the unanticipated consequences of particular roles or mixtures of roles in differing advisory contexts?

Inquiry should also be made into the incentive systems which affect the recruitment and participation styles of members of various advisory networks. The central questions are: Who is taken into account and why? Why do advisers get involved as they do? Does it make any difference whether motivation comes from professional esteem, monetary remuneration, political ambition, or whatever? Why does the attitude that "your work may have a direct effect on things that are happening in the real world" stir, if not inspire, many men to public advisory undertakings, while being of little or no significance to others? What are the advisory career ladders and concommitant incentive systems that lead from one policy field to the next, from one advisory role to the next?

Closely related to an examination of incentives is the problem of who is heard or who is "eligible" for participation in executive advisory systems. Advocates of "pluralism," "participatory democracy," and "maximum feasible community participation" are inclined to believe that representatives of those who are affected by public programs ought to be included in the advisory bodies and in the policy developments of those programs. The 1968 "Poor People's

---

[5] These two responses come from interviews conducted in the summer of 1967 with two chairmen of Presidential commissions.

March on Washington" and the students' demands for a voice in university decisions underscore this point of view. Daniel Moynihan's caveat to advocates of maximum participation may be worth noting:

> Clearly one of the most powerful forces right now in politics is the diffusion of middle class attitudes concerning participation: "I want to take part," "I want to help decide," "I want to be heard." These are animating more and more people, but perhaps the numbers of people who can be heard is limited.[6]

It may be proper to be concerned with the consequences of what happens when poor people or young people are selected for advisory service. What are the implications for the new participants, for the former elites and experts whose exclusive domain the advisory systems had formerly been, and what are the effects on policy outcomes? A prominent student of public administration insists that advisory committees should be appointed not on any basis of representation but according to expertise and nonpartisan qualifications:

> The individuals on these committees must be drawn directly from industry or the professions. Their fundamental purpose is to do away with that middleman, the politician. . . . The representative factor is of little consequence except as an indicator of the expert qualifications of the committeeman, the breadth of his experience, and his close touch with a profession or industry. When an economic or social interest has the vitality to sustain a responsible organization, this agency should be taken into account when spokesmen for this interest are selected. This connection, however, must be taken as indicative of the appointee's competence to advise rather than of his authority to represent.[7]

These contrasting views raise numerous questions about the relationship of politicians and experts, leaders and led, and also about linkages between national policy developments and what Lowi has labelled "interest group liberalism."[8] The number of important research concerns (only a few have been mentioned here) is readily apparent. We need only suggest that the use of role analysis coupled with extensive empirical work should yield greater understanding in this area—the "orphan of contemporary political science."

Advisory Systems and Comparative Political Analysis

"Case analysis" and the use of the case method have been the traditional and dominant research approaches to the study of the Presidency and executive

---

[6] Daniel P. Moynihan, "Toward the Year 2000," Workshop I, *Daedalus,* Summer, 1967, p. 663.

[7] E. Pendleton Herring, *Public Administration and the Public Interest,* New York, McGraw-Hill, 1936, pp. 359–360.

[8] Theodore Lowi, "The Public Philosophy: Interest Group Liberalism," *The American Political Science Review,* March, 1967, pp. 5–24.

politics. While this is surely understandable, the political science discipline is now at a juncture where reliance on the case method alone is no longer acceptable. A political science which genuinely seeks a rigorous and systematic understanding of executive politics must adopt a comparative approach and concentrate less on turning points and the idiosyncratic and more on the patterns of political behavior within the executive processes. As Banfield suggests, "Social science differs from most journalism and from most history in (among other things) concerning itself with what is typical rather than with what is unique."[9] Moreover, only comparative analysis will enable us to move beyond discussion of isolated political behavior and allow us to generalize about persisting patterns, styles, and roles which characterize Presidential and advisory system transactions.

Probably the greatest difficulty in placing executive politics research in a comparative framework stems from the widespread feeling that advisory processes vary too much from one administration to the next and depend so much on the style and ideology of the incumbent President. A description of the extent of some of this variability was offered by Somers when he contrasted the Truman and Eisenhower rapport with experts:

> The new Administration is finding it difficult to fill higher posts even when they are vacant. The big change lies more in the new relationship. In general—and nothing is altogether general in this highly varied picture—suspicion is directed primarily at the type of personnel so prominent in the past 20 years, the "planners," the "idea men," the people who translated vague policy objectives into substantive proposals, the intellectuals who kept contriving new ventures and new paths to explore. These people—"egg heads" is now the accepted term—are not in good standing, they will depart or be quiescent.[10]

Variability certainly does exist, but this is not to say that general patterns of intelligence gathering, policy formation, and executive leadership do not evolve over time and that these are not comparable. The burden of comparative political analysis is to develop criteria for comparison and then to engage in rigorously designed comparisons both over time (i.e., among succeeding occupants of a particular office or role) and across systems (i.e., among different countries and also among subsystems).

By and large, comparative analysis of presidents has been the province of biographers or journalists, who are generally inclined to compare "Presidential greatness," and the growth of the Presidency, or to discuss some of the flamboyant alter egos who have occupied highly visible White House advisory

---

[9] Edward Banfield, *Political Influence,* New York, Free Press, 1961, p. 11.

[10] Herbert M. Somers, "The Federal Bureaucracy and The Change of Administrations," *The American Political Science Review,* March, 1954, pp. 145–146.

posts.[11] These contributions are not to be lightly dismissed, for not only are these studies practically all we have, but also many of them are highly suggestive of salient questions deserving more thorough research analysis. An instructive example of this genre is a recently published volume entitled *The President's Men*, written by free-lance journalist, Patrick Anderson.[12] This developmental history of senior White House staff aides, from the administration of Franklin Roosevelt to that of Lyndon Johnson, attempts a critical comparison of White House advisory roles and seeks to show the importance of White House staffers in policy-making contexts:

> The complex, technical, fast moving nature of today's government is inevitably reducing the importance of outside advisers. By sheer force of personality, the outsider may impress the President with general strategies, but to have a continuing impact, the adviser needs to be on the scene twelve hours a day, reading the cables, studying intelligence documents, sounding out the bureaucracy, digging deeply into the facts and figures a hard pressed President needs. That is why the influence of outsiders is giving way to that of staff insiders—men like McGeorge Bundy, Bill D. Moyers, Theodore Sorensen, Joseph A. Califano, Jr.—whose value to the President rests less on their mastery of affairs of state than on their mastery of the endless details of state.[12]

Unfortunately, the author presents no evidence which confirms or rejects this initially outlined a priori thesis, rather he concentrates exclusively on portraying the men who played these top inside roles and on assessing how they related to the President and to other key actors in the Presidential advisory system. Nonetheless, Anderson's book does attempt a comparative perspective as well as a longitudinal dimension, and he is to be congratulated for his approach.

Just as there is need for more comparative examination of the strategies and roles of White House staff aides, so too there is need for greater clarification and comparative research of the varied advisory networks that channel intelligence and policy recommendations into the White House. We know, for example, that a variety of functions are performed by a myriad of outside advisory and consultative processes, but we have very little understanding about the differential impact and contributions of these groups and individuals. Does it matter whether the outside advisers are located in certain types of institutional

---

[11] See, for examples, Thomas A. Bailey, *Presidential Greatness*, New York, Appleton-Century Crofts, 1966, Louis Koenig, *The Invisible Presidency*, New York, Holt, 1960; Rexford Tugwell, *How They Became President*, New York, Simon and Schuster, 1964; Rexford Tugwell, *The Enlargement of the Presidency*, Garden City, N.Y., Doubleday, 1960; Patrick Anderson, *The President's Men*, Garden City, N.Y., Doubleday, 1968, Tom Wicker, *JFK and LBJ*, New York, Morrow, 1968. For one of the best volumes of historical biography see Richard Hofstadter, *The American Political Tradition*, New York, Knopf, 1948.

[12] Anderson, *op. cit.*, p. 2.

settings? Does the size of the advisory structure matter? What are the effects and consequences of competing advisory mechanisms or competing task force experiments? At present there are many parallel advisory groups, skewed with varying numbers of participants, perhaps also with varying numbers of "specialists" vis-à-vis "representatives," and in various milieux. And it may well be that examination of such differing mixes could lead to the verification or rejection of many of the now vaguely conceptualized propositions about alternative advice-generating options and their effects.

Comparative inquiry may also lead to an understanding of structural effects and constraints which influence advisory operations and advisory participation. For example, in a preliminary report of their comparative study of various riot commissions, Lipsky and Olson note the importance of commission ties with the executive:

> The virtual absence of criticism of the executive in commission reports cannot be explained on the basis of intervention by the executive in the deliberations of the commissions. Most creating executives of recent riot commissions did not exercise veto powers over the contents of commission reports. . . . The absence of criticism of the executive seems, rather, to be related to the commissions' dependence upon the executive in the implementation processes. And thus dependence on other centers of power is intrinsic to the process of recommendation implementation.[13]

In sum, our cumulative understanding of policy contributions and the policy effects of advisory processes will be advanced through the use of the comparative method.[14] This standard has become so widely acknowledged in the contemporary research community that little need be said here other than to note that a comparative framework will be a major requirement for the study of executive politics and executive advisory systems.[15] It is perhaps reassuring to note that allied substantive research areas are already located in such a comparative framework; it is now commonplace to have university courses in comparative legislative processes, comparative party politics, com-

[13] Michael Lipsky and David J. Olson, "On the Politics of Riot Commissions," paper delivered at the 1968 Annual Meeting of the American Political Science Association, Washington, D.C., September 3–7, 1968, p. 22.

[14] For instructive essays on comparative methodology see Harry Eckstein and David Apter, eds., *Comparative Politics,* New York, Free Press, 1963. For a discussion of the comparative method for intranational studies see Heinz Eulau, "Comparative Political Analysis: A Methodological Note," *Midwest Journal of Political Science,* November, 1962, pp. 397–407.

[15] For helpful steps in the direction of comparative studies of executive politics see Lewis J. Edinger, ed., *Political Leadership in Industrialized Societies,* New York, Wiley, 1967. For the use of a comparative approach in study of advisory groups see Norman Thomas and Harold Wolman, "Policy Formulation in the Institutionalized Presidency: The Johnson Task Forces," which can be found earlier in this book, pp. 124–143.

parative judicial behavior, and so forth. In due time, comparative executive politics will evolve as course material too.

Future Planning and Executive Politics

Social scientists and all manner of outside advisers are quite often flattered by what many policy makers think they can deliver. Advisers are continually being asked to "invent the future" or at least to speculate about alternative futures and about optimal policies for the resolution of society's most intractable problems. Probably no one is as eloquent in his demands as John Gardner when he counsels those in the university that the future of the nation as well as the future of the universities is at stake:

> I would not wish to see anything happen that would alter the character of the university as a haven for dissent and for creative, scholarly work. That must be preserved at all costs. But I believe that those parts of the university which are already involved in extensive interaction with the larger community are going to have to take that relationship more seriously than ever before. . . . We need in the university community a focussed, systematic, responsible, even aggressive concern for the manner in which the society is evolving—a concern for its values and the problems it faces, and the strategies appropriate to clarify those values and to solve those problems.[16]

That the notion of "future planning" has attracted a fashionable following (much like earlier followings of cybernetics and econometrics) is evidenced by the score of articles, books, conferences, and even societies which have adopted this as their central concern. To a great extent this movement is a response to the call that the academic and research community has a responsibility to anticipate the major policy requirements of future decades. Daniel Bell depicts the task as follows:

> . . . even though our society is becoming "future-oriented," we have no adequate mechanisms to anticipate, plan for, guide, or "invent" the future. In the last decades we have been overwhelmed by a number of fractious problems (Negro rights, poverty, pollution, urban sprawl, and so on) that, for lack of adequate foresight, have been dealt with in an *ad hoc* and piecemeal fashion. Since the contours of these problems have had to be taken as "givens" (that is, the cities have sprawled, the baby bulge is already in the colleges), there has been little leeway in formulating adequate solutions. The questions, therefore, are whether we can identify sufficiently far in advance the nature of the emerging problems, whether we can indicate the kinds of data or knowledge necessary for the formulation of alternative solu-

---

[16] John W. Gardner in a speech delivered at the University of Michigan Sesquicentennial Celebration, Ann Arbor, Mich., July 13, 1967.

tions, and whether we can design new institutions or methods to cope with these problems.[17]

We need to ask, in response, how will future-planning undertakings be related to the Presidential advisory system? What will the effects be on the nature of political participation in our cities and in the nation?[18]

Future planning as a movement and perhaps as an academic profession is very likely here to stay. But there are liabilities or potential difficulties that will be incurred by any overly hasty adoption of long-range plans or planning procedures. For speculation on this point, listen to Aaron Wildavsky's questioning of the implications of some of the new future-oriented budgetary tactics:

> Whether or not large-scale program budgeting would actually benefit the Chief Executive is an interesting question. It is not entirely clear that Presidents would welcome all the implications of program budgeting. It is well and good to talk about long-range planning; it is another thing to tie a President's hands by committing him in advance for five years of expenditures. Looking ahead is fine, but not if it means that a President cannot negate the most extensive planning efforts on grounds that seem sufficient to him. He may wish to trade some program budgeting for some political support.[19]

The debates revolving around the feasibility of an annual social report and some kind of Council of Social Policy Advisers deserve similar scrutiny. Up to now, political scientists have too often left such considerations to the members of other professions such as economists, management consultants, and statisticians. Will such developments alter the traditional balance between Congress and the Presidency? Will the present form of the Cabinet become obsolete? Will economic and societal accounting become privileged information or might it not be appropriate to disclose these figures much like the closing daily prices and averages of the stock market?

Closely related to such concerns are another set of questions about the role of the federal government in contracted research and in the particularly important societal function of technology transfer.[20] Illustrative of the policy questions that are at stake here are these specific problems:

[17] Daniel Bell, "Preliminary Memorandum to the Members of the Commission on the Year 2000," *Daedalus,* Summer, 1967, p. 652.

[18] For a valuable essay on the need to consider political participation as an important variable in planning for the future, see Robert A. Dahl, "The City in the Future of Democracy," *The American Political Science Review,* December, 1967, pp. 953–97.

[19] Aaron Wildavsky, "The Political Economy of Efficiency," *The Public Interest,* Summer, 1967, pp. 41–42.

[20] See Clarence H. Danhof, *Government Contracting and Technological Change,* Washington, D.C., The Brookings Institution, 1968; and also the review essay by Bruce L.R. Smith, "The Concept of Scientific Choice," *The American Behavioral Scientist,* May, 1966, pp. 27–36.

1. To what degree is technology transfer a responsibility of the federal government? Can transfer objectives be achieved without a federal policy?

2. How should this policy embody various points of view as to who should benefit directly and indirectly from public funds spent on federal Research and Development?

3. Which federal agency or group should control the information dissemination system, the financial incentive systems, or other such devices that will be used to facilitate technology transfer?[21]

It is impossible to separate the systematic study of "research for choice" and technology innovation from the study of the Presidential advisory system and also from the whole study of how ideas and new knowledge become translated into public policy changes.

Social Scientists and Executive Intelligence

Presidents Kennedy and Johnson both recognized the importance of intellectuals and specialists and tried, to the best of their abilities, to attract able men to their administrations and able consultants to their advisory networks. More than in any previous administration, White House special assistants and Cabinet members established working relations with the academic and research communities with the goal of securing new ideas and new recruits. After the initial Johnson years, praise for these efforts was often lavish:

> Whatever the eventual terms and conditions of their roles, it is quite clear that the intellectuals are in American politics to stay. None of the major programs of the Great Society is workable without their participation. The economists on the Council of Economic Advisors, the scientists and social scientists in the Pentagon, sociologists and psychologists in the Office of Economic Opportunity, the city planners in the new Department of Urban Affairs—these are very much the signs of the times. Indeed, those government departments which have not yet "intellectualized" themselves—such as Commerce and Agriculture—are finding their political power dwindling, their status in the public eye diminishing, and their very existence being questioned.[22]

White House aides noted that university-based professionals readily accepted, and rarely asked to resign from advisory affiliations, even during active campus protests against United States foreign policy. No doubt, however, they were somewhat selective in their initial recruiting. Some explained that the glamour and personal status associated with White House consulting

[21] Edward E. Furash, "The Problem of Technology Transfer," in Raymond A. Bauer and Kenneth J. Gergen, eds., The Study of Policy Formation, New York, Free Press, 1968, p. 328.

[22] Irving Kristol, "The Troublesome Intellectuals," The Public Interest, Winter, 1966, p. 5.

were often prevailing influences. ("This is the White House calling. The President has asked me to ask if you would serve on. . . .") Others mentioned that professional responsibility includes these obligations as well as membership in the appropriate professional associations. An additional factor is probably the belief that one's area of expertise might actually contribute to better public policy.

The federal government has increasingly become a user of the research of the social sciences as well as that of the physical sciences. The Defense Department, State Department, Council of Economic Advisors, and even HEW and HUD have social scientists on their staffs and scattered throughout their advisory networks. But the relationships between social science communities and the White House remain less than satisfactory to a great many social scientists. Above and beyond the major ideological obstacle of United States involvement in Vietnam, four general areas of disquietude may be singled out:

1. Tension, or potential tension, between research autonomy and policy advisory activity

2. Unnecessary secrecy surrounding the White House advisory system

3. Adequate funding for behavioral and social science research

4. Uneasiness of role differentiation between politicians and professional political scientists

The once fashionable notion of a "policy science profession" has recently undergone greater probing and questioning. After the now celebrated cancellation of Project Camelot, some people have decided that the very phase "policy science" may be a contradiction in terms. Suggesting that policy making and scientific exploration are distinctively different in style and standards, Irving Louis Horowitz questions the possibility of any easy (or at least rapid) union between policy and science:

> The great failing of a policy science approach is that it has not recognized that the price of rapid professionalism and integration is high. By raising the banner of the "policy sciences of democracy" this approach minimizes the autonomous and critical aspects of social science development. Without this autonomic aspect to science, one cannot really speak either of a profession or of an occupation. There are standards in a social science and levels of performance within each science that link its practitioners apart from their actions or reactions toward policy questions. When a breakdown of autonomy occurs, when policy questions or ideological requirements prevail, the deterioration in the quality of the social sciences is a certain consequence. Policy places a premium on involvement and influence; science places a premium on investigation and ideas.[23]

Inevitably, questions arise about the degree of secrecy appropriate to

[23] Irving Louis Horowitz, "Social Science and Public Policy: Implications of Modern Research," Horowitz, ed., *The Rise and Fall of Project Camelot,* Cambridge, The M.I.T. Press, 1967, pp. 373–374.

White House advisory processes. Many social scientists have been disappointed and irritated by the heavy-handed security precautions that seem to have become commonplace in the contemporary Presidential advisory system. One White House political analyst found that "inventiveness and creativity" were inhibited by President Lyndon Johnson's insistence that secrecy surround all task force and Presidential commission activities:

> No ranking academician or even industrial leader with whom I had ever been acquainted wanted his best ideas hidden under a bushel. Secrecy is not an ingredient of a viable campus or democracy. It defeats the proliferation of thought which is the essence of progress. Having prepared the way for a domestic social revolution in the early days of his Presidency, Johnson's oppressive administrative manner unfortunately helped inhibit its fulfillment.[24]

Critics have held that task force and commission reports should become public documents at the end of a year's time. For Presidents, it is argued, should not have the right to monopolize or "patent" policy proposals or new ideas. It was this type of situation that led Moynihan to suggest that there was a "crisis of confidence" and that both the Congress and the public deserved some new institutional device which would make public the best ideas for policy development and evaluation. We might conjecture that citizen advisory boards could be established which would report directly to the people of the country, much in the manner of an "advocate planner." In some respects the Carnegie Corporation has sponsored this approach in its studies of secondary schooling, higher education, and public television. Carnegie's "commissions," while not entirely autonomous, perform many of the same roles and functions as the White House commissions, but are much less constrained to secrecy by the political pressures inherent in the Presidential advisory system.

Another delicate matter in the social science—White House relationship is the question of the level and process of financing social and behavioral research. Senator J. William Fulbright boldly alludes to the problem when he states that:

> The bonds between the government and the universities are . . . an arrangement of convenience, providing the government with politically usable knowledge, and the university with badly needed funds.[25]

Proposal after proposal has been offered in an attempt to improve the financing of basic research in the behavioral sciences.[26] Debates in Washington and

[24] Hugh Sidey, *A Very Personal Presidency*, New York, Atheneum, 1968, pp. 256–257.

[25] Senator J. William Fulbright, as quoted in Irving Louis Horowitz, "Social Science Yogis and Military Commissars," *Trans-action*, May, 1968, p. 29.

[26] Dante B. Fascell (U.S. House of Representatives), "Behavioral Sciences and the National Security," in Horowitz, ed., *op. cit.*, pp. 177–195.

in the academic professions primarily center on the advantages of expanding the National Science Foundation (NSF) to include large-scale funding of social science research versus establishing some new type of National Social Science Foundation. Unfortunately both Congress and the executive branch too often assess the utility of social science research with the same criteria used for research in the natural sciences. With visions of rockets and space ships in mind, they ask about the applications of social and behavioral research. The "pay-offs" from the social sciences are not now, nor are they ever likely to be, as visible or dramatic. Moreover, the political consequences of some of the research in the behavioral sciences is likely to be highly controversial. Social scientists should be wary of overstating their case or of promising results which will require many years for development.

A National Academy of Sciences report on the behavioral sciences has suggested that social science should receive substantially greater federal funding and representation within the National Science Foundation and the White House Office of Science and Technology. In a widely publicized policy stand, the report urged a reversal from the present policy of neglect of the behavioral sciences and called for the establishment of a National Institute for Advanced Research and Public Policy as a forum for exploring, outside of regular channels, the theoretical and methodological problems of applying knowledge to social action.[27] This is a welcome challenge, and it may well serve as the future agenda for policy reorganization and a more sensitive approach to the needs of the behavioral sciences. This should motivate social science researchers, who in the past have often been students of the role of natural scientists in government, to turn their attention now to their own roles in national politics and in executive advisory systems.

Not unrelated to the questions of a definition of a "policy science" profession and adequate funding of the social sciences is the proper professional differentiation between politicians and political scientists. In an era in which there is considerable talking across vocational and professional boundaries, it is important for us to examine the quality and quantity of these interactions. What types of skills are required to communicate effectively about one's research to members of policy-making circles? What types of competence and understanding are required of Presidential advisers for the purpose of listening and giving intelligent attention to the research community? Is there a need for a profession of brokers who would translate and communicate basic research results into practical applications and policy-making vocabulary? Our knowledge of these possibilities is, at present, embarrassingly limited. In an instructive review of how Max Weber confronted several of these same dilemmas, Harry Eckstein nominates the following topics for careful future research:

[27] See the discussion of this report: John Lear, "Public Policy and the Study of Man," *Saturday Review,* September 7, 1968, pp. 59–62.

a) the nature of the professional cultures of politicians and political scientists, (both of which vary over certain ranges);

b) the channels and volume of interaction among them;

c) who actually interacts in these channels on both sides, with what frequency and in what manner;

d) the strains that arise in the interactions;

e) the nature and behavior of individuals and institutions that especially intermix the two vocations (such as political scientists in actual public service and politicians recruited into academic careers); and

f) the experience in public service of men who use training schools in public affairs as springboards to their careers.[28]

To "know oneself" and the role of one's profession in the American executive intelligence system is a worthy admonition to those political scientists who aspire to the larger investigation of political leadership and executive politics. This is, however, certainly a first step. For although we have indicated above some worthwhile questions for the study of executive advisory processes, the general field of executive advisory systems stands in need of a much broader frame of reference. In sum, then, the field of executive politics and executive advisory systems suggests itself as susceptible to more systematic inquiry. Though problems of conceptualization and quantification will be more difficult than in many related fields, the imperative of understanding societal leadership should encourage those researchers who are adventuresome as well as concerned.

---

[28] See Harry Eckstein, "Political Science and Public Policy," in Ithiel de Sola Pool, ed., *Contemporary Political Science*, New York, McGraw-Hill, 1967, p. 162.

Selected
   Bibliography

Books

Alsop, Stewart, *The Center: People and Power in Political Washington*, New York, Harper & Row, 1968.

> A journalistic version of the Washington political advisory and influence system during the Lyndon Johnson Administration.

Altshuler, Alan A., ed., *The Politics of The Federal Bureaucracy*, New York, Dodd, Mead, 1968.

> A collection of recent research on the federal bureaucracy and the executive branch of government.

Anderson, Patrick, *The President's Men*, Garden City, N.Y., Doubleday, 1968.

> A Washington free-lance writer presents a fascinating descriptive account of the roles played by key White House staff assistants and the ways in which Presidents employed their top staff advisers from 1932–1967.

Barber, James D., *Power in Committees: An Experiment in the Governmental Process*, Chicago, Rand McNally, 1966.

> Although this is a study of community financial boards, it is suggestive of some theoretically interesting assessments of power and system politics in government by small committee.

Bauer, Raymond A., and Kenneth J. Gergen, eds., *The Study of Policy Formation*, New York, Free Press, 1968.

> A collection of essays which assess and discuss contemporary

developments in research methods used in studying public decision making and policy formulation.

Bauer, Raymond A., Ithiel de Sola Pool, and Lewis A. Dexter, *American Business and Public Policy: Politics of Foreign Trade,* New York, Atherton Press, 1963.

> An informative analysis of interactions among business and the Washington policymaking community with focus on the politics of foreign trade from 1953 to 1962.

Bauer, Raymond A., ed., *Social Indicators,* Cambridge, The M.I.T. Press, 1966.

> A probing exploration of the uses of social indicators and social systems accounting.

Bernstein, Marver H., *The Job of the Federal Executive,* Washington, D.C., The Brookings Institution, 1958.

> Somewhat dated, but still an insightful exploration of how senior civil servants view their jobs, their responsibilities and their relationships to major political institutions.

Braybrooke, David, and Charles E. Lindblom, *A Strategy of Decision: Policy Evaluation as a Social Process,* New York, Free Press, 1963.

> A theoretical approach to the study of decision making and policy politics.

Burns, James MacGregor, *Presidential Government,* Boston, Houghton Mifflin, 1966.

> A delineation of three styles of Presidential leadership and an outline of the liabilities and assets of the modern enlarged Presidential establishment.

Cater, S. Douglass, *Power in Washington,* New York, Random House, 1965.

> An informed Washington reporter's view of policymaking and coalition formations in the nation's capital.

Chamberlain, Lawrence H., *The President, Congress and Legislation,* New York, Columbia University Press, 1946.

> An adventuresome attempt to assess the relative influences of Congress and the Executive upon public policy developments between 1880 and 1940.

Clokie, Hugh M., and J. William Robinson, *Royal Commissions of Inquiry,* Stanford, Stanford University Press, 1937.

> A comprehensive history and description of British reliance on Royal Commissions.

Cohen, Bernard C., *The Press and Foreign Policy,* Princeton, Princeton University Press, 1963.

> One of the best treatments of the two-way relationship between the press and top national policy makers.

Cornwell, Elmer E., Jr., *Presidential Leadership of Public Opinion,* Bloomington, Indiana University Press, 1965.

> The best contemporary volume on Presidential public relations, White House press conferences, and so forth.

Corwin, Edward S., *The President: Office and Powers,* rev. ed., New York, New York University Press, 1957.

> One of the standard texts delineating the Constitutional sources of Presidential powers, generally considered to be an overly formalistic account of the Office of the Presidency.

Domhoff, G. William, *Who Rules America?,* Englewood Cliffs, N.J., Prentice-Hall, 1967.

> A rather polemical elitist interpretation of how the upper class controls and governs American political and economic institutions.

Downs, Anthony, *Inside Bureaucracy,* Boston, Little, Brown, 1967.

> A compact presentation of hypotheses and theories about behavior in large bureaucratic agencies, with numerous illustrations from the federal bureaucracy.

Dror, Yehezkel, *Public Policymaking Reexamined,* San Francisco, Chandler Publishing, 1968.

> A thorough review of various rational and incremental policy and decision-making models coupled with the author's own advocacy of an "optimal" model of policy making within a policy science framework.

Dulles, Allen, *The Craft of Intelligence,* New York, Harper & Row, 1963.

> A former CIA Director attempts to explain the role of the U.S. intelligence operation and the relevance of strategic intelligence for foreign policy decision making.

Edinger, Lewis J., ed., *Political Leadership in Industrialized Societies,* New York, Wiley, 1967.

> One of the first systematic attempts to promote comparative analysis of executive political leadership with several suggestive research frameworks.

Ewald, William R., ed., *Environment and Policy: The Next Fifty Years,* Bloomington, Indiana University Press, 1968.

> A stimulating set of papers and commentaries commissioned on behalf of the American Institute of Planners' Fiftieth Year Consultation containing particularly useful contributions by Herbert Simon on "Research for Choice" and Alan Altshuler on "New Institutions to Serve the Individual."

Fenno, Richard F., *The President's Cabinet,* Cambridge, Harvard University Press, 1959.

> The best critical study to date of President-Cabinet relations and the functions which the Cabinet performs.

Finer, Herman, *The Presidency, Crisis and Regeneration,* Chicago, The University of Chicago Press, 1960.

> A vintage reformer notes our gamble on a solitary President and proceeds to formulate a variety of Presidential reforms including a plan to create eleven Vice-Presidencies to assist the overburdened Presidency.

Flash, Edward S., Jr., *Economic Advice and Presidential Leadership: The Council of Economic Advisers,* New York, Columbia University Press, 1965.

> A useful analysis and history of the CEA and its varied success as White House adviser.

Gilpin, Robert and Christopher Wright, eds., *Scientists and National Policy-Making,* New York, Columbia University Press, 1964.

Insightful essays by political scientists and science advisors exploring the relatively new roles which scientists are playing in the development of national science policy.

Green, Harold P., and Alan Rosenthal, *Government of the Atom*, New York, Atherton Press, 1963.

An excellent study of the creation of new institutions to meet changing roles and responsibilities in the national government.

Greenberg, Daniel S., *The Politics of Pure Science*, New York, New American Library, 1967.

An account of the growing ties between science and government in the post-World War II years with a number of short illustrative case studies.

Gross, Bertram M., ed., *A Great Society?*, New York, Basic Books, 1968.

An informative collection of academic appraisals of the problems and prospects of a Great Society and the requisite type of political and policy leadership which might facilitate a responsive and enlightened society.

Hanser, Charles J., *Guide to Decision, The Royal Commission*, Totowa, N.J., Bedminister Press, 1965.

An examination (and favorable appraisal) of how the British employ blue-ribbon public commissions to investigate sensitive public policy matters.

Haviland, H. Field, Jr., et al., *The Formulation and Administration of United States Foreign Policy*, Washington, D.C., The Brookings Institution, 1960.

This is a study of the problems and perspectives involved in U.S. foreign policy making and execution, sponsored by the Senate Foreign Relations Committee and conducted by the Brookings Institution.

Herring, E. Pendleton, *Presidential Leadership*, New York, Farrar, Straus, 1940.

Although somewhat out of date, this volume contains insightful analyses of Presidential entourage and Executive–Legislative relationships.

Herring, E. Pendleton, *Public Administration and the Public Interest,* New York, McGraw-Hill, 1936.

> A classic discussion of federal bureaucracy in general and regulatory commissions in particular and their role in service not to special interests, but in the "public interest."

Hilsman, Roger, *Strategic Intelligence and National Decisions,* New York, Free Press, 1956.

> One of the best introductions and treatments of the role of secret intelligence in national security policy making by a political scientist with career experience in military and intelligence fields.

Hirschfield, Robert S., ed., *The Power of the Presidency,* New York Atherton Press, 1968.

> A valuable gathering of articles on the concepts and controversy of Presidential power, utilizing historical and contemporary viewpoints as well as several of the major Supreme Court decisions that have affected Presidential leadership.

Hitch, Charles J., *Decision-Making for Defense,* Berkeley, University of California Press, 1965.

> Hitch popularized the now celebrated "operations research" and "systems analysis" techniques while serving as a top official under Secretary Robert McNamara in the Defense Department. This volume discusses these procedures and their functions.

Hobbs, Edward H., *Behind the President,* Washington, D.C., Public Affairs 1954.

> An out-of-date, but useful historical review of many of the White House support staffs during the Truman and Roosevelt Administrations.

Hofstadter, Richard, *The American Political Tradition,* New York, Knopf, 1948.

> Here a historian takes a close and critical look at the inflated interpretations of Presidential political leadership.

Hunter, Floyd, *Top Leadership, U.S.A.,* Chapel Hill, University of North Carolina Press, 1959.

> An attempt to show that a "power elite" governs America, relying, in part, on the much contested "reputational" method of elite identification.

Huntington, Samuel P., *The Common Defense,* New York, Columbia University Press, 1961.

> An important study of various factors and political involvement strategic to national defence policy making.

Jackson, Senator Henry M., ed., "Jackson Subcommittee Papers on Policy-Making at the Presidential Level," *The National Security Council,* New York, Praeger, 1965.

> An informative collection of staff reports, as well as testimony from leading participants in the Truman and Eisenhower Administrations and outside observers of Presidential policy making.

Jacob, Charles E., *Policy and Bureaucracy,* New York, Van Nostrand, 1966.

> A good introductory study of national policy making and bureaucratic behavior with many useful illustrative discussions.

Kallenback, Joseph E., *The American Chief Executive,* New York, Harper & Row, 1966.

> A comparative treatment of the varied roles and responsibilities of the Presidency and the governorships in American political systems.

Kaufmann, William W., *The McNamara Strategy,* New York, Harper & Row, 1964.

> A sympathetic yet perceptive description of former Defense Secretary Robert S. McNamara's Pentagon use of PPBS and cost/effectiveness research teams and research analyses.

Kennan, George F., *Memoirs, 1925–1950,* Boston, Atlantic-Little, Brown, 1967.

> A prize-winning personal record of a diplomat and, in later

years, a frequent White House adviser on foreign policy and security matters.

Kent, Sherman, *Strategic Intelligence,* Princeton, Princeton University Press, 1949.

Recognized as a classic introduction to national intelligence requisites and strategies.

Koenig, Louis W., *The Chief Executive,* rev. ed., New York, Harcourt, Brace & World, 1968.
One of the best textbook treatments of the American Presidency and the growing number of roles and responsibilities expected of our chief executive.

Koenig, Louis W., *The Invisible Presidency,* New York, Holt, 1960.

An examination of President–alter ego relationships from Alexander Hamilton to Sherman Adams.

Laski, Harold, *The American Presidency,* New York, Harper & Row, 1940.

An Englishman takes a hard look at the American chief executive in a series of highly readable lecture-essays.

Lasswell, Harold D., and Daniel Lerner, eds., *The Policy Sciences,* Stanford, Stanford University Press, 1951.

Lasswell deserves great credit for his long-time promotion of a policy orientation for empirical and behavioral social science research. This collection of essays illustrates some of the possibilities and some of the methodological prospects.

Levitan, Sar A., and Irving H. Siegel, eds., *Dimensions of Manpower Policy: Programs and Research,* Baltimore, The Johns Hopkins Press, 1966.

An example of "policy science" examinations of program and research strategies in a very strategic domestic policy sphere.

Lindblom, Charles E., *The Intelligence of Democracy,* New York, Free Press, 1965.
An important discussion of bargaining and mutual adjustment strategies involved in democratic decision-making systems.

Lindblom, Charles E., *The Policy-Making Process,* Englewood Cliffs, N.J., Prentice-Hall, 1968.

> A short introduction to some of the theoretical problems and practical consequences of contemporary national policy making processes.

Lyden, Fremont J., and Ernest G. Miller, eds., *Planning Programming Budgeting: A Systems Approach to Management,* Chicago, Markham Publishing Co., 1967.

> A very useful collection of papers offering both an introduction and examination of PPB analysis with major focus on the management of federal programs.

McConnell, Grant, *Steel and the Presidency, 1962,* New York, Norton, 1963.

> One of the best case studies of Presidential relations with big business, using the steel price crisis of April, 1962 as the context.

Mann, Dean, and Jameson W. Doig, *The Assistant Secretaries: Problems and Processes of Appointment,* Washington, D.C., The Brookings Institution, 1965.

> A survey of the variety of recruitment and socialization processes used in staffing sub-Cabinet positions.

Marcy, Carl, *Presidential Commissions,* New York, King's Crown Press, 1945.

> An early survey of the legal basis and types of Presidential fact-finding, administrative, and investigatory commissions.

Martin, John Bartlow, *Overtaken by Events,* Garden City, N.Y., Doubleday, 1966.

> A highly readable and insightful autobiographical account of Ambassadorial and Presidential special emissary assignments and involvement with the politically volatile Dominican Republic during the early and mid-1960s.

May, Ernest R., ed., *The Ultimate Decision,* New York, Braziller, 1960.

> A study of several Presidents and the use of "Commander-in-Chief" authorities during strategic international conflict periods.

Monsen, R. Joseph, and Mark W. Cannon, *Makers of Public Policy: American Power Groups and Their Ideologies,* New York: McGraw-Hill, 1965.

> Treats a diverse collection of reputed power groups and includes chapters on the "intellectuals" and "the civil bureaucracy."

Neustadt, Richard E., *Presidential Power,* New York, Wiley, 1960.

> One of the best-known studies of Presidential politics, suggesting an administrative-politics model for assessing the personal and political effectiveness of Presidential leadership.

Novick, David, ed., *Program Budgeting,* "Program Analysis and The Federal Budget," Washington, D.C., U.S. Government Printing Office, 1965.

> This RAND-sponsored research serves as a general introduction to cost/analysis or cost/utility program budgeting, with several specific policy areas, such as education and the space program used for examples.

Peabody, Robert L. and Nelson W. Polsby, eds., *New Perspectives on the House of Representatives,* Chicago, Rand McNally, 1963.

> A very useful collection of research articles relevant to an understanding of Congressional policy politics.

Perlman, Mark, *Labor Union Theories in America,* New York, Harper & Row, 1958.

> This volume contains a detailed discussion of early U.S. Commissions on Industrial Relations providing informative case histories of these Congressionally legislated commission studies.

Price, Don K., *The Scientific Estate,* Cambridge, Harvard University Press, 1965.

> One of the best discussions of the role which scientists are playing in government, politics, and future planning.

Rainwater, Lee, and William L. Yancey, *The Moynihan Report and The Politics of Controversy,* Cambridge, The M.I.T. Press, 1967.

> A provocative account, along with abundant source materials, of the role of social scientists and national policy discussions on civil rights, involving Daniel P. Moynihan's Report on

The Negro Family and the 1964 White House Conference "To Fulfill These Rights."

Rivers, William L., *The Opinion Makers,* Boston, Beacon Press, 1965.

An analysis of the operations and biases as well as the influence of the Washington press corps.

Roberts, Charles, *L.B.J's Inner Circle,* New York Delacorte Press, 1965.

A reporter's interpretation, accompanied with multiple profiles, of White House staff members and staff assignments during the early Johnson Administration.

Rosenman, Samuel I., *Working With Roosevelt,* New York, Harper & Row, 1952.

Written by a former Special Counsel and chief speech-writer for FDR, this volume offers an instructive view of the role of speech writers and brain trusts during the middle and late Roosevelt years.

Rossiter, Clinton, *The American Presidency,* New York, Harcourt, Brace & World, 1956.

A highly popular and readable short introduction to the various tasks of the Presidency together with an appraisal of the evolution of the modern Presidency.

Sayre, Wallace S., ed., *The Federal Government Service,* Englewood Cliffs, N.J., Prentice-Hall, 1965.

This is a revised series of papers, originally written in 1954, which still provide one of the best introductions to the prospects and dilemmas of the federal government service.

Shanks, Michael, *The Innovators: The Economics of Technology,* Baltimore, Penguin, 1967.

A survey of the growing use of management consultants, policy research institutions (in and out of government) and the general framework within which new ideas and new techniques are translated into goods and processes.

Smith, Bruce L. R., *The RAND Corporation: Case Study of a Non-Profit Advisory Corporation,* Cambridge, Harvard University Press, 1961.

A useful history and exploration of the functions and roles of the RAND Corporation which additionally considers some of the important implications and consequences of reliance on "not-for-profit" advisory institutions.

Sorensen, Theodore C., *Kennedy,* New York, Harper & Row, 1965.

One of the best recent Presidential biographies by a former White House special counsel.

Stein, Herman D., *Social Theory and Social Invention,* Cleveland, The Press of Case Western Reserve University, 1968.

The results of a colloquium probing the relations between social science general theory and domestic social public policy.

Sundquist, James L., *Politics and Policy: The Eisenhower, Kennedy, and Johnson Years,* Washington, D.C., The Brookings Institution, 1968.

An analysis of national policy problems and national policy response during the 1952–1968 period by one who actively participated in many of the policy processes and policy responses during that time.

Warner, W. Lloyd, *et al., The American Federal Executive,* New Haven, Yale University Press, 1963.

A survey of government officials with emphasis on their status, social backgrounds, and career orientations.

Wenk, Edward, ed., *The Office of Science and Technology,* Washington, D.C., U.S. Government Printing Office, 1967.

A survey of the White House science support staff prepared by the Science Policy Research Division of the Legislative Reference Service, Library of Congress for the House Committee on Government Operations.

White, Leonard D., *The Federalists,* New York, Crowell Collier & Macmillan, 1948.

White, Leonard D., *The Jeffersonians,* New York, Crowell Collier & Macmillan, 1951.

White, Leonard D., *The Jacksonians,* New York, Crowell Collier & Macmillan, 1954.

White, Leonard D., *The Republican Era,* New York, Crowell Collier & Macmillan, 1958.

> White's histories are an invaluable source for learning about the growth and development of the Presidency and the executive branch of government.

Wiesner, Jerome B., *Where Science and Politics Meet,* New York, McGraw-Hill, 1965.

> A collection of speeches, testimony and other observations on the formulation of science public policy by President Kennedy's chief science adviser.

Wildavsky, Aaron, *The Politics of the Budgetary Process,* Boston, Little, Brown, 1964.

> A valuable look at the strategies used by the Bureau of the Budget as well as by those who must deal with this central support staff in the Executive Office of the President.

Wilensky, Harold L. *Organizational Intelligence,* New York, Basic Books, 1967.

> A valuable contribution to an understanding of the role of experts, knowledge, and intelligence processes as used by agencies, such as the Council of Economic Advisers and the Central Intelligence Agency, and by private industry.

Young, James S., *The Washington Community, 1800–1828,* New York, Columbia University Press, 1966.

> An exceptionally interesting account of the evolution of the early Washington political community, with emphasis on the development of Presidential relations with Congress and the Bureaucracy.

Articles

Allison, Graham, "Conceptual Models and The Cuban Missile Crisis: Rational Policy, Organizational Policy and Bureaucratic Policy," a paper delivered at the Sixty-fourth Annual Meeting, American Political Science Association, Washington, D.C., September 3–7, 1968.

Argyris, Chris, "Some Causes of Organizational Ineffectiveness Within the Department of State," Center for International Systems Research, Department of State, Washington, D.C., January, 1957.

Bell, Daniel, "Notes on the Post-Industrial Society," two parts, *The Public Interest*, Winter and Spring, 1967, pp. 24–35 and pp. 102–118.

Brown, David S., "The President and the Bureaus: Time for a Renewal of Relationships?," *Public Administration Review*, September, 1966, pp. 174–182.

Brown, David S., "The Public Advisory Board as an Instrument of Government," *Public Administration Review*, Summer, 1955, pp. 126–204.

Bundy, McGeorge, "The Presidency and Peace," *Foreign Affairs*, April, 1964, pp. 353–365.

Davis, James, and Randall B. Ripley, "The Bureau of the Budget and Executive Branch Agencies: Notes on Their Interaction," *The Journal of Politics*, November, 1967, pp. 749–770.

Drew, Elizabeth B, "On Giving Oneself a Hotfoot: Government By Commission," *Atlantic Monthly*, May, 1968, pp. 45–49.

Dror, Yehezkel, "Policy Analysts: A New Professional Role in Governmental Service," *Public Administration Review*, September, 1967, pp. 197–203.

Eckstein, Harry, "Political Science and Public Policy," in Ithiel de Sola Pool, ed., *Contemporary Political Science*, New York, McGraw-Hill, 1967, pp. 121–165.

Edinger, Lewis J., "Military Leaders and Foreign Policy-Making," *American Political Science Review*, June, 1963, pp. 392–405.

Ellis, William W., "The Federal Government in Behavioral Science," Special Report, *The American Behavioral Scientist*, May, 1964.

Epstein, Leon D., "Parties as Policy Makers," in his larger study, *Political Parties in Western Democracy*, New York, Praeger, 1967, pp. 264–275.

Evans, Allan, "Intelligence and Policy Formation," *World Politics*, October, 1959, pp. 84–91.

Fairlie, Henry, "Thoughts on the Presidency," *The Public Interest*, Fall, 1967, pp. 28–48.

Gill, Norman, "Permanent Advisory Committees in the Federal Government," *The Journal of Politics*, November, 1940, pp. 411–435.

Gross, Bertram, et al., "What, Another Hoover Commission?," *Public Administration Review*, March/April, 1968, pp. 168–180.

Hammond, Paul Y., "Foreign Policy-Making and Administrative Politics," *World Politics*, July, 1968, pp. 656–671.

Harris, Fred R., "Political Science and the Proposal for a National Social Science Foundation," *American Political Science Review*, December, 1967, pp. 1088–1095.

Henry, Laurin L., "The Presidency, Executive Staffing and the Federal Bureaucracy," a paper delivered at the 1967 Annual Meeting, American Political Science Association, Chicago, Ill., September 5–9, 1967

Horowitz, Irving Louis, "Social Science Yogis & Military Commissars," *Transactions*, May, 1968, pp. 29–38.

Huntington, Sam, "Strategic Planning and the Political Process," *Foreign Affairs*, January, 1960, pp. 285–299.

Kaysen, Carl, Harry G. Johnson, and Mancur Olson, "Economics and Public

Policy," a three-part discussion, *The Public Interest,* Summer, 1968, pp. 68–119.

Kopkind, Andrew, "The Future Planners," *The New Republic,* February 25, 1967, pp. 19–23.

LaPorte, Todd, "Politics and 'Inventing the Future': Perspectives in Science and Government," *Public Administration Review,* June, 1967, pp. 117–127.

Leiserson, Avery, "Scientists and the Policy Process," *American Political Science Review,* June, 1965, pp. 408–416.

Lipsky, Michael, and David J. Olson, "On the Politics of Riot Commissions," a paper delivered at the Sixty-fourth Annual Meeting, American Political Science Association, Washington, D.C., September 3–7, 1968.

Lear, John, "Public Policy and the Study of Man," *Saturday Review,* September 7, 1968, pp. 59–62.

Lisagor, Peter, "How New Laws Are Conceived," *Nation's Business,* August, 1967, pp. 19–20.

Lowi, Theodore J., "American Business, Public Policy, Case Studies and Political Theory," *World Politics,* July, 1964, pp. 677–715.

Lowi, Theodore, "The Public Philosophy: Interest Group Liberalism," *American Political Science Review,* March, 1967, pp. 5–24.

Mansfield, Harvey C., "Federal Executive Reorganization: Thirty Years After the President's Committee on Administrative Management," a paper delivered at Sixty-fourth Annual Meeting, American Political Science Association, Washington, D.C., September 3–7, 1968.

Marx, Gary, "Report of the National Commission: The Analysis of Disorder or Disorderly Analysis?," a paper delivered at Sixty-fourth Annual Meeting, American Political Science Association, Washington, D.C., September 3–7, 1968.

Moynihan, Daniel P., "A Crisis of Confidence?," *The Public Interest, Spring,* 1967, pp. 3–10.

Neustadt, Richard E., "Presidency and Legislation: Planning the President's

Program," *American Political Science Review,* December, 1955, pp. 980–1021.

Olson, Mancur, Jr., "The Relationship of Economics to Other Social Sciences: The Province of a 'Social Report,' " a paper delivered at the Annual Meeting, American Political Science Association, Chicago, Ill., September 8, 1967, revised July, 1968.

Otten, Alan L., "Tasks and Forces," *The Wall Street Journal,* February 10, 1967, p. 8.

Parmenter, Tom, ed., "Special Report—The Case For and Against a National Social Science Foundation," *Trans-action,* January/February, 1968, pp. 54–76.

Price, Don K., "Staffing the Presidency," *American Political Science Review,* December, 1946, pp. 1154–1168.

Ripley, Randall B., "Interagency Committees and Incrementalism: The Case of Aid to India," *Midwest Journal of Political Science,* May, 1964, pp. 143–165.

Seligman, Lester G., "Presidential Leadership: The Inner Circle and Institutionalization," *Journal of Politics,* August, 1956, pp. 410–426.

Semple, Robert B., "Signing of Model Cities Bill Ends a Long Struggle To Keep It Alive," *New York Times,* November 4, 1966, pp. 1, 44.

Sigel, Roberta S., "Citizen Committees—Advice *vs* Consent," Trans-action, May, 1967, pp. 47–52.

Simon, Herbert A., "The Changing Theory and Changing Practice of Public Administration," in Ithiel de Sola Pool, ed., *Contemporary Political Science,* New York, McGraw-Hill, 1967, pp. 86–120.

Smith, Bruce L. R., "The Concept of Scientific Choice," *The American Behavioral Scientist,* May, 1966, pp. 27–36.

Smith, Bruce L. R., "The Future of the Not-for-Profit Corporations," *The Public Interest,* Summer, 1967, pp. 127–142.

Thompson, James C., Jr., "Why Vietnam? An Insider Looks Back for Answers," *Washington Post,* April 14, 1968, pp. B1, B4.

Tugwell, Rexford G., "The President and His Helpers—A Review Article," *Political Science Quarterly,* June, 1967, pp. 253–267.

Ways, Max, "Intellectuals and the Presidency," *Fortune,* April, 1967, pp. 147–149, 211, 212, 214, 216.

White, Theodore H., "The Action Intellectuals," three part series, *Life,* June 2, 9, and 16, 1967.

Wildavsky, Aaron, "The Political Economy of Efficiency," *The Public Interest,* September, 1968, pp. 3–48.

Index

A

Abelson, Philip H., 303
Academic community, 133, 239, 280, 331–333
  as source of ideas, 94–95, 222
  See also Intellectuals
Acheson, Dean, 8, 150–151, 153–155, 273, 279
Ackley, Gardner, 30, 128
  quoted, 31
ACT, 244
Action documents, *ad hoc* commissions and, 114–115
Ad hoc commissions, 101–116
  advantages of, 104–106
  characteristics of, 101–102
  departmental, 102
  disadvantages of, 106–110
  importance and prevalence of, 103–104
  membership on, 105–107, 110–111
  organization of, 107
  reports of, 113–114
  use of, 102, 116
  special problems in, 110–115
Ad Hoc Committee on Public Welfare, 253–255
Adams, Henry, quoted, 221
Adams, Sherman, 16
Administration, good, 156
  intellectuals and, 156
  stagnation in, 156–162
Administrative Assistants, 15, 22
Advice, 163, 166
  machinery of, 221–224
Advisers, 159, 169, 223
  Presidential, *see* Presidential advisers
Advisory Board on Economic Growth and Stability, 263, 265

Advisory bodies, 222, 250–256, 307–308
  on education, 223
  on science, 295–304
  tripartite, 250–251
Advisory Council on Economic Security, 250
Advisory politics, 321–325
  Cabinet and, 25–28
Advisory systems, 325–329
Agencies, 5, 109, 296
  ad hoc commissions and, 104, 107, 112–113
  and policy making, 125, 127, 129, 131, 262–263, 293
  quasi-independent, 290
  and task forces, 138
Aid to Dependent Children (ADC), 251, 253–255
Aircraft nuclear propulsion program (ANP), 50, 53
AFL–CIO, 34, 119, 215
Analysis, policy making and, 167
Anderson, Patrick, quoted, 327
Anshen, Melvin, quoted, 79
Antipoverty bill, 210
Anti-Poverty Task Force, 100
Appleby, Paul, quoted, 65
Appointments Secretary, 14
Appropriations, 63–64, 80, 183, 289
  for aid programs, 287
  for foreign affairs research, 275
  military, 177–179
Arms Control and Disarmament Agency, 56
Arnold, Fortas & Porter, 152–154
Arnold, Thurman, 152, 154
Atomic Energy Commission (AEC), 42, 53, 196